The Soviet Rural Economy

This book uses both econometric modelling and descriptive analysis to present a theoretical and analytical picture of the Soviet rural economy that encompasses its past, its present condition, and its future prospects. The contributors offer views and approaches that represent a departure from traditional perspectives in a continuing effort to achieve a better understanding of Soviet agriculture and to stimulate further research. This book's interdisciplinary approach will make it useful for economists, agricultural economists, and students and teachers of Soviet and Eastern European area studies.

The Soviet Rural Economy

Edited by
Robert C. Stuart

Rowman & Allanheld
PUBLISHERS

ROWMAN & ALLANHELD

Published in the United States of America in 1984
by Rowman & Allanheld
(A division of Littlefield, Adams & Company)
81 Adams Drive, Totowa, New Jersey 07512

Library of Congress Cataloging in Publication Data
Main entry under title:

The Soviet rural economy.

   Includes bibliographical references and index.
   1. Agriculture—Economic aspects—Soviet Union—
Congresses.   2. Agriculture and state—Soviet Union—
Congresses.   3. Rural development—Government policy—
Soviet Union—Congresses.   4. Soviet Union—Economic
policy—1917-   —Congresses.   5. Soviet Union—
Rural conditions—Congresses.   I. Stuart, Robert C.,
1938-
HD1992.S5944   1983   338.1'0947   83-9668
ISBN 0-86598-092-6

   84 85/ 10 9 8 7 6 5 4 3 2 1

Printed in the United States of America

Contents

Preface

The present book on the Soviet rural economy is the outgrowth of a long-standing perception about Western analysis of the Soviet rural economy in general and Soviet agriculture in particular. That perception, simply put, is that the demand for knowledge about the Soviet rural experience has in general outstripped the available supply of knowledge.

This imbalance seems to arise for at least three basic reasons. First, the Western demand for knowledge about the Soviet rural economy has been and remains strong. This demand results in part from the fact that the study of rural society/economy in the Soviet historical and institutional setting is of substantial interest to social scientists pursuing basic questions about rural development. At the same time, however, the rural sector has been and continues to be a crucial component of the overall Soviet economy and hence must be understood if we are to assess Soviet performance now and in the future.

Second, the number of specialists devoting some or all of their attention to the Soviet rural economy is quite small.

Third, the limitations facing researchers, for example, data limitations, have restricted progress in the field, particularly the extent to which empirical evidence can be brought to bear upon basic theoretical concepts long since tested and analyzed in market economic systems.

With this justification in hand, I began to consider a different and difficult question: How best could I induce authors to make contributions to a book, contributions that would not only enhance our basic knowledge of the Soviet rural economy, but also take us beyond traditional boundaries and provide a basis for further research? The answer, I perceived, lay in the implementation of five basic propositions, all of which have become cornerstones of the present book.

First, no major effort was made to cover all or even most of the topics that might be useful in a book devoted to the Soviet rural economy. It has been my experience that when one tries to "fill gaps" by producing a piece of research in a short period of time, the result is generally of limited worth. Thus where it could not be easily avoided, imbalance was viewed as acceptable.

Second, considerable emphasis was placed upon the selection of scholars whose work might represent a departure from tradition. This bias was in no way a rejection of the traditional, but rather part of an effort to improve our knowledge through new methods, improved data bases, and new perspectives.

Third, emphasis was placed upon obtaining participation by scholars of a wide variety of ages, approaches, and disciplines. In part, this emphasis was thought appropriate for the achievement of departures from tradition.

Fourth, the contributors to this book were in no way constrained or limited by predetermined guidelines. On the contrary, it was hoped that the contributors would feel free to focus on whatever they thought important with whatever method or approach seemed appropriate in the particular circumstances.

Fifth, while a conference would be a useful mechanism for preparation and delivery of the research project, emphasis would be placed upon using the conference mechanism to improve the quality of the research and to do so through substantial revision of all papers based upon conference discussion and subsequent critical analysis of all papers.

Cast in this perspective, the outcome presented here represents diversity rather than conformity, and imbalance rather than balance. Furthermore, it represents the culmination of a long effort at writing and revision, one that it is hoped will serve as a stimulus to further work, not as a survey of past events.

Obviously the present book represents the inputs of many persons and a number of institutions. At the outset, I would like to thank James Millar and Paul Gregory, both of whom provided wise counsel at an early stage and on a continuing basis.

Naturally, support for such a venture is essential. In this context, I express my gratitude for the financial support of the United States Department of Agriculture, and in particular assistance provided by Kenneth Farrell, Anton Malish, and David Schoonover, all of whom were instrumental in making sure that this book could in fact appear. In the same vein, thanks go to the University of Houston Center for Public Policy for the provision of both material and administrative support.

For a superb job of presentation of the conference, I would like to thank Abbott Gleason and the staff of The Kennan Institute for Advanced Russian Studies, The Wilson Center, Smithsonian Institution, Washington, D.C.

I would be remiss if I did not thank the participants: those who delivered papers, those who chaired sessions at the conference, and those who participated from the floor. Finally, I would like to express my gratitude to the authors for their patience and understanding over the past two years as I badgered them for one revision after another, and to Matthew Held, Susan Thornton, Jim Le Maire and the staff of Rowman & Allanheld, who patiently waited for the final result.

It is with sadness that I must note the absence of a paper by Professor Arcadius Kahan, whose untimely death in March of 1982 removed from among us a colleague and scholar.

Belle Mead, N.J.
January, 1983

Introduction: Perspectives on the Russian and Soviet Rural Economy

Robert C. Stuart

It would clearly be presumptuous to think that a single essay could summarize the state of our knowledge on Russian and Soviet agriculture. Yet if a volume of essays is to make a contribution to that knowledge, clearly the content of these essays must move beyond the available literature. The reader, therefore, must be in a position to assess the findings of research in each topical area, to isolate the important questions that remain to be answered, and to consider each essay's contribution to answering those questions. In addition, the assessment should be carried out with knowledge of the available research tools and the data to which the tools will be applied.

Certainly it would be a grandiose task to expect each reader to develop the sort of assessment suggested above. At the same time, however, it would be quite unnecessary and inappropriate for this introductory essay simply to summarize each contribution. The articles can and do stand on their own, and each reader is capable of considering those that may be of particular interest. What contribution, then, can this introduction make for the benefit of the reader?

Rather than attempting to assess the extent of current scholarship about Russian and Soviet agriculture, let us consider a much narrower, but nevertheless useful, framework. Suppose we consider two questions: First, why do we conduct research on Russian and Soviet agriculture? Second, what specific questions do we seek to answer, and in what ways do data and methodological considerations constrain us in the real world?

The purpose of this introductory sketch of Russian and Soviet agriculture is to place each of the following essays in its proper context. Specifically, we will consider each contribution, seeking to elaborate those questions that are important to the topic at hand; the advances in our knowledge made by the essay; and finally, the sorts of issues that remain unresolved. The emphasis will be upon the context in which each essay arises.

RUSSIAN AND SOVIET AGRICULTURE: THE DEMAND FOR KNOWLEDGE

There are two dominant reasons for our interest in Russian and Soviet agriculture. First, the Soviet agricultural model and its prerevolutionary underpinnings serve as an important component of a major economic system, a system fundamentally different from those with which we in the West are traditionally familiar. Thus prior to and after the Revolution of 1917, indeed until the late 1920s, alternative strategies of economic development for Russia and the Soviet Union were the focus of interest and frequently of discussion. Ultimately, choices were made; and institutional arrangements, incentives, and economic policies of a very different nature, namely those of centrally planned socialism, were chosen and implemented. Our interest centers not only on the nature of the choices perceived to be available and the manner in which specific alternatives were in fact chosen, but also on the degree to which the ultimate choices in fact influenced observed patterns of economic development. Underlying this interest, then, are the presumptions that the particular choices made influenced observed outcomes, and that the nature of those influences are of interest. But of interest to whom and in what context?

Consider, as an example, the case of currently less developed nations. Although Western (and some Soviet) observers have viewed Soviet agricultural performance as less than impressive, nevertheless the Soviet industrialization experience and its collective and state agricultural model are frequently appealing to underdeveloped countries, especially to those countries where rapid industrialization is a paramount objective. In this context, one would want to focus upon the nature of the Soviet agricultural system and the extent to which that system might be applicable in a different setting.

A second and obviously related source of interest in Russian and Soviet agriculture might be essentially pragmatic. Consider another example. In the present day and indeed in prerevolutionary times, the Soviet Union (and Russia) is a major consumer and a major producer of food products and, as such, a major factor in the world food balance. Any effort to understand that balance and to project its future trends must necessarily include the Soviet agricultural scenario. In short, it is necessary to understand how Soviet agriculture works, and how well it works.

Our pragmatic "need to know" about Soviet agriculture has necessarily influenced the nature of our research and the specific sorts of questions for which we have sought answers. At the same time, the search for answers has frequently been constrained, if not by methodological limitations then by the absence of data. However, if we are to develop a meaningful picture of this different agricultural system, then we must take some risks, try some new approaches, and apply the best methods and skills available to those data that we have. Thus we must look at the past and the present, and we must do so with both theoretical and empirical investigation.

This essay will follow the outline of the volume. Thus we begin with a discussion of the early years, the periods immediately preceding and following the Revolution of 1917. Thereafter, we turn to an examination of contemporary Soviet agriculture, including examination of recent performance patterns and projections for the 1980s.

THE SUPPLY OF KNOWLEDGE: THE EARLY YEARS

Although it may be somewhat artificial to isolate particular periods in economic history, our initial interest in this volume centers on what we have described as the early years, that is, the period from the 1880s through the Revolution of 1917, and thereafter through the 1920s. What are the important issues of this early era?

First, throughout the early years, agriculture in particular and the rural economy more generally formed the dominant sector of the Russian and later Soviet economies. This dominance could be observed by almost any indicator, such as labor and capital shares or value of output. Thus reference to the Russian and Soviet economic development of the early years must consider agriculture.

Second, it is well known that Soviet agriculture underwent a dramatic transformation in the late 1920s and early 1930s through the process of collectivization. Thus it was at the end of the early years that a new era began, an era characterized by new organizational arrangements, new incentive arrangements, and new policies. To what extent did the experience of the prerevolutionary and precollectivization agricultural scenario play a role in the ultimate choices that were made and the manner in which those choices were implemented?

Given the importance of agriculture in the Russian and subsequent Soviet arrangements, it is not surprising that the matter of agriculture's role in economic development would be a matter of continuing discussion. In particular, the question of agricultural performance would be a key issue. Much of the material in the first section of this volume is devoted to an examination of this central issue—how well did agriculture perform in the early years, and to what extent did performance or perceptions of performance influence the choices made?

Turning first to the prerevolutionary years, many analysts have focused upon the Russian rural economy for the light that such an investigation might shed upon political and economic forces leading to the Revolution of 1917, the base upon which postrevolutionary agricultural development would proceed.[1] Was Russian agriculture backward and unproductive, operating under the vestiges of feudal arrangements, inadequate inputs, lack of appropriate technology, and so on; or were the beginnings of a modern agricultural sector already observable in the 1880s?

In recent years, a number of scholars, including Kahan, Gregory, Wheatcroft, Davies, and others have attempted to reexamine the record of the early years.[2] What is the prevailing view of this era, and what do we learn from this reevaluation?

As Paul Gregory points out in his contribution to the present volume, the traditional view of prerevolutionary Russian agriculture is schizophrenic.

On the one hand, many have argued that the Emancipation Act of 1861 and the changes instituted thereafter did not provide the watershed of a new era and did not, therefore, provide the underpinnings for modernization in the rural sector. Thus it is argued that agriculture as a dominant but generally stagnant sector became a major factor in developments that led to the Revolution of 1905 and changes thereafter. In turn, this dismal picture of the prerevolutionary era forms part of the basis which subsequent postrevolutionary (1917) changes would be justified.

At the same time, if one examines simple aggregate statistics, there are some measures by which the performance of the Russian economy and Russian agriculture in particular appear to have been generally strong in the post-1880 period. Russia was a major grain producer (the world's leading grain producer at the time of the Emancipation Act of 1861) and a major exporter of grain products. How well did Russian agriculture perform in the years preceding the Revolution of 1917, and to what extent and with what justification did the performance of these early years influence later events?

Paul Gregory looks specifically at the extent to which changes in rural levels of living (as has been argued) were a factor leading to the Revolution of 1905. Examining a number of traditional indicators, Gregory argues that contrary to the popular conception, living standards in rural Russia increased considerably during the 1880s and 1890s. The conclusion, therefore, is that the materials available to date should at a minimum provoke a reconsideration of the events and outcomes of this era.

A more positive picture of Russian agricultural performance would necessarily lead to a reexamination of the role of agriculture in subsequent events and especially the role that agriculture might have been expected to play in subsequent economic development.

The postrevolutionary and precollectivization era, the years between 1917 and 1928, has been the subject of considerable interest. This interest stems in large part from an attempt to determine the nature of the forces that led to the implementation of a drastic change in Soviet agriculture, namely collectivization, in the late 1920s and early 1930s. Economists have tended to argue that during the postrevolutionary years up to 1928, state-peasant relations in the Soviet Union were generally abrasive. Thus in the face of a need to harness agriculture in the service of industrialization under less than ideal conditions, collectivization was a mechanism to exert control and, above all, to extract the surplus from the peasants. Accordingly, it has traditionally been argued that whatever the associated costs, the economic rationale of collectivization was the extraction of the surplus to finance industrialization; thus the peasants bore the major brunt of Soviet forced-draft industrialization of the 1930s and subsequent years.

In his contribution to the present volume, Mark Harrison examines some of the traditional explanations for the abandonment of the NEP arrangements.[3] In particular, he focuses upon the contrasting views of NEP as first, inconsistent with rapid socialist industrialization; second, inconsistent with further (though slower) industrialization; and finally, a purely political option. Harrison concludes that the abandonment of NEP was indeed a political action, but that it had an economic logic, the desire of the state to enforce changes in the agricultural sector consistent with rapid socialist industrialization.

Thus much of the discussion of this paper deals with what turns out to be a crucial theme of the period, the state of Soviet agricultural production and the degree to which prevailing arrangements and performance could be viewed as consistent with the objective of rapid socialist industrialization. Of no lesser importance is Stalin's perception of reality on these issues.

Thus, as was true for the prerevolutionary years, agricultural performance during the NEP period (and indeed thereafter) is a matter of central concern for the proper understanding of events and options. Typically, agricultural performance has been seen in rather simple terms, namely grain output and grain marketings. Grain is the crucial product of the agricultural sector, and its distribution is of basic importance, not only for the contribution that it might make to improved living standards and thus economic development (the central focus of the prerevolutionary period), but also for the direct contribution that it might make to the development process, the issue that became dominant during the development discussions of the 1920s.

Steve Wheatcroft tackles the difficult question of assessing the actual state of Soviet agricultural production and distribution during the 1920s and early 1930s in his discussion. What do the numbers tell us about Soviet agricultural production in this period?

After a consideration of existing indices of Soviet agricultural production (the Soviet indices and the Johnson-Kahan index), Wheatcroft develops his own estimates of both grain and livestock production. The Wheatcroft indices differ in construction from other indices primarily in terms of the degree of inclusion and the product and regional weighting used to develop an aggregate production index.

Wheatcroft provides the empirical evidence to support two important conclusions. First, he concludes that Soviet agricultural performance (production) in the 1920s was generally worse than has typically been argued. Second, he concludes that the decline in output during the early years of collectivization (the early 1930s) was greater than had previously been thought. Finally, Wheatcroft examines grain production on a regional basis, a matter of importance to our understanding of this period, since a great deal of the discussion about collectivization and its impact and results has focused upon regional differentials, the so-called grain surplus and grain deficit regions, and the nature of production arrangements in each.

In a sense, then, the Wheatcroft results could be viewed as support for a quite traditional interpretation of the events of the 1920s and 1930s, that poor agricultural performance was indeed an economic factor in the collectivization decision, but that the outcome was more negative than might have been anticipated.

As we have already noted, Western interest in the Soviet experiences of the 1920s and 1930s has focused upon the rationale, mechanics, and outcome of collectivization. Until recently, much less attention has been focused upon microeconomic issues and, in particular, how organizational arrangements were changed and national economic planning introduced.

Eugene Zaleski attempts to fill this gap with an examination of Soviet agricultural planning in the early years. Zaleski deals with planning in a number of important and interrelated dimensions. First, he examines the nature of planning, as applied to both the character and the pace of collectivization. Second, he examines both production and procurement planning arrangements of the late 1920s and early 1930s. Zaleski's conclusions are important for our reevaluation of the rationale for, and outcome of, the collectivization decision. If, as has been argued, we should consider collectivization to have been, at least in part, a political decision with a long-term perspective of the socialist transformation of the countryside, then, Zaleski would argue, the poor economic performance of Soviet agriculture in the early 1930s could be viewed as a temporary necessity or expedient—a price that had to be paid to obtain better long-term results.

Zaleski draws an important conclusion from his analysis, that we ought to pay more attention to the late 1930s, a period in which we might view collectivization without the excesses of collectivization.

It is unlikely that the controversies surrounding the early years of Russian and Soviet agricultural development will soon subside. Indeed it is to be hoped that the essays in this volume can make a positive contribution to continuing discussion.

THE SUPPLY OF KNOWLEDGE: APPROACHES TO SOVIET RURAL DEVELOPMENT

It is not difficult to find a framework in which to cast, and thus to explain, the role of agriculture in the process of economic development. There are many competing explanatory models, varying in such basics as prevailing climatic conditions, the initial level of economic development, the availability of various inputs, the assumed dynamics of the development process, the organizational arrangements chosen, and so on.[4] Typically the role of agriculture in the development process has been cast in terms of the contribution that agriculture can make and the nature of the transformation that must take place as economic development proceeds.

Thus it is argued that during the early stages of the development process, agriculture as the dominant sector must contribute toward development. This contribution is usually product (for processing, consumption, and/or export) and labor, the latter being provided to the industrial sector. As labor departs, factor substitution, typically capital for labor in agriculture, maintains the growth of agricultural output.

In this simplified form, the picture of a contribution by agriculture has been applied to the Soviet case and provides what James Millar would term the "standard story" of collectivization. What is this story, and how has it been challenged?

The essence of the standard story is as follows: Collectivization had an economic rationale, which was the provision to the state of an agricultural "surplus" for the purpose of financing the industrialization drive. Thus, as noted earlier, the popular conception pictures the squeeze on the peasants, which, along with a neglect of agriculture, enabled the state to extract the means for promoting industrialization.

Thus both the peasants and the workers bore the burden of industrialization. Not until the 1950s and the rise of Nikita Khrushchev would the neglect be reversed, in a series of policy changes designed to begin the crucial process of agricultural transformation, as Soviet leaders would describe it, *intensification*.

The contributions by James Millar, Frank Durgin, and Alfred Evans challenge at least two of the three perceptions outlined above. What is the nature of the challenge?

Millar, on the basis of his reconstruction of the data provided from archives by the Soviet economist Barsov, argues that collectivization did not appreciably change the magnitude of the resource flow between agriculture and nonagriculture; thus the major economic rationale for collectivization, provision of an expanded net agricultural surplus for industrialization, falls to the ground.[5] As Millar points out, the picture that he presents is for a limited, though important, period of time. Basically, Millar concludes that we ought to reassess our picture of collectivization in light of the possibility that it was a policy mistake on all counts.

Frank Durgin challenges the "neglect" theory of agriculture in Soviet economic development, but he does much more. As noted above, it has become customary to "periodize" the development of Soviet agriculture and to tie particular policies to particular leaders—the "Stalin era," "the Khrushchev era," and so on. Durgin makes two points that present the long-term picture of Soviet agriculture from a new perspective.

First, Durgin argues that a careful reading of the literature of the Stalin and Khrushchev years will reveal that in fact Stalin was not the ruthless suppressor of agriculture and Khrushchev the great liberalizer of agriculture. In fact, many of the programs associated with the Khrushchev years, for example, expansion of irrigation and changes in organization and management, were in fact products of the earlier Stalin years. In short, Durgin argues that Soviet agricultural policies may in fact have a far greater degree of continuity through time than is commonly ascribed to them.

Second, Durgin suggests that if one examines the extent to which Khrushchev policies in fact originated in the Stalin years, the "neglect" theory is in fact simplistic. This view is in fact harmonious with the Millar position that by a number of measures, Soviet agriculture was a net recipient of resources from nonagriculture during the early and crucial years of collectivization in the 1930s.

If the papers by Millar and Durgin tend to cast doubt upon traditional Western interpretations of the role of agriculture in Soviet economic development, Alfred Evans argues that from the point of view of structural transformation, the long-term developmental patterns of Soviet agriculture might well be cast within a rather traditional framework. Thus he states that as the transformation of the countryside has taken place, specialization has increased, and labor has departed for employment in the urban industrial sector, to be replaced by capital in the rural sector. Consistent with these changes are concomitant organizational changes, especially the introduction of the agro-industrial complex, a relatively recent development.

THE SUPPLY OF KNOWLEDGE: THEORY AND ANALYSIS

Thus far discussion has concentrated on the past, particularly on agricultural performance, the impact of the record upon policy, and the effects of changing policies on performance. In an examination of contemporary Soviet agriculture, what are the important issues of the contemporary era, and to what extent do we have useful answers to pressing questions?

Once again, for many observers of the contemporary Soviet agricultural scene, performance is the focus of interest. This interest stems in part from the poor harvest record of the 1970s, a period in which the Soviet Union became a rather persistent net importer of grain; it also relates to the long-term prospects and projections of future performance. Will Soviet agriculture continue to be the Achilles heel of the Soviet economy, as some would argue? Or is it increasingly on a modern footing, capable of meeting the food and fibre needs of the country?

While one can imagine many indicators by which performance could be assessed, two directions of investigation are of particular importance: First, how well is the Soviet population provided with basic food needs? Second, in the provision of these basic needs, how well are the traditional inputs, land, labor, and capital, being utilized?

The Western view of contemporary Soviet argiculture is, to a degree, schizophrenic, in the manner that the Western view of early Russian agriculture is. The predominant view is that Soviet agriculture simply does not work very well.[6] What does this generally mean? Supplies of foodstuffs to the marketplace are generally sporadic; while there have been increases over time, they remain generally inadequate. In addition, agricultural productivity is typically viewed as being low, as a policy of limiting price increases at the retail level necessitates large state subsidies. Finally, the private sector is seen as the ideologically unpalatable saving grace of the agricultural sector.

These undesirable outcomes are pinpointed to a number of familiar causal factors, including climatic problems, lack of appropriate incentives, poor planning, cumbersome organizational arrangements, and lack of proper attention to matters of scale and specialization.

At the same time, however, critics of this negative posture point out that there have been significant long-term increases in the output of agricultural products in the Soviet Union, steady dietary improvement, and an agricultural transformation that fits rather closely to a number of approaches to the role of agriculture in the development process.[7]

In theory, it should be possible to resort to the facts to resolve this dispute and thus uncover Soviet agricultural reality. Unfortunately our task is by no means this simple, though recent theoretical and empirical research is beginning to provide better answers to the questions that we pose. What are the improvements?

In the past, it has frequently been necessary to assess Soviet agricultural performance by reliance upon partial indicators, simply because data limitations precluded development of a more accurate though more complex picture. Thus it has been usual to look at yields per unit of land area as an indicator of the effectiveness of resource use, an indicator particularly difficult to interpret in a land-rich, if climate-poor country.

Further, despite a tendency to view the kolkhoz as an inherently poor performer vis-à-vis the sovkhoz, data by farm type, by product, and by region have typically been inadequate, precluding the sort of analysis that would isolate the influence of differing organizational arrangements.

Finally, to take another example, most would argue that the distribution system in the Soviet Union is very poor. Thus it is quite possible to have excess demand for certain food products in urban markets, while these products spoil from lack of storage, poor transportation, improper processing, and so on. But who can cite even minimal data on the distribution system? It is very difficult to assess the contribution of this factor to overall agricultural performance, since one must rely upon anecdotal evidence from the Soviet press and the complaints of Soviet citizens.

One methodology that has proven very effective for the analysis of agricultural production is the production function. This approach, using simple econometric techniques, views a product as generated by several inputs, typically land, labor, and capital. Thus we can generate a more realistic picture of the production process, relating output to a number of inputs, rather than a single input such as land.[8]

The production function method allows examination of the relationship between inputs and outputs, the nature of differences in this relationship across regions, and changes in the relationship through time. Furthermore, the question of substitution of factors, that is the replacement of labor by capital as labor departs for the urban (industrial) sector, can also be investigated.

In the past, the production function analysis of Soviet agriculture has generally been conducted on the basis of highly aggregated data. The present contributions adopt a different perspective.

Elizabeth Clayton develops a production function on a regional basis, not by the more usual yet controversial republic classification, but on the basis of agricultural production conditions. It is not surprising that when compared with an aggregate production function for agriculture, regional production functions show statistically significant differences, suggesting that gains can be achieved from shifting input-output patterns on a regional basis.

One theme that permeates the Western literature on Soviet agriculture, but which is very difficult to examine and analyze in an empirical framework, is the matter of organizational arrangements and their impact upon agricultural performance. Specifically, is the sovkhoz, supplied as it is with state inputs, a more efficient form of organization than the kolkhoz, or is there a degree of decentralization of decision making in the kolkhoz that might offset the benefits of state financing?

Michael Wyzan examines Soviet agricultural production from the production function approach by disaggregating the analysis by farm type. In spite of the growing similarities between the two types of organizations, Wyzan considers the hypothesis that in fact the kolkhoz behaves in a manner similar to the labor managed firm. This hypothesis is generally not confirmed by empirical evidence, which conforms to the Western view of the kolkhoz as being largely within Soviet planning mechanisms and arrangements.

Wyzan finds that differences in production by farm type are much less important than past discussions of this subject would suggest. Surprisingly, the kolkhoz does better than the sovkhoz in a number of instances, especially with better yields and generally better prospects for the growth of output. The sovkhoz, Wyzan finds, is clearly superior in the indicator of labor productivity, though this difference (as with some other differences) can in part be explained by the fact that the sovkhoz has access to better nonlabor inputs such as capital and land.

There is yet another Western view of Soviet agricultural production that remains to be empirically examined. It has frequently been asserted in the Western literature that Soviet agriculture is not very specialized, by farm type, region, or both. Put another way, on-site inspection and anecdotal evidence would suggest that to a degree most Soviet farms tend to raise most crops and to engage in the raising of animals. Is this picture accurate, and if so, why does Soviet agriculture not pursue the gains to be achieved from specialization?

A simple interpretation of economic theory would suggest the following conditions for the most efficient usage of resources: The production of agricultural output should be shifted from high-cost to low-cost regions. Furthermore, such a pattern of reallocation should continue until, at the margin, the cost of producing, let us say, potatoes in region A, is the same as the cost of producing potatoes in region B. Cost minimization would be appealing in the Soviet (or any other) case to the extent that two conditions are met: First, appropriate cost data must be available such that cost differences by region, farm type, etc. can be determined. Second, this information must be available to those who make production decisions, whether on the farm, in the planning agency, or some combination of the two.

In the past, it has been difficult to examine this question of specialization, largely because of the lack of appropriate data. However, for a selected but important region, the Ukraine, Kenneth Gray examines the question of specialization.

Once again, the production function approach is used to examine a basic but very important question: To what extent is there rational specialization (as defined above) in the production of sugar beets, vegetables, and sunflowers in the Ukraine?

The analysis suggests that there is evidence (with some exceptions) to suggest that, with the exception of sunflowers, there is a good deal of rationality in the specialization trends observed. Thus there is a tendency, in the Ukraine, to grow the crops mentioned in those regions most favorable to their production. However, as Gray notes, the available data make it very difficult to isolate qualitative differences in inputs, a matter pervasive in production function analysis, and especially important in the case of the land input. To the extent that data limitations may be relaxed in the future, it will be possible to use this approach to examine the rationality of specialization on a much broader scale in Soviet agriculture.

Let us turn to another important facet of Soviet agriculture, the utilization of labor. In a broad sense, patterns of labor allocation in Soviet agriculture are rather close to theoretical expectations outlined earlier. As the Soviet economy has developed, the supply of labor available to the agricultural sector has dwindled, and population has migrated from the rural to the urban areas. The present picture is that of an aging rural population (from which the agricultural labor force must in large part be drawn) as youth migrate to the better opportunities of the urban areas. Furthermore, it has been noted that the sex imbalance, in part a result of World War II losses and migratory patterns, leaves a predominantly female rural labor force, one that has been attracted to the private sector at the expense of the public sector. With growing official interest in the private sector as a means to provide necessary food supplies, will it be possible to attract sufficient labor to the socialized sector, or might it be necessary to mandate minimum contributions, as in the past? What are the regional implications of this problem; do the nature and magnitude of incentives matter; and if so, in what ways do they matter?

The theory of labor force participation as applied to market economic systems is generally adequate to provide useful answers to these sorts of questions. Unfortunately, in the Soviet context, the available data are typically inadequate. However, with recent demographic trends in the Soviet Union, the matter of labor force participation and the nature of forces influencing that participation take on added importance.

In his contribution to the present volume, Clark Chandler builds and applies a model of the Soviet collective farm labor force. Although the model is restricted by a number of theoretical and practical considerations, nevertheless the conclusions are instructive and suggestive of possible future approaches to the analysis of the labor force problem. What are the major conclusions?

Chandler notes that, in general, the labor force behavior of Soviet collective farmers is strongly affected by economic variables, and, as we might expect, sex differences are important. He finds that the private sector is not an important claimant of the male labor force, while for women the picture is much more complicated. The evidence suggests that for women the private sector is indeed an important claimant of time, a result that confirms past (though partial) analysis of this question.

These conclusions deserve extension and elaboration, especially in an era when the growth of the rural labor force is destined to be very slow, when participation rates are already very high, and when there is limited potential for factor substitution. The major problems here are the lack of necessary data and the growing complexity of organizational arrangements in the Soviet countryside through the emergence of the agro-industrial complex, which is discussed in the following section.

THE SUPPLY OF KNOWLEDGE: PERFORMANCE AND PROSPECTS

It will be quite obvious to the reader of this volume that Soviet agriculture has undergone important transformation, while its performance remains a matter of controversy. Although the flamboyancy of the Khrushchev era may have been replaced by the tedium of the Brezhnev era, one might do well to adopt the advice of Frank Durgin to examine the underlying policies for an analysis and interpretation of events in Soviet agriculture.

From the outset, we have argued that consideration of Soviet agriculture should include examination of organizational arrangements, policies, and incentives. In the final section, the authors examine all three facets of Soviet agriculture, with the intent of assessing change and the possible impact of change upon future performance patterns.

Turning first to the matter of incentives, Western observers of Soviet agriculture have always argued that material incentives are very important, but that they are typically inadequate. This inadequacy, it is argued, stems from several characteristics of the Soviet agricultural system, but two in particular are thought to be dominant. First, many would agree that in the kolkhoz and maybe to a lesser degree in the sovkhoz, it is very difficult to relate the reward received to the effort expended. The traditional use of the labor day mechanism on kolkhozy is a case in point.

Second, it has also been argued that incentives are inadequate in the simple sense that their magnitude is limited (in part by socialization of the means of production) and, above all, cannot be converted into the goods and services that Soviet rural consumers desire, such as better housing and consumer durables. To what extent are these observations accurate?

Gertrude Schroeder undertakes an examination of the incentive question in the general and important issue of levels of living in rural areas. Within the limitations of existing data and with comparisons to the urban setting, Schroeder derives two important conclusions. First, and consistently with Soviet policies in this area, the level of living in Soviet rural areas has risen rapidly in the past twenty years, reaching toward the levels achieved in Soviet urban areas. Second, however, in a number of dimensions Soviet rural living standards lag; in the future, the growth of these standards is likely to be slow relative to past growth. To the extent that it is the change or expectation of change that is important to the Soviet rural dweller, these results deserve attention in the projection of future labor force participation and effort. Indeed, to the extent that material gain is an important element in explaining labor force behavior, it is interesting to speculate on why past gains have not resulted in better effort, and what impact the projected leveling of future gains might have in an increasingly tight labor supply scenario.

As has already been emphasized, the nature of organizational arrangements in Soviet agriculture is a theme that has been of central importance to Western analysts. This interest stems in part from the particular arrangements chosen, the kolkhoz and the sovkhoz. More generally, however, it stems from the perception that, in contrast to a decentralized market economy, organizational change can be implemented more rapidly and possibly more effectively in the centralized and planned economy. This view seems to have been confirmed by organizational changes in earlier years, frequently sudden and often controversial. In recent years, however, the style may have changed, but the substance is there. Indeed the important recent development of the agro-industrial complex in its various forms has been relatively quiet and has reflected agricultural development patterns observed in other economic systems, both socialist and nonsocialist.

Altough there have been various forms and degrees of "industrial" type activity (manufacturing, processing, repair, etc.) in Soviet rural areas for many years, the recent era has witnessed a sharp expansion of this type of activity. Of particular importance is the adoption of a framework that may in large part change the Soviet farm production process, specifically the isolation of its components, from inputs at one end to the marketing of farm products at the other end.[9]

Valentin Litvin examines the issues related to the process of agro-industrial integration. He notes that while there is considerable variation by type, the general process of agro-industrial integration has been pervasive for a number of regions and over a variety of sectors, for both crops and livestock. Litvin examines both the economic and the social aspects of the integration process, emphasizing that many of the problems arise from traditional economic difficulties in the Soviet economic system, for example, problems in the material technical supply system or the basic differences betwen the kolkhoz and the sovkhoz. Although integration is seen to be a continuing component of Soviet agricultural policy, Litvin argues that renewed emphasis upon the private sector is evidence of official skepticism about the outcome of integration. This skepticism, he argues, is founded upon observed difficulties with existing integrated complexes in areas such as shortage of capital and managerial problems.

Although the process of agro-industrial integration has been a dominant theme in recent years, other organizational issues have been raised. Everett Jacobs addresses a number of related issues, including changes in agricultural planning, organization at the microeconomic level (the issue of the link), and the final implementation of khozraschet in the sovkhoz. From an examination of these issues and policy changes of recent years, Jacobs concludes that there has been a strong trend toward centralization of decision making in Soviet agriculture. Clearly this is a theme of great importance and one that bears watching in the future.

Although Jacobs (and indeed many Western economists) would argue that Soviet agricultural performance could be improved with genuine decentralization of decision making, he concludes that this option might only be considered as a drastic reorientation under continuing bad performance. Indeed the view that there is a degree of centralization of decision making is probably consistent with the integration campaign and a persistent view in the Soviet Union that agricultural management can in fact be cast along the lines of industrial management at advancing stages of economic development.

Throughout this introduction, certain themes have been given special emphasis. One such theme has been the need to understand Soviet agriculture, not just from a scholarly interest and perspective, but especially from a very practical viewpoint. This need to know has been constrained both by the methods of analysis available and the data limitations, constraints that we have elaborated with respect to many of the contributions in this volume. In the concluding paper by Daniel L. Bond and Donald W. Green, much of what has been said comes together, for Bond and Green use sophisticated modelling within the limitations of the method and available data, attempting to give us a picture of the immediate future. Given our stock of knowledge about Soviet agriculture, and expressing this stock in a formal picture (model) of Soviet agriculture, what scenarios can we project for the performance of Soviet agriculture in the 1980s? Specifially, the trends that we would like to observe are changes in both inputs and outputs for both crop and animal production.

Obviously the skeptical observer might argue that forecasts of agricultural production, where many unknown factors such as climatic changes can be influential, must be inherently unstable. Bond and Green use the production function approach, discussed in some detail at an earlier stage, to develop a number of alternative scenarios based upon varying assumptions. What are the alternative scenarios, and what do they tell us about future Soviet agricultural performance?

Bond and Green project that for the period 1981–85, the average annual output of grain in the Soviet Union will be 217 million metric tons, a figure somewhat lower than that projected in the five-year plan for this period. This projection, in combination with low initial grain *stocks* and a desire to build livestock herds and to maintain minimum inventory levels of grain, will, it is argued, generate average annual grain imports of 26 million metric tons. These projections are consistent with the maintenance of the livestock sector, with only modest gains in meat production, gains somewhat below those projected in the Soviet five-year plan.

Is weather, one of the unpredictable factors that we mentioned, an important consideration in these projections? Bond and Green have developed an alternative scenario upon the assumption of weather conditions better than those underlying the above projections. This good weather scenario projects an additional domestic availability of grain of 15 million metric tons (annual average); but because of wastage and spoilage, the reduction of imported grain for the livestock sector is only modest, and domestic production is still well below domestic demand.

RUSSIAN AND SOVIET AGRICULTURE: A REAPPRAISAL?

We have argued that in many dimensions, our demand for knowledge about Russian and Soviet agriculture has typically exceeded the supply. The demand has persisted not only on the basis of scholarly interest in the particular organizational arrangements and policies applied in the Soviet case, but also on the basis of the Soviet position in the world food balance. At the same time, data limitations have frequently precluded the sort of sophisticated analysis that would dramatically improve our basic understanding of Soviet agriculture and facilitate projection of future trends. Cast in this perspective, Western interest remains substantial, but our picture substantially unchanged. Soviet agriculture inherited a backward system, which was radically tansformed under Soviet rule, only to be exploited in the service of economic development, thus producing the contemporary Achilles heel of the Soviet economy.

Would a reappraisal be justified? To be sure, our knowledge of Soviet agriculture has improved through time, and it would be unfair to judge our present knowledge upon either the simplistic summary presented above or the selected and partial coverage of the present volume. But if we examine our picture of Soviet agriculture against such a background, and if we include the substantial volume of recent work in the field, would it be reasonable to suggest that a new and different picture is emerging? If so, what is the nature of this picture, and in what directions will it move?

Although it would be unreasonable to suggest that one can identify a sharp and decisive shift in our knowledge of Soviet agriculture, it would be quite appropriate to observe that in a number of important areas, new findings have emerged, findings that, when refined and reexamined, will undoubtedly cast Russian and Soviet agriculture in a perspective rather different from that currently prevailing.

Returning to our earlier, somewhat arbitrary classification of time periods and our focus upon organizational arrangements, policies, and incentives, we can put together a picture of Russian and Soviet agriculture that differs in important respects from that presented in summary fashion above.

Thus we may well argue in the future that Soviet agriculture did not inherit a relatively backward agriculture from its Tsarist predecessors, but that the turmoil of the immediate pre- and postrevolutionary years—that is, from the early 1900s through the 1920s—limited the extent to which earlier modernization trends could in fact continue. While it is quite clear that there were alternatives, and possibly very good alternatives, to collectivization, Western analysis probably understates the importance of the political/ideological element in the Soviet objective function substantially. Cast in this light, collectivization was not a mechanism that changed the rural contribution, but simply continued it, along with that provided by the growing industrial sector.

This scenario suggests that we are developing a new picture of the Russian and Soviet development pattern, and especially the role of agriculture in that pattern. At the same time, as we extend this picture into the contemporary era, we are plagued by a relative vacuum for the years of the 1930s through the 1950s.

This vacuum is the result of a number of factors. In part, other questions have been of greater interest to scholars. Also, there has been a particular paucity of data for these years, and especially for the 1940s. However, our image of an exploited agriculture's contributing a sharply expanded surplus in the 1930s, in combination with the view of sudden and important changes under Khrushchev, allowed us to assume that the intervening years were just "more of the same," with necessary (but largely unresearched) adjustments for the war experience. Finally, contemporary research, to the extent that it utilizes increasingly sophisticated methods for which large amounts of data are necessary, tends quite understandably to focus upon recent years as data have become more available.

But what about our picture of contemporary Soviet agriculture? Interestingly enough, it is probably reasonable to suggest that our reappraisal is most noticeable in a historical context. However, our picture of contemporary Soviet agriculture is also improving and changing.

A perusal of recent research within and beyond the present volume would certainly suggest that we are developing a more substantive picture of the production conditions of Soviet agriculture and the influence of important variables upon those conditions—for example, differences by farm type, by crop, and by region. Our ability to capture the peculiarities of Soviet distribution arrangements remains limited.

On balance, this new picture probably gives us two sorts of messages. First, it gives us messages about specific and interesting questions, such as whether women can be induced to work in the socialized sector, or the rationality of potato production in various regions, for example. It is hoped that this sort of analysis will be generalized in the future.

The second message that it gives, however, is that Soviet agriculture, on balance, and if one allows for all of the important prevailing constraints, probably performs rather better than has been traditionally argued. From the point of view of improving Soviet agricultural performance, this message is positive, in the sense that it identifies and empirically investigates the importance of the various constraints, whether these are natural conditions, incentive arrangements, policies, or whatever. At the same time, the message is ominous for our interest in the world food balance, since it implies that improvement in Soviet agricultural performance, even if we do understand the constraints, will be difficult and expensive to achieve.

Is this an old picture in new clothing? Not really. We have traditionally argued that Soviet agriculture is a neglected sector that does not perform very well. The implication is a very positive one, namely that the reversal of that neglect, through more investment, more appropriate organizational arrangements, or whatever, will reverse the record of poor performance. But if we find out that in fact there has not been neglect, and that performance is better than we thought but still inadequate to meet domestic demand, the message is much less positive, for it does not imply the existence of easy remedies.

NOTES

1. See, for example, Lazar Volin, *A Century of Russian Agriculture* (Cambridge, Mass.: Harvard University Press, 1970).

2. See, for example, Paul R. Gregory, "Grain Marketings and Peasant Consumption, Russia, 1885–1913," *Explorations in Economic History* 17, no. 2 (April 1980): 135–64.

3. For a discussion of the NEP period, see Eugene Zaleski, *Planning For Economic Growth in The Soviet Union, 1918–1932* (Chapel Hill: University of North Carolina Press, 1971).

4. For a survey, see Yujiro Hayami and Vernon W. Ruttan, *Agricultural Development: An International Perspective* (Baltimore: The Johns Hopkins University Press, 1971).

5. See James Millar, "Mass Collectivization and the Contribution of Soviet Agriculture to The First Five-Year Plan: A Review Article," *Slavic Review* 33, no. 4 (December 1974): 750–66.

6. See Paul R. Gregory and Robert C. Stuart, *Soviet Economic Structure and Performance,* 2d. ed. (New York: Harper & Row, 1981), chapter 7.

7. Charles K. Wilber, "The Role of Agriculture in Soviet Economic Development," *Land Economics* 45, no. 1 (February 1969).

8. For recent work in this area, see, for example, Elizabeth M. Clayton, "Productivity in Soviet Agriculture," *Slavic Review* 39, no. 3 (September 1980): 446–58; Michael L. Wyzan, "Empirical Analysis of Soviet Agricultural Production and Policy," *American Journal of Agricultural Economics* 63, no. 3 (August 1981): 475–83.

9. Robert C. Stuart, "Aspects of Soviet Rural Development," *Agricultural Administration* 2 (1975): 165–78.

PART ONE

Issues in Russian and Soviet Agrarian History

1

The Russian Agrarian Crisis Revisited

Paul R. Gregory

The agrarian crisis theory of the 1905 Russian revolution is well established in the Western and Marxist literatures. Its principal thesis is compelling and logical: The revolution of 1905 was caused in large part by an "agrarian crisis." Symptoms of the agrarian crisis were rising land prices, the growing arrears in peasant redemption payments, the famine of the early 1890s, declining per capita land holdings of obshchina members, and reports of peasant impoverishment in grain-deficit provinces. It appears entirely reasonable to conclude, on the basis of such evidence, that the 1905 uprising was the Russian peasant's way of reacting to an impossible economic situation.

Supporters of the agrarian crisis interpretation of the 1905 revolution are drawn from various disciplines and political camps. Prominent Western economic historians such as Alexander Gerschenkron, Alec Nove, and Lazar Volin subscribe to the agrarian crisis school.[1] Both Nove and Gerschenkron draw parallels between Witte's agrarian policies and those of Stalin and detect some rather strong resemblances between Witte and Stalin with regard to taxation and agricultural exports. In their view, industrial capital formation was financed by forced reductions in peasant living standards. A majority of Western historians appear to subscribe to the agrarian crisis hypothesis.[2] To quote a typical conclusion: "Heavy taxes had exhausted the peasant population's ability to pay and had driven all of Russian agriculture into an endemic crisis."[3] The agrarian crisis hypothesis fits well into the Marxian dialectic and is a prominent feature of Lenin's writings on prerevolutionary Russia. The 1905 revolution is seen by Marxist-Leninist writers as a reaction by exploited peasants and downtrodden industrial workers to growing immizerization.

CHALLENGES TO THE AGRARIAN CRISIS THEORY

The neatness and convenience of the agrarian crisis hypothesis have made it a part of the received doctrine on prerevolutionary Russia. It provides an entirely logical explanation of an important political event, and it is a point of view that can draw support from both Marxist and Western scholars. For this reason, the agrarian crisis hypothesis remains firmly entrenched in most standard histories of prerevolutionary Russia.

What I attempt to do in this paper is to demonstrate that the empirical evidence does not support the agrarian crisis theory unless very strong and unusual income distribution effects are present. Rather, I suggest that the Russian peasant was experiencing a rising standard of living during the industrialization era starting in the 1880s. Growing peasant immizerization was not the cause of the 1905 revolution. Instead, historians must look to other, less convenient explanations of the 1905 revolution.

Evidence of an Agrarian Crisis

Much of the debate on the agrarian crisis has not used direct evidence on rural living standards. Instead, evidence has been brought forth on tax arrears, excise tax payments, and the like.[3] Stronger support of the agrarian crisis hypothesis would be direct evidence of declining rural living standards in the decades preceding the 1905 revolution. In fact, Alexander Gerschenkron supports the agrarian crisis position with his finding of a decline in per capita wheat and rye available for domestic consumption between the early 1870s and late 1890s.[4] If the index of real per capita rural income could be shown as dropping or stagnant over the decades preceding the 1905 revolution, the agrarian crisis hypothesis would appear justified. This type of evidence would be more conclusive than the data on peasant tax arrears, land rental rates, and so on, that have been used to this point to demonstrate an agrarian crisis.

It is not possible to obtain a "good" comprehensive index of rural real per capita income of Russian peasants. The conceptual difficulties and data problems are simply too severe. In the end, one must rely on partial indicators of rural living standards; so the issue is which partial indicator is more reliable than others. The most relevant data that are available are for grain production and technical crops. Reliable livestock, dairy, hunting, fishing, and vegetable production statistics are few and far between, as are data on peasant purchases in retail markets. Moreover, data on peasant earnings in nonagricultural pursuits are sketchy, if not nonexistent. Official series of wages of hired farm labor are available and have been used with reference to the agrarian crisis question,[5] but a wage series such as this would be a quite unreliable guide to rural living standards.

The wealth of data gathered on grain production is explained by the crucial role of grain exports, which prompted tsarist statistical authorities to do their best to gather data on grain production, grain exports, and grain transport. I would suggest that the most reasonable empirical approach to the agrarian crisis issue is through the grain market.

What this means from a research perspective is that inferences concerning peasant living standards must be based upon trends in grain. This is true even though retained grain products accounted for only 50 percent of retained farm consumption.[6]

Aggregate statistical series provide an alternate approach to the use of grain statistics. One can perhaps examine growth rate trends of the aggregate economy and infer from them growth rates of rural real incomes. The justification of this approach would be as follows: The agricultural population made up some 85 percent of the Russian population and some three-fourths of the Russian labor force at the turn of the century.[7] It is therefore unlikely that trends in rural real incomes would differ substantially from economywide trends. In order for urban real incomes to grow at rates substantially above rural real incomes, restrictions on rural-urban migration would have had to be quite severe to prevent the natural flow of population in response to real wage differentials. It is for this reason that structural restrictions on rural-urban migration play such an important role in the Gerschenkron model. The demonstration of a "dual" Russian economy of primitive agriculture and modern industry was also prominent in Lenin's writings.

In this paper, I shall examine three types of evidence. First, the available estimates of Russian per capita national income are studied on the grounds that in a predominantly rural economy, aggregate real income is a reasonable proxy for rural real income. Second, evidence on agricultural output and exports is investigated. The assumption underlying this approach is that agricultural output and agricultural incomes tend to move together. Third, the detailed evidence on grain marketings and grain production is scrutinized to determine whether per capita grain consumption of the rural population was rising or falling during the period under investigation.

THE EVIDENCE: AGGREGATE TRENDS

Let me begin with a survey of the empirical evidence on aggregate indicators of real per capita incomes for the period 1870 to 1905.

Per Capita National Income, Goldsmith

The best-known study of Russian national income is that of Raymond Goldsmith.[8] Goldsmith was prevented by data deficiencies and time constraints from preparing a complete set of national income accounts. Instead, Goldsmith prepared two series, one on crop production (grains and technical crops), the other on factory industrial production and mining. His agricultural production series for the period 1870 to 1904 is for the fifty European provinces. Goldsmith's results are recorded in Table 1.1.

What do the Goldsmith estimates tell us about the Russian agrarian crisis? They reveal that per capita agricultural output was likely stagnant between the early 1870s and early 1880s, but grew substantially on a per capita basis from the onset of the industrialization era in the 1880s to 1905. Factory production grew at rapid rates throughout this period but accelerated between the 1880s and 1904. In sum, the Goldsmith study fails to provide support for the agrarian crisis hypothesis. According to Goldsmith, both agricultural and factory production were growing faster than popula-

Table 1.1   Indexes of Agricultural Production, Factory Production, and Population, Goldsmith, 1870-1904, 50 European Provinces (1870-74 = 100)

period	crops	factory production	total population	rural population
1870-74	100	100	100	100
1883-87	117	217	120	117
1900-04	185	588	156	151

Source: Raymond Goldsmith, "The Economic Growth of Tsarist Russia, 1860-1913," *Economic Development and Cultural Change* 9, no. 2 (1961).

tion from the 1880s to 1904, albeit with considerable annual fluctuations. As aggregate figures, the Goldsmith data tell us little about regional trends or about the distribution of this income between large estates and small peasant households; but it seems unlikely for an economy growing on a per capita basis to experience income distribution effects so perverse that per capita growth was not shared by a substantial percentage of the population.

National Income: Gregory

I have just completed a study of Russian national income during the industrialization era of Russia, and these findings also shed light on the agrarian crisis hypothesis. The Goldsmith study of national income was incomplete for several reasons. The Goldsmith study was based upon the two indexes reported above; other components of Russian national income were inferred from very sketchy data. Also, Goldsmith's agricultural indexes are not for empire territory for the entire period under investigation. Goldsmith had to rely heavily on data for the fifty European provinces and thus to understate the growth of agricultural production for the Russian empire. Further, Goldsmith used gross agricultural production series despite the existence of alternate series on net production.

My results are reported in Table 1.2.

Table 1.2   Growth of Russian National Income, 1883-1913 (annual growth rates)

period	agriculture	industry +	trade and services	national income
1883-87 to 1897-1901	2.55	5.45	2.50	3.4
1897-1901 to 1909-13	3.0	3.6	2.8	3.1

Source: Paul Gregory, *Russian National Income, 1885-1913* (Cambridge: Cambridge University Press, 1982).

The Russian population grew at an annual rate of slightly over 1.5 percent between 1883 and 1901 (the urban population at a rate of some 2.5 percent). My results are supportive of the Goldsmith series in suggesting that there was substantial per capita growth of real income during the decades preceding the 1905 revolution. Growth rates of agricultural output after the turn of the century were not much different from those from 1883 to 1900.

Varzar's Index

A third source of aggregate evidence is an index of per capita output of consumption goods, prepared but never published by the prominent Russian statistician, V. E. Varzar. Varzar's index consists of physical output series weighted by 1913 prices. It includes goods that are obviously consumer goods such as grains, animal products, and textiles, but also includes some producer goods such as pig iron and copper. Thus the Varzar production index is by no means ideal. Varzar's index is reported in Table 1.3.

AGRICULTURAL PRODUCTION SERIES, THE EVIDENCE

The population of the Russian empire grew at an annual rate of slightly over 1.5 percent between 1885 and 1905. The rural population accounted for 85 percent of the total, and the growth rate of the rural population was just slightly under 1.5 percent per annum. The question therefore is: Did Russian agricultural output grow faster or slower than the Russian population?

Two indexes of agricultural production were cited in Tables 1.1 and 1.2. Both rely heavily on the official Ministry of Interior series of grain production. They differ in territorial coverage, and one (the Goldsmith series) is a gross production series and the other (Gregory) is a net production series. This latter difference is not inconsequential because the ratio of net to gross production rose substantially between 1885 and 1913.[9] The increase in the net to gross output ratio is not a rare phenomenon (a change of similar magnitude occurred in Germany). Territorial adjustments are also important because agricultural production grew more rapidly outside the fifty non-European Russian provinces. Therefore, indexes that cover the non-European provinces yield higher rates of growth.

Table 1.3 **Varzar's Index of Output of Consumption Goods, 1913 prices**

period	value of production mln. rubles	per capita output
1887	4298	48.0
1904	7057	60.6

Source: P. P. Maslov, *Kriticheski analiz burzhuaznykh statisticheskikh publikatsii* (Moscow: Nauka, 1955), p. 459.

The real complication in evaluating these agricultural production series is that no major study of intertemporal bias has ever been undertaken. The studies that do exist deal more with the degree to which crop figures must be raised for underreporting at one point in time, rather than with the issue of changing bias over time. It is always possible that improving coverage will impart an upward bias to any historical series, but so far the literature has failed to demonstrate that such a bias exists in the Russian series.

Both the Goldsmith series and my own series suggest that agricultural production grew more rapidly than the rural population between the 1880s and 1905. Both series grew at circa 2.5 percent per annum. According to both series, agricultural output per capita was growing at around 1 percent per capita. The available agricultural output series do not suggest declining output per capita in agriculture. Instead, they point to a rather substantial growth of per capita farm output when cumulated over twenty years. Extraordinary upward biases would be required to yield a declining per capita output series.

EXPORTS

One of the arguments for the agrarian crisis position is the fact that "hunger exports" were being forced from the rural population. It is argued that rising per capita agricultural output was not going to raise rural living standards. Instead, peasants, faced with an insurmountable tax burden, were forced to channel increases in output into the export market.

An examination of grain export statistics (which are likely the most reliable statistics cited in this paper) reveals that grain exports did indeed grow more rapidly than grain output. Between 1884 and 1904, grain exports grew at an annual rate of circa 3.5 percent, as compared to an annual growth rate of grain output of 2.5 percent.[10] The ratio of grain exports to grain output therefore rose at an annual rate of around 1 percent during the period under investigation.

Do increasing grain exports mean that peasants were being "forced" by oppressive taxes to part involuntarily with their grain production? This is not necessarily the case. By marketing grain, peasants were simply following the classic pattern of exchanging cash crops for manufactured goods and other farm products. Such exchanges, if voluntary, typically raise, rather than lower, standards of well-being. The question is therefore: Were such exchanges voluntary? It is doubtful that the state possessed sufficient power in the countryside to force peasants to part involuntarily with their output. The evidence on tax arrears suggests that peasants treated direct tax obligations rather casually. Theoretically fixed tax payments showed a strong positive correlation with agricultural incomes. It is hard to imagine the peasant community marketing grain in face of hunger in order to meet direct tax obligations. The state's reliance on indirect taxes supports the position that peasants could not be forced by direct taxes to market output against their wishes.

AGRICULTURAL CAPITAL STOCK

One useful indicator of rural living standards is the real reproducible capital wealth of the agricultural population. The real capital stock of a farm population consists of its livestock herds, farm equipment, inventories, and farm structures. Unfortunately, the most common indicator of rural wealth—livestock herds—is subject to a wide margin of error. The official series on livestock herds gathered by veterinary authorities and the Ministry of Agriculture is considered unreliable, and we cannot determine from this evidence whether per capita livestock holdings were rising per capita between the 1880s and 1904. Two recent studies come to quite different conclusions concerning per capita growth of livestock herds.[11]

We do have better data on trends in other forms of real capital wealth in Russian agriculture. The available estimates of the agricultural capital stock are recorded in Table 1.4.

The available capital stock series therefore suggest that the agricultural capital stock was growing more rapidly than farm population between 1890 and 1904. This is true whether one uses a slow or more rapidly growing series for livestock herds.

Rural Living Standards

National income series, agricultural production series, and agricultural capital stock series all point to rising per capita output between the 1880s and 1904. Such series, however, do not shed light on the regional and household distributions of the aggregate series. It is quite possible, for example, for one agricultural region to experience declining per capita output while the aggregate series is growing per capita. It is also possible for one agricultural population group, say small land holders, to experience declining per capita output while the aggregate series grows. The issue of regional disparities will not be addressed in this paper, but it no doubt has played an important role in the agrarian crisis debate.

Table 1.4   Annual Growth Rate of Agricultural Capital Stock, Russia, 1890–1914, 1913 Prices

1. Equipment and structures	2.7%
2. Equipment, structures, and livestock (Kahan)	1.8%
3. Equipment, structures, and livestock (Gregory)	2.0%

Sources: Arcadius Kahan, "Capital Formation during the Period of Early Industrialization in Russia 1890–1913," in *The Cambridge Economic History of Europe,* vol. VII, part 2 (Cambridge: Cambridge University Press, 1978), p. 300; Gregory, *Russian National Income, 1885–1913* (Cambridge: Cambridge University Press, 1982) Appendix 8 and Appendix 9. In column 1, the Gregory series on farm structures is used with Kahan's series on farm equipment.

It is not possible to break the various series down into estate series and small farm series. However, it is important to the agrarian crisis debate to establish whether aggregate per capita growth was shared by peasant farmers or emanated only from the large estates.

I have addressed this question in another paper.[12] I have attempted to calculate nonmarketed grain products available for consumption on the farm. In this calculation, I have attempted to adjust for inventory holdings, so as to rule out large inventory accumulations by the large estates. Grain retained for own consumption (given Adam Smith's adage about the demand for food being limited by the capacity of the stomach) should be roughly indicative of the farm population's consumption of grain products, at least in the "grain surplus" provinces. My results are summarized in Table 1.5.

These figures on retained food grains suggest growth rates well above the growth rate of the rural population. They also suggest a changing composition of retained farm products in favor of the "luxury" grain, wheat. In the 1880s, wheat was primarily produced for the market, and rye was consumed by the peasant family. By the turn of the century, farm families were retaining significant portions of their wheat crops—a fairly clear sign of rising per capita income.

A DUAL ECONOMY?

The agrarian crisis thesis could still hold in the face of some of the contrary evidence related above if these were indeed a strong "dual" economy at work in the tsarist economy. This dual economy would consist of a backward and primitive peasant agriculture and an advanced industrial economy. For such a dual economy to exist, there would have to be some mechanism for limiting the flows between the two sectors, particularly flows of population and labor force. The dual economy thesis is based, in part, on the notion that the emancipation placed such severe restrictions on mobility that large income differentials could emerge between agriculture and industry. In this way, the farm population was forced to shoulder the burden of industrial investment.

What evidence is there of a dual Russian economy? One can look at two sorts of evidence: evidence on urban and rural living standards, and evidence on relative agricultural-industrial productivity growth. In Table

---

Table 1.5   Retained Grain Products, 1913 prices, Russia (million rubles)

year	wheat	rye	barley	potatoes	total
1885–89	154 (100)	551 (100)	113 (100)	65 (100)	883 (100)
1897–1901	344 (223)	649 (118)	168 (149)	171 (263)	1332 (151)

Source: Paul Gregory, "Grain Marketings and Peasant Consumption, Russia, 1885–1913," *Explorations in Economic History,* 17 (1980): 147.

1.6, I assemble data on growth indexes of "urban" and "rural" real consumption. It goes almost without saying that these two indexes are quite inexact. The urban index assumes that all retail sales were to urban residents, and the rural component includes only retained farm products and rural housing services.

Table 1.6   Urban and Rural Consumption Expenditures (annual growth rates)

year	urban consumption	rural consumption	government
1885–89 to 1889–93	1.2	.4	.4
1889–93 to 1893–97	5.7	5.9	11.9
1893–97 to 1897–01	5.7	1.6	3.4
1897–01 to 1901–05	2.9	3.1	2.9
1885–89 to 1897–01	3.2	2.7	4.5

Source: Gregory, *Russian National Income, 1885–1913* (Cambridge: Cambridge University Press, 1982), Table 6–2.

The two indexes on "urban" and "rural" real expenditures fail to reveal a large divergence between urban and rural real consumption trends. Real rural consumption growth is likely underestimated, due to the allocation of all retail sales to the urban population.

The relative rate of growth of agricultural labor productivity in Russia and other countries is given in Table 1.7. A dual Russian economy would be shown by low relative rates of growth of agricultural labor productivity vis-à-vis other countries. As Table 1.7 indicates, Russian agricultural labor productivity growth does not stand out as being extraordinarily low relative to other countries.

CONCLUSIONS

The empirical evidence fails to support the agrarian crisis hypothesis. There is little evidence of declining per capita incomes or living standards in Russian agriculture between the 1880s and 1905. Instead, the picture is one of an agricultural population that was experiencing rising per capita income and living standards. The evidence presented in this paper is aggregative and does not rule out the possibility of declining per capita incomes in particular agricultural regions. In fact, the origins of the agrarian crisis hypothesis may ultimately be traced to certain agricultural regions that were suffering substantial declines in real incomes. For the empire as a whole, this did not appear to be the case.

The Western literature has always been ambivalent in its assessment of tsarist Russian agriculture. On the one hand, Russia's prominent role in the world grain market is cited as evidence of the strength of prerevolutionary Russian agriculture and the weakness of contemporary Soviet agriculture.

Table 1.7   **The Rate of Growth of Agricultural Labor Productivity ÷ Rate of Growth of Industrial Labor Productivity, Russia and Selected Countries**

Country	Period	Relative growth rate
Russia	1883–1913	.75
Germany	1850–1909	.67
France	1870–1911	.99
U.S.	1870–1910	.87
Japan	1880–1920	.86
Norway	1875–1910	1.00
Canada	1880–1910	.77
UK	1801–1901	.74

Sources: The French and Norwegian figures are calculated from Simon Kuznets, *Modern Economic Growth* (New Haven: Yale University Press, 1966), Tables 3–1 and 3–2. The German data are calculated from Walther Hoffman, *Das Wachstum der deutschen Wirtschaft seit der Mitte des 19. Jahrhunderts* (Berlin: Springer, 1965), pp. 33, 35. The Japanese figure is from Kuznets, "Notes on Japan's Economic Growth," *Economic Growth: The Japanese Experience since the Meiji Era* ed. L. Klein and K. Ohkawa (Homewood, Ill.: Richard D. Irwin, 1968), pp. 398–99. The Canadian, British, and American figures are from the following sources: O. J. Firestone, *Canada's Economic Development, 1867–1953*, Income and Wealth Series, vol. V (London: Bowes and Bowes, 1958), pp. 184–88; P. M. Deane and W. A. Cole, *British Economic Growth, 1688–1959* (Cambridge: At the University Press, 1962), pp. 142, 166; Stanley Lebergott, "Labor Force and Employment, 1800–1960," *Output, Employment and Productivity in the United States after 1800*, Studies in Income and Wealth, vol. 30 (Princeton: Princeton University Press, 1961), pp. 118–120; Department of Commerce, *Historical Statistics of the United States from Colonial Times to the Present*, F216–225.

On the other hand, the agrarian crisis hypothesis has typically painted a very bleak picture of the state of tsarist agriculture. It would appear that Russian agriculture performed much better than the proponents of the agrarian crisis hypothesis would have us think.

NOTES

1. Alec Nove, *An Economic History of the USSR* (London: Penguin, 1969), p. 19; Alexander Gerschenkron, "Agrarian Policies and Industrialization: Russia 1861–1917," *Cambridge Economic History of Europe* (Cambridge: Cambridge University Press, 1965); Lazar Volin, *A Century of Russian Agriculture* (Cambridge: Harvard University Press, 1970).

2. For a survey of the literature from the perspective of a historian, see Eberhard Mueller,

"Der Beitrag der Bauern zur Industrialisierung Russlands 1885–1930," *Jahrbuecher fuer die Geschichte Osteuropas,* 27 H.2, (1979): pp. 197–219.

3. R. Hennesy, *The Agrarian Question in Russia 1905–1907* (Giessen: W. Schmitz, 1977), p. 22.

4. On this, see James Y. Simms, Jr., "The Crisis in Russian Agriculture at the End of the 19th Century: A Different View," *Slavic Review* 36, no. 3 (1977). pp. 377–98.

5. S. Blanc, *Die Landarbeiterverhaeltnisse in Russland* (Zurich: Rascher, 1913), chapter 9.

6. Paul Gregory, "1913 Russian National Income—Some Insights Into Russian Economic Development," *Quarterly Journal of Economics* 90, no. 3 (August 1976). pp. 389–405.

7. Paul Gregory, "Economic Growth and Structural Change in Tsarist Russia: a Case of Modern Economic Growth?" *Soviet Studies* 23, no. 3 (1972), pp. 418–34.

8. Raymond Goldsmith, "The Economic Growth of Tsarist Russia 1860–1913," *Economic Development and Cultural Change* 9 no. 3 (April 1961), pp. 441–76.

9. Paul Gregory, *Russian National Income, 1885–1913,* (Cambridge: Cambridge University Press, 1982), Appendix 5.

10. *Sbornik statistiko-ekonomicheskikh svedenii po sel'skomu khoziaistvu Rossii i inostrannykh gosudarstv* 7 (Petrograd, 1915).

11. Arcadius Kahan, "Capital Formation during the Period of Early Industrialization in Russia 1890–1913," *Cambridge Economic History of Europe,* vol. VII, part 2 (Cambridge: Cambridge University Press, 1978), pp. 265–307.

12. Paul Gregory, "Grain Marketings and Peasant Consumption, Russia, 1885–1913," *Explorations in Economic History* 17, no. 2. (April, 1980). pp. 135–64.

2

A Reevaluation of Soviet Agricultural Production in the 1920s and 1930s

S. G. Wheatcroft

This paper is a reevaluation of the scale and value of Soviet agricultural production in the 1920s and 1930s and in comparison with the prerevolutionary period. Particular attention is paid to the complex of relationships within agriculture and to some of the regional dimensions of this complex. But work on this subject is far from complete. I have carried out a brief survey of available agricultural production indices for the whole USSR (all-Union indices) and have made preliminary all-Union estimates.[1] But more detailed work on each branch of agriculture is required before a final version with a detailed regional and sectoral breakdown can be computed.[2] Work is most advanced on analyzing grain production and utilization in detail up to the end of the 1920s.[3]

This paper provides a brief review of current knowledge on agricultural production; a guide to continuing research on this topic; and some preliminary results concerning preliminary all-Union agriculture production indices and a regional account of the complex of relationships associated with the production of the major agricultural product of this period—grain.

THE AVAILABLE INDICATORS ON THE SCALE OF SOVIET AGRICULTURAL PRODUCTION

In the 1920s and early 1930s several relatively short series of agricultural production statistics were produced in the USSR. These were connected with work on the balances of the national economy and the control figures.[4]

Apart from these earlier partial series, there are three series of agricultural production figures that cover a more lengthy period. These are (a) a former Soviet official (but presently discredited) series, which was published in the 1930s, (b) an American index calculated by D. Gale

---

This research on Soviet agriculture forms part of a project on Soviet Economic History that is financed by the British Social Science Research Council.

Johnson and Arcadius Kahan in 1959, and (c) a new revised Soviet index, which was also first published in 1952.[5]

The former (1930s) Soviet official gross agricultural production series has to be pieced together from several sources and even then only spans 1913, 1929–35, 1937, and 1938.[6] It is not comparable with any of the series produced in the 1920s, although it is given in fixed 1926–27 prices. It is divided into arable and livestock sectors and a few major product groups within these sectors. But no regional figures are available.

The major feature of this series is the sharp rise in arable production from 1933. All the major Western experts working on Soviet agriculture in the 1930s refused to accept the veracity of this indication of growth. The existence of a "biological" yield distortion in the data from 1933 to the early 1950s has now been accepted in the Soviet Union.

The American series calculated by Johnson and Kahan was worked out at a time before the official Soviet figures had been revised.[7] The American index was based upon just eleven products. Official physical product evaluations were used for all of these apart from grain, the physical quantity of which was deflated in line with a fairly obscure Soviet hint, and with the generally held belief that such a deflation was necessary. When Johnson came to revise the index and compare it with the official Soviet index in 1963, he then substituted the revised Soviet grain production figures for his earlier estimates and added a 1913 indicator.[8] In order to calculate aggregate totals, the eleven products were weighted with fairly crude 1926–27 fixed prices taken from the 1929–30 control figures. No regional breakdown was given.

The current Soviet index of agricultural production first appeared in the 1958 annual statistical handbook, published in 1959.[9] This is an index based on 1913 = 100. Values are given for arable and livestock production as well as for gross agricultural production. It is evaluated in fixed 1926–27 prices for all years up to 1950 and appears to be based on the former 1930s series, with adjustments being made for 1933 and subsequent yield data, with revised coverage of livestock produce for the 1920s, and with a revision of the pre–World War I indicator. Both the first two points would add to the reliability of the index, but there still remain considerable problems of intertemporal comparability, between the 1920s and the 1930s and between both of these and the prerevolutionary period.

Two important conclusions follow from an analysis of the available data. First, there are some fairly important differences between the new official series and the Johnson and Kahan series. The main differences are that (1) Johnson and Kahan had a much more favorable evaluation of the level of production in 1930 than did the official Soviet index; (2) they considered the 1913–1928 growth to have been less than indicated in the official index; and (3) the absolute low point in production came in 1932 and not 1933. As will become apparent below, my results differ even more strongly from the official series than do the Johnson and Kahan series. Second, very little detail about agricultural production on a regional basis is currently available. This topic will be dealt with in some detail in the present study.

TOWARD A REEVALUATION OF SOVIET AGRICULTURAL PRODUCTION

The first step in the reevaluation of Soviet agricultural production is to get as clear as possible a definition of the nature of agricultural production and its coverage. We have to ensure that we are in a position to make a meaningful quantitative evaluation of those detailed aspects of production and production flows that we wish to analyze. Then we have to consider these quantitative evaluations in physical terms, in order to assess the reliability and comparability of these evaluations. Finally, these physical evaluations have to be transferred into value units for further aggregation. I will begin by proposing a working definition of the agricultural system.

The Agricultural System: Product Coverage and Product Flows

In this paper I consider two aspects of the agricultural system, the production and distribution of all the different kinds of agricultural produce throughout the country as a whole and the production and distribution of one product, grain, throughout the different regions of the USSR.

Product Coverage and All-Union Distribution

Figure 2.1 presents a model of Soviet agriculture indicating the main directions of product flows between the different sectors within agriculture and the flows between agriculture and the other parts of the economy and social system.

The arable sector includes the production of grains, potatoes, vegetables, technical crops, and fodder. All of these, with the exception of fodder, were included in the Johnson and Kahan calculations. The livestock sector includes milk, meat, eggs, and wool, which were all included in the Johnson and Kahan index; but it also includes changes in the herd stocks (as regard both draft animals and meat stock), the production of manure, and hides.

The major differences in product coverage between my index and the Johnson-Kahan index are the inclusion of a larger number of products that are used primarily within agriculture itself in my index. My gross agricultural production figure is therefore less commodity-oriented than their figure.

Geographical Coverage of the Agriculture System

Figure 2.2 divides the country into five major regions with fairly distinct production and utilization characteristics. These regions were based on major classifications used in the 1920s with reference specifically to grain production and utilization, but they nevertheless have fairly general significance.

Two of the regions are consumer regions: the Northern Consumer Region (NCR), comprising the Moscow Industrial Region, the North, North-West (Leningrad Industrial Region) and BSSR, and the Southern Consumer

Figure 2.1
"MODEL" of agricultural interrelationships

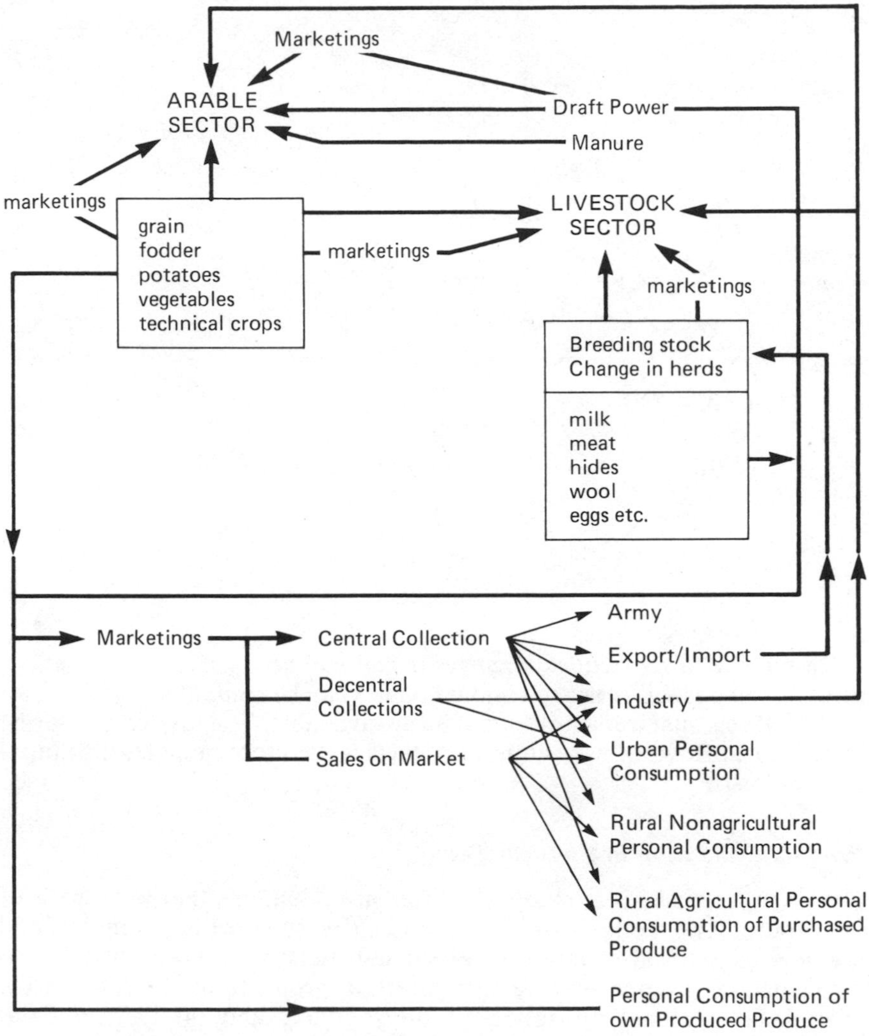

*Note: Marketings refer to all forms of marketings,
i.e., state collections, free market, hiring
out of animals, etc.*

Region (SCR), comprising Transcaucasia and the Central Asian republics.
The three producer regions are the Southern Producer Region (SPR), com-
prising the Ukraine and North Caucasus, the Central Producer Region
(CPR), comprising the Central Agricultural Region and the Volga Region,
and finally the Eastern Producer Region (EPR), comprising the Urals,
Siberia, the Far Eastern Region, and Kazakhstan.

Figure 2.2
The pre-1939 area of the USSR, indicating the basic
producer and consumer regions used in this study

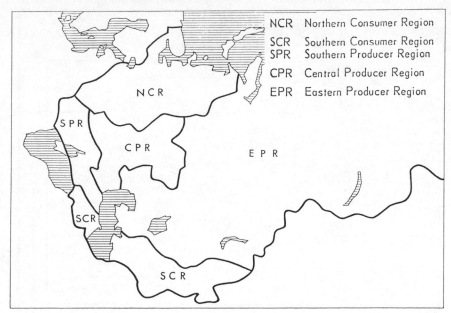

NCR   Northern Consumer Region
SCR   Southern Consumer Region
SPR   Southern Producer Region
CPR   Central Producer Region
EPR   Eastern Producer Region

Despite the fairly frequent changes in regional boundaries in this period, roughly comparable series of regional figures can be computed[10] and at least until 1935 regional transportation data are available. The task of measuring interregional flows of agricultural products is therefore quite feasible (until 1935 at least).

Product Evaluation in Physical Terms

The procedure used is to study: (1) different evaluations that were made of the product, the methods of evaluation and reasons for adjustments, and the general political situation in which statisticians were working; (2) indirect data associated with factors affecting production; (3) data on the overall and regional utilization of the produce; and (4) indirect data, associated with product availability.

Product Evaluation, Changes in Evaluation and Political Atmosphere

Arable production was initially estimated by Soviet statisticians on the basis of sown area statistics, average expected yields (for most of the 1920s, this was the accepted prewar level of yields), a condition factor (normally a figure on the 0–5 scale reflecting how much the harvest was above or below average). The level of harvesting losses was incorporated in the level of average expected yield. Corrections were justified on statistical grounds on the basis of knowledge of utilization, a belief that peasants and local statisticians always tended to conceal the true level of production, and trial surveys. Several methods of trial harvesting and threshing were used before the development of the *metrovka* method in the early 1930s (this used a 1-meter square device to collect sample harvests from the fields for threshing). After 1933 the *metrovka* measurements began to be substituted directly for the yield assessment instead of being used as a mere control method. The trial harvesting and threshing carried out by the *metrovka* method involved no or very little harvest losses and so was an indication of the "biological" rather than the barn yield. But it did not necessarily represent a totally new level of distortion. Trial threshings and many other methods had been used earlier to bid up the harvest evaluations. And earlier the use as the basic average level upon which to apply condition corrections of a prewar yield figure, which had been substantially corrected upwards, had also resulted in large upwards corrections. For most of this period it appears to me that the statistical reason for making adjustments to the evaluation of arable production was in any case far less important than the political reasons. I will return to the political reasons later.

During this period, livestock production was evaluated on the basis of changes in the age and sex structure of the different animals in the herd; average yields of nonterminal produce and their wastage; and average slaughter weight indicators for the slaughtered contingent and their wastage. If anything, livestock produce calculations were more difficult than arable ones, but there was considerably less conflict over them.

Throughout the 1920s there were major discussions between the statisticians and the planners over the different evaluations of agricultural production in general and of arable production in particular. The State Planning Commission (Gosplan) consistently favored higher evaluations than the Central Statistical Administration (TsSU) over both current and prerevolutionary arable production.[11]

Given the political atmosphere of the times and the striving for higher and higher plans,[12] agricultural production statistics had taken on "real political significance," as Ordzhonikidze once remarked.[13] Under such circumstances the resolution of the conflict between the statisticians and the planners was more of a political than a scholarly question.

As early as 1926, the task of evaluating the scale of agricultural production was taken out of the hands of TsSU and placed in the hands of an Expert Council of representatives from various interested agencies, who voted on what size crop should be accepted. But even this Expert Council failed to produce politically acceptable figures in 1929, when a correction to production was politically necessary to justify an increase in planned grain collections.[14] However, after the purging of the Expert Council, the arrest and disappearance of its most prominent member and the transfer of TsSU into a mere accounting sector of Gosplan, the statisticians became less vocal in their opposition to proposed corrections.

For several years the task of making evaluations of agricultural production fell directly upon a department of Gosplan (the Statistical Economics Sector of Gosplan was renamed the Department of National Economic Accounts in 1931, in order to emphasize its subordination to the plans).

Osinskii, the major political figure involved in statistics, later characterized this as a period dominated by "the psychology of planning constructivism; since the plan must be fulfilled and over-fulfilled it follows that the planned figure is ultimately substituted for the result even though this does not always correspond with reality."[15]

In 1932 the central statistical agency (now known as TsUNKhU) was strengthened and given more independence from Gosplan, and Osinskii returned to its directorship.[16]

In 1932 and the first part of 1933, Osinskii did appear to succeed in producing more independent and objective evaluations and even in building up his own independent network of harvest evaluation inspectors—the interregional committees for harvest evaluations (MRK)—under the Central State Committee for harvest evaluations (TsGK), under his own chairmanship. But during the 1933 harvest campaign Molotov and Stalin took direct action to circumscribe Osinskii's committees, to put pressure on local harvest evaluations through local party groups and particularly through the newly created political departments.[17] This resulted in a great inflation in evaluations. The original 1933 mechanism for this inflation was simply local subjective evaluations, but the continuation of this level of inflation soon became institutionalized in the form of substituting the biological yield or quasi-biological yield for barn yield evaluations.

The 1933 and subsequent biological yield distortions appear therefore not so much as the initiation of a distortion, but as a method of continuing a distortion already present, the removal of which was being threatened.

Evaluations of the output of the livestock sector in the 1920s were less closely affected by political factors. Unlike grain, whose marketings were planned by the state from the early 1920s, livestock produce marketings remained almost exclusively private until the late 1920s. TsSU was consequently allowed to keep control over these evaluations throughout this period.

The decline in meat weight of the herds was apparent in 1928–29,[18] following the severe grain collections crisis of spring 1928; but for a while in the late 1920s and early 1930s the figures for the production of the livestock sector were offered exclusive of changes in the meat weight in the herds. These therefore indicated increases in the level of production of the livestock sector in the catastrophic years of 1928–29 and 1929–30, when the level of production including the loss in weight of the herds was falling very dramatically.[19]

The leading TsUNKhU livestock expert was later to complain about the mistaken tendency to confuse livestock output (*vykhod*) with livestock production.[20] He went on to say that there were still serious methodological as well as technical problems associated with livestock production evaluation and he even presented a revised scheme of how he considered the calculation of livestock production should be changed. Several of the elements that he recommended have subsequently been adopted, such as giving considerably more emphasis to changes in the meat weight of herds. But other eminently sensible suggestions have not been accepted, such as including the value of rearing draft animals and breeders and of changes in their stock. These were two aspects of livestock production that were very important and appear to me to be directly analogous to tractors or machine tools, whose value is certainly included in the value of gross industrial production. Their exclusion is to some extent symbolic of a tendency to underestimate the complex internal interrelationships within agriculture, but it must be admitted that Western economists are also guilty of this tendency.[21]

Nimitz is correct in claiming that the currently accepted series of meat and milk production data are not comparable with the data of the 1930s,[22] because in the latter meat included only cow meat, pig meat, and sheep meat, and milk included only cow's milk. (Incidentally, a large share of the increase in nonmain animal meat in the early 1930s indicated in the current data must have been due to the consumption of horse meat). But I would disagree with Nimitz's claim that the inclusion of offal has changed the data; the apparent change in the ratio of meat to slaughter weight for the main three animals was due to the classification of bacon, ham, and sausage meat as offal.[23]

Comparing the postrevolutionary and prerevolutionary data is very complicated. I have argued that there was initially little statistical justification for adding a large correction to the prerevolutionary arable data; that this correction was added by Gosplan mainly to assist them in bidding up their evaluations of the harvests of the 1920s; but that it has to be accepted to maintain comparability with harvest evaluations of the late 1920s. The removal of this correction in the 1930s and a further deflation of these figures in the 1950s is consequently unjustifiable and makes the data noncomparable with the currently accepted figures for the 1920s.[24]

Comparisons of prerevolutionary and postrevolutionary livestock produce are highly uncertain because of the uncertain nature of prerevolutionary livestock figures. The official attitude has been to reject the standard prerevolutionary livestock registration statistics totally and to accept the level of livestock as indicated by the 1916 livestock census as being more indicative of the prewar level. But the Soviet economist A. L. Vainshtein has argued, convincingly, that the prewar level of livestock was much higher than the 1916 level and that consequently considerably higher correction figures should be accepted.[25]

Indirect Data Associated With Factors Affecting Production

Unfortunately work along these lines has not progressed far enough yet for any great reliability to be placed on these elements. But they are mentioned here for the sake of completeness and to provide an indication of what work is being carried on and where it is hoped to lead.

The effects of agro-meteorological data on yields, the level of veterinary diseases on animal wastage, and the level of livestock feed data on livestock numbers may all be considered as relationships that could provide us with background data.

The Overall Utilization of the Produce

An investigation of the total utilization of the produce will ensure that very large errors will not be made. Under normal circumstances the reliability of production figures based on utilization cannot be very high, certainly not as high as the reliability of direct production data. But these were not normal circumstances, for we are dealing with fairly large distortions in production data. Moreover, in the 1920s, very detailed balances of production and utilization were drawn up, and special statistical investigations were made to improve knowledge of general utilization norms. In any case, an understanding of utilization is important in itself and for an understanding of the scale of marketing production.

In the 1920s there was a whole sector of TsSU under the distinguished statistician A. E. Lositskii, and they organized a whole series of sample survey consumption and feed investigations. As zemstvo statisticians before the revolution, Lositskii and his colleagues were already heirs to a great tradition of detailed peasant budget studies. During the first world war the government had employed many of these statisticians in working out food consumption plans. After the revolution, when they were given their own statistical office, they set about enthusiastically gathering their utilization data. If anything, Lositskii was too enthusiastic in his claims and too ambitious about his consumption and utilization balances.[26] They often served as the basis for inflating already high production figures. Great care has to be taken in using them, and it should be remembered that balances can always be drawn at the level sought by the statistician. But they are nevertheless a unique source of data. Much detailed state-collection, transportation, and industrial utilization data are available. Population figures and livestock figures can be estimated from the demographic censuses and the far more frequent livestock censuses. Changes in food consumption per capita and consumption of feed per capita of livestock-type, in comparison with their late 1920s levels, are somewhat problematical, but there are few scattered indicators upon which to base hypotheses.

Seed utilization is relatively straightforward, given abundant sowing data and the assumption that seed ratios did not change much.

Wastage and stock changes are the greatest problems. We do have the 1920s data, but these were very controversial questions even then. As I emphasized above, great care has to be taken with these data, possible margins of error have to be carefully watched, and even then only approximate indicators can appear.

Indirect Data Associated to Some Extent With Product Availability

Finally we come to the kolkhoz market price data, which may be considered relatively free-market price data. These can serve as useful indicators of changing availability over time and by region of the different products.

They should, however, be used in conjunction with the utilization balance data to ensure that there is nothing significant happening to change matters on the demand side.

The detailed results of these analyzed production and utilization series are to appear as SIPS *Discussion Papers*.

Product Evaluation in Value Terms

From the late 1920s until 1933 there was considerable inflationary pressure on the private market for agricultural goods, while state collection and state retail prices were kept more or less stable. This could only be achieved by fracturing the markets, by making deliveries to the state obligatory, and by rationing retail sales. The deflationary measures of 1933 (the great increase in state retail prices and the sharp reduction in money supply) produced a stability in agricultural prices that remained more or less to the end of the decade. The gap between state retail prices and market retail prices closed, but both were at a level considerably higher than in the 1920s. For state collection versus market prices, the position was very different. State collection prices remained at the very low 1920s level for grain, although there was a considerable improvement in the prices for industrial crops and livestock produce. There was a slight moderation in the severity of the very low state grain collection prices, by means of quality and assortment bonuses and of slightly higher prices for decentralized state purchases (*zakupki*) that were authroized after the fulfillment of the state deliveries plan. But the difference between the state collection price and the private market price remained very large. (Of course private market sales could only be carried out after the fulfillment of the state collection plan.)

The multiplicity of prices, the existence of severe market restrictions, and the great inflation of the late 1920s and early 1930s have all contributed to making the task of measuring agricultural production especially difficult. Agricultural production can either be measured in fixed prices or in current value terms, by using the prices actually current in different markets at different times. This paper is primarily concerned with evaluations in fixed prices.

Most fixed-price evaluations in this period were in 1926–27 prices[27] and there are sound reasons for this. In 1926–27 the agricultural markets (both stage collections and retail) were not as artificially divided as they were later to be. Consequently the differences between the state and private prices were not very large,[28] and so the overall average price was not very susceptible to changes in the shares of marketed and nonmarketed production.

The all-Union 1926–27 prices for individual products are readily available in the 1929–30 control figures, and this source was used by Johnson and Kahan.[29] Less aggregated regional prices, however, can be calculated only for grain from this source. The 1926–27 regional prices for grain in the major regions are given below:

    NCR   81.9 rubles per ton
    SCR 105.2 rubles per ton
    SPR   53.4 rubles per ton

Table 2.1   Gross Agricultural Production in Physical Terms (preliminary results)

| | Grain Variants | | Potatoes | Vegetables | Wild Hay | Sown Hay | Oil Seeds | Sugar beet | Flax Fibre |
	High	Low							
1909/13	79.9	68							
1913	92.7	79	29.9	8.6			0.7	10.8	0.3
1924	51.4	44	35.3					3.5	0.3
1925	72.5	62	38.4		58.9	4.9	2.2	9.1	0.3
1926	76.6	66	42.8		65.0	5.7	1.6	6.4	0.3
1927	71.7	62	42.5	10.4	65.5	8.5	2.2	10.4	0.2
1928	73.3	63	45.2	10.5	67.6	10.5	2.1	10.1	0.3
1929	71.7	62	45.1	10.6	56.8	12.9	1.8	6.3	0.4
1930	78	67	44.6	13.9	47.1	13.7	1.6	14.0	0.4
1931	68	62	40.6	16.8	51.1	16.9	2.5	12.1	0.6
1932	68	62	37.2	17.6	41.9	14.7	2.3	6.6	0.5
1933	74	68	44.0	21.8	41.6	12.0	2.4	9.0	0.5
1934	75	68	44.2	20.0	41.4	11.1	2.1	11.4	0.5
1935	80	75	53.8	16.8		(13.4)	1.9	16.2	0.6
1936	66	60	44.7			(16.6)	1.5	16.8	0.6
1937	100	95	58.7			(16.5)	2.1	21.9	0.6
1938	76	70	37.5			(21.9)	1.7	16.7	0.5
1939			36.0					16.9	0.5
1940			70.0					18.2	

Note: The above data are in million tons, except for eggs (in milliard units) and hides (in millions).

CPR   50.9 rubles per ton
EPR   48.6 rubles per ton
USSR   57.8 rubles per ton

Major shifts in the importance of different regions in production could lead to an increase in the overall 1926–27 grain prices if the NCR and SCR became more important, and a decrease if they became less important in all-Union production.

My calculations, weighting regional production figures with these different prices, have indicated that regional changes would increase the overall average value of grain production by 1–5 percent in the period 1927–1936 (due to the relative increase in the share of NCR and SCR in total production) and decrease it by 2–4 percent in 1937–40 (as the share of NCR and SCR fell sharply).

Unfortunately a much more complex procedure is necessary to establish the regional significance and regional values for nongrain products.

Table 2.1 (continued)

	Cotton	Change in Draft Stock	Change in Meat Stock	Meat	Milk	Eggs	Large Hides	Small Hides	Wool	Manure
1909/13		(0.2)	(0.2)	3.9		9.5			0.18	11.7
1913	0.5		0.2	4.0	25.1	10.2			0.18	
1924		+1.4	+0.3	3.3	26.3				0.13	10.7
1925	0.6	+2.1	+0.4	3.7	28.2	9.6	11.1	59.2	0.15	11.3
1926	0.6	+2.4	+0.3	4.1	30.5	10.5	12.1	61.6	0.16	12.0
1927	0.7	+1.9	+0.3	4.3	30.6	10.5	13.4	62.5	0.18	12.5
1928	0.8	+1.1	−0.3	4.9	31.0	10.8	17.3	69.5	0.18	17.6
1929	0.9	−4.4	−1.6	5.8	29.8	10.1	23.2	89.9	0.18	11.3
1930	1.1	−3.9	−1.7	4.3	27.0	8.0	17.6	75.3	0.14	9.3
1931	1.3	−6.7	−1.0	3.9	23.4	6.7	16.7	75.1	0.10	7.9
1932	1.3	−3.0	−0.9	2.8	20.6	4.4	12.9	50.1	0.07	6.7
1933	1.3	−0.9	0	2.3	19.2	3.5	10.1	40.6	0.07	6.6
1934	1.2	+0.2	+1.0	2.0	20.8	4.2	7.0	30.5	0.07	7.4
1935	1.7	+0.8	+1.6	2.3	21.4	5.8	7.2	28.9	0.08	8.3
1936	2.4	0	+0.1	3.7	23.5	7.4	10.2	35.6	0.10	8.9
1937	2.6	+0.8	+1.0	3.0	26.1	8.2			0.11	9.4
1938	2.6		+0.7	4.5	29.0	10.5			0.14	10.1
1939	2.7		−1.0	5.1	27.2	11.5			0.15	9.2
1940	2.6		+0.1	3.9	26.6	10.2			0.15	10.3

Note: The above data are in million tons, except for eggs (in milliard units) and hides (in millions).

RESULTS

So far only very incomplete and preliminary results are available. A rough set of all-Union figures has been calculated and weighted with all-Union 1926–27 prices and is presented below in comparison with the current official Soviet series and the Johnson and Kahan series. More detailed regional figures characterizing the complex of relationships associated with grain production and utilization are also presented.

All-Union Aggregated Results

Table 2.1 presents the series of quantitative evaluations of the eighteen different product groups and two variants of grain that have been included in our reevaluation of Soviet agricultural production. The sources of the main data for inclusion in two of the main product groups (grain and potatoes) are given in Appendices 3 and 4 to this paper. More detail on these sources and methods, the sources for the other products, and possibly some revisions will appear in later SIPS Discussion Papers.

Table 2.2 shows major examples of the fixed 1926–27 prices that have been used to convert the above product series into value terms.

Table 2.3 presents an indication of the value of each of these product series in 1926–27 prices and presents subtotals for the nonlivestock and livestock subsectors and for total gross agricultural production.

Table 2.4 presents a comparison of the results of this preliminary reevaluation with the current official Soviet index and with the earlier Johnson and Kahan reevaluations.

The SIPS series differs from the other series in being generally lower in the period 1929–32 and higher after 1935. This applies to both the arable and livestock sectors. The trough in both arable and livestock production comes in 1932, whereas for the official series it comes a year later in 1933.

As regards comparisons with the prerevolutionary situation, the SIPS series indicates that there was far less growth between 1913 and 1928 in both arable and livestock produce than is indicated by the official series or by the Johnson-Kahan series.

Regional Production and Utilization Relationships: The Example of Grain[30]

This section presents some of the work we have been undertaking on regional agricultural developments, looking at the crucial changes in the

---

Table 2.2   1926/27 Prices for Agricultural Products

Grain	57.8 rubles per ton
Potatoes	26.7 rubles per ton
Vegetables	41.9 rubles per ton
Wild hay	24.5 rubles per ton
Sown hay	44.3 rubles per ton
Oil seeds	82.2 rubles per ton
Sugar beet	10.4 rubles per ton
Flax fibre	351 rubles per ton
Cotton fibre	279 rubles per ton
Meat	481 rubles per ton
Milk	62 rubles per ton
Eggs	3 kopecks each
Large hides	10.4 rubles per ton
Small hides	2.5 rubles per ton
Wool	209 rubles per ton
Manure	1.1 rubles per ton

Source: Calculated from data in *Statisticheskii spravochnik SSSR 1928* (1929), pp. 274–81.

Table 2.3a Gross Agricultural Production in Million Rubles (1926/27 prices) (preliminary results)

	High Variant		Low Variant										All Arable	
	Grain	Straw and Chaff	Grain	Straw and Chaff	Potatoes	Vegetables	Wild Hay	Sown Hay	Oil Seeds	Sugar beet	Flax fibre	Cotton	High	Low
1909/13	4618	323	3930	275									(8460)	(7724)
1913	5358	375	4566	320	798	403	1400	400	159	112	117	131	9252	8405
1924	2971	208	2543	178	943									
1925	4191	293	3584	251	1025	596	1443	217	298	94	105	158	8420	7771
1926	4427	310	3815	267	1143	478	1593	253	221	67	95	153	8740	8085
1927	4144	290	3584	251	1135	403	1605	377	281	108	84	201	8628	8029
1928	4237	297	3641	255	1207	502	1656	465	293	105	114	229	9105	8467
1929	4144	290	3584	251	1204	497	1392	571	263	65	127	241	8794	8195
1930	4508	316	3873	271	1191	563	1154	607	265	146	153	311	9214	8534
1931	3930	275	3584	251	1084	685	1252	749	384	125	104	360	9030	8668
1932	3930	275	3584	251	993	619	1027	651	348	68	175	355	8441	8071
1933	4277	299	3930	275	1175	774	1019	532	366	94	192	367	9095	8724
1934	4335	303	3930	275	1180	784	1014	492	335	118	187	328	9076	8643
1935	4624	324	4335	303	1437	930	1224	594	314	168	193	482	10290	9980
1936	3815	267	3468	243	1193	563	1515	735	283	175	204	674	9424	9053
1937	5780	405	5491	384	1567	727	1500	731	343	227	200	719	12199	11889
1938	4393	307	4046	283	1001	513	1600	970	205	174	192	725	10170	9709
1939	4393	307	4046	283	961	448	1600	1000	301	176	176	748	10110	9737
1940														

Source: See S. G. Wheatcroft, A Reevaluation of Soviet Agricultural Production, CREES Discussion Paper, SIPS series (forthcoming).

Table 2.3b Livestock Produce in Million Rubles (1926/27 prices)

	Changes in draft stock	Changes in meat stock	Meat	Milk	Eggs	Large Hides	Small Hides	Wool	Manure	All Livestock
1909/13	+72	+96	1876	1449	284	100	140	38	226	4326
1913	+104	+96	1924	1498	300	104	142	38	228	4486
1924	+140	+144	1592	1582	258	100	136	27	209	4239
1925	+210	+209	1765	1696	281	115	148	32	221	4735
1926	+240	+120	1967	1834	307	126	154	34	234	5079
1927	+190	+120	2083	1840	309	139	156	37	244	5181
1928	+90	−149	2357	1864	317	180	174	38	246	5181
1929	−440	−746	2790	1793	297	241	225	38	221	4480
1930	−390	−794	2073	1624	235	183	188	29	182	3385
1931	−670	−476	1876	1407	196	174	188	20	154	2917
1932	−300	−414	1347	1238	130	134	125	14	131	2446
1933	−90	0	1106	1154	103	105	102	13	129	2660
1934	+20	+467	962	1251	123	73	76	13	145	3173
1935	+80	+789	1106	1287	169	75	72	17	162	3801
1936	0	+63	1780	1413	218	106	89	21	174	3913
1937	+80	+491	1443	1569	240	120	100	22	184	4303
1938	+100	+346	2165	1744	308	110	90	29	197	5149
1939	+50	−495	2453	1635	339	100	90	31	180	4461
1940	−10	+58	1876	1600	301	100	90	37	701	4303

Source: See S. G. Wheatcroft, A Reevaluation of Soviet Agricultural Production, CREES Discussion Paper, SIPS series (forthcoming).

Table 2.3c   All Agricultural Production

	High Variant	Low Variant
1909/13	(12786)	(12050)
1913	13738	12891
1924		
1925	13155	12506
1926	13819	13164
1927	13809	13210
1928	14286	13648
1929	13274	12675
1930	12599	11919
1931	11947	11585
1932	10887	10517
1933	11755	11384
1934	12249	11816
1935	14091	13781
1936	13337	12966
1937	16502	16192
1938	15319	14948
1939	14521	14150
1940		

Source: See S. G. Wheatcroft, A Reevaluation of Soviet Agricultural Production, *CREES Discussion Paper,* SIPS series (forthcoming).

regional production and utilization of grain, particularly in the 1920s as compared with 1913, and in the crucial years of the Soviet industrialization drive from 1928 to 1931.

Despite a slight increase in the production of grain in the two consumer regions in the 1920s, there was still insufficient grain produced to offset the increase in demand in those areas. By the late 1920s the Northern and Southern Consumer Regions still needed to import about a quarter of their needs (they produced about 15 million tons a year and needed to import about 5 million tons).

In the late 1920s the three producer regions were already finding it extremely difficult to satisfy these domestic needs, let alone provide large export surpluses.

Before the revolution, the Southern Producer Region (SPR) had been supplying more than 8 million tons of grain a year surplus to its own requirements. These had been mainly exported abroad. But in the late 1920s a combination of factors resulted in the quantity of available surpluses being about 4 million tons less than before the revolution. The level of production was 1–3 million tons below the prewar level, the increase in population led

Table 2.4 Agricultural Production by Major Sectors: Official, Johnson and Kahan, and SIPS Estimates, 1909/13–1940 (1928 = 100)

	Gross Agricultural Production				Arable Production				Livestock Production		
			SIPS				SIPS				
	Official	J and K	High	Low	Official	J and K	High	Low	Official	J and K	SIPS
1909/13			90	88			93	91			83
1913	81	86	96	94	85	85	98	99	73	87–83	87
1928	100	100	100	100	100	100	100	100	100	100	100
1929	98	101	93	93	99			97	94		87
1930	94	104	88	87	108		101	101	73		65
1931	92	92	84	85	108		99	102	68		57
1932	86	82	76	77	107	91	93	95	55	61	48
1933	81	85	82	83	103		100	103	47		51
1934	85	85	86	87	107		100	102	53		62
1935	96	96	99	101	118		113	118	63		74
1936	88	90	93	95	101		104	107	70		76
1937	108	113	116	119	128	131	134	140	80	71	83
1938	97	99	107	110	103		112	116	88		100
1939	98		102	104	107		111	115	87		86
1940	114	120			132				83		

Sources: Official: Official Soviet series in *Sel'skoe khozyaistvo SSSR*, Moscow: Statistika, 1960, p. 79. J and K: D. Johnson and A. Kahan, "Soviet Agriculture: Structure and Growth," *Comparisons of the United States and Soviet Economies*, part 1, Washington: U.S. Government Printing Office, 1959, pp. 204–6; and D. Johnson, "Agricultural Production" in *Economic Trends in the Soviet Union*, eds. A. Bergson and S. Kuznets, Cambridge: Harvard University Press, 1963, p. 208. SIPS: Wheatcroft's estimates, see text of this paper.

to a rise in personal consumption by 0.6–1.0 million tons, and there was an uncertain and probably higher level of livestock feed consumption.

Before the revolution the main source of grain surpluses for the domestic market was the Central Producer Region (CPR), which produced about 5 million tons of grain surplus to its own requirements. This region had been suffering somewhat from overpopulation even before the revolution, and it suffered most seriously from the drought and famine in the early 1920s. Production levels here in the late 1920s were still about 3–5 million tons below the prewar level, mainly due to the sown areas being still 15 percent lower. The famine and wretched conditions led to much migration, so there was little growth in population in this region. Livestock levels were also much lower than before the revolution, but since those animals that did exist were probably better fed, it is doubtful whether there was any reduction in demand from this source. Overall, therefore, surpluses from this region were only about 1–2 million tons in the 1920s (i.e., 3–4 million tons lower than in 1913).

The Eastern Producer Region was the only one that showed any improvement with regard to grain production and surpluses over this period. Before the revolution it provided less than 1 million tons of grain surpluses. In the 1920s there was a very sharp increase in production of about 30–40 percent, or 4–5 million tons, in comparison with 1909–13. The population rose substantially in this region, by 4–5 million by the late 1920s, and so would have required an additional 1.5 million tons of grain. The livestock level was still much lower than before the war, but again it is uncertain whether this meant that the level of livestock consumption of grain was lower. Overall there were consequently about 1–2 million tons of surplus grain from this region, as opposed to less than 1 million tons before the revolution.

Taken together then, the three producer regions would probably, under normal circumstances, have been in a position to provide about 5 million tons of grain surpluses in the late 1920s. This would normally have been just sufficient to provide for the current requirements of the two consumer regions in the late 1920s, but it would not have provided any further surplus for an increase in demand from these regions or for exports.

Unfortunately, two factors disturbed this potential balance. First, the government attempted to enforce grain exports through increased state collections, second, in 1928 the SPR suffered from an exceptionally bad spell of winter killings, which destroyed 40 percent of the winter sowings, lowered production there by about 5 million tons, and effectively removed the SPR as a surplus-producing region for that year.[31] This led to extreme strain on the already tight utilization balance, the application of extreme measures in state grain collections, and the subsequent decline in livestock. It also pushed the regime into the momentous step of rapidly collectivizing agriculture. The 1928 harvest was fairly high in the EPR, and record collections were made from this region (more than 2 million tons). The severity of the system of forced grain collections was such that it effectively ruined the growth potential of both arable and livestock farming in the EPR. Not only did livestock levels plummet, but so did the levels of grain production and extraregional marketings. It was not until 1934 that the level of production in this region rose again to its 1926 and 1928 level (over 16 million tons) and extraregional marketings to over 1 million tons (in fact 2 millions).

The position in the SPR and CPR was more complicated as a result of the influence of the fine weather conditions of 1930, which produced exceptionally high harvests that allowed large collections to be made. This provided a false indicator of the successes of collectivization and of the forced grain collections system. The export of grain surpluses produced in that year (almost 10 millions tons was exported in the calendar years 1930 and 1931), instead of building up reserves, had disastrous consequences for Soviet agriculture in the following years.

There was little subsequent growth in production in these areas in the early and mid 1930s, but they nevertheless took the full brunt of providing the surpluses for the growing population in the consumer regions. This they were able to do only at the expense of their own consumption, with extremely unfortunate consequences, both for the rural population itself and for livestock husbandry.

CONCLUSIONS

This paper has attempted to provide a review of current research designed to reevaluate Soviet agricultural production nationally and regionally. I conclude that the level of arable and livestock production in the 1920s was much lower in comparison with the prewar data than is currently accepted, either in the Soviet Union or in the West. Moreover, the decline in both arable and livestock sectors by 1932 was more severe than indicated by other sources and actually resulted in a level of production lower than the prewar level.

The discrepancies resulted mainly from the different evaluations in physical terms of the level of production of the main products (particularly grain) in the prewar and subsequent period. It is doubtful whether the finer tuning achieved by the inclusion of any more minor products or by using less crude aggregates would have contributed much.

My regional analysis of grain production and utilization relationships provides, I hope, a different dimension to our understanding of the complexities of the grain problem in these years.

NOTES

1. An earlier version of this survey and estimate, "Soviet Agricultural Production, 1913-1940," (CREES, University of Birmingham, informal working paper) was presented and discussed at a CREES Soviet Industrialisation Project Series (SIPS) Seminar in 1978.

2. These will be appearing as *CREES Discussion Papers* (SIPS series).

3. See S. G. Wheatcroft, "Grain Production and Utilisation in Russia and the USSR before Collectivisation," (Ph.D. thesis, University of Birmingham 1980), and "Grain Production Statistics in the USSR in the 1920s and 1930s," *CREES Discussion Papers,* SIPS No. 13, Birmingham University (1977).

4. For 1923/24 in prewar prices and with a regional breakdown: *Balans narodnogo khozyaistva SSSR 1923-1924g., Trudy TsSU,* XXIX (Moscow: 1926); for 1928, 1939, 1930 in 1928 prices: *Materialy po balansu narodnogo khozyaistva SSSR za 1928, 1929, i 1930 gg.* (Moscow: 1932); for 1913 and 1922/23 in prewar prices: B. A. Gukhman, *Produktsiya i potreblenie SSSR: K Narodno-khozyaist-vennomu balansu (1922/23 khozyaistvennyi god)* (Moscow: 1925); for 1913, 1924/25, and 1925/26 in prewar prices: *Kontrol'nye tsifry narod-nogo khozyaistva na 1925/26 god* (Moscow: 1925); for 1923/24, 1924/25, 1925/26, and 1926/27 plan in prewar prices: *Kontrol'nye tsifry narodnogo khozyaistva na 1926/27 god* (Moscow: 1926); for 1924/25, 1925/26, 1926/27, and 1927/28 plans in prewar prices: *Kontrol'nye tsifry narodnogo khozyaistva SSSR na 1927/28 god* (Moscow: 1928): for 1925/26, 1926/27, 1927/28, and 1928/29 plan in 1925/26 prices: *Kontrol'nye tsifry narodnogo khozyaistva SSSR na 1928/1929 god* (Moscow: 1929); for 1925/26, 1926/27, 1928/29, and 1929/30 plan in 1925/26 prices: *Kontrol'nye tsifry narodnogo khozyaistva SSSR na 1929/1930 god* (Moscow: 1930); for 1925/26, 1926/27, and 1928/29 prices and with a regional breakdown: *Sel'skoe khozyaistvo SSSR: 1925-28* (Moscow: 1929).

5. See Table 4.4 for a presentation of these data in comparison with the author's estimates.

6. *Sotsialisticheskoe stroitelstvo SSSR* (Moscow: 1936), pp. 232-37; *Sel'skoe khozyaistvo SSSR* (Moscow: 1939), p. 281. See Appendices 1 and 2.

7. D. Johnson and A. Kahan, "Soviet Agriculture: Structure and Growth," U.S. Government Printing Office, *Comparison of the United States and Soviet Economies,* part I, (Washington, 1959), pp. 201-37.

8. See D. Johnson, "Agricultural production," in *Economic Trends in the Soviet Union,* eds. A. Bergson and S. Kuznets (Cambridge, Mass.: Harvard University Press, 1963), p. 208.

9. *Narodnoe kyozyaistvo SSSR v 1958g* (Moscow: Statistika, 1959), p. 350. A slightly fuller series appeared in *Sel. Khoz. SSSR.* (Moscow: Statistika, 1960), p. 79, and a few explanatory notes were included in the next agricultural and statistical handbook, published in 1971, *Sel. Khoz. SSSR* (1971), pp. 681-85.

10. See S. G. Wheatcroft, "Grain Production and Utilisation," vol. 3, for an example of how these regional series are derived.

11. There was less conflict over how much production had dropped in comparison with the prewar level than over what these actual levels were. This should be remembered when later attempts are made to adjust the prewar figures and leave the postrevolutionary figures as they are.

12. R. W. Davies and S. G. Wheatcroft, "Further Thoughts on the First Soviet Five-Year Plan," *Slavic Review* no. 4 (December 1975): 790-802.

13. S. Ordzhonikidze, *Statyi i rechi* vol. 2, (Moscow: 1957), pp. 177-78.

14. See S. G. Wheatcroft, "Views on Grain Output, Agricultural Reality and Planning in the Soviet Union in the 1920s," (M. Soc. Sci thesis, University of Birmingham, 1974), pp. 167-69.

15. V. V. Osinskii, *Polozhenie i zadachi narodno-khozyaistvennogo ucheta* (Moscow: 1932), p. 5.

16. For an account of Osinskii's earlier period as director of TsSU, see S. G. Wheatcroft, "Statistics and Economic Decision-Making in the USSR under Stalin," (Working paper, CREES, University of Birmingham, 1979), pp. 6, 17. Available on request from the author.

17. for more details, see Wheatcroft, "Grain Production and Utilisation," pp. 9-11.

18. *Kontrol'nye tsifry nar. khoz. na 1929/30* (Moscow: 1929), pp. 534-35.

19. *Narodnoe khozyaistvo SSSR na poroge tret'ego goda pyatiletki i kontrol'nye tsifry na 1931g* (Moscow: 1931), p. 253.

20. A. Nifontov, *Produktsiya zhivotnovodstva* (Moscow: 1937), pp. 104-5. Of course, 1937 was a very different year, and such "confusion" in 1937 would have led to an underestimation of livestock production and not to its overestimation.

21. See, for instance, Berger and Londsberg, *American Agriculture, 1899-1939,* (New York: National Bureau of Economic Research, 1942), pp. 95-96. Another interesting similarity with Soviet statisticians is their reluctance to include stock changes that have a negative value.

22. Nancy Nimitz, "Soviet Statistics of Meat and Milk Output: A Note on The Comparability over time," RAND Research Memorandum, The Rand Corporation, RM 2326 (Santa Monica: 1959).

23. *Ibid.,* pp. 8–9; *Sots. stroi. SSSR* (Moscow: 1936), p. 215.

24. S. G. Wheatcroft, "The Reliability of Russian Pre-War Grain Output Statistics," *Soviet Studies* No. 2 (April 1974): 157–80; S. G. Wheatcroft, "Grain Production and Utilisation," vol. 1.

25. A. L. Vainshtein, 'Iz istorii predrevolyutsionnoi statistiki zhivotnovodstva', *Ocherki po istorii statistiki SSSR,* iii (Moscow: 1960): 86–115.

26. Wheatcroft, "Grain Production and Utilisation," vol. 2, pp. 505–526.

27. The 1923/24 balance and other early works used prewar prices, and the 1928, 1929, and 1930 balances of the national economy used 1928 prices.

28. On an All-Union basis, state collection prices even in 1926/27 appear much lower than private market prices. But this is mainly due to regional differences. Most collections occurred in the producer regions where prices were low anyway. A comparison of prices within these regions indicates that the state prices were not unduly low.

29. See *Kontrol'nye tsifry nar. khoz. SSSR na 1929/1930* (Moscow: 1930), pp. 581–82, Johnson and Kahan, "Soviet Agriculture," p. 204.

30. This section relies heavily on the conclusions from my thesis and the data on grain production and transportation given in appendices to the thesis.

31. S. G. Wheatcroft, "The Significance of Climatic and Weather Change on Soviet Agriculture (with particular reference to the 1920s and 1930s")," (*CREES Discussion Papers,* SIPS No. 11, University of Birmingham, 1977).

Appendix 1 Gross Agricultural Production in the USSR According to Various Series

	1913	1928	1929	1930	1931	1932	1933	1934	1935	1936	1937	1938	1939	1940
1930s series (in milliard rubles) 1926/27 prices)														
Gross Agricultural Production	12.6		14.7	14.0	13.9	13.1	14.0	14.6	16.1		20.1	18.5		
Arable	8.0		9.1	9.6	9.9	9.8	11.1	11.3	12.2		15.1	12.7		
Livestock	4.6		5.7	4.4	4.1	3.3	3.0	3.3	3.9		5.1	5.8		
Indices:														
Gross Agricultural Production	100		117	111	110	104	111	116	128		160	147		
Arable	100		114	120	124	123	139	141	153		189	159		
Livestock	100		124	96	89	72	65	72	85		111	126		
Current series														
Gross Agricultural Production	100	124	121	117	114	107	101	106	119	109	134	120	121	141
Arable	100	117	116	126	126	125	121	121	138	118	150	120	125	155
Livestock	100	137	129	100	93	75	65	72	86	96	109	120	119	114
Johnson's series														
Gross Agricultural Production	100	116		106					105		127		118	
Arable	100	118		122					129		161		130	
Livestock	100	115		90					81		95		107	

Sources: 1930s series: See Appendix 2.
Current series: *Sel'skoe khozyaistvo SSSR* (Moscow: Statistika, 1960), p. 79.
Johnson's series: Bergson and Kuznets, eds., *Economic Trends in the Soviet Union* (Cambridge: Harvard University Press, 1963), p. 208.

Appendix 2   Soviet Official Indicators Published in 1930s of Gross Agricultural Production and its Major Components (in million rubles at 1926/27 prices)

	1913	1929	1930	1931	1932	1933	1934	1935 (prelim.)	1936	1937	1938 (prelim.)
Gross Agricultural Production	12,607	14,745	14,008	13,944	13,072	14,017	14,591	16,097		20,123	18,529
Arable production	8,028	9,059	9,602	9,851	9,779	11,054	11,308	12,194		15,070	12,694
Grain	3,841	3,348	3,741	3,415	3,461	4,490	4,547	4,677		6,352	5,270
Industrial Crops	782	876	1,059	1,242	1,092	1,147	1,088	1,362		1,746	1,728
Potatoes and vegetables	n.a.	1,866	2,23	2,281	2,292	2,569	2,471	2,672		n.a.	
Fruit	n.a.	392	342	414	387	372	432	484		n.a.	n.a.
Other	n.a.	2,577	2,229	2,499	2,547	2,476	2,770	2,999		n.a.	n.a.
Livestock production	4,579	5,686	4,406	4,093	3,293	2,962	3,282	3,903		5,054	5,835
Milk	n.a.	2,050	1,857	1,610	1,414	1,318	1,431	1,518		n.a.	n.a.
Meat and lard	n.a.	2,376	1,723	1,583	1,193	964	866	1,024		n.a.	n.a.
Hides and leather	n.a.	457	389	355	253	256	229	235		n.a.	n.a.
Wool	n.a.	184	142	99	70	65	68	82		n.a.	n.a.
Other	n.a.	618	294	447	362	361	689	1,044		n.a.	n.a.

Note: n.a. = not available

Sources: 1913: *Sots.sel.khoz. SSSR* (1939), p. 86.
   1929–1935: *Sots.stroi SSSR* (1936), pp. 232–33.
   1937 and 1938: *Sel.khoz. SSSR* (1939), p. 281.

Note: n.a. = not available

Appendix 3 The Level of Grain Production in the USSR According to Different Series (in million tons)

| | TSSU | | Pre-1926 reform | | | TsUNKhU | | Current Soviet | Johnson and Kahan | SIPS | |
	USSR less SCR	All USSR approx.	Gosplan	Expert (a)	Council (b)	(a)	(b)			High	Low
1908/12											
1909/13	(68.0)	71	75.3				67.6	65.2		79.9	68
1913			93.2				80.1	76.5		92.7	79
1916	61.5	64.5									
1924	42.7	45.7	51.7	51.6						51.4	44
1925	63.4	66.6	71.9	72.4	72.7				72.7	72.5	62
1926				76.3	76.6				76.6	76.6	66
1927				74.1	71.7				71.7	71.7	62
1928					71.5	73.3	73.3		73.3	73.3	63
1929						71.7	71.7		71.7	71.7	62
1930						83.5	83.5		83.5	78	67
1931							69.5		66.0	68	62
1932							69.8		63.0	68	62
1933							89.8	68.4	67.1	74	68
1934							89.4	67.7	67.3	75	68

(continued on next page)

Appendix 3 (continued)

| | Pre-1926 reform TSSU | | | | | | | | | SIPS | |
	USSR less SCR	All USSR approx.	Gosplan	Expert (a)	Council (b)	TsUNKhU (a)	TsUNKhU (b)	Current Soviet	Johnson and Kahan	High	Low
1935							90.1	75.0	69.3	80	75
1936							82.7		60.0	66	60
1937											
1938							120.3	97.4	91.9	100	95
1939							95.0		70.7	76	70
1940											

Sources:

Pre-1926 reform: TsSU: 1916, 1924 and 1925 USSR less SCR, and 1924 and 1925 all USSR: see *Abrégé des données statistiques de l'URSS* (Moscow: 1925), pp. 61–68. For 1909/13 in relation to 1916: see *Trudy TsSU*, XVIII (Moscow: 1924): pp. 131–33.

Pre-1926 reform: Gosplan: N. M. Vishnevsky, "Khlebo-furazhnii balans," in *BSE*, IV (1926): p. 479. (Similar figures for the 1920s appear in *Kontrol'nye tsifry narodnogo khozyaistva SSSR na 1925/26g.* (1925), pp. 74–75).

Expert Council: (a) *Ezhegodnik po khlebnoi torgovli*, No. 1 (Moscow: 1928), pp. 83–85. (b) *Statisticheskii spravochnik SSSR 1928* (Moscow: 1929), pp. 178–79.

TsUNKhU: (a) *Narodnoe khozyaistvo SSSR* (1932), pp. 172–73. (b) I. D. Laptev, *Razmeshchenie sotsialisticheskogo zernovogo khozyaistva* (Moscow: 1940), pp. 30 and 72. On page 30 of Laptev all the listed grain production figures are given, with the exception of 1936. The 1936 yield is given on p. 72, and 1936 grain sown area is in *Posevnye ploshchady SSSR* (Moscow: 1939), p. 15.

Current Soviet: 1909/13, 1913, 1928–32, 1933–37, 1938–40 grain production: *Sel'skoe khozyaistvo SSSR* (Moscow: Statistika, 1960), p. 196. The annual production figures for the 1930s were calculated by the present author by applying deflators based on the kolkhoz barn yield/biological yield ratios for these years. For the kolkhoz barn yields see I. E. Zelenin, "Osnovnye pokazateli sel'skokhozyaistvennogo proizvodstva v 1928–1935gg" and M. A. Vyltsan, "Metody ischisleniya proizvodstva zerna v 1933–1941gg," in *Ezhegodnik po agrarnoi istorii vostochnoi evropy, 1965g.* (Moscow: 1970), pp. 464–73, 474–81. See also Yu. A. Moshkov, "Statistika sel'skohozyaistvennogo proizvodstva v SSSR," in *Massovye istochniki po sotsial'noekonomicheskoi istorii sovetskogo obshchestva* (Moscow: 1979), p. 219.

Johnson and Kahan: 1925–1938 from D. G. Johnson and A. Kahan, "Soviet Agriculture: Structure and Growth," in *Comparisons of the United States and Soviet Economies*, part 1, (Washington: U.S. Government Printing Office, 1959), p. 231. The 1913 figure comes from D. G. Johnson, "Agricultural Production," in *Economic Trends in the Soviet Union*, ed., A. Bergson and S. Kuznets (Cambridge: Harvard University Press, 1963), p. 206.

SIPS estimates: Two series of SIPS estimates have been made: high and low. The high estimate is based on the assumption that the pre-1926 Gosplan experts were correct and that large corrections were required to the prewar data and to the 1920s data. The official 1930 figure is assumed to be distorted even in terms of this high series and so has been deflated in line with the figures available for the utilisation of the 1930 harvest. (See *Materialy po balansu narodnogo khozyaistva SSSR za 1928, 1929, 1930 gg.* (Moscow: 1932), pp. 312–19.

The post-1933 biological yield harvests are also considered to be distorted in terms of this high series, but on the other hand the uncorrected barn yield figures are far too low to be comparable with the earlier highly inflated series. I have consequently taken a figure somewhere between these two. The low estimate is based on the assumption that the pre-1926 TsSU experts were correct in assuming that no or very little correction was required to the prewar data and that a relatively small correction was required to the 1920s data. The late 1920s evaluations of the Expert Council have consequently been deflated to bring them in line with the earlier pre-1926 TsSU evaluations, and even greater deflations have been applied to the 1930–32 data. From 1933 onwards I have assumed that this series is directly comparable with the barn yield harvest figures.

It should be pointed out that both these series indicate that the level of grain production in the mid-1920s was substantially lower than in 1909/13. It is only the comparatively recent practice of comparing uncorrected prewar data with highly corrected postrevolutionary data that has led to the belief that the level of grain harvest in the mid-1920s had reached the prewar level.

Appendix 4   Potato Production in the USSR According to Different Series (in million tons)

| | TsSU | | | | | | Johnson and | |
	USSR less SCR	All USSR	Gosplan	Expert Council	TsUNKhU	Current Soviet	Kahan	SIPS
1909/13						22.4		
1913			29.9			23.3	23.3	29.9
1916	20.3	(20.6)						
1924	29.9	30.2	34.8	32.8				35.3
1925	44.1	44.3	44.8	38.6			38.6	38.4
1926				43.0		41.1	43.0	42.8
1927				41.2			41.2	42.5
1928				39.9	46.4		46.5	45.2
1929					45.6		45.6	45.1
1930					49.4	45.9	49.5	44.6
1931					44.8		44.8	40.6
1932					43.1		43.1	37.2
1933					49.3		49.2	44.0
1934					56.2	48.5	51.0	44.2
1935					51.0		69.7	53.8
1936					65.9	44.6	51.0	44.6
1937					63.8	58.7	65.6	58.7
1938					43.1		41.9	37.5
1939						47.9	51.3	36.0
1940								70

Sources:

TsSU: 1916, 1923–25: *Abrégé des données statistiques de l'URSS*, (Moscow: 1925), pp. 66–69.

Gosplan: 1913, 1924, 1925: *Kontrol'nye tsifry narodnogo khozyaistva SSSR za 1925/26g*, (Moscow: 1925).

Expert Council: 1924–26: *Statisticheskie obozrenie*, 1928, No. 11, p. 22. 1925–28: *Statisticheskie spravochnik SSSR 1928g.* (Moscow: 1929), pp. 204–5.

TsUNKhU: 1928–36: *Sel'skoye khozyaistvo SSSR 1935g*, (Moscow: 1936), pp. 471, 1428. 1937–38: *Sel'skoye khozyaistvo SSSR* (Moscow: 1939).

Current: 1909–13, 1913, 1924–28, 1929–32, 1933–37, 1936, 1937, 1938–40 from *Sel'skoe khozyaistvo SSSR* (Moscow: Statistika, 1960), p. 201.

Johnson and Kahan: Johnson and Kahan, "Soviet Agriculture: Structure and Growth," in *Comparisons of the United States and Soviet Economies*, (Washington: U.S. Government Printing Office, 1959), p. 231.

SIPS variant: Accepts the earlier large Gosplan production figure of 29.9 million tons for 1913. This figure included both field-grown potatoes (20.4 million tons) and allotment-grown potatoes (9.5 million tons) according to Gukhman, (B. A. Gukhman, *Produktsiya i potreblenie v SSSR* (Moscow: 1925), p. 130). The TsSU figure of 19.9–22.4 million tons covers only field-grown potatoes. A small deflation has been made to the 1929–32 data and a larger deflation to the post-1933 potato harvest data to convert the biological yield data to a more comparable barn yield series. More details will be given in a forthcoming SIPS Discussion paper.

Appendix 5   Grain Production by Region (unadjusted, in million tons)

	NCR	SCR	SPR	CPR	EPR	USSR
1909/13	10.9	(3.2)	27.4	24.6	11.9	78.0
1920	8.2	(3.2)	18.6	13.2	8.7	51.9
1921	10.1	(3.2)	13.8	9.7	7.0	43.8
1922	10.9	(3.4)	17.7	18.0	7.1	57.1
1923	9.5	(3.4)	20.8	15.3	7.8	56.8
1924	10.4	3.5	15.9	11.9	10.2	51.9
1925	11.2	3.5	27.0	17.7	13.4	72.8
1926	11.4	3.6	24.1	21.5	15.8	76.4
1927	11.4	3.2	24.7	20.1	13.5	72.9
1928	10.9	3.8	18.8	21.5	17.5	72.3
1929	11.9	3.8	24.6	19.4	12.1	71.7
1930a)	12.6/	4.0/	29.8/	22.4/	14.8/	83.5/
b)	11.7	3.7	27.6	20.8	13.7	77.4
1931	11.5	4.0	26.1	18.6	9.4	69.5
1932a)	11.7/	3.1/	21.1/	21.7/	12.3/	69.9/
b)	11.7	3.1	19.0	19.5	11.1	65.0
1933	11.3	3.7	21.7	19.4	10.9	67.0
1934	12.7	4.2	16.4	20.7	16.4	70.4
1935	13.5	3.9	22.6	22.6	14.1	76.7
1936	(10.0)	(2.0)	(14.4)	(19.7)	(13.0)	59.1
1937	11.8	1.9	29.3	33.0	19.8	95.8
1938	7.4	2.6	24.3	16.6	23.4	74.3
1939	8.6	3.2	29.7	16.2	16.9	74.6
1940	9.6	2.8	32.0	25.9	16.2	86.5

Note: These figures have not been adjusted for intertemporal comparability. As explained in the text, the removal of the entire biological yield distortion for the post-1933 period probably makes these figures too low in comparison with the earlier figures; this is why these all-Union figures differ from the SIPS series.

Sources: 1909/13–1929: S. G. Wheatcroft, *"Grain Production and Utilisation in Russia and the USSR before Collectivisation,"* vol. 3, (Ph.D. thesis, University of Birmingham, 1980, p. 99.

1930a), 1931 and 1932a): *Sotsialisticheskoe stroitel'stvo SSSR,* (Moscow: 1934).

1930b): Total from Moshkov (Moscow: 1966), pp. 230–31; regions estimated by present author.

1932b): Estimate by the present author.

1933–1940: Complex estimation from sown area data and regional kolkhoz barn yield data, 1932–1933 from I. E. Zelenin, "Dinamicheskie obsledovaniya kolkhozov za 1933–1934gg," in *Istochnikovedenie istorii sovetskogo obshchestva,* vyp. I (Moscow: 1968), p. 350; 1937–1940 from Yu V. Arutunyan, *Sovetskoe krestyanstvo v gody velikoi otechestvennoi voiny,* (Moscow: 1970), pp. 430–31. 1935 barn yields are estimated from 1935 biological yields and the relationship between 1933 and 1934 barn and biological yields. 1936 barn yields are estimated on the assumption that a low overall figure was needed.

Appendix 6   **Regional Grain Transportation Balances (despatches net of receipts, in million tons).**

	NCR	SCR	SPR	CPR	EPR	USSR
1901	− 2.9	+ 0.2	+ 4.6	+ 2.3	+ 0.2	+ 4.5
1913	− 4.3	+ 1.3	+ 8.3	+ 3.3	+ 0.8	+ 9.3
1920	− 1.8	+ 0.1	+ 0.1	+ 0.3	+ 0.3	− 0.5
1921	− 0.9	+ 0.1	+ 0.0	− 0.0	+ 0.1	− 0.7
1922	− 1.3	+ 0.1	+ 0.8	− 0.2	+ 0.3	− 0.8
1913	− 3.9	− 0.5	+ 8.7	+ 4.9	+ 0.8	+ 10.0
1922/23	− 1.5	− 0.2	+ 1.4	+ 0.9	+ 0.9	+ 0.6
1923/24	− 2.3	− 0.2	+ 3.8	+ 1.0	+ 0.2	+ 2.7
1924/25	− 2.5	− 0.4	+ 1.7	+ 0.2	+ 1.5	+ 0.6
1925/26	− 4.0	− 0.8	+ 4.8	+ 0.9	+ 1.1	+ 2.1
1926/27	− 3.8	− 0.7	+ 3.3	+ 2.1	+ 1.7	+ 2.7
1927/28	− 4.3	− 0.9	+ 2.9	+ 1.7	+ 1.1	+ 0.6
1928/29	− 3.6	− 0.8	+ 0.3	+ 2.0	+ 2.1	− 0.2
1929/30	− 4.0	− 1.0	+ 3.7	+ 2.2	+ 0.2	+ 1.0
1930	− 2.7	− 1.0	+ 5.6	+ 2.9	− 0.1	+ 4.8
1931 excluding foreign trade	− 4.1	− 1.3	+ 2.3	+ 3.6	+ 0.2	0
foreign trade			(+ 4.1)	(+ 1.0)		+ 5.1
including foreign trade	− 4.1	− 1.3	+ 6.4	+ 4.6	+ 0.2	+ 5.1
1932 excluding foreign trade	− 3.7	− 0.9	+ 1.9	+ 3.4	+ 0.7	0
foreign trade			(+ 1.2)	(+ 0.3)		+ 1.5
including foreign trade	− 3.7	− 0.9	+ 3.1	+ 3.7	+ 0.7	+ 1.5
1933 excluding foreign trade	− 3.1	− 1.3	+ 1.2	+ 3.4	+ 0.7	0
foreign trade			(+ 1.3)	(+ 0.4)		+ 1.7
including foreign trade	− 3.1	− 1.3	+ 2.5	+ 3.8	+ 0.7	+ 1.7
1934 excluding foreign trade	− 0.4	− 1.5	+ 1.8	+ 4.0	− 0.1	
foreign trade			(+ 0.6)	(+ 0.2)		+ 0.8
including foreign trade	− 0.4	− 1.5	+ 2.4	+ 4.2	− 0.1	+ 0.8

(continued on next page)

Appendix 6   (continued)

	NCR	SCR	SPR	CPR	EPR	USSR
1935 excluding foreign trade	− 4.4	− 1.2	− 0.1	+ 3.5	+ 2.0	
foreign trade			(+ 1.2)	(+ 0.3)		+ 1.5
including foreign trade	− 4.4	− 1.2	+ 1.1	+ 3.8	+ 2.0	

Note: These data include foreign trade unless otherwise stated.

Sources: 1901, 13, 20–22: *Trudy TsSU,* XIX, vyp. II (1925): 6–11.
1913, 22/23–26/27: G. Vasilyev in *Statisticheskoe obozrenie,* no. 8, (1928), 68, 72.
1928/29, 1929/30 and 1930: *Narodnoe khozyaistvo SSSR* (Moscow: 1932), p. 268; excluding foreign trade: 1931 *Dinamika i geografiya gruzovogo dvizheniya na putyakh soobshcheniya SSSR (1928–31gg),* (Moscow: 1932), pp. 15–17.
1932 *Sotisalisticheskoe stroitel'stvo SSSR,* (Moscow: 1935), pp. 265–66.
1933 *Transport i svyaz SSSR v 1933g,* (Moscow: 1934), pp. 107–12.
1934 *Sotsialisticheskoe stroitel' stvo SSSR,* (Moscow: 1936), p. 493.
1935 *Gruzooborot zheleznodorozhnogo i vodnogo transporta za 1935g,* (Moscow: 1936), p. 1.

3

Why Was NEP Abandoned?

Mark Harrison

INTRODUCTION

The New Economic Policy pursued by the Soviet state from early 1921 to the summer of 1929 can be defined as the regulation of the economy's development by means of a series of balances between socialist and presocialist forms of production, centralized administrative planning and decentralized commodity exchange, industrialization and agricultural development, worker and peasant interests. As for the objectives of policy, here too there was a balance between those who saw NEP as a temporary compromise unlikely to be sustainable in the long run, and those who endowed it with the far more long-range significance of a system of transition to socialism. By the summer of 1929 these balances had become hopelessly disrupted, and after this point Soviet development entered a new phase of forced, rapid industrialization on the basis of a highly centralized economy, excluding or subordinating petty commodity forms.

Why was NEP abandoned? Ths question has been answered in three different ways, of which the third appears to me to be the most satisfactory. The first view is that NEP was abandoned because it had become inconsistent with any further industrial development, and its abandonment was compelled by this economic logic. The second view, which reacts against the first, is that NEP was still consistent with a wide variety of alternative development patterns, including the industrial development actually achieved in the interwar Five-Year Plans. Therefore the abandonment of NEP reflected no economic logic, but was a byproduct of brute political struggles and the formation of the Stalinist political system. The third view is that NEP was inconsistent with the extremely rapid industrialization actually undertaken from 1928 onwards, but did contain the possibility of alternative development patterns involving a lesser commitment to industrial growth. If this was the case, the abandonment of NEP was neither compelled by the logic of the economic situation (according to the first

Department of Economics, University of Warwick, England. The author is grateful to Mr. Peter Law, Professor Robert C. Stuart, Dr. Stephen Wheatcroft, and others for helpful comments. An earlier version of this paper has been published as "Why Did NEP Fail?" in *Economics of Planning* no. 2, (1980).

view) nor an irrational byproduct of a bureaucratic struggle (according to the second), but was the outcome of a political conflict over the course of Soviet economic development that involved real, mutually exclusive alternatives.

The main source of authority for the first view, that NEP had become inconsistent with any further socialist industrial development, was Stalin, who in 1928 identified the small-scale, petty commodity character of agriculture under NEP as a principal constraint on economic growth:

> in our country the principal holders of grain available for the market are the small and, primarily, the middle peasants. This means that not only in respect to gross output of grain, but also in respect to the production of grain for the market, the USSR has become, as a result of the October Revolution, a land of small peasant farming, and the middle peasant has become the "central figure" in agriculture. . . . [T]he abolition of landlord (large-scale) farming, the reduction of kulak (large-scale) farming to less than one-third, and the change to small peasant farming with only 11 per cent of its output available for the market, under the conditions of the absence in the sphere of grain growing of any more or less developed large-scale farming in common (collective farms and state farms), was bound to lead, and in fact has led, to a sharp reduction in the output of grain for the market as compared with pre-war times. It is a fact that the amount of marketed grain in our country is now half of what it was before the war, notwithstanding the fact that gross output of grain has reached the pre-war level.[1]

This view, formulated in 1928 on the basis of 1926–27 statistics, was the foundation for the view that industrial development could only proceed by replacing small-scale agricultural commodity production with large-scale production and the direct appropriation of surplus products by the state. In itself, of course, this view did not dictate the pace and methods of the transition, which were set in the unfolding of the economic and political crisis of 1928 and 1929.

Since 1928, Stalin's view has been subject to three main revisions, which are examined below. The first is that it embodied an underestimate of the productive potential of the small-scale peasant agriculture produced by the October Revolution. The second is that the grain crises of 1928 and 1929 were, at least in part, provoked by the planners themselves; policy adjustments would have permitted rapid industrial growth to be reconciled with NEP. The third is that actual Soviet growth in the first Five-Year Plan period involved significant avoidable costs; a continuation of NEP would have avoided these costs while still producing the results. Taken together, these revisions back up the view that the abandonment of NEP was irrational, serving only Stalin's lust for power. Each contains essential elements of truth, although all of them have at times been overstated.

HOW GREAT WAS THE PRODUCTIVE POTENTIAL OF PEASANT AGRICULTURE?

Did Stalin underestimate the productive potential of peasant farming in a socialist economy? Today some historians continue to emphasize the constraints imposed on agricultural development by the inefficiencies of land parcellation; the medieval three-field strip system and repartitional tenure; the parochial, backward peasant culture.[2] This picture of unchanging backwardness may be an unrealistic stereotype.

Until recently the sharpest focus of historical scrutiny fell on rural-urban grain transfers. Undoubtedly the level of grain marketings in the 1920s really was much lower than before the first World War.[3] In the sixties a Soviet challenge was mounted against the statistics used by Stalin in 1928, arguing that they understated grain marketings during NEP, but the challenge was probably misdirected.[4] Grain marketings may have deteriorated by as much as half, comparing the midtwenties with the years before the war. But the focus upon grain marketings alone is one-dimensional and in fact misleading, since in other respects Soviet agriculture revealed unprecedented vitality under NEP.[5]

The evidence is that both yields and harvests of grain grew rather rapidly until the mid-twenties, by which time they had roughly matched the prerevolutionary benchmark. Recovery was less marked than current Soviet data would imply. It was also uneven, being least marked in the traditional grain-surplus regions of the south and center; producer and consumer demands, which also grew rapidly, kept the grain balance under constant tension.[6] Meanwhile, however, the degree of agriculture's monocultural dependence upon extensive grain cultivation was diminishing, and resources previously devoted to grains were being shifted into other arable and nonarable sectors. The arable hectarage devoted to relatively input-intensive, high-yielding commodity ('industrial') crops had doubled. The country's livestock herds had recovered quickly from wartime losses and, after recovery, continued until 1928 to grow at an annual rate of 3–4 percent compared to the sluggish prerevolutionary precedent of under 1 percent. Quantitative growth in livestock herds until 1928 was accompanied by improved milk and meat yields.[7] These encouraging trends to some extent exacerbated the difficulties on the grain front, and in any case were sharply checked in 1928. Farm technology remained backward, and yields vulnerable to environmental fluctuations. But the picture of peasant farming under NEP as stagnant and unresponsive to new opportunities is sharply refuted.

The decline in grain marketings relative to prerevolutionary standards reflected improvements in the rural economy in consumption as well as production. There was a healthy reaction against the abnormally high levels of grain extraction previously demanded by tsarist policies for financing investment and public expenditure. If grain marketings had contracted,

> the cause . . . was not the liquidation of large-scale production in agriculture, which had brought not a contraction but growth in agricultural production. The cause was the growth in peasant consumption. This growth in fact amounted to the attainment by consumption standards of a level at which the normal reproduction of labour-power of the direct producer in agriculture could take place—the chief productive force which, before the revolution, had been exhausted and degraded by kulak and landlord exploitation.[8]

In other words, as a result of the October Revolution, Soviet agriculture had gone through a transition from a combination of large-scale and small-scale producers, to overwhelmingly small-scale farming. But the disappearance of the large-scale, high-yielding producer had not meant the rise of the small-scale, low-yielding subsistence farmer. The small-scale farmers themselves were developing intensive, high-yielding branches of diversified commodity production and were claiming a greater share of their own output for both production and consumption purposes in order to bring this about. Such a prospect had been envisaged by Lenin many years earlier: the most rapid development of agriculture's productive forces would come on the basis of the petty producer, with increased yields and large-scale productive forms arising through an organic process of development—not implanted or enforced from above.[9] At the same time, of course, neither Lenin nor his successors had solved the practical problem of finding socialist forms for such an organic process.

COULD NEP HAVE BEEN BETTER MANAGED?

The second revision to the view that NEP was doomed by the end of the 1920s concerns the extent to which the grain crises of 1928 and 1929 were provoked by the mismanagement of economic policy. For the year 1926–27, state procurement prices for grain had been lowered, sharply altering the relative advantage to the peasants of grain cultivation in favor of shifting resources further into industrial crops and livestock herds. Although the procurement price of grain was allowed to drift upward again in 1927–28 and 1928–29, the relative advantage for sellers of livestock products that had been created in mid-NEP was not eliminated; in the latter market the state remained a minority purchaser and was unable to hold down its own demand price. The imbalance of relative prices in favor of nongrain products was also noticeable in comparison to the prewar conjuncture.[10] From the viewpoint of grain procurement planning, it was a clearly irrational course.[11]

The difficulties of the grain procurers were further exaggerated by the management of aggregate demand in the economy. By the latter 1920s *goods famine,* i.e., chronic excess demand for manufactures, was endemic in the Soviet economy. Peasant commodity producers, unable to use money balances accumulated from the sale of foodstuffs in order to purchase manufactures, withdrew from both markets. Attempts to remedy the situation by increasing grain procurement prices in autumn 1928 only increased the excess of rural monetary demand. An inflationary gap had developed, which could only be closed by a reduction in rural and urban living standards (or both), or by postponing current investment plans. By 1926–27 gross investment in Soviet large-scale industry had considerably exceeded the standard set by prewar growth; the industrial capital stock was growing at rates exceeding 10 percent per annum, although expansion was patchy across the major industrial sectors, badly coordinated, and reflected serious problems of absorption of new technology.[12] Industrial growth was itself contributing to the economic tensions, partly through the investment demand for plant and machinery. But a significant part of the industrial growth, which ranged between 17 and 22 percent per annum between 1925–26 and 1928–29, was still being accounted for by the reemployment of unused fixed capacity. The resulting demand for working capital, of which in physical terms agriculture was the most important source, was also contributing to the strained situation.

It has been argued that policy adjustments would have reduced the strain, relaxed the constraints, and allowed rapid industrial growth to continue within NEP. Preobrazhensky, not an advocate of NEP but seeking room for maneuver within it, criticized the domination of the economy by competitive market forces, as a result of which the surplus product of peasant farming was being retained within the petty commodity sector. His solution was to challenge the competitive market forces with a combination of political force and market power. The state should use its political and economic monopoly to redistribute the surplus product of the petty commodity sector towards socialized industry. The method that he advocated was a combination of direct and indirect taxation, which would compel the peasants to sell their products at unfavorable terms of trade.[13]

Discussion of the impact of increased indirect taxation of the peasantry has often failed to distinguish its macroeconomic and microeconomic effects. Some additional burden of indirect taxation would have helped to close the inflationary gap opened up by ambitious industrial investment plans. An increase in the supply price of manufactures would have choked off excess demand for them, and an unchanged quantity of manufactures supplied to the rural market at a higher price would have called forth increased marketings of grain. The opposite policy of price reductions on manufactures, if not combined with a simultaneous reduction in industrial investment plans, would have intensified the inflationary disequilibrium and the breakdown of market relations. The "goods famine" was a more immediate cause of peasant withdrawal from product markets in 1927 and 1928 than the equilibrium response of peasants to terms of trade that are only relevant when trade actually takes place and all markets are cleared (for more analysis of this point, the interested reader is referred to the Appendix at the end of the chapter).

Beyond the restoration of macroeconomic balance, would further increases in indirect taxation have increased or reduced net marketings of grain? On the basis of microeconomic reasoning, Millar argues, rather categorically, "that the peasants were not self-sufficient and that a turning of the general terms of trade against them would have increased marketings, not just production."[14]

In this case greater indirect taxation would have stimulated the peasants to greater productive and sales effort and would have achieved an unambiguous increase in net rural-urban product transfers. To the extent that this was feasible, alternative policies could have secured the regime's economic objectives within NEP, marking out a superior solution to the Stalinist one.[15]

Millar's view rests on two foundations. The first is the hypothesis that peasants exhibited an inelastic demand for income or some kind of target-income motivation.[16] This idea was elaborated by Chayanov, who obtained the result by assumption,[17] and there is little evidence to support it.[18] The second foundation is the hypothesis that peasants exhibited an inelastic demand for manufactures.[19] Millar finds important support here from the work of Guntzel on the 1922–23 scissors crisis.[20] However, I remain skeptical of the possibility of statistical identification of an equilibrium peasant response to changes in the terms of trade, whether in the early twenties (when imbalances were extreme, when there were large exogenous fluctuations in production combined with grave statistical deficiencies, and when the state controlled only a small part of the rural market for manufactures),[21] or in the middle and later twenties, where my own empirical investigations have not led to any conclusions.[22]

The more conventional view that, other things being equal, worsened terms of trade led peasant farmers to reduce their sales, finds negative support in the highly successful surplus appropriation policies of tsarist governments, which had to combine indirect with direct taxation. Direct taxation was organized through a battery of coercive rural institutions, ranging from the manorial system and medieval commune to the standing rural militia, and was designed to compel peasants to market produce at unfavorable prices. Preobrazhensky did not envisage a return to such measures, and Nove suggests that this was the very point of his self-criticism before the 17th CPSU Congress in 1934 ("Collectivisation, that was the point! Did I anticipate collectivisation? I did not.")[23] Without new forcible institutions of direct taxation, the effects of indirect taxation would be contradictory. Use of the market power of the state industrial sector to shift the terms of trade against peasant farming would mean higher price-cost margins per unit of industrial production and, up to a certain point, an increase in the total surplus-product realized within the state industrial sector. Excess aggregate demand would be reduced or eliminated. But in the short run it would mean lower rural living standards and consumer demand, lower industrial turnover and employment, and therefore more inequality of urban incomes, access to jobs, and access to the means of consumption.

Finally, the objectives of indirect taxation of manufactures could always be thwarted while peasants had access to markets not fully controlled by the state. Indirect taxation of manufactures would be nullified if the state could not drive down livestock product prices while it was successfully lowering grain prices. Indirect taxation would be evaded if peasants could turn to petty rural industries supplying manufactures in competition with nationalized producers. Additional administrative measures would be needed to enforce state monopolies in the supply and purchase of these commodities and meant the end of NEP.

COULD RAPID INDUSTRIALIZATION HAVE BEEN RECONCILED WITH NEP?

The third revision to the view that NEP was doomed by the end of the 1920s can be put as follows. Actual Soviet industrialization was unprecedentedly rapid. However, the Stalinist policies of forced collectivization and overambitious planning resulted in grave economic losses along the way. Had these losses been avoided, the same economic transformation could have been achieved with a much smaller burden upon the peasantry and working class. This smaller burden, it is argued, would have been consistent with the NEP framework.

In what sense did Stalinist policies result in avoidable losses? It has been argued that these were of two kinds: the destruction of assets and the misallocation of resources. On the first score we know that Stalin's agricultural policies resulted in the loss of half the country's livestock herd between 1928 and 1932. It is less clear whether the slaughter of livestock that brought this about was occasioned by peasant responses to forced collectivization or by the reallocation of grain flows from animal consumption to state procurement for human consumption. In either case the result was the same. Supplies of meat and milk dried up but bigger quantities of inferior foodstuffs were made available for urban consumption. At the same time, increased quantities of manufactures, particularly tractors using precious steel and engineering resources, had to be supplied to agriculture to make good the deficit of animal draught power. As a result of these factors, combined with petty commodity transfers on the free "kolkhoz market" that proved impossible to suppress and were legalized at an early stage, collectivization did not achieve any significant increase, either in the net transfer of resources from agriculture to industry or in the net financial contribution of agriculture to investment in the economy as a whole.[24] Since actual Soviet industrialization did not require these magnitudes to rise much, if at all, above their 1928 levels,

> a continuation of the New Economic Policy of the 1920s would have permitted at least as rapid a rate of industrialization with less cost to the urban as well as to the rural population of the Soviet Union.[25]

On the second score of resource misallocation, Gisser and Jonas have argued that Stalinist policies in agriculture resulted in a shortfall in total factor productivity growth beneath that obtainable under other arrangements. Using a two-sector (agriculture and nonagriculture) model with Cobb-Douglas production functions, Kaplan's indices of historical inputs and outputs, and Bergson's estimates for factor shares, they calculate that between 1928 and 1940 total factor productivity in agriculture declined at 0.1 percent per year. Had it risen at the rate achieved by United States agriculture in the interwar period, reflecting enhanced freedom and incentives to innovate imported technology, then Soviet agricultural output growth would have been raised from 1.6 to 2.7 percent per year; alternatively, if agricultural output growth were held to the historically achieved level, sufficient labor supplies could have been released to Soviet industry to raise industrial output growth from the achieved 8.1 percent to 10.67 percent per year. They conclude:

> industrialization without the "super-industrializers" could have occurred at the same rate or even a more impressive rate than actually happened . . . . The acceptance of the Stalin-Preobrazhensky path led to unnecessary sufferings on the part of the Soviet population and misallocation of resources . . . . It seems that Bukharin was right after all.[26]

It has also been argued that avoidable efficiency losses resulted from the Stalinist industrial strategy. Some years ago Holland Hunter suggested that the Soviet economy between 1928 and 1941 was a case study in excessive "tautness." "Taut" planning, involving the setting of highly ambitious, probably unattainable growth targets, may be necessary to achieve high industrial growth rates in a developing economy. By this means, resources are mobilized, reserves are uncovered, and slack is eliminated. As a result the production frontier is pushed out more rapidly than would result from a process of planning for what is already known to be "realistic." However, if taken too far, the approach of taut planning results in cumulating imbalances and sharply reduced growth achievement; in this case, "further relaxation of aggregate targets would yield still higher rates of achieved improvement."[27] This diagnosis, at any rate with respect to industrial development in the First Five-Year Plan, is shared by Barsov:

> the level of accumulation in 1931 and 1932, above all considering the reduced level of agricultural production, was in all probability excessively high and scarcely yielded optimal conditions for solving the problems of the most rapid industrialization of the country. It seems to me that approximately the same effect in increasing industrial production and heavy industrial growth could have been achieved by allocating a somewhat smaller share of the national income to investment, increasing resources for consumption and creating optimal conditions for material incentives and growth in the productivity of social labour.[28]

More recent work by Hunter has also supported the view that the First Five-Year Plan was excessively taut and strained the economy. Hunter attempted to measure the expansion potential of the 1928 Soviet economy on the basis of the technical norms and environmental expectations of the First Five-Year Plan "optimal" variant, using a six-sector linear programming model. He found that:

> No allocation of resources among the six sectors and over the several plan years would enable the terminal-year levels of capital and output to be reached, along with the intended levels of household consumption and other final uses. Even with the plan period extended to six, seven or eight years, the full set of official targets is unachieveable.[29]

Model imperfections, leading to both understatement[30] and overstatement[31] of plan infeasibility, have been acknowledged. But it is hard to object to the measured conclusion:

> if Bolshevik targets are reinterpreted as calling for a very substantial increase in the economy's capacity (especially in industry and construction), put in place as quickly as conditions permitted, then the estimates . . . suggest that these Bolshevik objectives might have been achieved without the Draconian methods that Stalin used. A number of alternative paths were available, evolving out of the situation existing at the end of the 1920s, and leading to levels of capacity and output as good as those achieved by, say, 1936, yet with far less turbulence, waste, destruction, and sacrifice.[32]

Thus consideration of Stalinist policies both for agriculture and for industrial planning lends support to the view that heavy avoidable wastage was involved.

But this conclusion falls far short of a much more far-reaching proposition that is sometimes held to follow, which states that the same industrial growth could have been achieved, and the wastage avoided, while retaining the NEP framework. Could the greater allocative efficiency that is presumed to be a feature of NEP have provided the necessary conditions for historically achieved rates of Soviet industrial development? Some kinds of economic reasoning take this to be the logical conclusion. They are clearly reflected in the views of Gisser and Jonas and of Millar: since actual Soviet performance in the thirties was based upon degraded efficiency and/or damaged resources, another arrangement that would have enhanced efficiency and averted the pure losses ascribed to collectivization would generate enhanced performance. The "other arrangement" is assumed to be NEP and a decentralized mixed economy. Along with this view goes a picture of the Soviet economy of 1928 as a rather flexible system containing a large number of possible trade-offs.

Some criticisms of this view are misjudged (as an example, Vyas rejects it primarily by refusing to contemplate all options in between extreme superindustrialization and economic stagnation: "it all depends on what one means").[33] A more serious challenge comes from the second line of reasoning—also followed by Vyas—which emphasizes sectoral bottlenecks and consumption commitments in the later NEP economy. It is argued that the economy had become quite rigid and overdetermined, and that while an array of moderate industrialization and balanced development possibilities were still consistent with NEP, rapid industrialization required institutional change in order to operate on binding constraints. In particular, even without the distortions and losses involved in the Stalinist style of policy making, the achieved level of Soviet growth rates required a major shift from consumption to accumulation.

What degrees of freedom faced Soviet planners, given the resources and the social relations actually existing in 1928? At the beginning of the First Five-Year Plan the Soviet economy was already in "a very tight situation"; "Shadow prices in the first year are extremely high."[34] This strained situation was primarily the result of carrying out existing industrial development plans, ambitious but still modest compared with the targets set in 1929 and 1930. Increasing disequilibria were being introduced into the NEP economy by attempts to industrialize rapidly without prior institutional change. To carry through the advanced targets of the First Five-Year Plan "optimal" variant necessitated radical changes in the allocation of resources, which could not have been financed by greater efficiency and the avoidance of waste. In Hunter's experiment, he asked whether it was possible to meet the "optimal" terminal-year capital stock targets in five years, allowing consumption per head to vary but requiring it to be spread evenly over the five-year period. Given the optimistic assumptions of the planners, the problem was soluble.

The trouble with this solution, of course, is that it would have reduced household consumption from its 1928 level of 21.2 billion rubles to about 15.7 billion rubles in 1929 . . . . One thinks of the surgical operation that was technically successful although the patient died.[35]

On the other hand

If we set a consumption floor that requires constant per capita household consumption, there is no feasible solution, even over an eight-year plan period. The Soviet economy was tightly constrained at the end of the 1920s, and there was no easy way to build an altered structure. Experiment indicates that roughly a 9 per cent cut in household consumption would have freed enough resources to set the growth model in motion.[36]

In summary,

Lower growth rates and slower structural shifts might have brought the Soviet economy out of its strained situation by the middle 1930s, and might have done so fairly smoothly. A milder set of targets would still, of course, have required some difficult changes. The regime would have had to coax more off-farm output from the peasants, raising the level of 1928 procurements by perhaps 4 per cent per year. It would also have been necessary to divert a larger share of the national income away from consumer goods and into capital formation. In the face of difficulties arising from the world depression, poor harvests or construction delays, the plan period might have had to be stretched out.[37]

It should be noted that Hunter's most recent ten-sector, variable-technology linear programming (KAPROST) model of interwar Soviet growth is less pessimistic. Given technical norms and environmental expectations derived from the First Five-Year Plan "optimal" variant, the model is able to match achieved Soviet industrial growth, while allowing consumption per head to rise sharply in the first two-year period after 1928. In the following two-year period it falls back, then resumes a meteoric rise. The injection of real trends in the world trading environment, Soviet defense spending, and agriculture has catastrophic results on consumption levels after 1930.[38] Assessment of this model and its projections is not complete,[39] and it is not yet certain whether it can be used to answer the questions that concern me here.

The need to shift resources out of consumption and out of agriculture is also reflected in Vyas's approach to structural change in the Soviet economy. He concludes that the building of an altered structure could not have been achieved without an initial decline in the industrial wage. Reconstruction requires an increased share of investment's going to heavy industry. With growing industrial employment, static or falling labor productivity, and an unchanged allocation system in agriculture, the real wage must decline in terms either of foodstuffs, or of consumer manufacturers, or both:

substantial declines in real wages were inevitable, given the objectives of the Soviet regime . . . hence it is misleading to suggest that the sharp declines that took place during the course of the actual [first Five-Year Plan] were merely the result of breakneck speeds of industrialisation and rapid collectivisation.[40]

Ultimately it seems very difficult to have reconciled the existing commitment of resources both to household consumption and to peasant agricultural production in 1928 with the fixed and working capital requirements of subsequent industrial growth. Gisser and Jonas's suggestion of a way out through possible increases in foreign investment is not realistic.[42] Therefore, in Ellman's words collectivization was not without logic:

> Comparing 1932 with 1928, collectivisation did *not* increase the net agricultural surplus . . . . It did, however, increase procurements of grain, potatoes and vegetables, thus facilitating an increase in urban employment and exports, swing the terms of trade between agriculture and the state in favour of the state, and facilitate the rapid increase in the urban labour force . . . . In this period collectivisation appears as a process which enabled the state to increase its inflow of grain, potatoes and vegetables and its stock of urban labour, at the expense of livestock and the rural and urban human population.[43]

Cooper, Davies, and Wheatcroft also emphasize the importance of the physical form of the gross transfer of inferior wage-goods out of agriculture (as opposed to the net flow of investment finance) as a condition of industrial growth, secured by collectivization. They point out that, had the 1928 livestock herd been maintained through the 1930s, it would have demanded an additional diversion of grains from human to animal consumption, reaching a maximum of 19 percent of the actual harvest in 1933-34.[44] In the same spirit, Vyas calculates that, had the actual trend of declining agricultural marketings between 1926-27 and 1928-29 been projected to the end of the First Five-Year Plan, on the basis of the "minimal" and "optimal" employment targets, the industrial wage in terms of food would have declined by 22 or 25 percent. In the event, industrial employment grew far in excess of the "optimal" variant, while there were drastic unforeseen declines in meat and milk marketings. Nonetheless, because collectivization ensured supplies of basic foodstuffs to industrial workers though not to peasants, the actual decline in the industrial wage in terms of food up to 1932 was held to 26 percent.[45] This is because by means of collectivization, agriculture "was transformed into a residual sector which absorbed shocks (e.g. bad harvest)."[46]

WHY WAS NEP ABANDONED?

In summary, therefore, it is difficult to agree with Millar that the NEP economy was consistent with industrialization on the scale of the 1930s, and that therefore the decision to abandon NEP was irrational. The crisis and abandonment of NEP followed directly from decisions to give priority to rapid industrialization. The evidence supports the view that:

> the New Economic Policy led to an expanding economy, but . . . the rate of industrial expansion feasible within NEP was far lower than that actually achieved during the first two five-year plans.[47]

The NEP economy could have yielded further economic expansion and restructuring of production relations, with rather less industrial growth, more agricultural revolution, and more attention to living standards. The latter tasks could not be reconciled, however, with the task of rapid, large-scale industrialization.

The abandonment of NEP reflected the needs of a state committed to rapid, large-scale industrialization to reduce the commitment of resources to agriculture and to enforce reduced living standards on both town and country. This was a political choice, but it had an economic logic. On the other hand it was a choice, not compelled by historical inevitability or destiny, so that it is difficult also to agree with Vyas, whose view (the exact opposite of Millar's) is that "the decision of mass collectivisation was made in response to the logic of objective circumstances."[48] There were alternatives to the Stalinist route, which would still have led to a socialist society. However, the crisis of NEP was a real, systemic crisis caused by the system's being called upon to fulfill industrial tasks probably not within its production and consumption possibilities.

NOTES

1. Joseph Stalin, *Leninism* (London: Allen, 1940), pp. 208-9 ("On the Grain Front").

2. Alec Nove, "The 'Logic' and Cost of Collectivization," *Problems of Communism* (July–August 1976): p. 56; Arvind Vyas, *Consumption in a Socialist Economy: the Soviet Industrialisation Experience 1929-1937* (New Delhi: 1978), p. 95.

3. Soviet agricultural produce was either consumed in kind on the farm or marketed. Of the marketed quantity, part would be retained within agriculture to supply food-deficit households, or retained within the village but transferred to rural small-scale manufacturers and service workers. The remainder would be available for transfer to the urban industrial and service sector and other purposes of state. Some of the latter would eventually find its way back to the countryside in processed form or as resupply for deficit areas. Unless otherwise indicated, I use the term "grain marketings" as a shorthand for the net rural-urban transfer of grains. For rigorous definition of these categories and their relationship to such concepts as "agricultural surplus," see James R. Millar, "Soviet Rapid Development and the Agricultural Surplus Hypothesis," *Soviet Studies* 22, 1 (July 1970): pp. 83-84; Michael Ellman, "Did the Agricultural Surplus Provide the Resources for the Increase in Investment in the USSR During the First Five Year Plan?" *Economic Journal* 85, 4 (December 1975): p. 851.

4. Iu. A. Moshkov, *Zernovaia problema v gody sploshnoi kollektivizatsii sel'skogo khoziaistva SSSR* (Moscow: Moscow University, 1966), pp. 20-24; E. H. Carr and R. W. Davies, *Foundations of a Planned Economy*, vol. I (Harmondsworth, Penguin, 1974), p. 971.

5. Moshkov, *Zernovaia problema*, pp. 19-20.

6. S. G. Wheatcroft, "A Re-Evaluation of Soviet Agricultural Production in the 1920s and 1930s", *Kennan Institute for Advanced Russian Studies Occasional Paper No. 125*, Washington, D.C. (April 1981), pp. 15-21.

7. V. P. Danilov, *Sovetskaia dokolkhoznaia derevnia: naselenie, zemlepol'zovanie, khoziaistvo* (Moscow: Nauka, 1977), pp. 279-301.

8. A. A. Barsov, *Balans stoimostnykh obmenov mexhdu gorodom i derevnei* (Moscow: Nauka, 1969), p. 23.

9. V. I. Lenin, *Collected Works*, vol. 3 (London–Moscow: 1964), p. 33 (Preface to the Second Edition of "The Development of Capitalism in Russia").

10. V. P. Timoshenko, *Agricultural Russia and the Wheat Problem* (Stanford: Stanford University Press, 1932), p. 178.

11. A. N. Malafeev, *Istoriia tsenoobrazovaniia v SSSR* (Moscow: Mysl' 1964), p. 115.

12. J. M. Cooper, R. W. Davies, and S. G. Wheatcroft, "Contradictions in Soviet Industrialisation" (CREES, University of Birmingham, 1977), pp. 4-5.

13. E. Preobrazhensky, *The New Economics* (Cambridge: Oxford University Press, 1965), pp. 91–112.

14. James R. Millar, "What's Wrong with the 'Standard Story'?" *Problems of Communism* 25, 4 (July–August 1976): p. 59.

15. James R. Millar, "A Note on Primitive Accumulation in Marx and Preobrazhensky," *Soviet Studies* 30, 3 (July 1978): p. 393.

16. James R. Millar, "A Reformulation of Chayanov's Theory of the Peasant Economy," *Economic Development and Cultural Change* 18, 2 (January 1970), pp. 219–29.

17. In Mark Harrison, "Chayanov and The Economics of the Russian Peasantry," *Journal of Peasant Studies* 2, 4 (July 1975): pp. 393–396. I follow Chayanov's theoretical analysis of the elasticity of supply of family labour. I am grateful to Abu Abdullah of the Chr. Michelsen Institute, Bergen, for explaining to me in correspondence how this treatment assumes the result that it appears to demonstrate. See also Mark Blaug, *Economic Theory in Retrospect* (London: 1964), p. 291; Mark Harrison, "Soviet Peasants and Soviet Price Policy in the 1920s," *Soviet Industrialisation Project Series* No. 10 (CREES, University of Birmingham, 1977), p. 22.

18. Harrison, "The Economics of the Russian Peasantry," *Journal of Peasant Studies* 2, 4 (July 1975): pp. 400, 412.

19. James R. Millar, "What's Wrong," p. 52.

20. Corinne Guntzel, *Soviet Agricultural Pricing Policy and the Scissors Crisis of 1922–23* ([Urbana] Ph.D. Thesis, University of Illinois, 1972).

21. V. P. Dmitrenko, "Bor'ba sovetskogo gosudarstva za ovladenii derevenskim rynkom v pervye gody NEPa," *Voprosy istorii* (no. 9 September, 1964): pp. 58–63.

22. Harrison, "Soviet Peasants and Soviet Price Policy in the 1920s," p. 18.

23. Alec Nove, *An Economic History of the USSR* (Harmondsworth: Penguin, 1972), p. 220.

24. Barsov, *Balans stoimostnykh;* A.A. Barsov, "NEP i vyravnivanie ekonomicheskikh otnoshenii mezhdu gorodom i derevnei," in M. P. Kim (ed.), *Novaia ekonomicheskaia politika: voprosy teorii i istorii* (Moscow: Nauka, 1974); James R. Millar, "Mass Collectivization and the Contribution of Soviet Agriculture to the First Five-Year Plan," *Slavic Review* 33, 4 (December 1974) pp. 750–66; Ellman, "Did The Agricultural Surplus,"; Michael Ellman, "On a Mistake of Preobrazhensky and Stalin," *Journal of Development Studies* 14, 3 (April 1978), pp. 353–56.

25. Millar, "What's Wrong," p. 766.

26. Mischa Gisser and Paul Jonas, "Soviet Growth in Absence of Centralized Planning: A Hypothetical Alternative," *Journal of Political Economy* 82, 2, Part I (March/April 1974): pp. 346–47.

27. Holland Hunter, "Optimal Tautness in Development Planning," *Economic Development and Cultural Change* 9, 4, Part I (July 1961): p. 568.

28. Barsov, *Balans stoimostnykh,* p. 96.

29. Holland Hunter, "The Over-Ambitious First Soviet Five-Year Plan," *Slavic Review* 32, 2 (June 1973): p. 251.

30. *Ibid.,* pp. 252–53.

31. R. W. Davies and S. G. Wheatcroft, "Further Thoughts on the First Soviet Five-Year Plan," 33, 4 *Slavic Review* (December 1974): 790–92; Vyas, *Consumption,* pp. 152–53.

32. Hunter, "Optimal Tautness," pp. 252–53.

33. Vyas, *Consumption,* p. 165.

34. Hunter, "Optimal Tautness," p. 289.

35. *Ibid.,* pp. 251–52.

36. *Ibid.,* p. 252.

37. *Ibid.,* pp. 253–54.

38. Holland Hunter, "Soviet Investment Choices in the Thirties—Constraints and Costs," Paper presented at the Second World Congress of Soviet and East European Studies (Garmisch: 1980), p. 10.

39. Mark Harrison, "Testing Soviet Economic Policies 1928–1940: A Comment," Paper presented at the Second World Congress of Soviet and East European Studies (Garmisch: 1980).

40. Vyas, *Consumption,* p. 147.

41. Gisser and Jonas, "Soviet Growth," p. 344.

42. Michael R. Dohan, "The Economic Origins of Soviet Autarky 1927/28–1934," *Slavic Review* 35, 4 (December 1976): pp. 624–25.

43. Michael Ellman, "Did the Agricultural Surplus," p. 859.

44. Cooper, Davies, and Wheatcroft, "Contradictions," pp. 10–11.

45. Vyas, *Consumption,* p. 144.

46. Ellman, "Did the Agricultural Surplus," p. 859.

47. Cooper, Davies, and Wheatcroft, "Contradictions," p. 1.

48. Vyas, *Consumption,* p. 171.

APPENDIX

In the conditions of the late 1920s a worsening of the terms of trade facing the Soviet peasantry would probably have moved the economy toward equilibrium and at the same time increased the flow of agricultural products (including grain) onto the rural-urban market, at least in the short run. This result does not require the rather strong assumptions behind the Millar hypothesis of inelastic peasant demand for manufactures and would be obtained even if, comparing one equilibrium position with another, the normal peasant response to a worsening of the terms of trade in the short run was to withdraw from the product market.

Why this is so can be seen in the following terms. Suppose that we can portray rural-urban trade in terms of a "representative" peasant household, abstracting from differentiation of households by assets, access to markets, and preferences. Suppose also that the household's sales and purchases of goods are decided separately from production decisions, the outcomes of which for the given period are already known. In equilibrium the representative household trades bundles of foodstuffs for bundles of manufactures, as shown in Figure 3.1

Figure 3.1

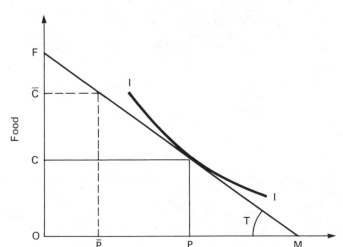

Mfrs

The harvest is fixed at OF. At terms of trade T, the resulting budget line is FM, and the household's highest attainable indifference curve is II. The household consumes OC of its food production, sells CF, and purchases OP manufactures in exchange.

In Figure 3.1, however, if the quantity of manufactures supplied to the rural market is constrained at level $O\overline{P}$, this result will be prevented. Unable to purchase OP manufactures, the household will only sell $\overline{C}F$ food. $C\overline{C}$ and $\overline{P}P$ measure the unrealized food sales and the frustrated demand for manufactures ("goods famine"), respectively.

What happens if the authorities permit the terms of trade to drift against the peasant? A possible result is shown in Figure 3.2. A worsening in the household's terms of trade from T_0 to T_1 shifts the budget line from FM_0 to FM_1. If we were comparing two equilibrium positions, we would find a fall in the demand for manufactures, while the supply of marketed foodstuffs would rise or fall depending on the price- and income-elasticity of the demand for manufactures (the Millar hypothesis would suggest an increased supply of marketed foodstuffs.). Figure 3.2 shows the strong case for my argument—the Millar hypothesis does not hold, and worsened terms of trade shift the tangency of indifference curves with the budget line in such a way that the equilibrium supply of food would fall from FC_0 to FC_1.

However, in reality the starting point is not one of equilibrium. Under initial conditions of goods famine, the supply of manufactures was constrained at $O\overline{P}$. At the initial terms of trade this elicited the marketed food supply $\overline{C}F$. At the new terms of trade the excess demand for manufactures is eliminated. At the same time the marketed food supply has increased from $\overline{C}F$ to C_1F, even though the quantity of manufactures offered in exchange has remained unchanged.

Figure 3.2

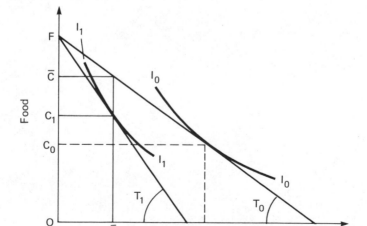

Mfrs

In fact, if we start from a position of excess demand for manufactures, then a small worsening of the terms of trade facing the peasants will always increase their marketed supply of foodstuffs in the short run. This result holds irrespective of the elasticity of peasant demand for manufactures, so long as the demand for manufactures does not fall below constrained supply. If the change in the terms of trade is more than large enough to relax the constraint, the elasticity of peasant demand for manufactures will influence the outcome; if the Millar hypothesis (inelastic demand) holds, the marketed supply of foodstuffs will continue to increase; but in the opposite case, the supply of foodstuffs will start to fall again if the price of manufactures goes on rising beyond the point required to eliminate the goods famine.

Policy makers trying to correct a goods famine disequilibrium, but ignorant of underlying peasant demand elasticities, can be more confident of the appropriateness of small price changes than large ones. They have to bear in mind that, the greater the elasticity of peasant demand for manufactures, the smaller will be the change in the terms of trade required to restore equilibrium on the rural-urban market, and the easier it will be to "overshoot." In addition, the greater the elasticity of peasant demand for manufactures, the smaller will be the increase in market supply of foodstuffs resulting from the restoration of market equilibrium.

Policy makers must also bear in mind two restrictions of the foregoing analysis. First, the analysis took the harvest as given and considered only short-run behavior in the product market, abstracting from the influence of the terms of rural-urban trade upon the incentives to labor and invest in agriculture. Second, it showed a possible course of correction of a goods famine disequilibrium by means of turning the terms of trade against the peasants, but it did not consider whether this course should be preferred to reducing very ambitious industrial investment plans and relaxing the supply-side constraint on the availability of manufactures in the rural market.

4

The Collectivization Drive and Agricultural Planning in the Soviet Union

Eugène Zaleski

INTRODUCTION

In Western works, a great deal of attention has been devoted to the study of Soviet agriculture; however, agricultural planning has received much less attention. This reduced interest in agricultural planning can in part be explained by the crude and complicated nature of Soviet agricultural planning, especially during the collectivization drive and the First Five-Year Plan period. During the early years of Soviet agricultural planning, several processes occurred simultaneously:

- The process of transition to more comprehensive and general plans, for both the annual and five-year periods
- The process of transition from flexible planning, characteristic of market socialism, toward imperative planning
- The integration of targets for the socialization of agriculture into the agricultural plans
- The use of a sort of "dual planning" where both plan targets and the tools of plan implementation were included in annual and five-year plans, typically developed and expressed as separate plans issued by the highest Soviet authorities and concerning collectivization, the production process, and relations between agriculture and its customers

In order to present these various aspects of Soviet agricultural planning in the early thirties, it is convenient to examine separately the indicators relating to production and procurement planning for Soviet agriculture, the targets for collectivization inside and outside of Soviet plans, and finally, the fulfillment of concrete targets for agricultural production and procurement.

PRODUCTION AND PROCUREMENT INDICATORS IN SOVIET AGRICULTURAL PLANNING

The available sources do not allow us to know exactly the nature of the agricultural indicators included in Soviet plans before and during the Five-

Table 4.1   Fulfillment of the Agricultural Targets of Annual Plans, 1928/29–1932

Series	Units	1928/29 Planned (1)	Actual (2)	(2) as Per Cent of (1) (3)	1929/30 Planned (4)	Actual (5)
Agriculture						
Total value of production (1926/27 prices)	mill. rub.	16,188	14,745[e]	91.1	16,736	14,008[e]
Vegetable production (1926/27 prices)	mill. rub.	10,719	9,059[e]	84.5	10,545	9,602[e]
Animal production (1926/27 prices)	mill. rub.	5,469	5,686[e]	104.0	6,107	4,406[e]
Harvests						
Grain, total (biological yield)	th. m. t.	74,500	71,742	96.3	88,900	83,545
Wheat	th. m. t.	22,440	18,880	84.1		26,920
Rye	th. m. t.	19,580	20,360	104.0		23,600
Barley	th. m. t.		7,214			6,770
Oats	th. m. t.		15,739			16,620
Corn	th. m. t.		3,018			2,665
Harvests of Technical Crops						
Raw cotton	th. m. t.	861	864	100.3	1,452	1,113
Sugar beets	th. m. t.	10,600	6,248	58.9	14,900	14,019
Sunflowers	th. m. t.		1,764		2,609	1,629
Flax fiber	th. m. t.		361		416	436
Hemp	th. m. t.		465			414
Potatoes	th. m. t.	43,600	45,630	104.7	51,300	49,448
Animal Production						
Meat and fat	th. m. t.		4,553[e]			3,215[e]
Milk	th. m. t.	31,000	29,335[e]	94.6		26,572[e]
Eggs	bill.	11.0	10.0[e]	90.9		7.2[e]
Wool	th. m. t.		178.8[e]			141.0[e]

Notes:
[a] from 1929 harvest obtained in 1930
[b] from 1930 harvest obtained in 1931
[c] from Davies, *The Socialist Offensive*, p. 104.
[d] from Davies, *The Socialist Offensive*, Table 13, p. 437.
[e] refers to the calendar year in which the fiscal year given in the column head ended.
     For additional details, see Zaleski, *Planning for Economic Growth*, p. 348 and 355–57.

Year Plan period. The first known documents are the Control Figures for the years 1925/1926 and for the following years until 1929/1930. For the first three years, these plans (Control Figures) were published in a very crude and reduced form. They included the main production targets and the so-called marketed production (not including sales within the village) in

Table 4.1 (continued)

	1931				1932	
(5) as Per Cent of (4) (6)	Planned (7)	Actual (8)	(8) as Per Cent of (7) (9)	Planned (10)	Actual (11)	(11) as Per Cent of (10) (12)
83.7	18,272	13,944	76.3		13,072	
91.1	12,804	9,851	76.9		9,779	
72.1	5,468	4,093	74.8		3,293	
93.9	97,860	69,484	71.0	81,484	69,873	85.8
		20,500			20,250	
		21,990			22,020	
		5,177			5,026	
		10,959			11,242	
		4,745			3,426	
76.7	2,102	1,290	61.4		1,271	
94.1	21,437	12,052	56.2	22,200	6,561	29.6
62.4	2,900	2,506	86.4		2,268	
104.8	568.2	553	97.4	666	498	74.8
		342			262	
96.4		44,850			43,124	
	3,273	2,861	87.4		2,294	
	30,663	24,806	80.9		20,558	
	10.56				4.2	
	159.2	98.0	61.5		69.0	

Sources: R. W. Davies, *The Socialist Offensive: The Collectivization of Soviet Agriculture, 1929–1930* (London and Basingstoke: Macmillan, 1980), p. 104 and Table 13, p. 437. Eugéne Zaleski, *Planning For Economic Growth in The Soviet Union, 1918–1932* (Chapel Hills: University of North Carolina Press, 1971), pp. 339–39.

(continued on next page)

value terms for the total and also expressed in physical units. Most of the products included in these early plans are presented in Tables 4.1 and 4.5.

A more elaborate version of these plans can be found in the annual plan for 1929/1930 and in the First Five-Year Plan for the period 1928/1929–1932/1933. For vegetable and animal products included in

Table 4.1   (continued)

| | | 1928/29 | | | 1929/30 | |
| | | Planned (1) | Actual (2) | (2) as Per Cent of (1) (3) | Planned (4) | Actual (5) |
Series	Units					
Market Production						
Grain	mill. m. t.		10.22		15.00	
Raw cotton	th. m. t.					
Sugar beets	th. m. t.		8,050			
Flax fiber	th. m. t.					
Potatoes	th. m. t.					
Meat and fat	th. m. t.		1,276			
Milk and dairy products	th. m. t.		6,800			
Wool	th. m. t.		58.2		63.0	
Procurements						
Grain: total	th. m. t.		16,081[a]		23,200[d]	22,139[bd]
centralized	th. m. t.	13,900	14,900[ac]			
Raw cotton	th. m. t.					
Sugar beets	mill. m. t.					13.2
Sunflowers	th. m. t.		810[e]			
Flax fiber	th. m. t.					
Hemp	th. m. t.					
Potatoes	th. m. t.					
Meat and fat (live weight)	th. m. t.		1,820			1,305[e]
Meat and fat (dead weight)	th. m. t.		1,197[e]		912	797[e]
Milk	th. m. t.		2,100			1,300
Eggs	mill.		2,074			
Wool	th. m. t.		44[e]			52[e]

Notes:
[a] from 1929 harvest obtained in 1930
[b] from 1930 harvest obtained in 1931
[c] from Davies, *The Socialist Offensive,* p. 104.
[d] from Davies, *The Socialist Offensive,* Table 13, p. 437.
[e] refers to the calendar year in which the fiscal year given in the column head ended. For additional details, see Zaleski, *Planning for Economic Growth,* p. 348 and 355–57.

Table 4.1, the annual plan for 1929/1930 and the first five-year plan also include the amount of land sown, yields, and the distribution by main regions.

The First Five-Year Plan also includes, in some detail, the plan for collectivization as well as plans for total production, marketed production (separately for individual peasants, kolkhozy and sovkhozy) for all the years from 1927/1928 to 1932/1933 and for the main regions. These targets also appear in the annual plan for 1929/1930.

The final version of the Five-Year Plan also includes several balances and

Table 4.1   (continued)

	1931			1932		
(5) as Per Cent of (4) (6)	Planned (7)	Actual (8)	(8) as Per Cent of (7) (9)	Planned (10)	Actual (11)	(11) as Per Cent of (10) (12)
					20.31	
					1,202	
					6,120	
					318	
					8,984	
					935	
					4,088	
					41.0	
	24,161	22,839	94.5	20,540	18,775	91.4
				1,617	1,203	74.4
					6.1	
		1,351			563	
				375	287	76.5
				120	40	33.3
					4,642	
		2,114			1,203	
87.4		1,039			648	
		1,200			2,100	
					386	
		49			41	

Sources: R. W. Davies, *The Socialist Offensive: The Collectivization of Soviet Agriculture, 1929–1930* (London and Basingstoke: Macmillan, 1980), p. 104 and Table 13, p. 437. Eugène Zaleski, *Planning For Economic Growth in The Soviet Union, 1918–1932* (Chapel Hill: University of North Carolina Press, 1971), pp. 339–39.

estimates: the balance for the production and utilization of cereals and animal fodder (*khlebo-furazhnyj balans*), estimates of the need for mineral fertilizers, sowings of special plants (*sortovykh posevov*), land preparation (*zemleustrojstvo*), the financing of agriculture through various channels. The latter included: funds belonging to the kolkhoz and to individual peasants, funds of different state organizations, local budgets, the state budget and finally, credits.

In all plans elaborated until 1929/1930, financing appears as the main tool of their implementation. These plans are initially flexible, though after 1927/1928 they were given a formal obligatory character, elaborated by the Gosplan of the USSR in collaboration with republican and local authorities.

Even at this time, however, special plans elaborated by the government and the Party frequently appeared in the press, assuming more and more a compulsory character. These plans concerned several aspects of agricultural activity such as contracts (*kontraktacija*), (see for instance the Central Party Committee decision of August 26, 1929, and the government decision of October 7, 1929);[1] the sowing campaign (to be implemented by local authorities and also concerning private farming);[2] procurements of grain, livestock, meat, potatoes, and the work for harvesting.

One has the feeling that these special agricultural plans were not well integrated into the general plans elaborated by Gosplan even if they were intended to implement agricultural targets. They were usually announced by the Central Committee of the Communist Party and/or the Council of People's Commissars in the form of orders given to various Soviet authorities.

It does not seem as if the introduction of administrative and command planning starting with the annual plan for 1931 changed to any degree the number of planned indicators.[3] The main task of agricultural planning seems to have been given to the *Narkomzem* of the USSR (The Commissariat for Agriculture), created 7 December 1929, an organization which controlled the republican commissariats of agriculture. However, other organizations controlling agricultural activities such as *NarkomSovkhoz* and *Narkomtorg* also collaborated in this work.[4]

The main innovation of the 1931 plan seems to have been the presentation of the agricultural plan according to the Soviet authorities controlling the agricultural activities: *Zernotrest, Risotrest, Skotovodoeskij trest, svitrest, traktorocentr,* electrical power stations, and others. This manner of presentation was designed to facilitate the transmission of planned orders.

The procedure applied in the 1931 plan followed that established during the previous campaign. The quota imposed on every village was now elevated to the status of a "village plan," but continued to be fixed by the district authorities on the basis of a district plan or quota sent to them by the region. At the village level, subquotas were fixed for different groups of peasant households. As a substitute for mass emulation, the device of socialist competition was borrowed from industry and some "counterplans" also appeared where kolkhozy offered deliveries above those officially requested.[5]

It is difficult to appreciate the extent to which changes were introduced in the annual and Five-Year Plans since the introduction of command planning in 1931 because the published materials are not complete.

The published targets for the 1933 plan do not differ in coverage for the principal agricultural products, for regional distribution, for sown area, for yields from those found in previous plans.[6] More details are given for the work of the Machine Tractor Stations (MTS), for the work of the sovkhoz, for different kinds of kolkhozy (specializing in cattle, hogs, sheep, etc.), for deliveries of agricultural products and for the collectivization campaign.

The annual plan for 1933 was elaborated simultaneously with some earlier versions of the Second Five-Year Plan. It is therefore not surprising that the differences in planned and published indicators was not great. One should mention, however, the publication of the evaluation if fixed *fondy* in agriculture in 1933 prices for all planned years until 1937, as well as for agriculture as a whole and for the sovkhozy and MTS (given the collectivization drive, the residual should be for kolkhoz fixed capital).[7] Investments in agriculture are also mentioned with some detail and with more data given for investments under the control of *NKZem* and *NKSovkhoz* for energy, productive construction, housing and others.[8]

The most detailed plan published in the Soviet Union was the annual plan for 1935.[9] The main emphasis in published targets is on technical equipment for agriculture and especially for the MTS including the number of tractors, agricultural machines, fertilizers to be furnished, and the specification for kolkhoz and sovkhoz performance. The progress of collectivization is mentioned in the text as an outstanding achievement. However, the procurement plans and campaigns are not included in the published materials. They did figure, however, in the plan, but only in the internal documents of Gosplan.[10] The same policy was followed in the 1936 plan and the number of published indicators for agriculture did not change very much.[11]

The most comprehensive view of the planned indicators for agriculture is given in the instructions for the 1936 and 1937 annual plans.[12] The main conclusion is that we have at this time a very comprehensive agricultural plan done separately for vegetable and animal production, with all necessary technical measures. This plan is established according to the institutional forms of agricultural production with division by federal republics and regions. It also includes a special and large plan for procurements and for the consumption of agricultural products.[13]

It is interesting to compare the planned indicators for agriculture with the published figures. This can be done with ease for the 1936 annual plan, though it would be difficult to quote all of the planned indicators that have been withdrawn from the published figures. For all main agricultural targets (production in value terms, sown area, yields, technical measures, animal production, etc.), only scattered information is given in the published plan for 1936, which, with the annual plan for 1935, is one of the most comprehensive in Soviet practice. Several institutional details (for example, production of nonagricultural people's commissariats or *ORS'y*) are ommitted. But what is most striking is the total exclusion of plans for procurements, plans to which the Soviet government gave such great emphasis during the thirties. In general, however, the plans are very detailed.

It is important to note that the extension of the number of indicators of agricultural activity in the Soviet plans was a rather imperfect mirror of the pressure exercised by the Party and by the Soviet government on the peasantry during the collectivization drive. The extraction of grain from the peasants played a crucial role in the Soviet system, assuming the character of a semimilitary requisitioning system and contributing toward the shaping of the Soviet economy as a *sui generis* war economy.[14] The procurement campaign was a difficult affair, using the energies of many agencies including the Politburo itself, which closely supervised all stages of the campaign.[15] Two stages of this campaign should be distinguished: procurements more or less compulsory but based formally on contractual obligations, and the transformation, since 1933, of the *zagotovki* (procurements) into a compulsory duty.

The procurements campaign of 1929/1930, for instance, was organized by a great number of decrees and institutions. Narkomtorg and Mikoyan, as People's Commissar for Trade, were in charge of the whole campaign, and no major change was made in the formal division of responsibilities among the various grain collection agencies. *Soyuzkhleb* collected grain from sovkhozy, and the milling levy from everybody. *Khlebocentr* was primarily responsible for collecting grain due under contracts from the kolkhozy and from the production associations of the individual peasants. The consumer cooperatives under *Tsentrosojuz* collected primarily from the unorganized peasants.[16]

The main innovation introduced by the government and Party decree of 19 January 1933 was the declaration that the *zagotovki* would become a compulsory state tax, a predictable norm, based upon the sown area and independent of the size of the crop.[17] A special Committee for Procurements (*Komzag*) was created for this purpose at the end of 1932 under the auspices of the highest administrative body (STO).[18] The *zagotovki* plans were based upon planned delivery targets approved or imposed by the Politburo and distributed (since 1931) for the big national regions. The Commissariats of local organs broke down the general figures into differential norms (so many quintals per hectare per crop) for their appropriate areas.[19] On the basis of such norms, specially constituted committees in the *raiispolkomy* finished the planning and assignment job by computing the amounts of grain to be imposed on every kolkhoz and, with the help of the *Selsovety*, on every private farmer.[20]

A parallel way of taking grain from the countryside was the extraction of *naturoplata* (payments in kind) by the machine tractor stations. Reporting only to its own hierarchy directed from the center, this administration was given priority over local Party and Soviet bodies. It was made responsible, from 1933, for managing the kolkhozy and the rural economy.[21]

It seems that production and procurement planning of agriculture were never entirely integrated. They occupied, in the official plan, two chapters, but this was only a formal aspect. As a matter of fact, the production plan elaborated through the institutional channels of Soviet agriculture and presented to Gosplan seemed to have a rather independent life in comparison with the struggle for grain and for the realizement of procurement plans, a day-to-day struggle requiring the mobilization of a large part of the state apparatus. Several "independent" plans for procurements appear during the whole period of the thirties in Soviet journals. For 1933, for instance, we can find five separate procurement plans (for grain, potatoes, again grain, meat, and milk and butter) and another plan for the payments in kind of the MTS. In the official *Soviet Sobranie Zakonov i Raspor-*

jazhenij (1933–1937) [Collection of laws and decrees], one can find each year a great number of decrees concerning *kontraktacija* (contract campaign) and compulsory deliveries and procurements for various kinds of agricultural products. Lengthy decrees for the sowing campaign, distributing the area to be sown for each region and for the kolkhoz, sovkhoz, and individual peasants were published every year.[22] Since these sowing obligations served as a basis for procurement duties, it is understandable that great emphasis was placed upon them by the government. In fact, as was stated by one Soviet official, the forced *zagotovki* pushed the government toward forced collectivization.[23]

THE COLLECTIVIZATION CAMPAIGN AND THE TARGETS OF NATIONAL ECONOMIC PLANS

The Policy for Socialization of Agriculture in the Last Phase of Preparation of the First Five-Year Plan

The socialization of agriculture was admitted as one of the important aims of the Fifteenth Party Congress of 2–19 December 1927. The government should definitely help poorer and middle peasants to establish collective farms of a different kind and to reinforce the pressure against the *kulaks*.[24] But, the way to unite small and dwarf peasant farms was to act gradually, not by pressure but by example and persuasion, in order to create large farms based on common, cooperative, collective cultivation of the land.[25]

This apparently moderate policy toward collectivization resulted also from the forms taken at this time by the collective farms. In May 1928, 69.9 percent of the collective farms were *TOZY*,[26] 26.3 percent were *Arteli*,[27] and 7.8 percent were *Communes*.[28] [29] At this time, according to Moshe Lewin, nobody intended to push the collectivization movement in an artificial way, meaning that it would be possible, given the available material and equipment.[30] The moderate attitude toward collectivization was several times stated by the highest Party organs in 1928. Indeed the Central Committee Plenum of July 1928 was dominated by the need to reassure the peasants, and Stalin announced shortly after the Plenum that "we need neither detractors nor eulogizers of individual peasant farming."[31] A document presented at the 15 December 1928 session of the Central Executive Committee once again presented collectivization as an issue for poor peasants, and, as Moshe Lewin states, nobody at this time considered this issue for a great part of the middle peasants.[32]

While pretending to adopt a moderate attitude toward private agriculture, the Communist Party under the pressure of Stalin introduced several measures creating tension and social struggles in the villages. The pretext was the struggle against the *kulak*. But, under this pretext, middle peasants and all opponents were discriminated against and the land could be confiscated at any moment. Middle peasants were often evicted from the *Selsovet* and their influence diminished. The fight against the *kulak* was also a pretext for the extraction of grain from the peasants during the pro-

curement campaign (following the introduction of *kontraktacija*), introduced first in 1927 for technical crops, and in 1928 for grain.[33] The "Ural-
Siberian method" with the personal participation of Stalin, consisting of arbitrary confiscation of grain, was enlarged to other regions, in spite of the
protests of "right wing" Politburo members such as Bukharin, Rykov, and
Tomsky.

The first attack (naming as yet no names) against "right wing devia-
tionists" came only in October and November of 1928 from Stalin. In the
winter of 1928/1929, the "Ural-Siberian method" was again applied to the
peasants and Stalin attacked Bukharin vigorously in the April 1929 Plenum
of the Central Committee.[34]

This strong difference of views about agriculture policy between the Party, headed by Stalin, and the "right wing" of Bukharin and Rykov, as the
head of the government, was not reflected in the plan figures. The annual
plan figures for 1928/1929, elaborated at the end of 1928, at the same time
as the final variant of the First Five-Year Plan for 1928/1929–1932/1933,
reflected still the moderate attitude admitted by the Fifteenth Party Congress of December 1927. In 1928/1929, the number of kolkhozy should
readh 38,000 against 32,506 in 1927/1928.[35] The moderation was also dominant in the final draft of the First Five-Year Plan. In 1932/1933, the gross
agricultural production of private farming should represent 87.0 percent,
and marketed agricultural production 77.1 percent of the total agricultural
production.[36] Four and one-half million peasant households, with twenty
million hectares of sown area should be organized into kolkhozy, mainly of
the TOZ type.[37] The sovkhoz should represent at the end of the Five-Year
Plan 2.9 percent of gross agricultural production and 8.0 percent of
marketed agricultural production.[38]

According to Moshe Lewin, the final version of the Five-Year Plan
forecasted the maintenance, for a long time, of private agriculture, for
which substantial help was planned.[39] A similar opinion has been expressed
by R. W. Davies, who states that collectivization was envisaged in all
statements of the Party leaders as a process that, even in major grain areas,
would take a decade or more. During this time, the massive supply of
agricultural machinery to the kolkhoz would provide the technical basis for
modern farming and offer an adequate inducement to individual peasants.[40]

The Collectivization Campaign and the Fight Against Kulaks
After the Adoption of the First Five-Year Plan

After the adoption of the Five-Year Plan in May of 1929, the gap between
the collectivization policy as presented in the plan and as followed in practice became wider. The agricultural plan was elaborated by Gosplan with
the cooperation of specialists of the Commissariat of Agriculture and of the
Cooperative Movement, but this was only a proposed policy and not
followed by the Party.[41] The Politburo and the Party Secretariat had their
own services dealing with agriculture and followed quite a different
policy.[42] This policy was based upon the thesis of Stalin about the class

struggle in the village, which was an instrument of the government in order to fight not against the capitalists, but against the opposition of the rural population, the dissatisfied workers and the Party members who were too much influenced by the spontaneity (*stikhija*) of the small bourgeoisie.[43]

This was the ideological justification for hard measures taken by the government against the peasants. One such measure was the fight against private dealers of grain paying higher prices. At the same time, the Party organized a campaign for an economic boycott of grain holders, creating tension in the village. Peasants considered guilty were thrown out of the cooperative, deprived of their supply of agricultural products in fixed prices, and amendments of *pjatikratka* (to pay five times as much) were applied to them.[44] In the second half of 1929, in selected grain areas, kulaks were also deliberately overassessed for grain deliveries, which were then expropriated for failure to obey.[45]

It is easy to understand that given these methods, collectivization progressed at a pace much faster than forecasted in the plan. Between June and October, 900,000 households joined kolkhozy, and the total number of kolkhoz households amounted to 1.9 million, with 8.8 percent of the sown area of the country.[46] But this amount was mainly represented by TOZY at 62 percent.[47] In some regions, collectivization was much more pronounced (North Caucasus, 19 percent; Lower Volga, 18.3 percent; Volga, 14 percent; and the Ukraine, 10 percent), thanks to the so-called measures of total (*splosnaja*) collectivization.[48] But, according to Moshe Lewin, until October of 1929, the peasants were not directly forced to join a kolkhoz.[49]

It is easy to understand that, under these conditions, the collectivization targets of the Five-Year Plan could not be maintained. If the Five-Year Plan forecasted five million households to be collectivized by 1932/1933, with 21–22 million hectares, the *Kolkhozcentr* planned 7–8 million households with 8 million hectares by 1930.[40] In this sense, the Five-Year Plan was completely out of date since the *Kolkhozcentr* intended to collectivize half of the rural population, with sown area tripled in comparison to the initial plan. The kolkhozy should deliver by 1933, 10 million tons of grain and satisfy the entire needs of the country.[51]

Given this policy, the annual plan for 1929/1930 was revised rather moderately. The original target of 2 million households to be collectivized in 1929/1930 was increased to 3,129,000 and the collective farm sown area from 6 million to 15.2 million hectares for the same year.[52]

The Offensive Against The Peasantry, or the All-Out Drive for Collectivization, December 1929/March 1930

At the very time when the text of the 1929/1930 plan was released, a complete revision of collectivization targets was developed. In an impassioned speech at the Sovnarkhom, Pyatakov assured that "extreme rates of collectivization of agriculture" should be adopted.[53] In a speech delivered on the twelfth anniversary of the Revolution, Stalin announced a "great turn" (*velikij perelom*) in the development of agriculture from "Small backward individual economy to large scale progressive collective agriculture.''[54] He emphasized strongly the change of mood among the peasants, arguing that they were joining collective farms not in small groups but in whole villages, whole rural districts (*volost*), and even whole groups of districts (*okrug*). Stalin's speech formed a part of a concerned campaign to encourage the enthusiasm of the Party cadres and to prepare the way for the Plenum of the Central Committee of the Communist Party to take place in November of 1929.

In his long speech of 15 November 1929 at the Party Plenum, Molotov argued that the pace of collectivization was "really frantic . . . . The North Caucasus would achieve more than 50 percent collectivization in 1929/1930, the Lower Volga was keeping up with this, and other major grain regions were not far behind.'' In the autumn of 1930, "we shall probably be able to see that collectivization will be completed in the 'main,' not only in a single region, like North Caucasus, but also in entire republics.''[55] He argued at the same time that the original Five-Year Plan must be ignored for all the main agricultural districts and regions.[56]

The resolution on the kolkhozy of the November Plenum did not go far and retained as a target only the size of the collectivized area of 15 million hectares to be achieved by the end of 1929/1930. But the pressure toward collectivization exerted by Stalin continued. At the beginning of December 1929, plans had been approved to complete collectivization of the main grain-surplus regions of the RSFSR by the middle of 1931 (by the end of 1930 in the Lower Volga Region and in a substantial number of other districts in the spring of 1930). Other regions also adopted more ambitious plans at this time.[57] It was argued at the Central Executive Committee session of 2 December 1929, by the chairman of the Lower Volga Executive Committee, that the comprehensive collectivization of the whole USSR should be achieved by 1929/1930.[58]

Different proposals for speeding up the collectivization drive had been advanced by the Politburo commission headed by Yakovlev, which was established on 5 December 1929. Its draft resolution, submitted on 22 December to the Central Committee, advocated that the overwhelming majority of the peasantry should be collectivized during the Five-Year Plan, with the collectivization of the main grain areas being completed in two to three years—that is, by the end of 1931 to the end of 1932. The 5 January 1930 Resolution "On the Rate of Collectivization and the Measures of Assistance by the State to Kolkhoz Construction,'' reduced the target dates for collectivization of the three main grain regions to one or two years—that is, by the end of 1931 to the end of 1932—and insisted that collectivization must be held back because tractors were not available, maintaining in brief form the warning against collectivization by compulsion.[59]

This last recommendation was certainly not respected during the all-out collectivization drive of January–February 1930. The resolution of various regional and local Party committees advocated the collectivization during a much shorter period, with political and police pressure being used on the peasants. The plan for the USSR envisaged that over 30 million hectares would be sown in the spring of 1930 by the kolkhozy. In the middle of February of 1930, the authorities estimated that the sown area of the kolkhozy would amount to 60–70 million hectares.[60] This movement had no relation to any planned targets for production. Another decision was also taken, which modified in a significant way the planned targets for collectivization. The text of the Five-Year Plan did not specify the nature of kolkhozy in which the 4.5 million peasants should be incorporated in 1932/1933.[61] Since, in 1928, the overwhelming majority of existing kolkhozy were of the *TOZ* type (about 70 percent),[62] one could expect that a non-compulsory increase in their number would not change basically their internal structure. For this reason, the decision of the Party at the end of 1929 to admit only the *artel* form represented a much more severe form of collectivization,[63] and a decisive step toward the expropriation of the peasantry.

It can be understood that for such a policy, persuasion alone would not be sufficient. The "voluntary principle" stated in the 5 January 1930 resolution was therefore replaced by terror exercised by local Party and OGPU authorities. The terror was particularly pronounced against the more wealthy peasants (*kulaks*) who were divided by a subcommission of the Politburo into three categories. The first category, described officially as "actively hostile," was selected directly by the OGPU and sent directly to concentration camps, while their families were subject to deportation to distant regions of the north, Siberia, and the far east.[64] The second category was selected in different ways, mainly "by general meetings of collective farmers and the poor peasants and *batraks* (landless peasantry) meetings."[65] They were described as "the most economically potent kulak households and deported outside the region (*oblast*) of their residence."[66] It is not known whether they could keep a part of their personal property.[67] Finally, the third category, regarded as the least noxious, were to be allowed to remain in the region but were to be given land of the worst kind.[68] It was admitted that this third category could be "reeducated" and they could be admitted into the kolkhoz as workers, with a possibility of full membership after five years.[69] The government prepared "control figures" (plans) for the number of kulaks to be expelled in each of the first and second categories. This number was divided by the regions among the *okrugs* and by the *okrugs* among the districts and villages. "Dekulakization" was more tightly controlled than collectivization. "Enthusiastic regional Party committees sometimes increased the quota set by the Central Party Committee."[70]

Temporary Retreat and Continuous Pressure for Collectivization

The hostile attitude of peasants toward collectivization with slogans such as "for Soviet power, without communist and kolkhozy" and women's mutinies (*babi bunty*)[71] motivated a momentary retreat in Stalin's policy. Stalin's "famous" article published in *Pravda,* 2 March 1930, entitled "Dizzy with Success: Problems of the Kolkhoz Movement," insisted on the voluntary principle in collectivization and deflected the responsibility to lower levels of Party and government administration.[72] A spontaneous exodus from kolkhozy followed, accompanied by drastic reductions of collectivization plans in grain surplus as well as grain deficit regions. The percentage of peasant households collectivized was reduced from 58 percent on 10 March 1930 to 21 percent on 1 October 1930.[73] The Sixteenth Party Congress of 26 June to 13 July 1930 reaffirmed the voluntary principle of collectivization, but declared that the grain problem had been solved in the main owing to the success of the kolkhozy and sovkhozy and called finally for further collectivization.[74] But it was argued that "the voluntary principle does not imply non-interference in the process of collectivization: collectivization must be encouraged, planned and organised."[75]

If the Party pressure for collectivization was maintained in the autumn of 1930, warnings that the "voluntary principle should be maintained" continued. No specific quotas for collectivization were set by central authorities and attempts by local authorities to adopt firm "control figures" for the number of households to be collectivized in each district were condemned. Nor was there any large-scale central campaign in the autumn of 1930 analogous to that of the first weeks of 1930.[76]

In any case, the targets of the annual plan for 1929/1930 concerning collectivization were largely overfulfilled, but the fluctuations during the year prove that this plan was completely disregarded. Instead of 3,129,000, the actual number of peasant households in collective farms was 5,000,000. Total collective farm sown area in the spring of 1930 was 43.4 million hectares, against 15.2 million planned for 1929/1930. However, at the end of the fiscal year 1929/1930, the area sown by collective farms was only around 30–32 million hectares.[77]

The 17–21 December 1930 Plenum planned a further advance in collectivization and "dekulakization" in 1931: 80 percent in the Ukraine, North Caucasus, Lower Volga, Central Volga; 50 percent in the remaining grain areas; 20–25 percent in grain-deficit zones. On average in the USSR for all branches of farming (grain, cotton, sugar beets, etc.), at least half of peasant households should be collectivized.[78] In spite of the "voluntary principle," continuous pressures and coercion were used against the peasants in order to force them to join the kolkhozy. Among methods used were arbitrary exactions known as "hard obligations" (*tvyordye zadanija*) to deliver vast quantities of grain to the state. If they failed to deliver the required amount, they were punished by the sale of their property, fines, imprisonment, etc. The attack was now on the "kulak and better-off peasants," and was clearly intended, in the winter of 1930/1931, to drive peasants back into the collective farms. This was repeated in 1931/1932. Some victims of these measures were deported, others evaded ever-growing delivery obligations by joining collectives "voluntarily."[79] The dominance of the *artel* in relation to other forms of kolkhozy became striking: in 1931 there were 91.7 percent *artels*, 4.7 percent *TOZY* and 3.6 percent *communes* out of the total number of kolkhozy.[80] A rough-and-ready system of piecerates was introduced to become the *trudoden* (work-day-unit) "legalized" by the decree of 5 July 1932.[81]

The December 1930 plans were rapidly surpassed, as well as those for the sown area of collective farms, for the collective livestock, and for deliveries to the state. By the beginning of July, 53.7 percent of peasant households had been included in the kolkhozy, increasing the 60.8 percent on 1 October 1932 and to 68.9 percent by 1 January 1934.[82]

The Second Five-Year Plan forecasted that at the end of the plan, all workers in rural areas would join the kolkhozy. Since this announcement, the pace of collectivization corresponded more or less to the annual targets: the annual plan for 1935 confirmed that the proportion of collectivized farms was 68.9 percent on 1 January 1934, 72.7 percent on 1 October 1934, 77.2 percent on 1 January 1935, and 80.8 percent on 1 April 1935.[83] The annual plan for 1936 stated that this percentage increased to 86.5 on 1 October 1935 and to 90 percent in 1936.[84]

The Second Five-Year Plan targets for collectivization were fulfilled and the Stalinist Constitution of December 1936 could announce the full collectivization of the country. This was only partially true, however, since in 1937, 93 percent of peasant households and 99 percent of cultivated land were socialized. But at the beginning of 1938, still 32.9 percent of all cattle, 17.2 percent of cows, 37.3 percent of sheep and goats, and 16.9 percent of pigs remained in private hands,[85] with important private production from the private plots of kolkhozniki, sovkhozniki, and others including products such as milk, eggs, and vegetables.[86]

PLANNING OF AGRICULTURAL PRODUCTION AND PROCUREMENTS DURING THE FIRST FIVE-YEAR PLAN

If we were to adopt the success criteria of Soviet authorities during the First Five-Year Plan, one would examine two categories of targets: collectivization of peasant households and procurements. If these indicators are not sufficient for an appreciation of Soviet performance in the long run, one cannot neglect, as the Soviets did during the collectivization period, the result of the overall agricultural production plans.

Production and Procurement Plans on the Eve of Collectivization

An overall outlook on Soviet agricultural and production plans for the year 1928/1929 is presented in Table 4.1.

It appears that the annual plan for 1928/1929 was well fulfilled for some industrial crops (raw cotton, potatoes, and rye), but rather poorly fulfilled for grain (total), animal products, and sugar beets. It must be noted, however, that the final draft of the First Five-Year Plan, approved in April–May 1929, increased slightly the targets for grain, sugar beets, and potatoes (see Table 4.2).

The overall fulfillment of the 1928/1929 annual plan reveals a considerable strain in the sectors associated with consumption.[87] These difficulties stemmed from agriculture, the failure to reach production targets being linked with the failure to meet the plan's provisions for investment in the privately owned sector of agriculture. The annual plan for 1928/1929

Table 4.2   Agricultural Goals of the 1928/29 and 1929/30 Plans

ANNUAL PLAN GOALS AS PERCENTAGE OF THE FIVE-YEAR PLAN FOR THE
CORRESPONDING YEAR

1928/29		1929/30	
Agriculture[a]		*Agriculture*[a]	
Potatoes	106.4	Raw cotton	133.2
Sugar beets	104.9	Flax fiber	124.2
Grain, harvested,		Sugar beets	120.1
total	101.3	Potatoes	110.5
Eggs	100.0	Grain, harvest,	
Milk	97.2	total	109.2
Raw cotton	96.7	Sunflowers	91.5
		Market production:	
		Grain	154.0
		Wool	79.1

PERCENTAGE OF FULFILLMENT OF 1928/29 AND 1929/30 ANNUAL PLAN GOALS

1928/29		1929/30	
Agriculture[a]		*Agriculture*[a]	
Potatoes	104.7	Flax fiber	104.8
Rye	104.0	Potatoes	96.4
Raw cotton	100.3	Sugar beets	94.1
Grain, total	96.3	Grain, total (biological	
Milk	94.6	yield)	93.9
Eggs	91.5	Raw cotton	76.7
Wheat	84.1	Sunflowers	62.4
Sugar beets	58.9		
		Agricultural procurements	
		Meat and fat	
		(dead weight)	87.4

[a]harvest and animal production

Source: Eugène Zaleski, *Planning for Economic Growth in the Soviet Union,
1918–1932,* (Chapel Hill: University of North Carolina Press, pp. 81, 84–85, 92.

forecasted 9.2 billion rubles of investment in the national economy, from
which 3.7 billion rubles should be in the private sector.[88] It can be estimated
that out of this private investment, 3.1 to 3.3 billion rubles were to be in-
vested in private agriculture.[89] Actual investment in current prices in private
agriculture was only 2.6 billion rubles in 1928/1929 and even less in
1928/1929 planned prices.[90] Thus the agricultural output not only failed to
meet the planned targets but even fell. The total grain harvest was 2.2 percent below that of 1928, which itself had shown a decrease. The harvest was
particularly poor for wheat (a drop of 14.1 percent), oats, corn, and
buckwheat groats. For sugar beets, the crop was catastrophic (38.4 percent

below 1928), and the crop of sunflowers, hemp, and potatoes also declined.[91]

The Soviet authorities attempted to cope with the crisis on the agricultural market by greatly increasing control by the state. By the spring of 1929, the coercion in collecting grain was extended to meat.[92] The collection campaign following the 1928 harvest was, however, a failure. In the agricultural year July 1928 to June 1929, total grain collected amounted to 10.8 million tons, less than in each of the two previous years (11.6 and 11.0 million tons). The decline in the centralized grain collections was even greater: only 8.3 million tons were received as compared with 10.6 and 10.1 million tons respectively in 1926/1927 and 1927/1928.[93] The government refused, however, to offer adequate material incentives to the peasants. The average price paid for grain by the private purchaser over the year 1928/1929 was double the price paid by the official collection agencies.[94]

Production and Procurement Planning in 1929/1930

The agricultural production plan for 1929/1930 was very ambitious. As can be seen from Table 4.2, almost all agricultural production targets exceeded the corresponding targets of the First Five-Year Plan. But the collectivization of agriculture was already an important part of the plan. So the aggregate investment target for agriculture was raised over the Five-Year Plan targets for 1929/1930 only by 4 percent, investment for the state-owned and cooperative sectors of agriculture was increased spectacularly by 182.6 and 56.8 percent respectively, while projected investments in the privately owned sector was reduced by 11.4 percent.[95] But the private sector of agriculture, with 2,657 million rubles of investment (in planned prices) still represented 61.9 percent of total agricultural investments of 4,293 million rubles planned for this year.[96] But nothing was done to help the private sector to fulfill its investment targets, and the collectivization drive acted in the opposite direction.

The poor fulfillment of the 1929/1930 agricultural plan can be seen from Tables 4.1 and 4.2. The failure was especially grave for animal production, with 72.1 percent of annual targets (in value terms) fulfilled. No figures were published about the results of the investment plan in the private sector. In the socialist sector, the investment plan for 1929/1930 was fulfilled at 102.8 percent, but it was for a small part of the total planned investment in agriculture.[97] One has to note that at this time, a disinvestment had taken place in the private sector in the form of reduction of livestock herds.[98]

The Soviet government took two main actions in order to deal with the crisis. The first was the temporary retreat, as shown by the reduction of the compulsory methods of collectivization mentioned above. The second was the increase in the amount of procurements.[99]

The procurement plan was not published until the campaign was almost complete, but partial plans published in June 1929 indicated that centralized procurements, including the milling levy, would amount to 12.5 million tons, which was later increased to 13.923 million tons.[100] No increase of the general price level paid to the peasants was forecasted. Organized procurements (milling levy, sovkhozy, contracts with kolkhozy and individual peasants) should provide 60 percent of the total, against 28 percent the previous year.[101] In fact, grain quotas were frequently imposed on the villages without even the pretense of a formal consultation with the village assembly (*skhod*).

In the agricultural year July 1929 to June 1930, the centralized procurements amounted to 14.9 million tons as compared with the plan of 13.9 million tons, and the total grain collected was 16.08 million tons.[102] The optimistic assessment about the 1929 harvest (79 million tons of grain initially estimated and 71.7 million tons finally obtained) justified higher procurement targets.[103] In fact, much higher procurement targets were introduced concomitantly with the reduction of the harvest in 1929 by 2.8 million tons of grain in comparison with the annual plan and 1.1 million tons in comparison with the preceding year (1928), representing a heavy burden imposed on the peasantry.

Production and Procurement Planning in 1930/1931

The 1931 annual plan for agriculture was certainly one of the most ambitious and was elaborated under new social conditions. The government was mainly preoccupied with the socialist sector, and 1931 was the first year during which methods of direct planning previously applied exclusively to industry were introduced into agriculture.[104]

The total figure for investment quoted in the 1931 annual plan for agriculture concerned exclusively the socialist sector: 5,287 million rubles, of which 3,642 were for the state-owned sector and 1,645 for the kolkhozy.[105] Industrial investments were also strongly influenced by planned deliveries to the socialist sector of agriculture. Increased deliveries of agricultural machinery, tractors, and fertilizers were supposed to consolidate the new regime of agriculture.

It can be seen from Tables 4.1 and 4.3 that fulfillment of the agricultural plan was particularly bad in 1931. The grain harvest was only 71.0 percent of the plan, even in terms of the "biological yields" greatly exaggerating the real results. The fantastic and unrealistic targets given for 1931 certainly explain a good part of the failure. The ongoing collectivization did not favor investments by individual peasants, and the investment in the socialized sector was fulfilled by 69.5 percent in the state sector of agriculture and by only 67.8 percent in the kolkhozy.[106]

The 1930/1931 (later 1931) procurement plan was based on the 1930 harvest. In order to justify high procurement targets, the Soviet government maintained for some time the initial estimates of 88 million tons harvested in 1930, a figure that was only in 1932 reduced to 83.5 million tons.[107] The grain procurement plan for 1930/1931 was very optimistic: about 23 million tons, including milling levy, about 7 million tons above the 1929/1930 procurement level. It was approved in July 1930 and remained in force throughout the campaign. This very high figure assumed that all, or almost all, marketed grain would be sold to the state. Out of this figure, 1.8 million tons should be delivered by sovkhozy, 10.1 million tons by the kolkhozy,

Table 4.3   Agricultural Goals of the 1931 and 1932 Annual Plans and Their Fulfillment

ANNUAL PLAN GOALS AS PERCENTAGE OF MAXIMUM GOALS OF THE
FIVE-YEAR PLAN

1931[a]		1932[b]	
Agriculture			
(harvests and animal		*Agriculture*	
production)		*(harvests)*	
Raw cotton	154.4	Flax fiber	128.1
Sugar beets	142.5	Sugar beets	127.8
Grain, total (biological		Grain	84.8
yield)	110.8		
Flax fiber	109.2		
Sunflowers	92.9		
Milk	82.7		
Wool	79.6		
Eggs	76.0		
Meat and fat	70.1		

PERCENTAGE OF FULFILLMENT OF 1931 AND 1932 ANNUAL PLAN GOALS

1931		1932	
Agriculture			
(harvest and animal		*Argiculture*	
products)		*(harvest)*	
Flax fiber	97.4	Grain, total (biological	
Meat and fat	87.4	yield)	76.4
Sunflowers	86.4	Flax fiber	74.7
Milk	80.9	Sugar beets	29.6
Grain, total (biological			
yield)	71.0		
Wool	61.5		
Raw cotton	61.4		
Sugar beets	56.2		
Agriculture			
(procurements)			
Grain	94.5		

[a]Percentage of maximum goals of the Five-Year Plan for 1930/31.
[b]Percentage of maximum goals of the Five-Year Plan for 1931/1932.

Source: Eugène Zaleski, *Planning for Economic Growth,* pp. 151, 193, 200, and 232.

5.8 million tons by peasants under contracts, 4.6 million tons by peasants not under contracts, and 0.7 million tons by the *kulaks.*[108]

Even if the procurement plan for 1930/1931 was not entirely fulfilled, 22.1 million tons of grain collected represented an important increase (6 million tons) over the previous year. Sovkhozy and kolkhozy delivered less than forecasted (1.37 and 6.71 million tons respectively), individual peasants a little more (11.93 million tons),[109] even though they (individual peasants) were subjected to all kinds of discrimination. But the big increase in procurements in 1931 was based on the exceptionally large crop of 1930, which could not be repeated.

Production and Procurement Planning in 1932 and the Results of the First Five-Year Plan

We do not have much information about production targets for agriculture in 1932 under the new regime of predominantly collectivized agriculture. We can see from Table 4.3 that agricultural production targets were higher than the Five-Year Plan targets for this year for industrial crops, but lower for grain. Investment goals for the socialist sector of agriculture were reduced in comparison to 1931 planned level if we calculate them in actual 1931 prices.[110]

The fulfillment of 1932 plan targets was even worse than in 1931 (see Table 4.3), and the plan for agricultural procurements was not fulfilled. The agricultural investment plan for the socialist sector was fulfilled by only 64.9 percent, the lowest level in the First Five-Year Plan period.

Given this situation, the Soviet government had to retreat from some communist ideological principles. Refusing to increase prices and to abolish rationing in the state and cooperative trade, the government resorted to an intermediate measure, creating the so-called "commercial sales" in state stores at prices determined by supply and demand, in order to absorb the excess purchasing power. The government also felt obliged to sanction an official free market in agricultural products. The following measures were taken toward this end in May of 1932:

- The government officially sanctioned sales by collective farms, collective farmers and individual peasants "at market prices."
- All discriminatory fiscal measures against collective farm trade were repealed and replaced by comparatively low taxes.
- The state substantially reduced its procurement of grain and livestock from collective farms, collective farmers, and individual peasants so that supplies destined for the collective farmmarket could be increased.[111]

The bad performance of 1932 made the overall performance of agriculture in the First Five-Year Plan particularly poor (see Tables 4.4 and 4.5). Given the tremendous importance of the grain harvest, its performance in 1932 looks particularly bad, even for results calculated in comparison with goals for 1931 in the minimum variant of the plan.

CONCLUSION

Both authoritarian command planning and the collectivization drive represented an important part of the Party and Stalin's program to get direct and unlimited control of the Soviet economy and society. For this reason, the simultaneous action of Stalin in both directions seems quite

Table 4.4   Fulfillment of Agricultural Goals of the Five-Year Plan

1932 Results as Percent of 1931/32 Minimum Goals		1932 Results as Percent of 1932/33 Maximum Goals	
Agriculture (harvests and production)		*Agriculture (harvests and production)*	
Flax fiber	118.6	Flax fiber	80.3
Raw cotton	87.1	Raw cotton	66.6
Potatoes	78.5	Grain	66.1
Grain	75.2	Potatoes	64.4
Sunflowers	67.5	Sunflowers	56.0
Milk	53.2	Hemp	43.7
Hemp	50.4	Milk	43.2
Meat	46.4	Meat	37.9
Sugar beets	40.8	Sugar beets	33.6
Wool	34.5	Wool	31.4
Eggs	27.5	Eggs	21.5
Argiculture (harvests and animal production)		*Agriculture (harvests and animal prodution)*	
Potatoes	242.8	Potatoes	194.9
Grain	142.0	Grain	103.6
Flax fiber	109.7	Flax fiber	69.1
Raw cotton	85.2	Raw cotton	64.2
Meat and fat	55.3	Meat and fat	38.8
Milk and dairy products	49.7	Milk and dairy products	33.5
Sugar beets	43.3	Sugar beets	33.2
Wool	36.4	Wool	26.6

Source: Eugène Zaleski, *Planning for Economic Growth,* p. 239.

understandable. But if one would try to follow the logic of this policy, the collectivization drive should have been planned in the same precise and detailed manner, as was intended for other parts of the economy, and integrated into the overall national economic plans.

It can be seen from what was presented above that the real image did not correspond to this utopian dream. The collectivization drive, even if intended to give the government the direct and detailed control of agricultural production and deliveries, disorganized rural life completely in the short run and was entirely contradictory to the concept of detailed central planning of the economy. What remained, in fact, from the central planning of agriculture was the coercive methods of extracting grain and other agricultural products from the countryside. But during the second five-year plan period, the detailed administrative planning corresponded well to the new collectivized structure of Soviet agriculture, with some important exceptions concerning the private plots and the kolkhoz market.

Table 4.5 Fulfillment of Agricultural Targets of the First Five-Year Plan, 1927/28–1932/33

Series	Units	Results in 1927/28 (1)	Goals for 1931/32 Minimum (2)	Goals for 1931/32 Maximum (3)	Goals for 1932/33 Minimum (4)	Goals for 1932/33 Maximum (5)	Results in 1932 (6)	(6) as Per Cent of (2) (7)	(6) as Per Cent of (5) (8)
Agriculture									
Total value of production (1926/27 prices)	mill. rub.	14,526	18,880	19,935	20,702	22,630	13,072	69.2	57.8
Vegetable production (1926/27 prices)	mill. rub.	9,216			13,232	14,469	9,779		67.6
Animal production (1926/27 prices)	mill. rub.	5,310			7,500	8,100	3,293		40.7
Harvests									
Grain, total (biological yield)	th. m. t.	73,120[a]	92,940	96,110	99,660	105,780	69,873	75.2	66.1
Wheat	th. m. t.	21,973[a]					20,250		
Rye	th. m. t.	19,296[a]					22,020		
Barley	th. m. t.	5,668[a]					5,026		
Oats	th. m. t.	16,482[a]					11,242		
Corn	th. m. t.	3,295[a]					3,426		
Harvests of Technical Crops									
Raw cotton	th. m. t.	821	1,460	1,610	1,677	1,907	1,271	87.1	66.6
Sugar beets	th. m. t.	10,140[a]	16,070	17,370	16,800	19,550	6,561	40.8	33.6
Sunflowers	th. m. t.	2,180	3,360	3,490	3,670	4,050	2,268	67.5	56.0
Flax fiber	th. m. t.	324[a]	420	520	480	620	498	118.6	80.3
Hemp	th. m. t.	460	520	570	530	600	262	50.4	43.7
Potatoes	th. m. t.	46,441[a]	54,900	58,080	60,040	66,980	43,124	78.5	64.4

	Unit								
Animal Production									
Meat and fat	th. m. t.	3,941	4,940	5,210	5,510	6,040	2,294	46.4	37.9
Milk	th. m. t.	30,489	38,610	41,730	42,430	47,590	20,558	53.2	43.2
Eggs	bill	10.0	15.3	16.1	17.6	19.5	4.2	27.5	21.5
Wool	th. m. t.	170	200.0	210.0	210.0	220.0	69.0	34.5	31.4
Market Production									
Grain	mill. m. t.	8.08	14.30	15.14	17.05	19.61	20.31	142.0	103.6
Raw cotton	th. m. t.	690	1,410	1,550	1,640	1,870	1,202	85.2	64.2
Sugar beets	th. m. t.	9,771	14,150	16,000	15,620	18,400	6,120	43.3	33.2
Flax fiber	th. m. t.	120	290	390	360	460	318	109.7	69.1
Potatoes	th. m. t.	2,690	3,700	3,880	4,190	4,610	8,984	242.8	194.9
Meat and fat	th. m. t.	1,350	1,690	1,900	2,070	2,410	935	55.3	38.8
Milk and dairy products	th. m. t.	5,161	8,220	9,750	9,812	12,180	4,088	49.7	33.5
Wool	th. m. t.	57.4	112.5	125.0	135.0	154.0	41.0	36.4	26.6
Procurements									
Grain	th. m. t.	11,000					18,775		
Raw cotton	th. m. t.	633					1,203		
Sugar beets	mill. m. t.	10.55					6.1		
Sunflowers	th. m. t.	1,072[a]					563		
Flax fiber	th. m. t.	135					287		
Hemp	th. m. t.	60					40		
Potatoes	th. m. t.						4,642		
Meat and fat (live weight)	th. m. t.	1,143[a]					1,203		
Meat and fat (dead weight)	th. m. t.						648		
Milk	th. m. t.	797[a]					2,100		
Eggs	mill.	1,900[a]					386		
Wool	th. m. t.	2,564[a]					41		

Note: [a]refers to the calendar year in which the fiscal year given in the column head ended. For additional details, see Zaleksi, *Planning for Economic Growth*, p. 348 and 355–57.

Source: Eugène Zaleski, *Planning for Economic Growth in the Soviet Union, 1918–1932* (Chapel Hill: University of North Carolina Press, 1971), pp. 311–13.

There is general agreement among Western economists that the results of the collectivization drive were disastrous for the Soviet economy. The figures presented in Tables 4.4 and 4.5 do not need many comments. One can add, that the most tragic result was the appearance of famine in the countryside. Alec Nove, in his *Economic History of the USSR,* states that "many died in the terrible early thirties. Eye-witnesses saw starving peasants, and I myself spoke to Ukrainians who remembered these horrors. Yet neither the local nor the national press ever mentioned the famine."[112] But what are the long-run consequences of these events?

The first consequence is a certain style of Soviet agricultural planning that has survived to the present. The distribution from above of detailed targets for agricultural production and activity, made in a bureaucratic way, is much more oriented toward control than production. The tremendous bureaucratic superstructure edified over the agricultural producers is still alive. In this situation, the only real incentives for agricultural producers are the legal or illegal evasion of the collective system: work on private plots, sales on the kolkhoz market, the more or less legal use of kolkhoz or sovkhoz property, and so forth.

Another survival of Stalin's policy of the early thirties is the unequal treatment of agriculture in Soviet plans. Plans for agricultural deliveries still have the highest priority, while other plans concerning agriculture are much less important. It is not an accident, if in all Soviet Five-Year Plans until now, the plans for agricultural production as a whole are strongly underfulfilled. They are simply not taken seriously, and agriculture as a whole still gets a low priority, even if in the last years, important investments have been planned for this sector.

Stalin's collectivization drive also had another consequence. The whole elite of successful peasants, cultivating land in an efficient way, was destroyed physically. Since the Russian peasantry was, for a long time, under the regime of serfdom, the more wealthy peasants (named *kulak* in order to create the "class struggle" in the village) represented the most dynamic part of the Russian peasantry, which succeeded in a short period in introducing an efficient peasant production. This dynamic part of the Russian peasantry, which could offer a basis for the future success of Soviet agriculture, was certainly not replaced by the Party bureaucrats of the kolkhoz administration.

NOTES

1. See *Ekonomichesja Zhizn SSSR* [Economic Life of The USSR], (Moscow: Gosudarstvennoe Nauchnoe Izdatelstvo "Sovetskaja Enciklopedija," 1961), pp. 216, 219.

2. See, for instance, the decree of 11 January 1929 about the sowing campaign in *Kollektivizaciia Selskogo Khoziaistva, 1927–1935* (Moscow: Izdatelstvo Akademii Nauk SSSR, 1957), pp. 110–116. About the 1930 sowing campaign of private farming, see the decree of 12 February in *Ekonomicheskaja Zhizn SSSR,* p. 233. The first sowing campaign organized by the state with individual targets distributed by the *Sel'sovety* and *Rajsovety* was organized in 1928. For a discussion, see Moshe Lewin, *Russian Peasants and Soviet Power: A Study of Collectivization* (London: George Allen and Unwin, 1968), p. 239.

3. *Narodno-khoziaistvennyi Plan SSSR na 1931 god* [National economic plan of the USSR for 1931] in *Doklad Gosplana SSSR Sovetu Narodnykh Komisarov SSSR* (Moscow-Leningrad: Gosudarstvenno Socialno-ekonomicheskoe Izdatelstvo, 1931), with a note: "not to be published."

4. It seems that since the creation of the *Narkomzem SSSR* the following principle of agricultural plan elaboration quoted in the form and indicators for the establishment of the 1936 plan was adopted: "The calculations of gross production of agriculture are done by all Peoples Commissariats and organizations. *N. K. Zem* elaborates the plan of gross production of the kolkhoz, of individual exploitation of kolkhoz peasants and of private farms. The plan for production of the sovkhoz is done by *N. K. Zem, N. K. Sovkhoz* and the Peoples Commissariat of the Food Industry of the USSR and should be presented into the Gosplan of the USSR according to sectors or Unions and in synthetic form for the Peoples Commissariat." *Ukazaniia i formy k sostavleiiu narodnokhoziaistvennogo plana na 1936 god* (Moscow: Izdanie Gosplana SSSR, 1935), p. 67.

5. R. W. Davies, *The Socialist Offensive: The Collectivisation of Soviet Agriculture, 1929-1930* (London and Basingstoke: Macmillan, 1980), p. 354.

6. *Osnovnye pokazateli vypolneniia narodno-khoziaistvennogo plana na 1936 god* [Main indicators of fulfillment of the economic plan for 1931], (Moscow: Centralnoe Upravlenie narodno-khoziaistvennogo Ucheta Gosplan SSSR, 1934), pp. 54-96, with a note: "not to be published."

7. *Vtoroi piatiletnii plan razvitia narodnogo khoziaistva SSSR (1933-1937 gg.)* [Second five-year plan for the development of the USSR national economy, 1933-1937], (Moscow: Izdanie Gosplana SSSR, 1934), vol. 1, p. 726.

8. *Ibid.,* pp. 640-41.

9. *Narodno-khoziaistvennyi Plan na 1935 god,* 2d. ed. [The national economic plan for 1935, second edition], (Moscow: Izdanie Gosplana SSSR, 1935), two volumes.

10. *Osnovnye pokazateli vypolnenija narodno-khoziaistvennogo plana* [Main indicators of the fulfillment of the national economic plan], a Gosplan monthly document for internal use.

11. *Narodno-khoziaistvennyi plan na 1936 god.* [The national economic plan for 1936], vol. 1 (Moscow: Gosplana SSSR, 1936), pp. 433-47.

12. *Ukazaniia i formy k sostavleniu narodnokhoziaistvennogo plana na 1936 god* (Moscow: Izdanie Gosplana SSSR, 1935). *Ukazaniia i formy k sostavleniiu narodnokhoziaistvennogo plana na 1937 god* [Instructions and forms for drafting the national economic plan for 1937], (Moscow: Izdanie Gosplana SSSR, 1936), pp. 89-136 and 373-90.

13. Including the calculation of marketed production, plans for deliveries of agricultural products, plans for decentralized procurements and plans for the utilization of the main (centralized) food products.

14. Moshe Lewin, "Taking Grain: Soviet Policies of Agricultural Procurements Before the War," in C. Abramsky (ed.), *Essays in Honour of E. H. Carr* (London: Macmillan, 1974), p. 281.

15. *Ibid.,* p. 281.

16. Davies, *Socialist Offensive,* p. 72.

17. Lewin, *Taking Grain,* p. 284.

18. *Soviet Truda i Oborony* [Council for labor and defense] was a kind of restricted committee of the Council of People's Commissars. For a discussion, see Eugéne Zaleski, *Stalinist Planning for Economic Growth, 1933-1952* (Chapel Hill: University of North Carolina Press, 1980), pp. 14-17.

19. Lewin, *Taking Grain,* pp. 297-98.

20. *Ibid.,* pp. 287-88.

21. Lewin, *Taking Grain,* p. 297.

22. See, for example, the sowing plan for 1933 in *Sobranie Zakonov i Rasporiazhenii,* 7 (February 10, 1933) article 43.

23. Lewin, *Taking Grain,* p. 284.

24. *Piatnadcatyi S'ezd VKP (b),* [Fifteenth congress of the communist party of the Soviet Union] (Bolshevik) in *KPSS v rezoluciiakh i resheniiakh s'ezdov, konferencii i Plenumov CK* [Communist party in the resolutions of congresses, conferences and plenum of the central committee], Part II (Moscow: 1953), pp. 347 and 351-52.

25. Stalin's speech at the 15th Congress as quoted in Alec Nove, *An Economic History of The USSR* (Harmondsworth: Pelican, 1982), p. 148.

26. Association for the Joint Cultivation of the Land. In this association the members retained ownership of their tools and implements, most of their livestock, and control over their land. They simply carried out some of the work jointly. See Nove, *Economic History*, pp. 149–50.

27. Cooperative use of the land, livestock, seeds and agricultural instruments but leaving the house and a land parcel in private ownership. At this time there were several kinds of artel: some paid members "by eaters" (in relation to mouths to feed), some in rough proportion to work done and some in accordance with the land and implements contributed. In some farms, a good deal of livestock was collectivized, in others much less. For a discussion, see Nove, *Economic History*, p. 163.

28. In the commune, everything was common: the land, materials and equipment. Some times even the housing and consumption were joint.

29. The proportion of TOZ, artel and communes are given by Moshe Lewin, *Russian Peasants and Soviet Power: A Study of Collectivization* (Paris: Mouton, 1968), p. 243 from the French edition. But, at this time the collectivized sector of agriculture represented a very small part of the total: Individual peasants, 97.3 percent of sown area, collective farms (TOZ, artels and communes), 1.2 percent of sown area and state farms 1.5 percent of sown area. See *Sotsialisticheskoe stroitelstvo SSSR* (Moscow: C. U. N. Kh. U. Gosplana SSSR, 1935), p. 39. In the gross value of production, the private sector of agriculture represented 98.6 percent, the state sector (sovkhozy), 0.9 percent and the cooperative sector, 0.5 percent. See S. G. Strumilin, E. I. Kviring, N. A. Kovalevskii and M. I. Bogolepov, *Osnovnye problemy kontrolnykh tsifr narodnogokhoziaistva SSSR na 1929/30 god* (Moscow: Gosudarstvennoe Izdatelstvo, 1930), pp. 174–75.

30. Lewin, *Taking Grain*, p. 245.

31. Nove, *Economic History*, p. 155.

32. Lewin, *Taking Grain*, p. 257.

33. *Ibid.*, p. 240.

34. Nove, *Economic History*, p. 155.

35. Lewin, *Taking Grain*, p. 247.

36. *Piatiletnii plan narodno-khoziaistvennogo stroitelstva SSSR* [Five-year plan for the development of the national economy of the USSR], 2d. ed. (Moscow: Izdanie Planovoe Khoziaistvo, 1929), vol. 1, p. 20.

37. No details on this question are published in the plan. Moshe Lewin mentions different opinions on the subject. According to the cooperative movement, the TOZ should be the main form of the kolkhoz, though others preferred the artel form. According to the five-year plan presented by the cooperative movement, out of 4.4 million peasant households to be collectivized at the end of the plan, 3.5 millions should be organized in the TOZ form. For a discussion, see Lewin, *Russian Peasants*, p. 317.

38. *Piatiletnii plan narodno-khoziaistvennogo stroitelstva SSSR* 2d. ed. (Moscow: Izdanie Planovoe Khoziaistvo, 1929), vol. 1, p. 20.

39. Lewin, *Russian Peasants*, p. 316.

40. Davies, *Socialist Offensive*, p. 404. It is interesting to note that even Sabsovic, the author of rather fantastic plans at this time, forecasted the end of collectivization only by the year 1943. See Lewin, *Russian Peasants*, p. 320.

41. Lewin, *Russian Peasants*, p. 320.

42. Even Bauman, the secretary of the Moscow Obkom and a deputy to Molotov in the rural department of the Central Committee, forecasted the end of collectivization in ten to twenty years. See Lewin, *Russian Peasants*, p. 320.

43. Lewin, *Russian Peasants*, p. 331.

44. *Ibid.*, p. 345.

45. Nove, *Economic History*, p. 162.

46. Lewin, *Russian Peasants*, p. 130 and Nove, *Economic History*, p. 161.

47. Nove, *Economic History*, p. 161.

48. The definition of the region of total (splosnaja) collectivization was rather vague. Sometimes it concerned a *raion* and at other times an *okrug* where 50 percent of the population

should be collectivized. According to some authors, the whole region should exceed this percentage. For others, these were regions where the majority of households were already organized into kolkhozy. On this see Lewin, *Russian Peasants*, p. 381.

49. *Ibid.*, p. 381.

50. *Ibid.*, p. 388.

51. *Ibid.*, p. 388.

52. Eugéne Zaleski, *Planning for Economic Growth in The Soviet Union, 1918–1932* (Chapel Hill: University of North Carolina Press, 1971), p. 102.

53. Davies, *Socialist Offensive*, p. 148.

54. I. V. Stalin, *Voprosy Leninizma* [Problems of Leninism], 11th. edition (Moscow: Gosudarstvennoe Izdatelstvo Politicheskoi Literatury, 1947), pp. 264–74.

55. *Splosnaja kollektivisacija:* translated as "total." See also the discussion in note 48 above.

56. Davies, *Socialist Offensive*, p. 164.

57. *Ibid.*, p. 180.

58. *Ibid.*, p. 182.

59. Davies, *Socialist Offensive*, pp. 200–201.

60. *Ibid.*, p. 233.

61. See above page 147.

62. See above page 145.

63. Nove, *Economic History*, p. 163.

64. Nove, *Economic History*, p. 167, quoting I. Trifonov, *Ocherki istorii klassovoi borby v SSSR v gody Nepa* [Outlines of the history of class struggles in the USSR during the Nep period], (Moscow: 1972), p. 237.

65. Davies, *Socialist Offensive*, p. 244.

66. Lewin, *Russian Peasants*, p. 421.

67. *Ibid.*

68. Nove, *Economic History*, p. 167.

69. Lewin, *Russian Peasants*, p. 421.

70. Davies, *Socialist Offensive*, p. 244.

71. *Ibid.*, p. 259.

72. *Ibid.*, p. 269.

73. Zaleski, *Planning for Economic Growth*, p. 102.

74. Davies, *Socialist Offensive*, pp. 332–34.

75. *Ibid.*, p. 334.

76. *Ibid.*, p. 380.

77. Zaleski, *Planning for Economic Growth*, pp. 102–3.

78. Davies, *Socialist Offensive*, pp. 380–81. According to *Planovoe khoziaistvo* 12 (1930), by the end of 1931, the share of the collectivized sector was to rise from 27.5 percent to "at least 50 percent" in the case of farms, from 32 percent to 47.3 percent in the case of area sown to grain and from 47.2 percent to 62.6 percent in the case of area sown to industrial crops and from 8 percent to 16.5 percent in the case of livestock.

79. Nove, *Economic History*, pp. 175–76.

80. *Ibid.*, p. 187.

81. *Ibid.*, p. 181.

82. Zaleski, *Planning for Economic Growth*, p. 174, and *Vtoroj piatiletii plan razvitia narodnogo khoziaistva SSSR (1933–1937 gg.)*, (Moscow: Izdanie Gosplana SSSR, 1934), vol. 1, p. 202.

83. *Vtoroj piatiletii plan*, p. 202, and *Narodno-khoziaistvennyi plan na 1935 god* 2d. ed. (Moscow: Izdanie Gosplana SSSR, 1935), vol. 1, p. 224.

84. *Narodno-khoziaistvennyi plan na 1936 god* 2d. ed. (Moscow, 1936), p. 206.

85. *Sel'skoe khoziaistvo SSSR* (Moscow: Gosstatizdat, 1960), pp. 263–64, and Nove, *Economic History*, p. 239.

86. Nove, *Economic History*, p. 239.

87. Zaleski, *Planning for Economic Growth*, pp. 88–89.

88. *Ibid.*, Table A-5, p. 369.

89. Estimated from Zaleski, *Planning for Economic Growth*, Table A-5, p. 369. Total in-

vestment in agriculture was 3.5 billion rubles, less 125 million rubles for the state sector and an unknown amount for the kolkhoz sector, the latter very small at this time being 1.5 percent of the total sown area (see note 29 above).

90. Zaleski, *Planning for Economic Growth,* Tables A-3, A-6 and A-7. It was estimated that the planned reduction of construction costs in private agriculture of 5 percent was not realized and that the price level did not change in relation to the year 1927/1928.

91. *Ibid.,* pp. 88–89.

92. Davies, *Socialist Offensive,* p. 49.

93. *Ibid.,* pp. 56–57.

94. About the methods of compulsory grain collection at this time, see pp. 146, 147, and 149.

95. Zaleski, *Planning for Economic Growth,* p. 94.

96. *Ibid.,* Table A-5, p. 371.

97. *Ibid.,* p. 374.

98. *Ibid.,* p. 138.

99. Ultimately, this increase should result from the expansion of the socialist sector of agriculture, but immediately the reinforcement of compulsory methods of procurement from the private sector was practiced.

100. Davies, *Socialist Offensive,* pp. 67–68.

101. *Ibid.,* p. 68.

102. *Ibid.,* p. 104.

103. *Ibid.,* pp. 64–7.

104. I. A. Gladkov, quoted in Zaleski, *Planning for Economic Growth,* p. 175.

105. Zaleski, *Planning for Economic Growth,* p. 371.

106. *Ibid.,* p. 374.

107. Davies, *Socialist Offensive,* pp. 345 and 349.

108. *Ibid.,* p. 347.

109. *Ibid.,* p. 437.

110. Zaleski, *Planning for Economic Growth,* pp. 365, 371 and 377. Total agricultural investment in the socialist sector amounted to 3645 million rubles in current prices of 1931. But, the 1931 plan in these prices was 5287 million rubles. The 1932 plan for the socialist sector of agriculture was in 1932 planned prices (which were 10 percent lower than actual 1931 prices) of 4360 million rubles.

111. Zaleski, *Planning for Economic Growth,* pp. 226–27.

112. Nove, *Economic History,* pp. 179–80.

PART TWO

Approaches to Soviet Rural Development

5

Views on the Economics of Soviet Collectivization of Agriculture: The State of the Revisionist Debate

James R. Millar

THE TRADITIONAL STORY

The traditional theoretical presentation of the model of Soviet rapid in-dustrialization in the 1930s was formulated by Alexander Erlich as a debate between two Bolshivik economists: E. Preobrazhenski, the "super in-dustrializer," and N. Bukharin, an advocate of balanced and thus moderate rates of growth of both agriculture and industry.[1] The debate turned on the belief that the peasantry exercised a "strangle hold on the food supply" and that it would not voluntarily submit to the rate of taxation implied by the needs of rapid industrialization. According to Erlich, the debate culminated in a true policy dilemma, one that could not be resolved within the framework of the NEP. It was resolved, instead, by Stalin's decision to col-lectivize agriculture.

The traditional appraisal of Stalin's solution is given succinctly by Bar-rington Moore, Jr.:

> While a heavy price was paid in human suffering, the main Bolshivik objective was achieved. The economic independence of the peasant was destroyed and a method created for getting grain to supply the cities and industry. A secondary gain was the release of manpower from the rural areas to the cities.[2]

This appraisal of collectivization has been seriously challenged on both theoretical and empirical grounds.[3] It is safe to say, in fact, that no one fully accepts the traditional story today, but general agreement on just what did happen and about how to model the process has not yet been attained.

There are, however, some important areas of agreement. It now appears that Bukharin was wrong in asserting that the peasantry would withdraw from the market in response to an adverse change in its overall terms of trade,[4] thereby undermining the industrialization drive Preobrazhenski had proposed. Preobrazhenski's plan to tax the peasantry as a primary way to finance industrialization might very well have worked, so long as the method used would have changed the terms of trade adversely for agriculture taken as a whole, that is, with respect to industry, and left relative agricultural product prices unchanged. Interestingly enough, however, the empirical evidence for the period of the First Five-Year Plan also shows that Preobrazhenski was himself probably wrong in thinking that "exploitation" of the rural sector was a necessary condition for rapid industrial growth. We now know that the terms of trade did not change against agriculture as a sector. Moreover, it is agreed that changes in the net surplus of agriculture, defined as the net contribution of agriculture to net investment in the economy as a whole,[5] cannot explain the enormous increase in rate and in investment that took place in the economy (although there remains serious disagreement about just how much agriculture did contribute to net investment before and after collectivization).[6] Consequently, the dilemma that Erlich identified was not really a dilemma at all, and thus the appropriateness of collectivization as a "solution" must also be in doubt.

The question is now: What model(s) best fits the actual process of early Soviet rapid development? It is on this head that revisionists of Erlich's story differ and differ substantially. My own view is that collectivization was purely and simply a mistake, without economic rationale whatever. Michael Ellman presents an alternative view, one that salvages an economic rationale for collectivization. Ellman subscribes to what can fairly be called a modified Preobrazhenski model of precipitive accumulation.[7] That is, Ellman concludes that collectivization played a positive role in the process of Soviet rapid development, although this role is not the same as that suggested by A. Ehrlich or other bearers of the standard story.

MICHAEL ELLMAN'S VIEW

Michael Ellman has provided a thorough and complete reevaluation of the period.[8] Let me specify his conception of the process of Soviet economic growth during the First Five-Year Plan. Ellman agrees that, no matter how you measure it, "collectivization did *not* increase the net agricultural surplus (measured in 1913 world market prices, 1928 Soviet prices or Marxist values)."[9] Ellman's own analysis weights intersector flows by input prices on the assumption that labor was the only input. He also assumes that prices of industrial products relative to agricultural products in 1928 in the Soviet Union did not reflect true "labor-content ratios" and must therefore be adjusted. The adjustment increases the relative weight of agricultural products in intersector flows and, as a result, yields a net outflow of resources to industry from agriculture during the First Five-Year Plan. Ellman's reweighting procedure also produces, however, a net agricultural surplus and a net outflow for the NEP period. As Ellman stresses, the change between the NEP and the First Five-Year Plan periods is insignificant.

Whether one uses Ellman's labor-content weights or unadjusted, constant 1928 prices, collectivization did not lead to an (algebraically) increased net surplus of agriculture. There is general agreement on this crucial point, which is sufficient to sink Erlich's interpretation completely. Ellman, however, obtains a positive net flow of resources to industry from agriculture for both the NEP and the First Five-Year Plan period with his labor content weights. Constant 1928 price weights yield a negative net flow for both periods. This difference in the sign of the net flow between agriculture and nonagriculture represents a real difference in the way that the role of agriculture in economic development is modelled.

As Ellman indicates, his analysis lends support to the Preobrazhenski model.[10] Where Preobrazhenski called for "exploitation" of the rural sector by the state and "self-exploitation" by the industrial workers of themselves as two sources of accumulation, only the second took place, if one evaluates the empirical evidence using Ellman's weights. That is, following Ellman, and contrary to the standard story, which assumed that *workers in the agricultural sector would be exploited for development of the industrial sector,* it turns out that it was the *exploitation of workers already in and of those transferred to industry from the rural sector* that explains Soviet rapid rates of capital accumulation. In Ellman's view, therefore, "primitive socialist accumulation" took place in the industrial sector, and the contribution of the peasantry was primarily that of contributing exploitable manpower to the industrial sector. In addition, according to Ellman, agriculture contributed an increased supply of basic wage goods and it provided substantial exports as well.

Ellman ultimately attributes these contributions of agriculture to collectivization. That is, he states that during the First Five-Year Plan, "collectivization appears as a process which enabled the state to increase its inflow of grain, potatoes and vegetables and its stock of urban labour, at the expense of livestock and the rural and urban human population." He goes on to say that the "two key mechanisms for obtaining the additional investment resources were collectivization (which made possible the increase in the volume of basic wage goods marketed by agriculture and the increase in the urban labour force) and the rapid inflation (which facilitated the fall in urban real wages)."[11] Ellman thus sees the policy of collectivization not as a mistake, but as having had certain redeeming features from a development perspective.

I find certain of Ellman's conclusions puzzling. The increased flow of grain and potatoes was, as Ellman admits, at the expense of livestock herds and thus livestock products. Some students of the late 1920s have argued that the growth of livestock herds was being encouraged by the rising relative price of livestock products—caused partly by government restraints on bread and grain prices. Even if it can be shown to have been necessary to change the composition of the population's diet back to a larger share of starches, as a prerequisite of rapid industrialization, why could this not have been done just as effectively and with much less waste and suffering by simply changing producer prices to favor grains and potatoes? There is substantial evidence showing that Soviet peasant farmers were sensitive to relative prices of farm output. A change in relative output prices might have been sufficient to increase the off-farm flow of grain and potatoes.

Moreover, any resulting reduction in livestock herds would have been more rational and less wasteful than that which resulted from the furious savagery collectivization provoked.

Ellman claims that collectivization was necessary to generate an adequate off-farm flow of labor, but he offers no evidence in support of the claim other than asserting that a large flow was required in the face of falling urban real wages. Obviously, part of the required additional labor was found among the urban unemployed, including women and the elderly, but the remainder had to be "mobilized" elsewhere. The first point to note is that no successfully developing country has experienced difficulty in generating a rural-to-urban flow of labor. In fact, in most cases problems have been posed instead by excessive outmigration from rural areas. In addition, the fall in urban-industrial real wages was induced in large part by the devastation of agricultural production occasioned by collectivization itself.

The inflation that was caused by this reduction in available food supplies certainly did the Soviet state no good. The state budget may benefit from an inflation that turns the terms of trade in its favor, thereby increasing its claim on economic capacity, but it does not stand to benefit from an inflation caused by a decrease in available food supplies or by resulting changes in the terms of trade in favor of farmers at the expense of urban workers. This is what collectivization brought about. The burden would seem to be on Ellman and others to show why a differentially favorable industrial wage would not have been both adequate and thus more desirable as a means to generate a suitable voluntary migration from rural areas.

As a matter of fact, most discussions of the flows of manpower generated by collectivization and rapid industrialization in the USSR have greatly oversimplified the process. Evaluation of these manpower flows from the standpoint of their contributions to development is more complex than has been assumed. It would require, for example, consideration of intra- as well as intersector flows. Some of the best farmers (the kulaks) left agriculture altogether. Others lost their lives. Still others were removed to marginal lands where their skills were less effective. The result in any case was a loss of skilled farmers and thus of productivity. Meanwhile, skilled workers and administrators from industry moved voluntarily into agricultural occupations to run the MTS and to manage and administer the new production system and the huge procurement bureaucracy that collectivization brought forth. Undoubtedly, the police and the military absorbed manpower also. It is highly likely that these industrial workers and managerial personnel were less productive in their new jobs than they had been in industry.

Other examples could be given of mobility leading to declines or even total losses in the productivity of manpower during the First Five-Year Plan.[12] The point here is that an assessment of the net impact of collectivization upon manpower flows has yet to be made, and the burden of showing that it was more favorable to Soviet economic development than an alternative would have been is on those who make the claim. It is not obvious *a priori*, except perhaps on very simple-minded assumptions about the distribution of surplus value between rural and nonrural sectors or the platitude that the new economy emerges from the old.

There is also a logical flaw in Ellman's argument with respect to the flow of labor out of agriculture. Ellman must shift the basis of sectoring from a type-of-product to a geographical (urban-rural) criterion in order to claim a manpower contribution. Doing so makes it impossible to maintain the industrial-agricultural distinction with which he began and which is necessary to measure the net surplus of agriculture. One can logically consider manpower as a "product" of a rural (or other) sector conceived as a geographical area. One could measure the net product flow from such a region as well, but the net surplus so obtained could not be associated uniquely with agricultural production. If one wants to ascertain the contribution of agriculture to growth, then one must adhere to a type-of-product criterion for sectoring the economy. It follows that any member of the population who is not employed, or who has a zero marginal product, is attributable to neither sector.

The development analyst cannot have it both ways. His model must adhere to a single sectoring criterion for any given evaluation. If one wants the "net surplus" to refer to net investment in the economy as a whole, as most two-sector development models imply, the net flow of manpower to and between sectors will, and can only legitimately, show up indirectly through impacts upon outputs and/or net product flows between sectors. Adding a net manpower flow to a net surplus measurement, as Ellman does, amounts to double counting caused by inconsistency in sectoring criteria.[13]

Collectivization did indeed help to drive people out of rural occupations, nonagricultural as well as agricultural. And it certainly contributed to the decline in real wages in both agricultural and industrial sectors, which in turn helped to drive previously unemployed wives, children, elders, plus the underemployed into industrial occupations, with the goal of maintaining real per capita (or per family) income. The point is, however, that there were alternative ways of accomplishing these ends, and the economic cost as well as the cost to the human population would appear to have been much less for almost any of the alternatives.

LABOR-SURPLUS MODELS

The model upon which Michael Ellman bases his case is a variant labor-surplus model. W. Arthur Lewis made this sort of model popular and it has had a large impact on the theory of economic development.[14] Lewis relied on a version of the traditional story of Soviet development, and his misunderstanding of the Soviet growth experience has had a great influence on the profession, and contributed, along with Erlich's, to the creation and propagation of the standard story that industrialization proceeded at the expense of agriculture in the USSR.

According to Lewis, what needs to be explained in any model of economic development is how the saving rate gets raised. His main contention is that the increase in the rate of saving out of national income has ordinarily been the result not of changing everyone's rate of saving, but of changing the distribution of income in such a way that "the incomes of the savers increase relatively to the national income. The central fact of economic development is that the distribution of incomes is altered in favor of the saving class."[15] The First Five-Year Plan certainly raised the rate of saving in the USSR—from about 15 percent of national income in 1928 to about 44 percent in 1932.[16] However, where Lewis was concerned with shifting income among private recipients to those who save more, that is, to the capitalists, in the Soviet case the shift was from the private to the public sector.

There are, then, certain immediately obvious similarities between an analysis based on the Lewis model and one based on Preobrazhenski's. The similarities derive from the fact that Lewis's model is a "classical" rather than a neoclassical model of development. If modified to fit the Soviet experience (and purged of certain rather bizarre discussions of inflationary financing), Lewis's model would appear to fit the Soviet experience better than Preobrazhenski's. The notion is that the typical developing country has unlimited supplies of labor in the short run, making it possible to increase both output, and thus investment, by putting idle labor to work. Since supplies of labor are unlimited, increasing employment does not raise the real wage in the growth sectors. Consequently, those initiating employment (in this case the state) stand to reap a disproportionate share of claims on the additional output—claims that could be utilized to increase the rate of capital accumulation.

The Lewis model does not require a decline in real wages for this to happen, merely a noticeable productivity gap in favor of industrial employments. Since collectivization did not lead to an adverse change in the terms of trade for agricultural producers, Lewis certainly could not have seen it as a potentially useful device. In fact, because it caused a decline in the capital stock in agriculture and thus increased labor demand in that sector (both directly to replace tractive power and indirectly by requiring administrators, enforcers, and skilled machinery operatives), collectivization could not possibly be a prescription of the Lewis model.

The problem with the Lewis model, however, is the same as for any model that bases growth upon a surplus of some sort: growth must be explained by increases in the surplus. In the case of surplus labor (as opposed to "surplus value" or "surplus product"), the surplus will eventually be absorbed, and, when it is, growth must come to depend upon different factors altogether if it is to continue. The Ranis and Fei model[17] is a good example of this, for somewhere between stage one and stage two, their model is converted from a classical model that depends upon absorbing surplus labor into a neoclassical model in which growth depends upon increases in total factor productivity in both the agricultural and the nonagricultural sectors.

Lewis provides a rationale for the necessity to change models in midstream growth by asserting that the nature of the development process itself changes with the process of successful development. Thus, the early stages of growth can be explained only by a classical model, and later stages are amenable only to neoclassical analysis. To my mind this has an advantage over a Marxist model, such as Preobrazhenski's, because it is much more awkward to force neoclassical considerations into the Marxist model than it is merely to switch models. Moreover, the gradual shifting emphasis in the Soviet economy over time from growth dependent almost exclusively upon growth of input quantities to growth based upon increases in total factor productivity does seem to illustrate Lewis's point of view.

The Lewis model is not really necessary, however. It is possible to conceive of growth within a modern analytic framework as having three components. Consider a typical production possibility frontier. First, growth can be quite rapid, if current output is inside the frontier, by merely increasing demand for output. Second, by changing the conventional definition of "full employment" (of both population and capital), as in wartime or through some similar stimulus to social transformation, the frontier itself may shift outward substantially instantaneously. These two components of growth correspond to Lewis's labor surplus stage. This analysis has the advantage, however, of allowing for the possibility of "surplus" capital as well as of labor. Subsequent growth, given the saving rate, which itself may be increased in the face of some great social purpose, will depend upon two factors: the growth of inputs in physical terms and the increase in total factor productivity. Within this framework, an economic rationale for Soviet collectivization may be found only as a process necessary for radical social transformation. Ellman apparently believes that this was the case (as did Erlich before him), but this needs to be established. Collectivization had so severe a negative impact upon the growth of agricultural output, upon the capital stock (and thus upon the demand for labor in agriculture and the demand for machines from industry), and upon the long-run capacity of the Soviet agricultural sector to achieve efficiency and increases in productivity, that the burden would seem to be on Ellman and those who agree with him to show why it was necessary.

ALTERNATIVE MEASURES OF AGRICULTURE'S CONTRIBUTION

I proposed a very different way of looking at the role of agriculture in 1970.[18] I do not refer here to the formula for ascertaining the net contribution of agriculture (i.e., the net contribution of agriculture to net investment in the economy as a whole). What I described were several alternative ways that are useful in thinking about the contribution of a sector of an economy to growth when it is fully agreed at the outset that no completely unambiguous measure is possible for a component sector of an interdependent system (that is, for any neoclassical model). Agriculture participates in growth if its output grows, and it participates in development if total factor productivity grows also, or if worker productivity grows thanks to the substitution of capital for labor. It is clear that Soviet agriculture participated in neither growth nor development during the First Five-Year Plan.

It has generally been assumed that Soviet agriculture failed to participate in growth and development because its contributions to other sectors were so great. However, we have seen that the *net product contribution* of Soviet agriculture, that is, the net flow of products, was either negative (using 1928 weights) or positive but unaugmented (using 1913 world market, or "Marxist" price weights). The *market contribution,* which is the extent to which a sector's purchases from other sectors help to finance that other sector's purchases from the first, of Soviet agriculture was clearly negligible or negative during the First Five-Year Plan. The same is true of the *finance contribution* of agriculture, which is the financial and terms-of-trade equivalent of the net product contribution. That is, the terms of trade, it turns out, changed in favor of agriculture, and it seems likely that the agricultural sector did not advance or return a significant amount of funds, if any, to industry. The truth appears to be, then, that by any measure, Soviet agriculture proved a dead weight on growth of the Soviet economy; and this was so, I propose, because collectivization was a massive policy error. It was a mistake from which no one stood to gain, including the state.

The contributions that Ellman and others have sought to attribute to collectivization belong instead to the introduction of the predatory agricultural procurement system—which helped to limit the losses collectivization brought about and thus raised the share of marketed output in the face of a decline in total output. While it is undoubtedly true that staunching the flow of blood from a severed artery is a "contribution" to health of the patient, the wound itself is not. Collectivization and the Stalinist agricultural procurement system of the 1930s stand in an analogous relation to one another. Taken together, the two measures offered no net contribution to Soviet economic growth.

NOTES

1. Alexander Erlich, "Preobrazhenski and the Economics of Soviet Industrialization," *Quarterly Journal of Economics* 64, no. 1 (February 1950).

2. Barrington Moore, Jr., *Terror and Progress—USSR: Some Sources of Change and Stability in the Soviet Dictatorship* (Cambridge: Harvard University Press 1966), p. 73.

3. See James R. Millar, "Soviet Rapid Development and the Agricultural Surplus Hypothesis," *Soviet Studies* 22, no. 1 (July 1970); "Mass Collectivization and the Contribution of Soviet Agriculture to the First Five-Year Plan: A Review Article," *Slavic Review* 33, no. 4 (December 1974); "A Debate on Collectivization: Was Stalin Really Necessary?" (with Alec Nove), *Problems of Communism* 25, 4 (July–August 1976) pp. 49–62; "Collectivization and Its Consequences: A New Look," *The Russian Review* 41, no. 1 (January 1982); and see also Michael Ellman, "Did the Agricultural Surplus Provide the Resources for the Increase in Investment in the USSR During the First Five-Year Plan?" *The Economic Journal* 85, no. 4 (December 1975).

4. James R. Millar, "A Reformulation of A.V. Chayanov's Theory of the Peasant Economy," *Economic Development and Cultural Change* 18, no. 2 (January 1970); Corinne Ann Guntzel, "Soviet Agricultural Pricing Policy and the Scissors Crisis of 1922-23" (Ph.D. diss., University of Illinois, 1972).

5. See Millar, "Soviet Rapid Development," especially pp. 82–85, for an exact definition.

6. Millar, "Mass Collectivization"; Ellman, "Did the Agricultural Surplus."

7. James R. Millar, "A Note on Primitive Accumulation in Marx and Preobrazhenski," *Soviet Studies* XXX, no. 3 (July 1978).

8. The basic new data upon which all revisionism is based were provided by A. A. Barsov in "Sel'skoe khoziaistvo i istochniki sotsialisticheskogo nakopleniia v gody pervoi piatiletki (1928-1933)" *Istoriia SSSR* no. 3, (1968) and *Balans stoimostnykh obmenov mezhdu gorodom i derevnei* (Moscow: Navka 1969). Alec Nove has also addressed the issues dealt with in this ar-

ticle, most notably in an unpublished paper, "The Contribution of Agriculture to Accumulation in the 1930s," which was co-authored by David Morrison and presented to a seminar in Paris in November 1981.

Morrison and Nove contend "that agriculture's contribution is in danger of being understated." by Millar and Ellman (p. 1). They argue that Barsov's data and presentation are faulty and that:

> The use of (say) 1928, 1913 or "labour-value" prices to measure what occurred in 1932 is inappropriate . . . . The use of 1932 prices, or any calculation purporting to show what happened to "terms of trade" between town and village between 1928 and 1932, is quite pointless (p. 2).

Although Nove and Morrison have quite legitimate and proper criticisms to make of some of Barsov's data and procedures, the general conclusion holds: there was no sharp change in the net flow of resources from or to agriculture that could "explain" the leap in net investment that accompanied rapid industrialization. Nove's refusal to use either adjusted or unadjusted price weights to measure this net flow is difficult to understand. His argument is not sound in my opinion, or else he is asking for an impossible degree of accuracy.

In general, Nove has been primarily concerned to show that the peasantry suffered a disproportionate welfare loss in consequence of collectivization and industrialization. The paper by Nove and Morrison goes a long way toward supporting this opinion, and I am prepared to accept the evidence. But this is beside the point when it comes to the question of where the real resources came from. The peasantry appears to have suffered, as did the urban population (albeit perhaps in lesser degree), needlessly. The whole point is that collectivization caused a net loss to all parties involved taken together.

9. Ellman, "Did the Agricultural Surplus," p. 859.

10. *Ibid.*, p. 860, n. 2.

11. *Ibid.*, pp. 859–60.

12. These flows of labor are described but not analyzed in R. W. Davies, *The Industrialization of Soviet Russia,* vol. 1, *The Socialist Offensive: The Collectivization of Soviet Agriculture, 1929–1930* (Cambridge, MA: Harvard University Press, 1980).

13. For a fuller discussion of these issues, see Millar, "Soviet Rapid Development."

14. W. Arthur Lewis, "Economic Development with Unlimited Supplies of Labour," *The Manchester School* 22 (1954); "Unlimited Labour: Further Notes," *The Manchester School* 26 (1958).

15. Lewis, "Economic Development with Unlimited Supplies of Labour," pp. 156 – 57.

16. Ellman, "Did the Agricultural Surplus," p. 845, Table 1.

17. Gustav Ranis and John C. H. Fei, "A Theory of Economic Development," *American Economic Review* 60, no. 4 (September 1961).

18. Millar, "Soviet Rapid Development," pp. 87–92.

6

The Relationship of the Death of Stalin to the Economic Change of the Post-Stalin Era
or
Was Stalin's Departure Really Necessary?

Frank A. Durgin, Jr.

INTRODUCTION

Alec Nove's well-known article entitled "Was Stalin Really Necessary?"[1] asked if the course of Soviet economic development during the Stalin era would have in any way changed if someone other than Stalin had been in charge. He hypothesized that it would not. In an analogous manner, this paper asks the question, "Was Stalin's departure necessary?"—i.e., would the many changes in agriculture and the marked improvement in the lot of the Soviet consumer that followed on the heels of Stalin's death been any less striking had he not died? It offers the hypothesis that it would not.

This hypothesis runs counter to the view long ingrained in the conventional wisdom in the West, which holds that the death of Stalin cleared the way for, and precipitated, a rapid change in economic priorities and policies, i.e., new to agriculture and a shift toward a larger share of the national income for the consumer. The underlying argument to be presented in this paper is that while the state of agriculture and the welfare of the consumer have decidedly improved in the post-Stalin era, it has merely been assumed, but never documented, that this improvement was in any way connected with Stalin's death. It will be shown that the increased inputs into agriculture, the marked expansion of agricultural output, and the concomitant improvement in consumer welfare,[2] are not fallouts of that death, but are simply the by-product of a continuation of trends, policies, and events set in motion by Stalin.

I am indebted to the University of Southern Maine for the Faculty Fellowship that supported the research for this paper, to Robert C. Stuart, Harry Shaffer, and Lynn Turgeon for valuable criticisms, and to Palmer Peters and Terry Devlin for typing.

CONSUMPTION AND INVESTMENT
IN THE POST-STALIN ERA

The single most distinguishing feature of the Stalinist economic policy was the pursuit of rapid industrialization via the only method (barring the receipt of foreign aid) by which it could be accomplished—the sacrifice of current consumption to investment and hence future consumption. Much has been written about the material deprivation of the Soviet consumer during the Stalin years and value questions have been raised about the substitution of planners' preferences for consumer sovereignty that made that investment effort possible.[3] Those aspects lie outside the realm of this paper, but as the conventional wisdom has it, Stalin's death precipitated a shift in priorities and moves by his successors to alleviate the lot of the suffering consumer. Bergson, for example, writes of "the stress on consumption that has obtained ever since Stalin died",[4] and Schroeder and Severin have written,

> Since the early 1950's, Soviet policies of the area of consumption and personal incomes have reflected a large scale effort to redress in part the gross imbalance in the economy which was Stalin's legacy.[5]

The empirical basis for the above and similar statements is the dramatic improvement in the well-being of the Soviet consumer in the immediate post-Stalin years, an improvement that continues unabated to the present. This improvement has been amply documented.[6] It has come about, however, not because consumption's share of the national income has been increasing, but rather in spite of the fact that consumption's share has been falling ever since Stalin died. It is simply the residual of an ever-expanding GNP, not the product of a shift in priorities.

One of the most salient but often overlooked features of the post-Stalin era has been the ever-decreasing share of GNP going to consumption and the ever-increasing share going to investment. As can be seen in Table 6.1, consumption's share of GNP fell progressively, from 62.4 percent of the total in 1950 under Stalin to some 56.5 percent in 1974 under Brezhnev. Investment's share during the same period doubled, rising from 14.8 percent of the total to 28.4 percent. The "imbalance" (if it can be labelled such) of the Stalin years seems not to have improved, but rather in a certain sense to have worsened.

The Investment Share

As the Greenslade estimates presented in Table 6.1 show, investment's share of the national output doubled during the period 1950–1974, rising from 14 percent to 28 percent of GNP. In order to compare the ever-increasing burden of investment during the post-Stalin years with that of the Stalin era, one has to turn to a different set of estimates, those by Moorsteen and Powell, which are presented in Table 6.2.

Because of differing definitions, these run higher than those of Greenslade, but also show a strong upward trend. If gross (as defined by

Table 6.1   Shares of Investment and Consumption as a Percent of GNP

	1950	1955	1960	1965	1970	1974	1978
Investment	14.8	19.4	23.9	26.0	27.0	28.4	31.0
Consumption	62.4	62.1	61.1	58.2	57.2	56.5	56.0

Source: Rush Greenslade, "The Real National Product of the U.S.S.R., 1950–1975" in the U.S. Congress, Joint Economic Committee, *Soviet Economy in a New Perspective* (Washington, D.C.: U.S. Government Printing Office, 1976), p. 177. 1978 figure from U.S. Congress, Joint Economic Committee *Allocation of Resources in the Soviet Union and China—1979* (Washington D.C.: U.S. Government Printing Office, 1980) (Part V), p. 11. This study forecasts that consumption's share will fall to 54 percent by 1985.

Moorsteen and Powell) investment took an average of 21 percent of the gross national product in the seven years preceding Stalin's death, it took an average of 26.6 percent during the seven years following his death. This 26.6 percent average for the entire seven-year post-Stalin period exceeds the peak of 26.2 percent reached in the single year 1935 at the height of Stalin's industrialization drive.

At no time since the death of Stalin has the priority of investment and the development of heavy industry been subordinated to consumption and the development of consumer goods industry. Malenkov did promise, and the Soviet people have benefitted from, higher levels of consumption. But Malenkov also emphasized that industrialization "was, and would continue to be, the basis of Soviet economic policy."[7] Malenkov's successor, Bulganin, taking up the same theme in 1955, stated that

> heavy industry is the source of a constant rise in the prosperity of the Soviet people. In developing heavy industry we have always followed and shall continue to follow the directives of the Great Lenin and the faithful continuator of his work, Joseph Vaissaronovich Stalin.[8]

Table 6.2   Investment Share in National Product (1937 prices)

Year	Value	Year	Value	Year	Value
1928	8.4	1938	18.5	1952	22.9
1929	2.9	1939	15.6	1953	21.9
1930	10.4	1940	12.3	1954	19.6
1931	14.4	1945	13.4	1955	22.9
1932	9.4	1946	15.1	1956	27.8
1933	16.0	1947	20.5	1957	26.2
1934	18.8	1948	18.5	1958	30.7
1935	26.2	1949	24.3	1959	30.6
1936	18.5	1950	21.6	1960	28.8
1937	21.1	1951	24.4	1961	30.6

Source: Richard Moorsteen and Raymond Powell, *The Soviet Capital Stock, 1928–1962* (Homewood, Ill.: Richard D. Irwin, 1966), p. 364.

And Bulganin's successor, Khrushchev, some two years later defended the continuing priority accorded to heavy industry and stated that the nation would not "deviate from the road marked out by Stalin"[9]—a position that he would reiterate in 1959.[10]

If the investment burden appears to have been eased by Stalin's successors, it is only in the sense that the investment of some 30 percent of 1978's $1,097.8 billion GNP, by virtue of the principle of diminishing marginal utility, inflicts a far less painful material deprivation than the investment of some 14–15 percent of 1950's much smaller $312 billion GNP.[11]

Consumption's Share of the National Income

In the intensity of our preoccupation with the "ruthlessness" of Stalin's industrialization drive, we in the West have lost sight of the fact that industrialization was and is pursued, not as an end in itself, but rather as a means of improving the well-being of the Soviet people in a setting of national security. "Improve the material and cultural well-being of the Soviet people" is the leitmotiv that ran through all of Stalin's pronouncements on economic matters. One of the prime charges he made in his well-known rebuke of Yaroshenko was that "Comrade Yaroshenko forgets that men produce not for production's sake, but in order to satisfy their needs."[12] Elsewhere in that same work he wrote:

> Insuring the maximum satisfaction of the continual growing material and cultural needs of society—that is the goal of socialist production: a continuing growth and development of socialist industry on the basis of an even higher technology that is the means for its attainment.[13]

While one may argue that the discount rate Stalin used in his calculus of industrialization was too low, it would be difficult to argue that his end goal was not an improvement in the lot of the Soviet consumer. It might also be noted that at no time did the percentage of national income Stalin diverted to investment approach the levels (36 percent) diverted from consumption in Japan and South Korea during the period of their rapid development and at periods of their history when their per capita incomes were no greater than that of the USSR.[14]

To use Stalin's emphasis on investment and the development of heavy industry as an indicator of anticonsumerism is to employ a nonsequitur. The first postulate of economic development is that it is only via the construction of lumber mills, clothing factories, and tractors that a nation can become better housed, clothed, and fed; and for that, more steel, machine tools, and locomotives are required. This postulate, it might be noted, is one that the current generation of U.S. economists has come to recognize as it hastens to embrace the tenets of the new "supply side" economics. As Khrushchev put it in 1959, defending the high priority he continued to accord heavy industry, "How can it be otherwise? In order to have sufficient consumer goods, the means of production are necessary first—we need metals, machines, etc."[15]

All of the Stalin Five-Year Plans called for significant increases in consumption. While consumption's share of the national income during the First Five-Year Plan was to fall from 77.4 to 66.4 percent, in absolute terms it was to increase by some 75 percent.[16] The Second Plan called for a 133 percent increase in the output of consumer goods and a twofold increase in the urban worker's consumption of food and manufactured products.[17] In the face of the developing military threats in the West and Far East, the ambitious consumption plans for the first two plans were lowered, and the Third Plan called for an increase in consumption of a somewhat lower, but yet respectable 69 percent (better than 10 percent per annum)—a plan that was shattered by the outbreak of World War II.[18]

The priority Stalin gave to consumption in the postwar period, as Eugène Zaleski has pointed out, was also high.[19] The cold war and the Korean conflict, however, forced the abandonment of the ambitious consumption targets. Rationing, it might be noted, was not abolished in Great Britain until 1954,[20] but Stalin abolished it in 1947 and followed through with a policy of annual reductions in the prices of consumer goods. As a result of the Stalin price cuts, the index of retail prices in 1952 was 50 percent that of the 1947 level.[21] These price cuts, in combination with the increases in wages, produced a 60 percent increase in the real wages of Soviet workers over the period 1948–1952.[22] Stalin's successor continued his price reduction policy for one year and then discontinued it.

While one can quite rightly argue that Stalin's ambitious plans for consumption were never met, it can also be argued that the goals of his successors have not been met. The consumer goods sector continues, as it did throughout the Stalin years, to serve as a buffer for shortfalls in planned inputs into the heavy industry and capital goods sectors—witness the fate of the recent plans for the expansion of civilian automobile production.[23] As recently as 1977, a Soviet economist felt compelled to write, "if the degree of fulfillment of plan targets for the commissioning of new plants in a number of branches falls between 80 percent and 85 percent, in branches producing consumer goods it is often less than 50 percent."[24]

The rise in consumption that became so visible following Malenkov's "New Look Speech" is a product of factors entirely unrelated to Stalin's death. The foremost of these is the fact that the nation's stock of capital in 1953 was some 50 percent higher than it had been in 1940,[25] a fact that gave planners a firmer base for rhetoric and a larger margin for economic maneuver. As Malenkov stated in his budget speech of August 1953,

> Until now, we did not have the possibility to develop the light and food industries at the same rate as heavy industry. At the present time we can and thus must . . .in every possible way accelerate the development of light industry.[26]

As a result of this enhanced capability, gains were made in production durables in the immediate post-Stalin era. This, however, was simply the by-product and logical consequence of the process of economic growth that had been set in motion by Stalin, i.e., the satisfaction of an ever-higher hierarchy of consumer wants. Many goods that had hitherto been produced in only insignificant numbers were now produced in larger quantities, and even very small increases in absolute terms translated into highly impressive percentage gains. Although amounting to an even smaller percentage of an expanding national income, the consumer goods sector was producing increasingly-larger absolute increments in consumption, which were becoming ever more perceptible to Soviet citizens and to Western observers. This increase notwithstanding, an examination of the following key trends relating to consumption makes it more difficult to argue that Stalin's successors have accorded increasingly higher priorities to current consumption:

1. As noted above, consumption as a percent of GNP has fallen continuously, from 62.1 percent in 1950 to 56.5 percent in 1974.[27]

2. The rate of expansion of consumer goods output fell in a manner that can be termed precipitous after the death of Stalin. According to Soviet sources, during the period 1950–53 the output of consumer goods expanded by 44 percent, while during the period 1955–58 it expanded by only 27 percent.[28] Estimates by Rush Greenslade show the rate of expansion of consumer goods output falling from an average of 5.9 percent per annum during the Fifth Plan, to 5.4 percent during the Sixth, to 4 percent during the Seventh, and to 3.8 percent during the Ninth.[29] Another study conducted for the JEC shows a fall in the rate of expansion of consumption in the USSR from 8.5 percent per annum during the Fifth Plan to 5.5 percent during the Sixth and to 3.7 percent during the Seventh.[30]

3. The consumer goods portion of industrial output has fallen from 31.2 percent of the total in 1950 to 29.5 percent in 1955, 27.5 percent in 1960, and on down to 25.9 percent in 1965—a level where it has remained, give or take a percentage point or two, for the past decade, standing at 26.2 percent in 1980.[31]

4. Investments in consumer goods industries (group B) as a percent of the nation's total investment effort have never reached the levels attained during the Stalin years, and the trend since his death has been downward. During the Second Plan, investment in group B industries reached 6.8 percent of the total, while the average for the three prewar Five-Year Plans was in excess of 6.37 percent,[32] a level never reached in any year of the post-Stalin era. During the Fourth Plan they accounted for 5.2 percent of the total investment, 4.5 percent during the Fifth, followed by a brief spurt during the Sixth Plan to 5.3 percent, falling to 4.8 percent during the Seventh, rising briefly to 5.3 percent during the Eighth, and falling to 4.8 percent during the Ninth, (in 1978), and 4.2 percent during the Tenth.[33]

While the illusion in the West is that the passing of Stalin ushered in a new day for the Soviet consumer, in terms of shares that day has not yet dawned. As has been demonstrated, throughout the entire post-Stalin era, consumption's share of the GNP has fallen; the rate of expansion of consumer goods production has fallen; the consumer goods portion of industrial output has fallen; and the percentage of total investment allocated to the consumer goods industries has fallen. In terms of shares, and the relation to the potential of the times, one could argue that the position of the Soviet consumer has deteriorated.

AGRARIAN POLICIES IN THE POST-STALIN ERA

It has now become deeply ingrained in the conventional wisdom of the West that Stalin "neglected" agriculture, i.e., that he accorded an overly low priority to investments in that sector. As regards agricultural investment, Stalin was "penurious compared to his successors," writes M. Gardner Clark, a renowned Western expert on Soviet agriculture.[34] James Millar, equally well-known, writes that Khrushchev attempted to reverse the effects of Stalin's "neglect and abuse" by increasing the share of investment funds allocated to the rural sector."[35] And Alec Nove, similarly writing about the effort of Stalin's successors to overcome "past neglects,"[36] cites the fact that total investment in agriculture rose from an average of under 3 billion rubles per year during the period 1951–1955 to 7.27 billion in 1961.[37] While it is true that the volume rose significantly, as in the case of consumption, when one looks to the shares for evidence of a significant and sustained shift in priorities toward agriculture, one does not find it. Agriculture's share of total investment in 1961 was exactly the same as it had been in 1950, 15 percent.[38]

Let us examine first trends in agriculture's share of total investment and second, the validity of the charge that Stalin "neglected" agriculture.

Trends in Agriculture's Share of Investment

In fairness to the authors cited above, it must be pointed out that agriculture's share of total investment did exhibit a short spurt in the years following Stalin's death, rising, as can be seen in Table 6.3, from 11.7 percent of the total during the Fourth Plan (1946–1950) to 14.1 percent during the Fifth (1951–1955), and to 14.2 percent during the Sixth (1956–1960). Our argument, however, is not that there were no increases, but only that

Table 6.3   Agriculture's Share of Investment

First Five-Year Plan (1928–1932)	15.5
Second Five-Year Plan (1933–1937)	11.8
3½ Years of Third Plan (1938–June 1941)	10.7
1 July 1941 to 1 January 1946	9.3
Fourth Five-Year Plan (1946–1950)	11.7
Fifth Five-Year Plan (1951–1955)	14.1
Sixth Five-Year Plan (1956–1960)	14.2
Seventh Five-Year Plan (1961–1965)	15.4
Eighth Five-Year Plan (1966–1970)	16.9

Source: NKhSSR V 1972, pp. 478–79.

whatever increases did occur were unrelated to Stalin's death. The spurt of investment during the Fifth Plan was due largely to the launching of the Virgin Land Program, which, as we will see in a subsequent section, seems to have been in the planning stages at the time of Stalin's death. And, as Volin has noted, "After 1955 the annual increases in agricultural investment slowed down."[39]

If instead of limiting the analysis to the brief five- or six-year period following Stalin's death, one extends it back into the 1940s, it becomes quite difficult on the basis of investment figures to defend the thesis that agriculture's priority has significantly heightened. An equally strong case could be made that efforts on behalf of agriculture were in fact weakened.

Examination of the figures in Table 6.3, discloses several facts. The trend toward an increasing share of investment clearly began a decade prior to Stalin's death. The rate of increase in agriculture's share slowed abruptly and came to a halt in the years following his death. Agriculture's share of total investment during the Sixth Plan (1956–1960), the first plan Stalin had no hand in formulating, was a mere one-tenth of 1 percent higher than it had been during the Fifth.

In addition, the following can be noted:

1. Agriculture's share of total investment was smaller in 1960 than it had been in 1950, i.e., 14.1 percent vs. 15 percent.[40]
2. Agriculture's share of total investment in the two-and-one-half-year five-year plans that followed Stalin's death never reached the levels it did during the First Plan.[41]
3. Agriculture's share of state investment (which excludes investment by kolkhozes) stood at 8.0 percent in 1960 vs. 10.2 percent in 1950.[42]
4. The state's share of agricultural investment (by the state and the kolkhozes), which during the period 1950–52 averaged some 55 percent, for the period 1954–56 remains substantially the same (54 percent), and for the period 1958–1960 averaged only 46 percent.[43]

If one turns to agriculture's share of fixed investment, one finds that although it increased in absolute magnitude, it declined as a percentage of total fixed investment, and in a manner that can be termed dramatic. As figures derived from estimates by Moorsteen and Powell (Table 6.4) show, agriculture's share of investment in equipment fell unrelentingly from a postwar high of 25.4 percent in 1950 to a low of 11.2 percent in 1961. As to agriculture's share of total investment in construction, there was a slight increase, with agriculture's receiving an average of slightly over 14 percent of the total construction share during the period 1946–53, and slightly over 15 percent during the period from 1954 to 1961. As to agriculture's share of total fixed investment (equipment and construction), this fell from a peak of 19.2 percent in 1950 to 12.6 percent in 1960 and 1961. A series presented by Folk Dovring, which begins with the year 1955, runs higher than these derived from the Moorsteen and Powell series, but also shows a fall in agriculture's share of fixed investment from 19.4 percent of the total in 1955 to 14.5 percent of the total in 1960 needs.[44]

Stalin's Neglect of Agriculture

In assessing the proverbial Stalin neglect of agriculture, one must give due consideration to the many and varied efforts, some of which can be termed as large-scale, that Stalin put forth on behalf of agricultural development. When these are examined and measured against the potential of the times, it would seem that they in many respects surpass by far those of his successors. Following are some often overlooked facts concerning inputs into agriculture under Stalin.

Production and Deliveries of Agricultural Machinery and Equipment

It was under Stalin's aegis that the USSR moved from a position of a non-producer and importer of tractors to become the world's largest producer of tractors. From 1929–1938 the Soviet tractor part rose from 34,000 to 483,500[45] while the park of grain combines rose from 7 to 153,500.[46]

An examination of figures on the state supply of agricultural equipment in the immediate postwar period also shows that Stalin did not neglect agriculture. As the figures in Table 6.4 show, agriculture's share of total investment in equipment rose from 9 percent of the total in 1947 to 24.4 percent in 1950. Although the nation's GNP was only some 25 percent greater in 1950 than it was in 1940,[47] deliveries of machinery to agriculture (in value terms) were some 650 percent above the 1940 level. Deliveries of tractors were five and one-half times the 1940 level in physical units, and more than four times the 1940 level in physical units, and more than four times the 1940 level in terms of 15 horsepower units.[48] Deliveries of grain combines were more than three times the 1940 level.[49] All of these increases are proportionately for larger than the increases in the nation's GNP and would seem to indicate that agriculture's priority was not a low one.

The Stalin Plan for the Transformation of Nature

Highly indicative of the importance Stalin accorded to agricultural matters, even in the capital short postwar period, are the efforts and considerable resources that were consecrated to the planting of forests and tree belts in the steep regions to protect the fields from dry winds blowing in from Asia and to attenuate the aridity of these regions. The "Stalin Plan for the Transformation of Nature," which Volin has characterized as "grandiose,"[50] was modelled after the U.S.'s reforestry and shelter belt program of the 1930s and called for the planting of national forests on the watershed divides and on the banks of the Volga and Don Rivers; the planting of some 5.7 million hectares of protective tree belts;[51] and the construction of some forty-four thousand ponds and reservoirs and the establishment of four-hundred-seventy forestry mechanization stations.[52] There has been considerable debate about the effectiveness of these tree belts, which now "present a familiar landscape to a traveler in the countryside."[53] At issue here, however, is not Stalin's effectiveness but rather his efforts.

Table 6.4   Agriculture's Share of Gross Investment (percent of)

Year	Total fixed capital investment	Total investment in equipment	Total construction
1928	17.4	24.3	15.4
1929	15.9	22.3	13.8
1930	14.0	22.4	10.7
1931	15.1	23.6	11.6
1932	11.9	18.2	8.9
1933	18.8	27.7	14.5
1934	17.2	27.6	12.9
1935	16.2	27.4	11.3
1936	15.0	25.3	10.4
1937	16.6	22.4	13.4
1938	14.2	17.2	12.3
1939	13.7	16.3	
1940	12.4	12.6	
1941	14.7	12.6	
1942	7.9	18.9	
1943	8.2	0	12.3
1944	8.3	0	
1945	8.4	4.3	
1946	11.4	6.0	
1947	12.8	9.0	14.1
1948	14.7	11.5	
1949	18.4	15.4	
1950	19.2	24.4	
1951	18.8	25.4	14.6
1952	17.3	24.3	13.1
1953	16.0	23.4	12.3
1954	16.3	21.3	13.9
1955	17.7	20.4	16.6
1956	16.4	18.9	15.9
1957	16.4	17.0	16.4
1958	16.1	16.4	15.8
1959	14.3	16.5	15.0
1960	12.6	13.5	14.0
1961	12.6	11.2	14.0

Source: Derived from figures given by Moorsteen and Powell, *Soviet Capital Stock,* pp. 429, 438, and 440.

Stalin's Irrigation Programs

It would also be a serious mistake to overlook Stalin's efforts to irrigate the Soviet countryside. And the importance he attached to that vital question rings unmistakably clear in his report to the seventeenth Congress in 1934. His dream was to irrigate the Trans-Volga regions, thereby providing the nation with "a large and absolutely stable grain base on the Volga which shall be independent of the vagaries of the weather."[54] The plan of the times called for the irrigation of between 10 and 11 million hectares.[55] The darkening international situation, however, brought a virtual halt to irrigation efforts. Nevertheless, the Soviet irrigated land area by 1940 had doubled and reached 8 million hectares.[56]

In 1950, Stalin resumed pursuit of his irrigation goal and ushered in what Volin has termed "a new era in Soviet irrigation".[57] That year work began on a series of large-scale hydroelectric projects involving the irrigation of nearly 15 million hectares. As Volin has written, "This new scheme of water development impresses one not only by its huge dimensions, but also by a significant geographical departure; the extension of irrigation into the European part of the country."[58] Because of design and engineering difficulties, work on the project slowed down after Stalin's death and the irrigated land area of the USSR in 1962 was only 0.7 million hectares larger than it had been in 1953.[59]

In 1963, in connection with the shift toward the intensification of agriculture forced upon the Soviets when they ran out of reserves of uncultivated land (discussed below), Khrushchev, in words highly reminiscent of Stalin's speech to the seventeenth Party Congress, called for expanding the nation's irrigation system to some 28 million hectares by 1980.[60] As in the case of Stalin's ambitious plans, that goal was not met. As of 1980, the irrigated land area had reached only 17.2 million hectares.[61] While it is true that the expansion of irrigated land area in the twenty-seven years following the death of Stalin exceeds that of the twenty-seven years preceding it, it must be borne in mind that the Stalin years were interrupted by four years of war, and that the work force, GNP, and capital stock of the sixties and seventies were manyfold multiples of those of the thirties and forties. The nation's GNP in the sixties and seventies was some five and seven-tenths and eleven times, respectively, as large as that of 1940, while the capital stock was respectively five and twelve times as large.[62]

Stalin's Virgin Land Program

Khrushchev's Virgin Land Program is another example often cited as an indication of the heightened priority Stalin's successors accorded to agriculture. When examined in the context of the short time span 1946–1954, it would appear to be so. But when examined in the context of the long sweep of Russian agricultural history from 1971 (or even 1880) on down through 1965, the Khrushchev program represents only a continuation of policies past. This point has been clearly documented by McCauley.[63]

If there is one unyielding constant running through the history of Russian agriculture from tsarist times through to the end of the Khrushchev era, it is the primary reliance on extensive farming and the unrelenting (albeit of varying intensity) conquest and cultivation of virgin lands as a means of expanding output. To feed a population that grew from 163 million in 1917 to 229 million in 1965, the Soviet sown area was expanded from 118 million to 209 million hectares.[64] Of that 91-million-hectare increase, some 38–39 million occurred during the Stalin years.[65]

In the closing days of the tsarist regime between 1881 and 1914, more than 20 million hectares of virgin land had been put to the plow. Stolypin, while acknowledging the difficulties of conquering them, spoke frequently of the "huge areas of virgin land fit for cultivation".[66] Lenin, prior to the Bolshevik takeover, had also spoken of the "huge" fund of available but yet uncultivated land.[67] The problem, as Lenin stated it after his arrival to power, was that the "huge areas of first-class land" in Siberia were "inaccessible because it lay far from the communications network," while several million hectares of virgin land in other areas remained unploughed, "since we do not have the draught animals and the necessary implements."[68]

By the late twenties the resources were available and Stalin, feeling that "the question of the cultivation of waste land and virgin land is of the utmost importance for our agriculture,"[69] responded to the grain crisis of that period by the establishment of some one-hundred-fifty large state farms on newly plowed land in the arid regions of the North Caucasus, Siberia, and Kazakhstan.[70] In connection with this project, Stalin at the Sixteenth Party Congress in 1930 was bragging that by the end of the First Five-Year Plan, those sovhozy would have "as large an area under grain as the whole Argentina today."[71]

At the same Congress, Ya. Yakolov, Stalin's Commissar for Agriculture, in a speech that Khrushchev seems to have borrowed some twenty-four years later, spoke of the 50–55 million hectares available for plowing up in Kazakhstan.[72] At the seventeenth Party Congress in 1934, Stalin returned again to his virgin land theme and the possibility of plowing up some 5 million hectares of virgin land in the "consuming" regions of Moscow and Gorky, which were at that time covered with shrub.[73]

By 1932 the Soviet sown area had increased by more than 24 million hectares over the 1928 level. Some 11 million of this increase had taken place in the newly formed sovhozes,[74] and by 1938 the sown area of Stalin's virgin land sovhozy had reached 15 million hectares.[75] Again during the period 1940–1944 another 16 million hectares of virgin and fallow lands were put under crop in the Eastern regions of the country.[76] In the immediate postwar period, there was a slowing down of the rate of expansion owing to shortages of labor and equipment. In Kazakhstan, between 1950–1953, however, some 2.1 million hectares of new lands were put to the plow, while in Western Siberia some 2.6 million hectares of new lands were brought under cultivation.[77] Thus, in three stages during the Stalin era, some 34–35 million hectares of new land were put to the plow and nation's sown area increased by some 39 million hectares. By way of comparison, some 40 million hectares of new lands were put to the plow during the Khrushchev era and the sown area expanded by some 50 million hectares. In relation to the possibilities of the times, the Stalin effort easily ranks on a par with that of Khrushchev. The capital stock and GNP Khrushchev had to work with was far more than double that available to Stalin.[78]

Furthermore, it seems that even the resumption of the virgin land efforts of the period 1954–1960 had its origins during Stalin's lifetime. A moment's reflection on the scale of the project leads one to conclude that it could not have been otherwise. In terms of land area plowed, distances, and volume of material, the project was, as Crankshaw has termed it, "really colossal" and "spectacular."[79] Already by the end of 1954, 17.6 million hectares of new land had been plowed up.[80] This, it might be noted, is an area one-third larger than the entire land area of England. The incremental harvest alone from these new lands in 1954 was 14.7 million tons;[81] or some 25 percent of the USSR's entire 1954 grain output.[82] To identify, procure, and move the necessary tractors, combines, parts, fules, lubricants, seed, and workforce over long distances into the new lands in the difficult conditions of the Soviet winter and spring and then plow, plant, and harvest required a very long planning lead. Some of the plowing, in fact, began in 1953, and, as McCauley points out, experimental plantings were carried out during 1953, and these could have occurred only in the spring of 1953.[83]

Toward the middle and late sixties there was a fundamental break with previous history, as the nation moved from extensive toward intensive farming as the primary basis for agricultural policy. This shift was forced upon Brezhnev as the nation approached the outer limits of potential of arable lands. It is a shift that economic exigencies would also have forced upon Stalin at some point, and there is ample evidence that he would have supported it. As early as the seventeenth Party Congress in 1934, he pointed out the two main lines for the expansion of agricultural output: "1. The line of the greatest possible expansion of crop areas . . . [and] 2. The line of . . . improved cultivation of the land . . . increasing the harvest yield and . . . if . . . necessary, to a temporary reduction in crop areas. . . . [T]he second line," he said, is "the only correct line."[84] But as that second line requires a far larger investment per unit of output, the shift to intensification (despite the directives of the nineteenth Party Congress) was by necessity postponed until the middle sixties, when the nation ran out of lands and had no other way out, and from an economic point of view, this certainly made sense. It is a shift that would have been made no matter who was in charge, even if that person had been Stalin.

Continuity in Post-Stalin Agrarian Policies

That one should find a basic continuity in the broad lines of Stalinian and post-Stalinian policies in the countryside should come as no surprise. There was very little change in the composition of the Party's ruling Central Committee between 1952 and 1956, and given the continuity of people in the key party and government posts dealing with agricultural matters, one would have little reason to expect radical change. A. I. Kozlov, who had served as chief of the Central Committee's Agricultural Section under Stalin, served in that post until March of 1955, was named Minister of Agriculture after Stalin's death, and continued in that post until September 1953, when he was named Minister of State Farms.[85] I. A. Benediktov, who had been Stalin's Commissar of Agriculture as early as 1938 and who had returned to that post after the war and served there until the death of Stalin, was renamed Minister of Agriculture when A. I. Kozlov departed from that post in September of 1953.[86] The key factor to any continuity of course would be

N. S. Khrushchev, who had been exerting a decisive influence on agricultural matters for some time prior to the death of Stalin.

The amalgamations, about which Khrushchev made so much fanfare, got under way in 1940 thirteen years prior to Stalin's death, and by 1953 the number of kolkhozes had been reduced from 236 thousand to 97 thousand,[87] while the average number of households per kolkhoz grew from eighty-one to twenty-two and the average sown area per kolkhoz grew from 492 to 1,407 hectares.[88] The process of amalgamations continued after his death, and by 1980 the number of kolkhozes had fallen to 25.9 thousand, the number of households per kolkhoz had grown to 492, and the average sown area had grown to 3,700 hectares.[89]

The prevailing ideology of the Stalin years was to raise the level of kolkhoz property to that of state property gradually. That goal has in no way been abandoned or diluted, but has been progressively realized through the formation of inter-kolkhoz enterprises and the unrelenting expansion of the state's share of agricultural employment and marketed farm output. In 1980 there were 9,638 enterprises owned jointly by kolkhozes, sovhozes, and other state enterprises, which had turned out a wide variety of products ranging from electricity to cement and canned goods.[90] The state's share of the agricultural workforce increased from 12 percent in 1953 to 46 percent in 1980;[91] its share of the sown area rose in the same period from 11.6 percent to 51 percent;[92] and its share of the marketed output rose from 14 percent in 1950 to 47 percent in 1980.[93] The private sector's share, on the other hand, fell from 4.4 percent of the sown area in 1953 to 2.8 percent in 1980,[94] and its share of the marketable output fell from 24 percent in 1950 to 12 percent in 1980.[95]

STALIN'S ROLE IN THE TAXATION AND PRICING REFORMS OF 1953

It is Malenkov's announcement in August of 1953 of the reform and reduction of the tax on the private plots and Khrushchev's announcement three and one-half weeks later of a reduction in the norms and an increase in the prices paid for obligatory deliveries by the kolkhozes and kolkhozniki that would seem to controvert the thesis of this paper and provide conclusive support for the prevailing view that the death of Stalin precipitated a turning point in the treatment accorded Soviet agriculture. That there were changes, sweeping changes in fact, is beyond dispute. My argument, however, is not that there were no changes, but only that the fact that they occurred after Stalin's death is entirely coincidental. As the most casual reading of Stalin's last will and testament, *The Economic Problems of Socialism,* reveals, it was Stalin himself who laid the theoretical foundations and cleared the way on both the economic and ideological planes for the break with the dogma of the past that occurred in August and September of 1953.[96] Without Stalin's authority, the reforms of August and September could never have occurred when they did, because in the setting of the post-Stalin era no one had sufficient statute or political security to argue, as

Stalin did, that certain concepts of Marx and Engels were invalid in the Soviet setting and should be "discarded"—an act without which the reforms of August and September could not have been carried out.

The sections that follow will examine each of the components of the 1953 package of tax and price reforms and how they relate to Stalin's views and also the matter of the timing of those reforms. While there are no stenographic reports of Central Committee meetings prior to Khrushchev's time, a priori reasoning, plus some bits of a posteriori evidence, lead inexorably to the conclusion that the reforms of 1953 were in the pipeline at the time of Stalin's death.

The Revision of the Taxation of Private Plot Activity

The tax law of August 1953 drastically simplified the methods of determining the amount of tax to be paid on private plot output (something Stalin would not have opposed); while its impact on the individual peasant was highly significant,[97] the loss in budgetary revenues stemming from the reduction was quite insignificant. The stated purpose of the reduction was to reverse a trend that had been under way since the end of the war toward a diminution in the volume of output emanating from the private plots and the decrease in the number of privately owned cows. It would thus seem to represent a break with previous attitudes toward the private plots. This shrinking of private plot activity, however, was not the result of any measures Stalin had taken to eliminate private plot activity. It was, after all, at his insistence that in 1930 the farmers were given the right to work private plots and then in 1932 to sell the output from those plots at free-market prices. It was also, as Volin points out, he who subsequently took the side of the kolkhozniki against the restrictionist tendencies that began to manifest themselves in some sections of the Party in the middle thirties.[98] It might also be borne in mind that private plot activity and private ownership of livestock reached their all-time postcollectivization highs during the Stalin era.

The reduction in private plot activity during the closing years of the Stalin era rather than being the result of efforts to discourage private plot activity was quite paradoxically the residual effect of his efforts to improve the lot of the consumer. The expanded value of food products sold through the government and cooperative retail network,[99] coupled with the approximate 10 percent annual reduction in food prices that had been effected since 1947, precipitated a decline in the kolkhoz markets' share of food product sales[100] together with declines in kolkhoz market prices.[101] Already in 1950, the index of food prices on the kolkhoz markets of the nation's seventy-seven largest cities stood at 98 percent of the 1940 level.[102]

This decline in kolkhoz market prices, in its turn, had put a severe squeeze on the profitability of private plot activity, a squeeze that was accentuated by the fact that in periods of declining prices the agricultural tax (on sown area, not profit) became increasingly regressive. It was "to correct" those unforeseen and unintended effects on private plot activity that the tax reductions of August 8 were put in effect.

The Price Reforms and Increases of September 1953

That the price reforms and increase of September 1953 opened up a new era of Soviet agrarian policy, an era vastly different from that of the Stalin years, is indisputable. The prevailing doctrine of the Stalin years was that prices could have no influence on either the volume or pattern of output under planned socialism.

This fact notwithstanding, it is interesting to note that pragmatism frequently overruled ideology and precipitated some rather thoroughgoing revisions of the wholesale price structure in 1949, 1950, and 1952. The post-1953 period, however, was clearly a new era. The "law of value" received its long overdue recognition, and price became one of the prime instruments of economic management in the countryside. Every year from 1953 to 1959, for example, not only were prices on agricultural output edged ever upward, but there was also a continual and significant shifting in the structure of those prices.[103]

This admission of the law of value (price) into the body of officially accepted dogma, however, was not the product of a tight turn rapidly conceived and executed in the brief six-month period following Stalin's death. It was the culminating product of a long and slow turn, which had been initiated some ten years earlier. The role of the law of value in the disturbing discrepancies between plans and results (particularly with respect to product mix) had, long before Stalin's death, made it apparent that the Soviets had indeed not "liquidated the law of value." That the law of value did continue to operate in Soviet society was becoming ever clearer; and the first indication that the guardians of the official doctrinal purity were ready to incorporate that fact into the official dogma came in the form of the famous 1943 *Pod Znamenem Marksizma* editorial: an editorial that, if not written by Stalin, at least had his blessings. The editorial stated that:

> The proposition that the law of value plays no role under socialism contradicts, by its very nature, the whole spirit of Marxist-Leninist political economy. It has barred the way to a correct understanding of those problems which are so acutely posed before us, not only questions of a theoretical nature, but also the practical problems of our economic policy.[104]

Stalin tightened the turn some 9 years later in the discussions on the new political economy text and in his *Economic Problems of Socialism*. The *Pod Znamenem Marksizma* editorial, while rejecting the notion that the law of value had been liquidated, hedged by stating that because of socialist institutions ("the distribution on the basis of the quantity and quality of labor") it operated in a "transformed form,"[105] Stalin, however, not only rejected the idea that the law of value had been liquidated, but attacked even the notion that it had been "transformed." "This is untrue. . . . Laws can not be 'transformed'. . . . [I]f they can be transformed then they can be abolished and replaced by other laws."[106]

Section two of his *Economic Problems of Socialism* was devoted to an explanation and justification of the existing commodity production and circulation in the USSR, i.e., the purchase-sale relationships between the farm cooperatives and the state, and the consumers and the state. His section three was devoted to a discussion of the Law of Value under socialism and reads as follows:[107]

> Wherever commodities and commodity production exist, there the law of value must also exist. In our country, the sphere of operation of the law of value extends, first of all, to commodity circulation, to the exchange of commodities through purchase and sale. . . . Here, in this sphere, the law of value preserves, within certain limits, of course, the function of the regulator.
>
> But the operation of the "Law of Value" is not confined to the sphere of commodity circulation. It also extends to production. True the law of value has no regulation function in our socialist production, but it nevertheless influences production, and this fact cannot be ignored when directing production. . . . Consumer goods are produced and realized in our country as commodities coming under the operation of the law of value. It is precisely here that the law of value exercises its influence on production. In this connection, such things as cost accounting and profitableness, production costs, prices, etc. are of actual importance to our enterprises. Consequently, our enterprises cannot, and must not, function without taking the law of value into account.
>
> The trouble is not that production in our country is influenced by the law of value. The trouble is that our business executives and planners, with few exceptions, are poorly acquainted with the operations of the law of value, do not study them, and are unable to take account of them in their computations. This, in fact, explains the confusion that still reigns in the sphere of price-fixing policy. . . .

Given Stalin's unmistakable discontent with, and his vigorous and scathing criticism of, the then existing system of prices, it is clear that even had he lived changes in the sphere of price policy would have been forthcoming. His role in provoking a discussion and recognition of the role of prices was a crucial one. The *sine qua non* of the utility vs. cost debates was a recognition of the fact that prices did in fact exert an influence, and Stalin's role in this matter was a crucial one, which has not been given its due recognition.

The publication of *The Economic Problems of Socialism* provoked the outpouring, beginning in 1953, of a large number of books and pamphlets devoted to the subject of "commodity production and the law of value under socialism." Some five years after Stalin's death and after he had become a "nonperson," the proponents of the view that the law of value did play a role under socialism were still but resting their arguments with quotes from Stalin's *Economic Problems of Socialism*. M. F. Marakova in a 1958 work, *Commodity Production and the Law of Value under Socialism,*[108] for example, quotes Stalin in ten places throughout his work in order to justify his position. A 1962 work by G. N. Khudokormov,[109] bearing the same title, albeit without quoting Stalin, copied Stalin's *Economic Problems of Socialism* arguments virtually verbatim.

The Extension of Commodity Production

The increases in the level of agricultural prices in the post-Stalin era, coupled with the increase in output they helped spur, produced an unprecedented expansion of the volume of commodity production. Between 1956 and 1959 the volume of kolkhoz receipts from sales to the government and cooperative procurement agencies more than tripled.[110] They increased 150 percent between 1959 and 1965, and then double again between 1965 and 1978. This would seem to run contrary to the vision Stalin had of the long run, in which the state and cooperative sectors would merge and commodity production would cease. The trend, however, is not contrary to his view of events in the short run, and a very large part of his *Economic Problems of Socialism,* together with his defense of the validity of the law of value under socialism, was devoted to arguments against those who, by citing Engels, were arguing that commodity production had no place in socialism.

The entire section 11 of *Stalin's Economic Problems of Socialism* was a discussion of commodity production under socialism. It was an argument against those "half-baked Marxists"[111] who took the position that the party had been wrong in preserving commodity production. In that section Stalin argued that much of what Engels had written regarding the socialization of the means of production and the abolition of commodity production was invalid in the Soviet setting and that the Soviets would also have to "discard certain other concepts taken from Marx's capital."[112]

In support of his defense of the necessity for preserving commodity production, he cited Lenin, who had once written that "in order to ensure an economic bond between town and country, between industry and agriculture, commodity production (exchange through purchase and sale) should be preserved for a certain period, it being the form of economic ties with the town which is alone acceptable to the peasants."[113]

Then, having wrapped himself in Lenin's cloak, he went on to refute those who said

> that commodity production must lead, is bound to lead, to capitalism all the same under all conditions. That is not true. . . . commodity production must not be identified with capitalist production. . . . Commodity production is older than capitalist production. It existed in slave-owning society, and served it, but did not lead to capitalism. It existed in feudal society and served it, yet, although it prepared some of the conditions for capitalist production, it did not lead to capitalism. Why then, one asks, cannot commodity production similarly serve our socialist society for a certain period?[111]
>
> The collective farms are unwilling to alienate their products except in the form of commodities, in exchange for which they desire to receive the commodities they need. At present the collective farms will not recognize commodity relation-exchange through purchase and sale. Because of this, commodity production and trade are as much a necessity with us today as they were, say thirty years ago, when Lenin spoke of the necessity of developing trade to the utmost.[114]

Could anyone have made a more powerful argument for the compatibility of commodity production and Soviet socialism than that made by Stalin? Is there any measure taken in the agricultural sector in the immediate post-Stalin period (1953 to 1958) that could not find both an economic and ideological justification in Stalin's arguments?

It is true that Stalin anticipated the eventual demise of commodity production and its "money economy."

> Of course, when instead of the two basic production sectors, the state sector and the collective-farm sector, there will be only one all-embracing production sector, with the right to dispose of all the consumer goods produced in the country, commodity circulation, with its "money economy" will disappear, as being an unnecessary element in the national economy.
>
> But, so long as this is not the case, so long as the two basic production sectors remain, commodity production and commodity circulation, must remain in force as a necessary and very useful element in our system of national economy.[115]

The Timing of the Reforms

Not only does one find that Stalin's last will and testament provides all of the theoretical underpinnings, both ideological and economic, for the reforms of 1953, but one finds also that a strong case can be made for the hypothesis that those reforms were in the pipeline at the time of Stalin's death. That case can be made on the basis of both a priori reasoning and some pieces of testimony by Khrushchev and Malenkov.

The case can be made on a priori grounds on the basis of two bits of reasoning: (1) the uncertainty of the immediate post-Stalin era was not conducive to the formulation of new initiatives; and (2) there was simply not enough time for the conceptualization and implementation of the complex reforms of August 1953 in the short five-month span of the time running from March to August 1953.

The Uncertainty of the Times

Given the tenseness of the political situation that prevailed until the demise of Beria in June of 1953 (described so well by Conquest[116]) it is doubtful that anyone would have wanted to "rock the boat." A joint Party-government message to the Soviet people, for example, on 7 March 1953,

> deemed it the most important task of the party and the government to insure uninterrupted and correct leadership of the whole life of the country, which in turn demands the greatest unity of leadership and prevention of any kind of disarray and panic, in order by this means to ensure unconditionally the successful implementation of the policy evolved by our party and government both in the domestic affairs of our country and in international affairs.[117]

In addition, given the many other concerns of the immediate post-Stalin period, as McCauley has pointed out

> Agriculture was not the first problem which claimed the attention of Malenkov in the weeks after Stalin's death. He was too much taken with other matters and may even have been a little out of touch with the exact situation. He did not attempt any new initiatives until after Beria's fall."[118]

If McCauley is correct, and there is every reason to believe that he is, then when would the measure of 1953 have been concocted? And even had

Malenkov attempted to institute the tax and price reforms of August and September 1953, it is highly doubtful that they could have moved through the pipeline in the short span of four months for the tax changes and five months for the price and delivery quota changes.

The alleged political purposes of the 1953 reform, the appeasement of a restless peasantry, could have been well served by uncomplicated, flat, across-the-board tax reductions and price increases. Instead there was a sweeping revision of the method of taxation as well as tax reduction. As regards the price increases, there was discrimination along product lines in the percentage of price increase. There was also discrimination as to both product and category of producer in the percentage of change in the obligatory delivery norms, with an increase in the norms for the kolkhozy for meat, wool, and milk.

The Time Constraint

Was it possible, technically or administratively, for the economic objectives of the tax cut and reform of August 1953 (stimulation of output, particularly of livestock, from the private plots) to have been formulated, the research necessary for setting regionally differentiated rates conducted, the budgetary estimates completed, and the tax law drafted and published in the span of five months? An affirmative response is difficult to defend.

In addition to the above a priori evidence, there is also some supporting a posteriori evidence to the effect that the tax and price measures of August and September 1953 were in the works prior to Stalin's death. Khrushchev, in his famous "secret" but widely publicized report to the Twentieth Party Congress on "The Crimes of the Stalin Era,"[119] states that he served on a special commission Stalin had set up to develop a resolution on "Means Toward Further Development of Animal Breeding in Kolkhozes and Sovkhozes."[120] The decree of September 1953 that reformed the norms and prices on obligatory deliveries, it might be noted, bore substantially the same title—"Means Toward Further Development of Animal Breeding in the USSR."

Although it weakens our position, it must be pointed out that Khrushchev also stated that the commission's recommendations were rejected by Stalin in February 1953. While Khrushchev does not state whether the proposals were rejected because the recommended price increases were too steep or not liberal enough, it is clearly the former that he implies. He states that Stalin, while reviewing the project, proposed that the taxes paid by farmers should be raised by 40 million rubles. It was Stalin's view, according to Khrushchev, that the peasants were so well-off that each kolkhoz worker would have to sell only one more chicken to pay the tax in full.[121]

Khrushchev's report, it must be remembered, however, is a largely self-serving document. As Roy Medvedev has noted, "One of the most serious charges against him (Khrushchev) was that while condemning the cult of Stalin, he had begun to propagate a cult of his own . . ."[122] As in his memoirs,[123] the picture that Khrushchev paints of Stalin is that of a dolt—a highly amusing dolt at that. "Everyone in Russia," for example, "who interested themselves even a little in the national situation saw the difficult situation in agriculture, but Stalin never noted it . . . ."[124]

Roy Laird has effectively dealt with this point elsewhere and pointed out that Stalin was acutely conscious of the backwardness of Soviet agriculture and had warned prior to his death that unless the backwardness was overcome, it would "hamper the continued growth of the productive forces of our country more and more as time goes on."[125] Furthermore, Khrushchev's assertion that Stalin had argued that the kolkhozes were so well-off that they could easily afford an increase of some 40 billion in the annual take of the agricultural tax does not square with Stalin's argument in 1952 that the kolkhozes were too poor to take over the MTS, which at that time had a total inventory of equipment considerably less than 20 billion rubles. Stalin's arguments against proposals by two of his economists, A. V. Sanina and V. G. Vehzner, to sell the MTS equipment to the kolkhozes were first and foremost economic, not ideological. "Are our collective farms capable of bearing such an expense?" he asked.

> No, they are not, since they are not in the position to undertake the expenditure of billions of rubles which may be recouped only after a period of six or eight years. Such expenditures can be borne only by the state . . . . What would be the effect of selling the machine and tractor stations to the collective farms . . .? The effect would be to involve the collective farms in heavy loss and then ruin them."[126]

Finally there is Malenkov's letter of resignation, in which he sees "particularly clearly [his] guilt and responsibility for the unsatisfactory state of affairs in agriculture," and goes on to praise the many important measures worked out by the Central Committee to overcome the lag in agriculture:

> Among such important measures is, undoubtedly, the reform of agricultural taxation, regarding which I think it opportune to say that it was carried out on the initiative of and in accordance with the proposals of the Central Committee of the Communist Party of the Soviet Union."[127]

CONCLUSION

This paper has attempted to show that the Western conventional wisdom that holds that Stalin's death paved the way for an increase in attention to, and resources for, agriculture and consumption is in error. While the evidence introduced is not sufficiently strong to build a perfectly airtight case, it is clearly strong enough to compel a reexamination of many of the assumptions underlying Western analysis of policies toward agriculture and the consumer in the post-Stalin era. The conventional wisdom holds that there were shifts in the trend lines of many economic aggregates in the years following Stalin's death. If, however, one were to ask the proverbial man in the moon to give a rough estimate of the date of Stalin's death on the basis of trends in the relative shares of investment going to agriculture, to group A and group B industries, and the share of national income going to investment and consumption, he would be utterly unable to do so.

NOTES

1. *Encounter* XVIII, no. 4 (April 1962): 86–92. Reprinted, together with Nove's subsequent exchange of views on the subject with Leopold Labedz, in *The Soviet System in Theory and Practice,* ed. Harry G. Shaffer (New York: Appleton-Century-Crofts, 1965), pp. 62–83.

2. The dependence of consumer welfare on the state of agriculture is very high in the USSR. Some 75 percent of all goods sold in Soviet retail trade are made from agricultural products. I. Ya. Karluk, *Agrarno-promyshlenyi Kompleks* (Moscow: Politizdat, 1981), p. 3.

3. For an excellent discussion of this question, see Paul R. Gregory and Robert C. Stuart, *Soviet Economic Structure and Performance* (New York: Harper & Row, 1974), pp. 10–12.

4. Abram Bergson, "Soviet Economic Showdown and the 1981–85 Plan," *Problems of Communism* (May–June 1981): 35.

5. Gertrude E. Schroeder and Barbara S. Severin, "Soviet Consumption and Income Policies in Perspective," in U.S. Congress, Joint Economic Committee, *Soviet Economy in a New Perspective* (Washington D.C.: U.S. Government Printing Office, 1976), p. 632.

6. See, for example, the study by G. Schroeder and B. Severin cited above; also the many excellent studies by Janet Chapman.

7. Speech of 12 March 1954; cited by Harrison Salisbury, *The New York Times,* 13 March 1954, p. 1.

8. Speech to the Supreme Soviet 9 February 1955, *The New York Times,* 10 February 1955, p. 4.

9. *The New York Times,* 30 March 1957, p. 4.

10. See Osgood Caruthers, *The New York Times,* 28 January 1959, p. 2.

11. 1978 figures taken from CIA, *Handbook of Economic Statistics, 1979* (Washington, D.C.; U.S. Government Printing Office, 1979), p. 22. 1950 figure derived from Rush Greenslade, "The Real National Product of the U.S.S.R., 1950–1975" in the U.S. Congress, Joint Economic Committee, *Soviet Economy in a New Perspective* (Washington, D.C.: U.S. Government Printing Office, 1976), p. 275.

12. J. V. Stalin, *Ekonomicheskiye Problemi Sotsialisma v SSSR* (Moscow: Gospolizdat, 1952), p. 80.

13. *Ibid.,* p. 78.

14. In Japan, for example, investment in 1968 reached a staggering 36 percent of GNP, according to data provided by the Japanese Planning Agency, cited by Martin G. Schnitzer and James W. Nordyke, *Comparative Economic Systems* (Cincinnati: South-Western Publishing Co., 1971), p. 314. Japan's per capita GNP in 1968 was $968 as compared with $1,200 for USSR. Seymour Kurtz (ed)., *The New York Times Encyclopedia Almanac,* 1970, (New York: The New York Times), pp. 870, 813.

15. Cited by Osgood Caruthers, *New York Times,* p. 12.

16. Maurice Dobb, *Soviet Economic Development Since 1917,* 4th ed. (London: Routledge & Keagan Paul Ltd., 1957), p. 235.

17. *Ibid.,* p. 269.

18. *Ibid.,* p. 292.

19. Eugene Zaleski, *Stalinist Planning For Economic Growth, 1933–1952* (Chapel Hill, North Carolina: The University of North Carolina Press, 1980.)

20. Sima Lieberman, *The Growth of European Mixed Economies 1945–1970* (New York, London: Schenkman Publishing Co., 1977), p. 70.

21. G. Malenkov, *Otchetnii Doklad XIV Cezdy Partii o Rabote Tsentralnovo Kommiteta TsKP (B).*

22. A study conducted for the Rand Corporation by Janet Chapman showed that the real wages of the Soviet workers rose from 56 percent of the 1928 level in 1948 to 90 percent of the 1928 level in 1952. Cited in the *New York Times,* 30 May 1954, p. 18.

23. For a description of the relegation of the consumer to a "second class position" during the Ninth Five Year Plan, see Roger Skurski, "The Role of the Consumer in Soviet Economic Development," *Soviet Union/Union Sovietique* 8, Part 2 (1981), pp. 252–66.

24. U. M. Ivanchenko, "Za Kruglum Stolom," *Voprosy Ekonomiki* 3 (1977): p. 31.

25. In 1937 prices, 452 billion rubles vs. 308 billion rubles in 1940; see Richard Moorsteen and Raymond Powell, *The Soviet Capital Stock, 1928–1962* (Homewood, Ill.: Richard D. Irwin, 1966), p. 359.

26. *New York Times* (August 10, 1953), p. 6.

27. See Table 6.1.

28. *Narodnoye Khozyaistvo SSSR v. 1958,* pp. 55–56 (hereafter *NKhSSSR).*

29. Rush Greenslade, *op. cit.,* p. 276.

30. Stanley H. Cohn, "General Growth Performance of the Soviet Economy," in U.S. Congress, Joint Economic Committee, *Economic Performance and the Military Burden in the Soviet Union* (Washington D.C.: U.S. Government Printing Office, 1970), p. 10.

31. *NKhSSSR v 1980,* p. 124.

32. During the First Plan, 6.3 percent, 6.8 percent during the Second Plan, and 5.8 percent during the Third. *NKhSSSR v 1977,* pp. 352–53.

33. *NKhSSSR v 1980,* pp. 336–37.

34. M. Gardner Clark, "Soviet Agricultural Policy," in *Soviet Agriculture: An Assessment of its Contributions to Economic Development,* ed. Harry G. Shaffer (New York: Praeger Publishers, 1977), p. 2.

35. James Millar in his introduction to James R. Millar, ed., *The Soviet Rural Community* (Urbana: University of Illinois Press, 1971), pp. xii–xiii.

36. Alec Nove, *The Soviet Economic System* (London: Allen & Unwin Ltd., 1977), p. 131.

37. *Ibid.*

38. 1950 figure from *NKhSSSR v 1963,* p. 453; 1961 figure, *NKhSSSR v 1962,* p. 434.

39. Lazar Volin, *A Century of Russian Agriculture From Alexander II to Khrushchev* (Cambridge: Harvard University Press, 1970), p. 349.

40. *NKhSSSR v 1962,* p. 453.

41. See Table 6.3

42. *NKhSSSR v 1963,* p. 545.

43. Derived from *Narkhoz v 1962,* p. 456.

44. Folk Dovring, "Mechanization in Soviet Agriculture," in James Millar, *The Soviet Rural Community,* p. 260.

45. J. Stalin, "Reports to the 17th and 18th Party Congress" in Joseph Stalin, *Leninism: Selected Writings* (New York: International Publishers, 1942), p. 326.

46. *Ibid.*

47. *NKhSSSR v 1970,* p. 381.

48. N. Anisimov, *Razvitiye Sel'skovo Khozyaistvo v Pyatol Pyatiletke* (Moscow: Gospolizdat, 1958), p. 134.

49. *Ibid.*

50. Lazar Volin, *A Century of Russian Agriculture* (Cambridge, Mass: Harvard University Press, 1970), p. 313.

51. *Ibid.*

52. Decree of 24 October 1948. Translated in *Notes et Etudes Documentaires* No. 1007, 23 February 1949. (*Paris:* Documentation Francaise).

53. Volin, *Century,* p. 319.

54. Volin, *Century,* p. 318.

55. Volin, *Century,* p. 319.

56. *NKhSSSR v 1980,* p. 239.

57. Volin, *Century,* p. 319.

58. *Ibid.*

59. In 1953 the irrigated land area was 8.7 million hectares. *NKhSSSR v 1958,* p. 441.

60. See his speeches of 14 August and 16 September 1963. N.S. Khrushshev, *Stroitel'stvo Kommunizma v SSSR i Razvitie Sel'skovo Khozyaistva* (Moscow: Politizdat, 1964), pp. 91, 125.

61. *NKhSSSR v 1980,* p. 239.

62. Capital stock in 1965 was 5 times that of 1940; GNP in 1915 was 5.7 times as large. Capital stock in 1975 was 11 times that of 1940; GNP in 1975 was 11 times as large. *NKhSSSR v 1980,* p. 37.

63. Martin McCauley, *Khrushchev and the Development of Soviet Agriculture: The Virgin Land Program 1953–1964* (New York: Holmes & Meir, 1976).

64. *Narodnoye Khozyaistvo SSSR Za 60 Let,* p. 303.

65. Sown area in 1953 was 157 million hectares. *NKhSSSR v 1965,* p. 308.

66. McCauley, "Khrushchev and the Development," p. 23.

67. *Ibid.,* p. 15.

68. *Ibid.*, p. 17.

69. See his address delivered at the conference of Marxist Students in the Agrarian Question, 17 December 1929. Reprinted in J. S. Stalin *Leninism: Selected Writings* (New York: International Publishers, 1942), p. 153.

70. Frank A. Durgin, Jr., "The Virgin Lands Programme 1954–1960," *Soviet Studies* XIII, no. 3 (January 1962): 255–56.

71. Maurice Dobb, *Soviet Economic Development*, p. 225.

72. For an excerpt, see McCauley, "Khrushchev and the Development," p. 24.

73. Reprinted in Leninism: Selected Writings, *op. cit.*, p. 320.

74. McCauley, "Khrushchev and the Development," p. 25.

75. F. A. Durgin Jr., "Virgin Lands," p. 256.

76. McCauley, "Khrushchev and the Development," p. 30.

77. *Ibid.*, p. 56.

78. Soviet GNP was 155 billion in 1934, 250 billion in 1940, and 558 billion in 1958. Moorsteen and Powell, *Soviet Capital Stock*, pp. 361–62.

79. Edward Crankshaw, "Russia's Food Supply," *The Listener*, 11 November 1954.

80. Annual Economic Report for 1954, *Pravda*, 21 January 1955.

81. See F. A. Durgin, Jr., "Virgin Lands," pp. 259, 264, who cites *Selskoye Khozyaistvo SSSR*.

82. *Ekonomika Selskovo Khozyaistva* no. 12 (1960): 8 and Khrushchev's speech of 23 February 1954.

83. McCauley, *op cit.*, p. 56.

84. Stalin, *Leninism*, p. 322.

85. Sidney I. Ploss, *Conflict and Decision-Making in Soviet Russia: A Case Study of Agricultural Policy, 1953–1963*, (Princeton, NJ: Princeton University Press, 1965), p. 67.

86. McCauley, "Khrushchev and the Development," pp. 50–51.

87. Robert C. Stuart, *The Collective Farm in Soviet Agriculture* (Lexington, Mass.: D.C. Heath and Company, 1972), p. 3.

88. *NKhSSSR v 1958*, p. 494.

89. *NKhSSSR v 1980*, p. 254.

90. *NKhSSSR v 1980*, p. 263.

91. *NKhSSSR v 1962*, p. 368; *NKhSSSR v 1980*, p. 282.

92. *NKhSSSR v 1958*, p. 396; *NKhSSSR v 1980*, p. 271.

93. *NKhSSSR v 1963*, p. 396; *NKhSSSR v 1980*, p. 208.

94. *NKhSSSR v 1958*, p. 396; *NKhSSSR v 1980*, p. 225.

95. *NKhSSSR v 1963*, p. 230; *NKhSSSR v 1980*, p. 208.

96. This is not to deny Stalin's role in foisting that dogma in the first instance.

97. The budgetary estimates were that the tax on the private plots would be reduced by some 4.1 billion rubles in 1953 and by some 8.2 billion in 1954. Although the 8.2 billion reduction amounted to only 1.1 percent of 1952 budgetary revenues, it amounted to over 80 percent of the yield of the tax on the private plots in 1952.

98. Volin, *Century*, p. 246.

99. The volume of food sales through this network in 1952 was more than double that of 1940. *NKhSSSR v 1959*, p. 723.

100. *Ibid.*, p. 707. The kolkhoz market share of total food sales in 1950 was 18.1 percent, compared with 20.2 percent in 1940.

101. See Marshall I. Goldman, *Soviet Marketing* (London: Collier-MacMillan Ltd., 1963), p. 88.

102. *NKhSSSR v 1959*, p. 970. Lynn Turgeon has argued that there is an inverse relationship between prices on the kolkhoz market and those in the government and cooperative retail outlets. See Lynn Turgeon, *The Contrasting Economies: The Study of Modern Economic Systems* 2d ed. (Boston: Allyn and Bacon Inc., 1969), p. 225.

103. See *Selskoye Khozyaistvo SSSR, Statisticheski Sbornik* (Moscow: Statisika 1960), p. 117.

104. *Pod Znamenem Marksizma*, nos. 7–8, (1943): pp. 70, 72.

105. *Ibid.*

106. J. Stalin, *Economic Problems of Socialism in the USSR*. (Moscow: Foreign Languages Publishing House, 1952), pp. 11–12.

107. *Ibid.*, pp. 19–20.

108. M. F. Makarova, *O Tavarnom Proizvodstve i Zakone Stoimosti Pri Sotsoializma* (Moscow: Gospolizdat, 1958).

109. G. N. Khudokormov, *O Tovarnom Proizvodstve i Zakone Stoimosti Pri Sotsializma* (Moscow: Visshaya Shkola, 1962).

110. They rose from 3.9 billion rubles in 1953 to 12.34 billion in 1959. In 1965 they reached some 21 billion rubles and in 1978 some 45 billion. *NKhSSSR v 1962,* p. 342; *NKhSSSR v 1978,* p. 258.

111. J. Stalin, *Economic Problems of Socialism* (Peking: Foreign Languages Press, 1972), p. 12.

112. *Ibid.,* p. 17.

113. J. Stalin, "Economic Problems.." *op cit.,* p. 13; Citing Lenin's "The Tax in Kind."

114. *Ibid.,* pp. 13–14.

115. *Ibid.,* pp. 15, 16.

116. Robert Conquest, *Power and Policy in the U.S.S.R.* (London: MacMillan & Co., 1961), p. 195.

117. "Problems.." *op. cit.,* p. 15.

118. Martin McCauley, "Khrushchev and the Development," p. 14.

119. This speech is reprinted in Edward Crankshaw, *Khrushchev Remembers* (Boston, Toronto: Little, Brown and Co., 1970).

120. *Ibid.,* pp. 610–11.

121. See Edward Crankshaw, *Khrushchev Remembers,* pp. 610–11.

122. Roy Medvedev, "The Stalin Question" in Cohen, *The Soviet Union Since Stalin* (Bloomington: Indiana University Press, 1980), p. 44.

123. See Edward Crankshaw, *Khrushchev Remembers.*

124. *Ibid.,* p. 610.

125. Roy D. Laird, "Soviet Goals for 1965 and the Problems of Agriculture," *Slavic Review* XX, no. 3 (October 1961): pp. 454–464. Reprinted in Harry G. Shaffer, *The Soviet Economy* (New York: Appleton-Century Crofts, 1963), pp. 144–45.

126. J. S. Stalin, *Economic Problems of Socialism,* pp. 94–95.

127. Translated in *The New York Times,* 9 February 1955, p. 2.

7

Changes in the Soviet Model of Rural Transformation

Alfred Evans, Jr.

INTRODUCTION

During the Brezhnev and Andropov periods the Soviet model of rural transformation has undergone a number of interrelated changes associated with the transition to a mature economy in the USSR. Powerful elements of continuity with previous rural economic and social policies persist. Soviet leaders are trying to make the framework inherited from the Stalin years work better. Yet in their attempts to achieve that objective, they have accepted significant modifications in the design and interrelationship of factors of rural change.

The Soviet model of rural transformation is a construct that forms a meaningful whole in the outlook of Soviet leaders. The model consists of objectives for rural economic and social change. Inferences about that model may be drawn from the statements of leaders, from the writings of Soviet ideologists and social scientists, from concrete policy commitments, and from the actual achievements of policy. However, we must be careful to keep in mind the distinction between hopes and reality. Objectives may not always be translated into consistent commitments of resources, and even the desired resource allocations may not always produce the intended results. The inconsistent execution of policy prescriptions and disappointing returns to policy outputs have plagued Soviet policies toward rural society in the Brezhnev period.

This essay attempts to place recent changes in Soviet policies toward agriculture and rural society in a comparative perspective, in order to make it possible to understand such changes as the parts of a single, coherent pattern. The thesis of the essay is that changes in the Soviet model of rural transformation show evidence of efforts to assimilate trends typical of rural social and economic life in countries with mature industrial economies.[1] Common features of rural social and economic change in mature industrial

The author of this essay would like to express his gratitude to Robert Stuart, Barbara Severin, D. Loy Bilderback, Don Leet, and John Tinker for the valuable criticisms and suggestions they offered.

societies will be described. The conditions that have impelled revision in the Soviet approach to rural social and economic development will be suggested. Changes in the Soviet model of rural transformation since the middle 1960s will be reviewed. However, it will be noted that the success of the revised Soviet model of rural transformation is still in doubt.

COMMON FEATURES OF RURAL ECONOMIC AND SOCIAL CHANGE IN COUNTRIES WITH MATURE INDUSTRIAL ECONOMIES

The experience of societies with mature industrial economies reveals some common, general tendencies of change in agriculture and rural social life.[2] The first change in rural areas associated with the achievement of a mature industrial economy is an increase in the capital-intensiveness of agricultural production.[3] Capital assets per worker increase. While the number of workers in agriculture decreases, output per worker rises. Among all forms of agricultural capital, farm machinery and motorized vehicles tend to show the highest rate of growth. Mechanization of agricultural labor is associated with increasing investment in land improvement and agricultural chemicals.[4]

The movement to capital-intensive, mechanized agricultural production is connected with changes in the structure of the agribusiness sector.[5] The dependence of agricultural producers on other components of the agribusiness complex grows. Agricultural producers depend on larger amounts of off-farm inputs. Employment in the production of supplies for agriculture grows, and so does employment in the processing and marketing of agricultural products, though employment in agriculture itself declines. As industrial components play larger roles, there are greater awareness of interdependence within the agribusiness sector and greater need for administrative coordination within that sector. One of the major structural trends in American agribusiness has been the spread of various forms of vertical integration.[6] Greater interdependence and demands for higher-level integration are also the result of growing specialization in agriculture. It becomes more common for a farm to concentrate primarily on growing one crop or raising one type of livestock. Increases in specialization and interdependence mean continued increases in the commercialization of production; the proportion of each farm's production consumed or used on that farm falls, while the proportion of output that is marketed rises.

The greater integration of agriculture into an interdependent economy contributes to greater social articulation between urban and rural society.[7] Mechanization is usually associated with increases in the number of educated professionals in agriculture. People in specialized occupational roles within the village community accept outside networks as their reference groups. Commercialization and vertical integration bring more frequent contact between farm and nonfarm management. As economic specialization and social differentiation increase within the rural community, more services from outside the community are required. Institutional linkages with the outside world are integrated with local networks of communication. Increased social articulation also is encouraged by other intrusions of the mass society, such as education and mass communications. With increases in commuting and in the location of industry in rural areas, the rural nonfarm population grows. Nonfarm rural residents tend to have social characteristics and attitudes intermediate between those of urban dwellers and rural farm workers. The rural community, formerly isolated, is penetrated by the agents and culture of urban society.[8]

A mature industrial society experiencing the transition to agricultural intensification also seems to be characterized by the narrowing of urban-rural inequality.[9] Increases in material reward for agricultural workers are associated with growth in the productivity of agricultural labor. It becomes difficult to retain skilled workers and professionals in rural settings without social conditions that more closely approximate urban standards. Urban-rural differences in incomes and levels of consumption decrease. Increasing investment in education in rural areas is related to the demand for a skilled agricultural workforce, the need for a skilled industrial workforce (recruited partly from migrants from the countryside), and the insistence of professionals in rural locales on improved educational opportunities for their children. The difference between urban and rural residents in educational attainment narrows. Rural transformation is not limited to agricultural development, but involves a complex pattern of social change as well.

CONDITIONS LEADING TO CHANGE IN THE SOVIET APPROACH TO RURAL TRANSFORMATION

There seem to be four conditions behind the revision of the Soviet model of rural social and economic change. Those conditions are shared by mature industrial economies in general. Each condition was realized in the Soviet Union by the end of World War II or during the ensuing decade and a half. The most basic condition was the achievement of a substantial level of industrial development by the early 1950s. That attainment provided the means to support a higher level of investment in agriculture. It also was the result of a pattern of uneven development. In September 1953 Khrushchev voiced the conviction that the disparity between the rates of growth in the production of industry and agriculture was detrimental to further economic growth.[10]

A second condition recognized by Khrushchev was growth in the demand for food by the urban population of the USSR. The urban population of the Soviet Union had more than tripled between 1926 and 1952 as a result of rapid industrialization.[11] Increases in the wages of Soviet nonagricultural workers also accompanied the expansion of industrial production. The money wages of nonagricultural workers and service employees had risen consistently from 1928 to 1954. However, the real wages of nonagricultural workers and service personnel had declined from 1928 to 1948, during the first Five-Year Plan periods, World War II, and the years of postwar recovery. It was only after the late 1940s that real wages in nonagricultural employment in the USSR began to rise.[12] A sustained increase in the real wages of Soviet workers would be possible only with growth in the production of consumers' goods, including food goods. Further growth in the money incomes of workers' families would particularly stimulate demand for meat, dairy products, vegetables, and fruits. Without increases in the production of food, it would be difficult to offer incentives for increases in the productivity of nonagricultural labor.

A third condition relevant to the future of rural society was the exhaustion of most of the supply of underemployed labor in the Soviet countryside. That supply must have seemed inexhaustible at the time of the collectivization of agriculture. Even after the movement of 24 million people from the countryside to the cities during the 1930s, a substantial pool of underemployed laborers was left in the villages.[13] That surplus was largely wiped out by the war with Germany. Yet the migration from rural to urban areas would continue with further industrialization. Increases in agricultural production could be achieved, not by the introduction of larger amounts of labor, but only by obtaining more production from each available agricultural worker. The enhancement of the productivity of agricultural labor would require increases in the capital-intensiveness of agriculture.[14]

A fourth condition for change was the disappearance of the reserve of unused, arable land in the USSR. The expansion of the area of land used in agriculture was a traditional Russian tendency that continued after the Bolshevik Revolution. The last great burst in the expansion of agricultural land in the USSR occurred during the 1950s. Under Khrushchev, the land under cultivation in the Soviet Union increased about one-fourth. Khrushchev's virgin lands program was a temporary substitute for the full-scale intensification of the use of land already in production. However, by the early 1960s, the prospect of gaining further, substantial increases in agricultural production by adding to the extent of cultivated land had vanished. Natural conditions of temperature, precipitation, and terrain would have made the appropriation of other large areas of land for agricultural production uneconomical and would have added to the unreliability of annual agricultural production.

Continued industrial development, a growing urban workforce, and rising urban incomes compelled Soviet policy-makers to seek increases in agricultural production. The lack of opportunities to introduce more land or labor into agriculture created pressure for the *intensification* of agricultural development, or getting more output from each worker and each hectare of land. In February 1964 Khrushchev called for a decisive turn to the intensification of Soviet agriculture.[15] In terms of the commitment of resources to the intensification of agricultural production, more has been accomplished in the Brezhnev and Andropov periods.

CHANGES IN THE SOVIET MODEL OF
RURAL TRANSFORMATION

The most widely acknowledged change in the Soviet approach to rural transformation has been an increase in investment in the technology of agricultural production. Change in that area has been documented so well that only a brief review of the subject is necessary.[16] Increases in agriculture's share of total investment in the Soviet economy were achieved during the period of recovery after World War II.[17] Khrushchev sporadically encouraged the expansion of investment in agriculture. However, the most consistent and dramatic growth in the proportion of investments devoted to agriculture followed Brezhnev's address to the March 1965 Plenum of the Central Committee of the Communist Party of the Soviet Union.[18] What the Soviets refer to as the "redistribution of resources in favor of agriculture" has brought increases in agricultural mechanization. In the 1970s, emphasis on land improvement and the application of agricultural chemicals was heightened sharply. Capital investments in Soviet agriculture during 1976–1980 were, as Table 7.1 indicates, more than three times greater than in 1961–1965.[19] In 1978, Brezhnev exacted a commitment from the Central Committee to devote at least as high a proportion of total investment to agriculture in the Eleventh Five-Year Plan (1981–1985) as in the preceding plan.[20] In 1982, he emphasized the importance of continuing to place heavy emphasis on investment in agriculture under the Twelfth Five-Year Plan, during the late 1980s.[21] The growth in the capital-intensiveness of Soviet agriculture, shown in Table 7.2, may be expected to continue. However, some Soviet economists call for increases even beyond the planned investment in agriculture. In the mid-1970s two

Table 7.1　Capital Investments in Soviet Agriculture,[a] 1961–1980

Investments	1961–1965	1966–1970	1971–1975	1976–1980
Billions of rubles[b]	48.2	81.5	130.5	171.0
Share of total investments in Soviet economy	19.8%	23.4%	26.5%	27.0%

[a]Includes investments in the "whole complex of work" related to agriculture, such as repair services for agriculture, agricultural research, land reclamation, and the processing of agricultural products, as well as agricultural production itself.

[b]In 1976 prices

Sources: David M. Schoonover, "Soviet Agricultural Policies," in *Soviet Economy in a Time of Change,* ed. John P. Hardt (Washington: U.S. Government Printing Office, 1979), p. 93; *Narodnoe khoziaistvo SSSR v 1980 godu* (Moscow: Statistika, 1981), pp. 337, 340.

Table 7.2   Fixed Capital Per Worker[a] in Collective Farms and
State Farms of the USSR, 1965, 1970, 1975, and 1980

	1965	1970	1975	1980
Fixed capital per worker (rubles)	1,843	2,958	5,433	8,240

[a]Includes only agricultural productive capital; given for the end of each year; valued at purchase prices, without allowance for depreciation. The number of workers is obtained by adding the annual average number of collective farmers, participating in the socialized agriculture of collective farms, to the annual average number of state farm workers. See Eberhard Schinke, "Soviet Agricultural Statistics," in *Soviet Economic Statistics,* ed. Vladimir G. Treml and John P. Hardt (Durham, North Carolina: Duke University Press, 1972), pp. 253–256.

Sources: Editions of *Narodnoe khoziaistvo SSSR* for the years covered.

economists advocated a fivefold increase in the capital funding and energy provision of labor in agriculture.[22]

With growth in capital in agriculture have come demands for the restructuring of organization ties within agriculture, and between agriculture and other branches. Soviet economists have begun to think in terms of their equivalent of the agribusiness sector—the agro-industrial complex (APK). As the concept of the APK has been popularized, greater recognition has been devoted to the interdependence of agriculture and related branches.[23] It is acknowledged that Soviet collective farms and state farms draw a growing proportion of supplies from outside agriculture and ship a larger proportion of their produce to industry for processing. The point has been made that with further modernization of agriculture, the share of industrial branches in the agro-industrial complex will grow. Criticisms are directed at the current weaknesses of integration with the APK. Some scholars suggest unified organizational mechanisms for improving coordination and overcoming excessive departmentalism within the national agro-industrial complex.[24]

Restructuring of linkages between individual productive units within the agro-industrial complex also has been placed on the agenda. Specialization and concentration by agricultural enterprises are strongly endorsed by the consensus of Soviet economists and by the highest leadership.[25] It is said that the production of several different types of crops and animal products by each farm detracts from the efficient use of new technology. With greater specialization, quotas for any one product are to be assigned to a smaller number of collective farms and state farms. Though complaints of lagging in implementation of the goal have been heard, there is evidence of a trend toward greater specialization in Soviet agriculture since 1965.[26] Interfarm cooperation is described as a means of furthering specialization through the creation of associations to relieve existing farms of tasks that now disperse their efforts. The movement toward interfarm associations received Brezhnev's support in 1973 and was approved by a Central Committee resolution in 1976.[27] The number of workers in interfarm enterprises has increased substantially in recent years.[28] The pace of implementation of interfarm cooperation has proved disappointing to the leadership so far. However, it should be remembered that the leadership views itself as pressing for gradual, long-term change.

The Central Committee's 1976 resolution also offered official encouragement for vertical agro-industrial integration. The forms of agro-industrial enterprises and associations vary.[29] The objective in each case is to place several stages in production and processing under the same management. The spread of vertically integrated organizational forms has been slow. However, Robert Miller concludes "there can be little doubt that the regime regards vertically integrated agro-industrial combinations as the ultimate model for Soviet agriculture."[30]

In the current Soviet perspective, agriculture development is part of a broadly based program of rural transformation. One of the distinctive features of contemporary Soviet thought is the realization that change in rural areas cannot be achieved only as the consequence of modernization of agricultural production. Khrushchev shared with Stalin the faith that agricultural mechanization would generate changes in social structure. However, Soviet sources now acknowledge that investment in agricultural mechanization is ineffective without concomitant social advances in rural areas.[31] The model of rural trnasformation of the Brezhnev and Andropov periods stresses the interdependence of a wide range of economic and social factors.[22]

Increasing social articulation between urban and rural society is a major objective of the current model of change. Contemporary Soviet theorists refrain from making a sharp distinction between "urban" and "rural" society, while describing differences of degree between different types of population settlements.[33] The current tendency is to look upon the urban and rural sectors not as polar opposites, but as interrelated parts of a single society. Within the rural sector, the growth of social differentiation is said to lead to greater integration with the rest of society.[34] The argument is that increasing occupational specialization in agriculture leads to the proliferation of social groups among the rural, farm population. Those groups are increasingly differentiated with respect to skills and education. The implication is that rural residents are becoming more differentiated in attitudes also, so that many are losing traditional peasant consciousness. Rural professionals most closely resemble urban residents in education, reading habits, ownership of durable consumer goods, and lack of religious beliefs.[35] Rural specialists are seen as a link between the urban and rural population.

The penetration of urban influences into rural communities through education and mass communications is a traditional objective of the Soviet regime. Contemporary Soviet writers advocate the acceleration of that process.[36] The drive to make ten years of education available throughout the USSR in the 1970s clearly was aimed at universalization of secondary education in the countryside. The proportion of school construction taking place in rural areas increased after 1965, although the percentage of the population living in rural areas was declining.[37] The number of rural libraries, clubs, and movie theaters has risen.[38] The trend toward widespread ownership of television sets in rural areas since the early 1970s means greater exposure to mass communications from urban centers.

A variety of means are thought to further social integration between town and country. One of the benefits of agro-industrial integration is said to be closer social linkage between agricultural and nonagricultural workers. The employees of agro-industrial associations and enterprises are categorized as an intermediate group with a synthesis of social traits.[39] (However, research on the social consequences of vertical integration in the agro-industrial complex in the USSR is still in a preliminary stage.) Some authors favor the development of industrial subdivisions of collective and state farms as a means of providing work for farmers in the seasons of slackened agricultural activity.[40] The location of more industry in rural areas is now seen as essential for the development of towns as centers serving the rural population. The former view that "the Soviet countryside was to be as exclusively as possible an agricultural production area" has been abandoned.[41] The growth of the nonagricultural rural population is considered a positive tendency.[42] Nonfarm rural people now constitute two-fifths of all rural residents in the Soviet Union.[43] The increase in commuting (*maiatnikovaia migratsiia*) from the villages to the cities is described as a natural tendency of "urbanization" of the rural way of life.[44] Nonfarm rural dwellers and commuters from rural areas are depicted as agents of social articulation between urban and rural society. A gesture of encouragement for urban-rural social integration was offered with the regime's announcement in the mid-1970s of the decision to issue internal passports to collective farm members.[45]

The reduction of inequality between the urban and rural population in the distribution of material benefits is another objective of the current Soviet leadership. In his speech to the Twenty-Fifth Party Congress, Brezhnev referred to the "equalization of the material and cultural conditions of life of the city and countryside" as a programmatic goal of the Party.[46] Increases in the wages and incomes of Soviet agricultural workers have played a part in urban-rural equalization. The "revolution" in the earnings of collective farmers and state farmers began during the Khrushchev years, with the raising of the purchase prices paid to farms for agricultural products and the institution of practices ensuring greater stability in compensation for collective farm workers. The earnings of kolkhozniki and sovkhozniki from work in socialized agriculture rose quickly in the middle 1950s and early 1960s. As a result, differences in compensation between industrial and agricultural labor decreased markedly.[47] Further increases in wages in

Soviet agriculture were granted in the Brezhnev period. The old labor-day system was replaced by a scale of regular wages in collective farms similar to that in state farms. Increases in the Soviet minimum wage raised the earnings of unskilled farm workers. A national, state-regulated system of social insurance for collective farmers was introduced in 1965. Increases in pensions for retired collective farmers were enacted subsequently. The incomes of farm workers' families have continued to rise since 1965. However, the differences between wages in industry, state farms, and collective farms have remained fairly stable since the late 1960s.[48]

Khrushchev tried to stimulate agricultural production by increasing the earnings of collective farmers and state farmers. He expected that with the growth of agricultural production, collective farms and state farms would have more funds to invest in improving living conditions. A broader approach is offered by the current leadership. Wage increases alone will not retain qualified personnel in rural areas as long as living conditions there remain backward. Without the retention (*zakreplenie*) of educated specialists and trained mechanizers in rural areas, the industrialization of agriculture cannot succeed.[49] The problem of the inferior level of living in the villages must be attacked directly, in conjunction with measures for expanding agricultural production. While before it was argued that advances in production would cause a rise in the level of living, now it is said that improvement in the rural level of living is also necessary for growth in production.[50]

Trends toward equalization of a number of indicators of urban and rural living levels have been established in the USSR.[51] In 1965, the surtax on goods sold through rural cooperative stores was abolished. Since 1965, the increase in retail trade in rural areas, both in proportion to rural population and as a percentage of that in urban areas, has been speeded up.[52] A strong trend toward equalization of the volume of retail services per capita in urban and rural areas has set in. Ownership of several types of durable consumer goods, such as refrigerators, washing machines, and television sets, has become more common among rural families.[53] Urban-rural inequality in the possession of most consumer durables has decreased. The connection of rural homes with electrical networks was virtually completed during the 1970s.[54] The equipping of homes in the countryside with gas connections increased sharply after 1965 and began to approach the rate in urban areas.

Growth in public services in rural areas was achieved during the Brezhnev period, but in somewhat uneven fashion. Urban-rural inequality in enrollments in public nursery schools, kindergartens, and other institutions for preschool children decreased, though the gap between city and countryside remains very wide.[55] The drive to extend full secondary education to the villages has been associated with increases in rural educational attainments. Urban-rural inequality in rates of completion of secondary education has continued to decrease steadily.[56] Inequality between urban and rural residents in the proportion of the population having completed higher education remains extremely high. There is little evidence concerning trends in the relationship between urban and rural health care. The number of physicians in rural areas has risen only slightly since 1965, but the disparity in the availability of hospital care between urban and rural dwellers seems to have been reduced.[57]

The worst bottleneck in changing rural living conditions is construction. The Soviet Communist Party's Central Committee adopted a resolution in 1978 calling for greater attention to rural construction needs. A separate Ministry of Rural Construction was organized in 1969. However, plans for the reconstruction of rural settlements remain underfulfilled.[58] The building of new homes for rural residents has remained a low priority for public investments. There have been complaints of slowness in the construction of new centers of public services. Most seriously, no adequate program for providing improved roads for the Soviet countryside has as yet been undertaken. Poor roads and seasonal roadlessness are among the most important causes of the isolation of village communities.[59] Construction enterprises and associations have not been given the resources to cope with the necessary tasks; the construction industry is notoriously inefficient in the use of the resources allocated to it; and the construction of facilities used in production continues to have first claim on labor and materials.

CONCLUSION

The Soviet model of rural transformation recently has been subjected to changes reminiscent of trends in other industrialized countries. First, massive increases in investment in agriculture have brought growth in agricultural mechanization, in programs of land reclamation, and in the application of agricultural chemicals. Capital per worker in Soviet agriculture has increased rapidly. Second, Soviet economists and political leaders have shown awareness of the need for more effective coordination of the components of the agro-industrial complex. Interfarm cooperation and agro-industrial integration have become the watchwords of the day for Soviet agriculture. Specialization and concentration of production are among the primary objectives of organizational restructuring. Third, growth in the complexity of rural social structure is not merely tolerated, but is welcomed for its contribution to articulation between urban and rural society. Fourth, inequality between the urban and rural population has been reduced. To the trend after 1953 of decreases in the difference between the incomes of farm and nonfarm families have been added since 1965 trends of decreasing inequality in the provision of a number of goods and services to urban and rural dwellers. Though a pervasive sense of the inferiority of rural life is still felt in most areas of the USSR, signs of progress in decreasing urban-rural inequality are unmistakable.

The result of recent changes should be described, not as the creation of an entirely new Soviet model of rural transformation, but as the acceptance of revisions in the Soviet model of rural transformation. The approach of the current leadership represents a synthesis of features of Soviet tradition dating from the collectivization of agriculture and the establishment of central planning with elements common to the experience of many industrial societies. Now that the outlines of the revised Soviet approach to agricultural development and rural social change have emerged fairly clearly,[60] the question of the effects of blending efforts to imitate tendencies of change in other industrialized countries with the patterns of rural economic organization and the rural social heritage distinctive to the Soviet Union may be raised. The question of the results of such a blending is raised here; to attempt to answer it would require a much broader study. Only a few tentative remarks on the relationship between the Stalinist, Soviet tradition and recent changes in rural development policy will be offered.

Stalin established a pattern of uneven economic development in the Soviet Union. Unever development was accompanied by policies of exclusion of the peasants from the growing urban society, and increases in inequality between the urban and rural population.[61] The Brezhnev leadership sought to overcome unevenness of development. In a "developed socialist society" (a socialist system of the Soviet type, with a fairly mature industrial base) the potential created by decades of industrial growth is used to raise up the less-developed sectors of the economy. The regime strives to eliminate the inconsistencies between subsystems. Evening up of sectors of the economy is tied to attempts at the integration of previously excluded groups into the system. The developed socialist society is said to be distinguished by a higher level of wholeness or integration (*tselostnost'*).[62] But it should be remembered that in the Soviet Union, changes in the leadership's perceptions and prescriptions have run ahead of changes in practice.

Efforts of the current Andropov leadership and those of Brezhnev to overcome the results of uneven development have not been entirely successful. The psychological heritage of the Stalinist period in agriculture is not easily effaced.[63] While the Soviets are attempting to make a transition to highly mechanized, large-scale, vertically integrated agribusiness, a transition begun only in recent decades in Western countries, they still are trying to eradicate the attitudes associated with subsistence-oriented peasant farming, left behind in the West much earlier during the transition to small-scale, partially mechanized, predominantly commercial agricultural. The Stalinist pattern of neomanorial agriculture perpetuated traditional peasant attitudes. Collective farm peasants looked on the requirement of labor in socialized agriculture as a levy to which they had to submit in order to obtain permission to engage in private plot farming. The peasant family relied on its private plot, primarily for satisfaction of its own consumption needs, and also to provide most of its modest cash income. The state also used the *corvée* liberally, mobilizing large amounts of unskilled labor to perform occasional tasks on and off the farm. The tradition of the peasant household as the basic unit of labor-intensive, self-sustaining farming was reinforced by the system of agriculture of the Stalin years.[64]

Since 1953, Soviet leaders have increased the remuneration of labor in socialized agriculture. But incentives remain a key problem. The relationship between regard and the laborer's contribution to production is tenuous. It is not certain that increases in wages and the expansion of spending from social consumption funds are strengthening feelings of responsibility and initiative among the workers in Soviet state farms and collective farms. A prominent Soviet writer, Fëdor Abramov, argues that the contrary tendency has set in. He accuses collective farmers of regarding increased material benefits as a gift from the state. Abramov describes a psychology of dependency among farm workers and complains that pride in work has declined since the earlier days of peasant household farming.[65] As the proportion of agricultural production coming from private plots decreases, the need to rationalize incentives and success indicators in socialized agriculture becomes even more serious. The marginal returns to investment in agriculture are steadily decreasing. Pouring more resources into Soviet agriculture seems to reveal more clearly the inefficiency of its organization. However, while revisions in the Soviet model of rural transformation have included a significant reallocation of resources, they have not extended to fundamental structural changes.

NOTES

1. The term *mature industrial economy* refers here to a stage defined some years ago by W. W. Rostow as the *stage of maturity,* following the early decades of industrialization. It is not suggested here that the Soviet Union has reached the stage of advanced industrial society, which Rostow termed the stage of *mass consumption.* Rostow estimated that the USA reached the stage of maturity about 1900, while the Soviet Union attained that stage around 1950. Rostow, *The Stages of Economic Growth* (Cambridge: Cambridge University Press, 1960), pp. 9–10, 59.

2. The principal sources of the generalizations that follow are Everett M. Rogers and Rabel J. Burdge, *Social Change in Rural Societies,* 2d. ed. (New York: Appleton-Century-Crofts, 1972); Lee Taylor and Arthur R. Jones, Jr., *Rural Life and Urbanized Society* (New York: Oxford University Press, 1964); and Irwin T. Sanders, *Rural Society* (Englewood Cliffs, New Jersey: Prentice-Hall, 1977). To date, most of the comparative generalizations in rural sociology pertain to early trends of modernization in peasant societies. Relatively little study has been devoted to common trends in agriculture and rural society in mature industrial societies. Thus the generalizations offered below should be regarded as tentative, and in need of testing with respect to a wider range of countries.

3. Rogers and Burdge, *Social Change,* 129; T. Lynn Smith and Paul E. Zopf, Jr., *Principles of Inductive Rural Sociology* (Philadelphia: F. A. Davis Company, 1970), p. 233; Milton M. Snodgrass and Luther T. Wallace, *Agriculture, Economics, and Growth,* 2d. ed. (New York: Appleton-Century-Crofts, 1970), p. 105.

4. The relationship between investment in mechanization and investment in land reclamation and agricultural chemicals varies from one country to another. The distinction between labor-intensive and capital-intensive agricultural development by Yujiro Hayami and Vernon Ruttan, in *Agricultural Development: An International Perspective* (Baltimore: Johns Hopkins University Press, 1971), pp. 44–45, pertains to the relative abundance of different types of inputs for agriculture. That distinction suggests the need to keep in mind the point that, while there are some common features in rural social and economic activity in industrialized countries, there are also some important differences among such countries with respect to trends in rural areas.

5. Rogers and Burdge, *Social Change,* pp. 138–149; Taylor and Jones, *Rural Life,* pp. 219–21, 309–27; Gail L. Cramer and Clarence W. Jensen, *Agricultural Economics and Agribusiness* (New York: John Wiley and Sons, 1979), pp. 27–39.

6. *Vertical integration* refers to coordination under the same management of two or more stages in the supplying of materials, and producing, processing, and distributing products.

7. The term *social articulation* refers to social linkage or interaction between urban and rural society (Sanders, *Rural Society,* pp. 6–8). For analyses of trends of urban rural social ar-

ticulation, see *idem.*, pp. 152-158; Rogers and Burdge, *Social Change*, pp. 4-10, 278-80; Taylor and Jones, *Rural Life*, pp. 32, 57-63, 93-107.

8. The classic description of that phenomenon in the United States is by Arthur J. Vidich and Joseph Bensman, *Small Town in Mass Society* (Princeton, New Jersey: Princeton University Press, 1968).

9. Taylor and Jones, *Rural Life*, pp. 57, 418. However, it should be noted that even in an advanced industrial society such as the United States, despite a very high level of capitalization of agriculture, there remains a measurable gap between the urban and rural population in income, levels of consumption, and educational attainment.

10. Nikita S. Khrushchev, "O merakh dal'neishego razvitiia sel'skogo khoziaistva SSSR," Doklad na Plenume TsK KPSS, 3 September 1953, *Stroitel'stvo kommunizma v SSSR i razvitie sel'skogo khoziaistva,* vol. 1 (Moscow: Politizdat, 1962), p. 10.

11. *Ibid.*

12. Janet Chapman, *Real Wages in Soviet Russia Since 1928* (Cambridge, Mass.: Harvard University Press, 1963), p. 144.

13. M. A. Vyl'tsan, "Trudovye resursy kolkhozov v dovoennye gody (1935-1940 gg.)," *Voprosy istorii* (2 February 1973): 31. Losses of life in rural areas during the "liquidation of the kulaks" in the late twenties and early thirties and the Stalinist terror of the late thirties should also be noted.

14. Growing scarcity of agricultural labor after World War II encouraged the growth of capital in agriculture and increases in wages in agriculture. It might be noted that a sharp decrease in the number of draft animals in Soviet agriculture during the early nineteen thirties had been followed by an increase in the production of tractors. At each stage from the nineteen thirties on, increases in the mechanization of Soviet agriculture can be interpreted partly in terms of factor substitution.

15. Khrushchev, "Intensifikatsiia proizvodstva—glavnoe napravlenie v razvitii sel'skogo khoziaistva," Rech' na Plenume TsK KPSS, 14 February 1964, *Stroitel'stvo kommunizma v SSSR,* vol. 8, pp. 388-91.

16. Among many excellent summaries of trends in Soviet agriculture since 1965 are Keith Bush, "Soviet Agriculture: Ten Years Under New Management," in *Economic Development in the Soviet Union and Eastern Europe,* vol. 2, ed. Zbigniew M. Fallenbuchl (New York: Praeger, 1976), pp. 157-204; David W. Carey and Joseph F. Havelka, "Soviet Agriculture: Progress and Problems," in *Soviet Economy in a Time of Change,* vol. 2, ed. John P. Hardt (Washington: U.S. Government Printing Office, 1979), pp. 55-86; and David M. Schoonover, "Soviet Agricultural Policies," pp. 87-115.

17. See the article by Frank Durgin in this collection.

18. Leonid I. Brezhnev, "O neotlozhnyky merakh po dal'neishemu razvitiiu sel'skogo khoziaistva SSSR," Doklad na Plenume TsK KPSS, 24 March 1965, *Leninskim kursom,* vol. 1 (Moscow: Politizdat, 1970), pp. 66-100.

19. The reference here is to investments in agriculture and closely related services, as explained in connection with Table 7.1. The statement also would hold true if applied only to investments in agricultural production itself. *Narodnoe khoziaistvo SSSR v 1980 godu* (Moscow: Statistika, 1981), pp. 341.

20. "Central Committee Meets on Agriculture," *The Current Digest of the Soviet Press,* XXX, no. 27 (2 August 1978): p. 13 (hereafter *CDSP*). Of course the implementation of that decision would raise the actual amount of investment in agriculture in the current plan period.

21. Leonid I. Brezhnev, "O prodovol'stvennoi programme SSSR na period do 1990 goda i merakh po eë realizatsii," *Pravda*, 25 May 1982, pp. 1-2.

22. Aleksandr A. Barsov and Lev V. Nikiforov, *Agrarno-promyshlennye kompleksy i sblizhenie dvukh form sotsialisticheskoi sobstvennosti* (Moscow: Znanie, 1976), pp. 22-23. A Soviet sociologist has advised that "for the effective development of agriculture on an industrial basis it is necessary to increase its fixed capital by two and one half to three times by 1990." Vladimir I. Staroverov, "Preodolcnic sotsial'nykh razlichii mezhdu gorodom i drevnei," in *Sotsial'naia struktura razvitogo sotsialisticheskogo obshchestva v SSSR,* ed. M. N. Rutkevich (Moscow: Nauka, 1976), p. 107.

23. Barsov and Nikiforov, *Agrarno-promyshlennye,* pp. 17, 43; Lev V. Nikiforov, "Socioeconomic Problems in the Industrialization of Agricultural Production," *Problems of*

Economics XIX, no. 3 (July 1976): 85 (reprinted from *Ekonomicheskie nauki,* 1975, 3); "Central Committee Meets on Agriculture," p. 9.

24. Barsov and Nikiforov, *Agarno-promyshlennye,* pp. 27–29; Nikiforov, "Socioeconomic Problems," p. 87; I. N. Buzdalov, "Agrarno-promyshlennaia integratsiia kak uslovie i forma sotsial'no-ekonomicheskikh preobrazvanii v derevne," in *Problemy preodoleniia sotsial'no-ekonomicheskikh razlichii mezhdu gorodom i derevnei,* ed. E. I. Kapustin (Moscow: Nauka, 1976), pp. 95–96.

25. Barsov and Nikiforov, *Agarno-promyshlennye,* pp. 16, 33; G. Loza and I. Kurtsev, "The Growth of Productive Forces in Agriculture in the Tenth Five-Year Plan," *Problems of Economics* XIX, no. 10 (February 1977): 6–7 (reprinted from *Voprosy ekonomiki,* 1976, p. 7); Brezhnev, "O. neotlozhnykh. merakh," p. 15.

26. Kenneth R. Gray, "Soviet Agricultural Specialization and Efficiency," *Soviet Studies* XXXI, no. 4 (October 1979): 546–47.

27. Schoonover, "Soviet Agricultural Politics," pp. 106–108.

28. According to *Narkhoz 1980,* p. 262, the number of workers in interfarm enterprises (other than construction enterprises) increased from 78,700 in 1970 to 713,200 in 1980.

29. See articles by Valentin Litvin and Everett Jacobs in this volume.

30. Robert F. Miller, "The Politics of Policy Implementation in the USSR: Soviet Policies on Agricultural Integration Under Brezhnev," *Soviet Studies* XXXII, no. 2 (April 1980): 179.

31. P. Simush, "Social Changes in the Countryside," *The Soviet Review,* XIX, no. 2 (Summer 1978): p. 37 (reprinted from *Kommunist,* 1976, p. 16). Brezhnev, in "Central Committee Meets on Agriculture," p. 3: "In today's conditions, the development of the productive forces of agriculture is linked in an especially close way with the resolution of the social questions of rural life."

32. Theodore H. Friedgut, "Integration of the Rural Sector into Soviet Society," *Slavic and Soviet Series,* Tel-Aviv University, III, no. 1 (Spring 1978): 29.

33. Staroverov, "Preodolenie Sotsial'nykh," p. 102.

34. Iurii V. Arutiunian, *Sotsial'naia struktura sel'skogo naseleniia SSSR* (Moscow: Mysl', 1971), p. 335.

35. Ian Hill, "The End of the Russian Peasantry?" *Soviet Studies* XXVII, no. 1 (January 1975): 109–27.

36. Arutiunian, "Sotsial'naia struktura," pp. 142–144; A. V. Vorontsov, *Kul'turnyi progress sovremennogo sela* (Moscow: Znanie, 1979), pp. 48–50.

37. Friedgut, "Integration of the Rural Sector," pp. 31–32.

38. Staroverov, "Preodolenie sotsial'nykh, pp. 142–43.

39. Vladimir I. Staroverov, "Sotsial'nye rezul'taty i posledstviia mezhkhoziaistvennoi kooperatsii i agropromyshlennoi integratsii," *Sotsiologicheskie issledovaniia,* 1979, pp. 4, 63–76; Simush, "Differences Between Town and Country in Light of the Development of the Socialist Way of Life," *The Soviet Review* XVII, no. 1 (Spring 1976): 32–33 (reprinted from *Voprosy filosofii,* 1975, p. 3).

40. Karl-Eugen Wädekin, "The Nonagricultural Rural Sector," in *The Soviet Rural Community,* ed. James R. Millar (Urbana, Illinois: University of Illinois Press, 1971), p. 160; Simush, "Differences Between Town and Country," p. 31. However, there is still controversy over the wisdom of placing industrial subdivisions on the farms. For an exchange of views on the subject, see *CDSP,* XXXII, no. 47 (24 December 1980): 1–3.

41. Wädekin, "Nonagricultural Rural Sector," pp. 160.

42. *Ibid.*; V. M. Selunskaia, *Izmenenie sotsial'noi struktury sovetskoi derevni* (Moscow: Znanie, 1979), pp. 45–46.

43. Staroverov, "Preodolenie sotsial'nykh razlichii," pp. 113.

44. Wädekin, "Nonagricultural Rural Sector," pp. 171; I. M. Taborisskaia, *Maiatnikovaia migratsiia naseleniia* (Moscow: Statistika, 1979), p. 40.

45. Friedgut, "Integration of the Rural Sector," pp. 32. The internal passport is necessary for legal changes of residence in the USSR. Its denial to collective farmers in the nineteen thirties was a token of exclusion of peasants from urban society.

46. Leonid I. Brezhnev, *Leninskim kursom,* vol. 5 (Moscow: Politizdat, 1976), p. 503.

47. David W. Bronson and Constance B. Krueger, "The Revolution in Soviet Farm Household Income, 1953-1967," in *The Soviet Rural Community,* pp. 228–29. For a detailed

analysis of data on Soviet agricultural incomes and rural living standards, see the article by Gertrude Schroeder in this collection.

48. Alfred Evans, Jr., "Agricultural Policy and Urban-Rural Equalization in the Soviet Union" (Paper presented at the Annual Convention of the American Association for the Advancement of Slavic Studies, Columbus, Ohio, October, 1978).

49. Khrushchev was conscious of the difficulty of retaining specialists and mechanizers in rural areas. However, during the period of his leadership, the introduction of measures that brought about increases in the incomes of collective farmers and state farm workers was virtually the sole response to that problem by the regime. In the Brezhnev period, the regime has undertaken a broader, more multifaced (though still incomplete) response to the problem.

50. Lev. V. Nikiforov, "Preodolenie sotsial'no-ekonomicheskikh razlichii mezhdu gorodom i derevnei," *Voprosy ekonomiki* 2, (1975): 3-14; "Central Committee Meets on Agriculture," pp. 3, 11; Brezhnev, "O prodovol'stvennoi programme SSSR," p. 2.

51. Alfred Evans, Jr., "Equalization of Urban and Rural Living Levels in Soviet Society," *Soviet Union* VIII, no. 1. (1981): 38-61.

52. *Ibid.*, p. 50; includes only retail trade in state and cooperative stores. In 1979, retail trade per capita in rural areas was 44 percent of the rate in urban areas. *Narkhoz 1979,* p. 453. It should be noted that rural residents of the USSR buy about 40 percent of their nonfood goods in urban stores.

53. Evans, "Equalization of Urban and Rural Living Levels," p. 49. Ownership of television sets per 100 rural families rose from fifteen in 1965, or 47 percent of the urban rate, to seventy-one in 1979, or 80 percent of the urban rate; refrigerators, from three in 1965 (18 percent), to 55 in 1979 (57 percent); washing machines, from twelve in 1965 (41 percent) to fifty-six in 1979 (71 percent of the urban rate per 100 families). From figures in *Narkhoz 1979,* p. 434.

54. According to *Narkhoz 1975,* p. 182, by 1974 99 percent of collective farm households and state farmers' homes used electrical energy. However, while almost all rural homes now may be connected with one or another electrical network, the average usage of electrical energy in rural homes remains relatively low. Kira I. Taichinova, "Povyshenie zhiznennogo urovnia sel'skogo naseleniia," *Voprosy ekonomiki* (1974): 59. In Stalin's time, connecting a collective farm with a state electrical network was prohibited by law and punishable as a criminal offense.

55. Evans, "Equalization of Urban and Rural Living Levels," p. 55. In the late nineteen seventies, the rate of enrollment of children in permanent preschool institutions per one thousand of the population (of all ages) in rural areas approached half of that in urban areas. Figuring enrollment in relation to the number of preschool age children would heighten the disadvantage of rural areas, where children make up a larger proportion of the population.

56. *Ibid.,* p. 53.

57. *Ibid.,* pp. 55-56; A. G. Safonov, "Convergence of the Levels of Medical Services to the Urban and Rural Populations," *Soviet Sociology* XVII, no. 3, (Winter 1978-1979): 75-89 (reprinted from *Sovetskoe zdravookhranenie,* 1977, p. 1).

58. Iu. Mezhberg, "Sovremennye problemy pereustroistva sela," *Voprosy ekonomiki* 5 (1978): 78-88; A. I. Iakushov, *Preodolenie sushchestvennykh razlichii mezhdu gorodom i derevnei v usloviiakh razvitogo sotsializma* (Moscow: Vysshaia shkola, 1979), pp. 169-80; "Central Committee Meets on Agriculture," p. 11.

59. See the selection of articles, "Taking a Look at the Bad Roads Problem," *CDSP,* XXXIII, no. 41 (11 November 1981): 11-12.

60. It should be reemphasized that the revised Soviet approach to rural transformation that has been described in this essay is at present a mixture of aspirations and actual achievements.

61. James R. Millar, "Introduction: Themes and Counter-Themes in the Changing Rural Community," in *The Soviet Rural Community,* pp. xi-xii, refers to a "deliberate policy" in the Stalin period "of excluding the rural sector from the main sources as well as the benefits of economic development, which served to perpetuate the traditional social, economic, and religious institutions of rural life in the peasant isolate thereby created." Under Stalin, collective farm peasants did not receive regular wage payments of the sort received by workers in state enterprises; peasants were excluded from coverage by the state pension system; and peasants were denied the internal passports necessary for legal changes of residence. Evidence

on the rural level of living in the Stalin years is fragmentary and does not all point in the same direction. Inequality between the urban and rural population in incomes and in consumption of more desired food products probably increased between the early nineteen thirties and the early nineteen fifties. A surtax was imposed on goods sold in stores in rural areas. However, a tendency toward urban-rural equalization in exposure to primary education was under way during the Stalin years. Alfred Evans, Jr., "The Soviet Regime and the Transformation of Rural Society" (Paper presented at the Annual Convention of the American Association for the Advancement of Slavic Studies, Philadelphia, Pennsylvania, November, 1980).

62. Leonid I. Brezhnez, "O proekte konstitutsii (osnovnogo zakona) souiuza sovetskikh sotsialisticheskikh respublik i itogakh ego vsenarodnogo obsuzhdeniia," 4 October 1977, *Leninskim kursom,* vol. 6, p. 536.

63. Friedgut, "Integration of the Rural Sector," p. 32.

64. That tradition is sustained today by the cultivation of private agricultural plots by collective farm members and others. The share of farm families' incomes derived from work on private plots has decreased gradually. However, attempts by the regime to stimulate production from private plots (personal subsidiary farming), such as those announced by the Central Committee of the CPSU in 1981, may nurture a tradition that runs counter to the complex of other changes sought by the leadership. For the latest and most far-reaching program of encouragement of private plot farming, see "Resolution Boosts Aid to Private Farming," *CDSP,* XXXIII, no. 5 (4 March 1981): 15–17.

65. "The Way We Make Our Living," *CDSP,* XXXI, no. 46 (12 December 1979): 9–10, 14.

PART THREE

Contemporary Soviet Agriculture: Theory and Analysis

8

Factor Endowment, Variable Proportions, and Agricultural Modernization: Regional Production Functions for Soviet Agriculture

Elizabeth Clayton

INTRODUCTION

In recent years, the Soviet Union has given great attention to agricultural modernization and food production, but has experienced difficulty in achieving its goals efficiently, in part because the regions differ so much. The first section of this paper examines the concept of economic efficiency in production and relates it to production function analysis. The second section looks at the effect of factor endowments and regional factor proportions on the methods used to achieve production efficiency. A final section estimates regional production functions and concludes with an assessment of both the empirical estimate and the prospects for gains through the regional reallocation of factors.

AGRICULTURAL MODERNIZATION AND PRODUCTION EFFICIENCY

In recent years, the Soviet Union has modernized its agricultural system by expanding its claims on capital investment, changing its mode of production, and raising its status. Tractors have become ubiquitous, the wheat belt has shifted northward by 200 miles, and in research and development the Soviet specialists now outnumber the American. Even the prospects for changing the course of whole rivers so that they flow south, not north, now seems possible.[1]

Yet Soviet agriculture continues to be criticized for inefficiency, particularly in comparison to the United States. This static comparison between the two countries is rather unfortunate, as it ignores the growth rate of Soviet agriculture, which has rivaled that of the United States, and the very different climate and factor endowments.[2] (This is not to say that the comparison is at all devious or unjustified; it simply reflects the interest of the comparison's client, which is often the United States government.) A more complete comparison would account for not only the differences from nature, but also their relationship to modernization strategy. A broader question is whether some apparent inefficiencies might be justified as a part of modernization, or even as a necessary response to local conditions that differ from our own.

The charge of economic inefficiency may be further untangled by separating efficiency in consumption and in production. In Soviet food consumption, output has grown, but costs have grown faster and state retail prices have been stable, requiring massive government subsidies and resulting in queues.[3] These queues and shortages reflect inefficiency in distribution or consumption, even in the national wage policy, but they may be distinguished from a possible inefficiency in production on the farm. Further, even the production efficiency itself may be subdivided into economic and technical aspects. Economic efficiency in production demands that the output be produced at least-cost, and its analysis requires a detailed knowledge of the pricing structure of inputs and outputs[4] This is set aside in this paper to focus on technical efficiency, which requires knowledge only of the physical quantities of inputs.

Pure technical (or engineering) efficiency in farm production means that output can increase only from more inputs. Identically, it also means that it cannot increase from the same inputs as before, and that if this appears to occur then it signals impurities either in measurement or in conception. Such errors are almost unavoidable, since they include unknowns such as organization, or unpredictables such as rainfall. In addition, agricultural modernization yields a growth in output not so much by increasing inputs as by substituting manufactures (tractors or chemicals) for the traditional inputs of labor and land. A technical efficiency can occur not with only one input combination, but with many different combinations. For example, tomatoes may be harvested by hand or by machine; both methods are equally efficient in the sense that neither labor nor machine use may be decreased without losing some harvest. (Correspondingly, the single choice between technologies that is economically efficient will depend on relative costs and profitability.) To evaluate even the technical efficiency is difficult when the input proportions are changing in different directions.

The statistical concept that analyzes production efficiency while input structures are changing is the *production function,* where output depends on inputs that may be substituted for each other. A production function may seem an odd statistical tool to apply to the Soviet Union. It is incontestably a phenomenon of neoclassical economics, relying on assumptions of equilibrium and profit maximization that seem chimerical in the light of Soviet experience. It considers nothing at all about the level or composition of demand, focusing instead on the components of aggregate supply. At its simplest level, a production function may be an empty formalism expressing only the intuitively obvious fact that agricultural output cannot be increased without more imputs and that both should be fully measured.[5] Extended to the Soviet experience, it would predict that agricultural production will decrease if livestock are destroyed (as during collectivization) or that it will increase if fertilizer deliveries grow (as during the recent decade).

Nevertheless, the available production function studies also have a certain intuitive plausibility that commends them. First of all, they express a purely technical or engineering relationship and a willingness to separate the aspect of efficiency from the economic. Second, they are generalized and have been applied to the study of agriculture in a diversity of economic systems; thus the Soviet estimates can be compared to others.[6] Finally they classify our knowledge in a way that is fairly independent of ideology. If a first approximation to an efficiency study of Soviet agriculture is purely technical and independent of ideology, e.g., the nationalization of land, then a second approximation can more accurately separate the pure effects of public land ownership.

The production function is particularly appropriate for studying efficiency in a system where prices are known to be in disequilibrium, as in the Soviet Union. At the simplest level of estimation used here, price data are required only for aggregating output, and it can be assumed that they roughly reflect the relative national priorities. Inputs are simply measured in physical units. The result is comparable data that can be used to analyze regional differences in the allocation of resources and to approximate the gains possible from regional reallocation. In particular, the regions vary considerably in their basic factor proportions of land and labor, with consequences for both optimal farm modernization and technical efficiency. It is to these regional differences that this paper now turns.

FACTOR ENDOWMENT AND VARIABLE PROPORTIONS

The republics of the Soviet Union differ considerably in basic agricultural land-labor ratios, as shown in Table 8.1, where the republics are grouped by their ratios of hectares per worker. The world's agricultural systems can be classified as land-saving (such as Japan) or labor-saving (such as the United States), and Soviet regions may be similarly classified, with the land-saving Caucasus-Central Asian region (Group III) and the labor-saving RSFSR-Kazakhstan region (Group I). The western republics (Group II) fall between the two extremes.[7]

With different factor endowments, each group's growth strategy should reflect the tendency to save the basic resource that is in shortest supply; e.g., Group I, resembling the United States in its factor endowment, would conserve on labor and use land; its labor productivity would grow faster than its yield. Group III, resembling Japan in its factor endowment, would conserve on land and use labor; its yield would grow faster than its labor productivity. These policies have indeed been followed, and the relative land availability (Z/L of Table 8.1) is negatively correlated with yield ($r = -0.65$) and positively correlated with labor productivity ($r = +0.42$).[8] At the polar extremes, the Georgian SSR has adopted a land-saving strategy, and the Russian SFSR has adopted a labor-saving strategy.

Resource endowment and factor proportions are also related to optimal

Table 8.1   Land per Worker and Average Farm Size, State and Colletive Farms, Republics of the USSR, 1979 (in hectares)

	COLLECTIVE FARMS		STATE FARMS	
Region and republic	Land/ Worker	Farm Size	Land/ Worker	Farm Size
I. North				
RSFSR	11	4,700	11	5,500
Kazakhstan	15	10,800	23	15,000
II. West				
Ukraine	5	3,400	5	3,400
Belorussia	4	2,000	5	2,400
Moldavia	2	2,400	2	1,300
Lithuania	6	1,900	5	2,000
Latvia	7	2,600	6	2,900
Estonia	8	2,900	7	3,100
III. South				
Georgia	1	400	1	700
Azerbaidzhan	3	1,200	2	700
Armenia	2	500	2	600
Uzbekistan	1.5	1,700	3	2,700
Kirghizia	3	3,200	3	2,600
Tadjikistan	2	2,400	2	2,600
Turkmenistan	2	2,300	2.5	1,500

Definitions:
   Land: sown hectares of crop land
   Workers: annual number taking part in state or collective farm work
   Farms: number at the end of the year

Source: Narodnoe Khoziaistvo SSSR v 1979 g. (Moscow: Statistika, 1980), pp. 240, 290–91, 302–4.

farm size. A worldwide study of developing agricultural systems has shown that a larger farm size is associated with higher labor productivity and lower land productivity (yield), because the larger farms are more likely to replace labor by capital and to hold more land idle.[9] As shown in Table 8.1, Soviet agriculture follows this common pattern, in that the median from size on both collective and state farms is higher where the land per worker is higher. Of course, the average Soviet farm is still extremely large and the regional differences are only relative. Similar farms of very large absolute size (over 1,000 hectares) are found only in Venezuela, Peru, and Brazil. The larger size in the Soviet Union is preferred not only because of resource endowments, but because the socialist costs for administration and planning are lower for a few large farms than for many small farms on the same area. These are scale economies for the bureaucrats, not the farmers.[10]

The corollary relationship between resource endowment, farm size, and idle agricultural land cannot be fully discerned because there are gaps in the necessary data, but some anomalies can be noted by dividing ploughed land (*pashnia*) by all agricultural land (*ugod'ia*) to determine land use. Kazakhstan follows the expected pattern—farm size is large and land use is small (18 percent)—but the other republics do not. If land were more idle on the larger farms, then the Group I republics would have the most idle land, but only Kazakhstan does. If more land were used on the smaller farms, then the southern republics would have the least land idle, but they have the most. The west and the RFSFR use their land most intensively in this sense: between 60 and 80 percent of agricultural land is put to the plough. It is possible that land is held idle not only for fallow, but for a sort of socialist speculation, and that the south's idle land is held for future investment. Between 1960 and 1980, Central Asia's agricultural land base grew by 10 percent, while west's declined absolutely. Ploughed area was virtually constant in both regions.[11]

A second corollary from these relationships is that small farm (private plot) production is more appropriate in the south, where labor is in "surplus," and where it can be applied intensively. This is partially confirmed by Soviet experience; in the north (Group I), the share of agricultural land in private use is less than 3 percent, but in the south (Group III) it is greater than 6 percent. However, the greatest share is in the west (Group II), where 7 percent is held in private use on collective farms and 10 percent by worker-employees, usually on state farms.

Observing the impact of factor endowments on agricultural production provides some new insights concerning the oft-cited conclusion that the private plots in the Soviet Union are "more efficient" because they produce 23 percent of the nation's food on only 3 percent of its land.[12] Since output depends on both labor and land, the private plot production is more precisely described as labor-using and yield-increasing. It conserves on land, the resource in shortest supply, but uses generously the more available resource, which is labor. Its greater effectiveness is the sum of the high yield from land, the intensive use of labor, and the specialization in land-saving, labor-using, high-value products such as meat and vegetables.

In a national sense, the private and socialized sectors of Soviet agriculture may be analyzed as though they were two countries engaging in international trade, each with different factor endowments. A first prediction from this analysis would be the observed specialization of output in the two sectors—the private sector in land-saving products (especially animal husbandry) and the socialized sector in land-using products (especially grains). If the assumptions of trade theory are met, there will, over time, be a tendency toward factor and commodity-price equalization between the sectors even when the factors are not mobile, as is the case for land. This equalization occurs through product specialization and labor mobility.

A second prediction from trade theory based on factor endowments is that a particular specialization depends on *factor proportions,* or land per worker. In this light, the private sector can be more critically viewed as a residual employer for surplus labor as yet unabsorbed into the more industrialized economy.[13] There is some support for this view in the Soviet data. First, the recent relaxation of restrictions on private production have not appreciably increased its output. Overall the pool of agricultural labor has shrunk, and the national output on private plots has declined. Nevertheless, in those republics where the pool of agricultural labor has increased, the private plot production has also grown, e.g., in Azerbaidzhan, where private plot output increased by 43 percent between 1970 and 1979.[14] Thus, the private plots are a policy that is labor-using and job-creating.[15]

While the private sector may be separated from the socialized for analytical purposes, they are in one national agricultural system. They directly share a labor force, for at least one member of a family must be employed in the socialized sector if the family is to receive a plot. Other ties, not so obvious, link the sectors in the provision of young livestock and their feed, in contracts between socialized farm and private farmer, in public provision of irrigation water, and others. In the next section, agricultural output includes both the private and the public sectors, and regional factor endowments expand to include manufactured inputs, and not simply land and labor.

REGIONAL PRODUCTION FUNCTIONS

The discussion thus far indicates that Soviet agriculture is comprised of not one but three different regional production systems, differentiated on the basis of land and labor factor endowments. Agricultural land, of course, is immobile, and agricultural labor partially so. Nevertheless, manufactured inputs and some labor may be shifted between regions to increase technical efficiency, and new inputs may be chosen to enhance natural capabilities. In order to assess the possibility of gaining output from these policies, three production functions were estimated, one for each region, using the eleven-years (1965–75) data, and comparing it to a single all-Union estimate. In each case, the estimating equation was:

$$Q^* = A + b_1Z^* + b_2HP^* + b_3CHEM^* + b_4LABOR^* + b_5HERDS^* + e \text{ where}$$

(*) denotes a logarithm
Q is the value of output in 1965 prices
Z is sown hectares
HP is capital measured in horsepower capacity
$CHEM$ is delivered fertilizer in 100-percent nutrient units
$LABOR$ is the annual workforce on state and collective farms
$HERDS$ is the productive livestock inventory measured in cattle-equivalent units.[16] The results are shown in Table 8.2

As shown by a Chow test, the precision of the production function estimates is significantly enhanced by considering the Soviet agricultural system as three regional subsystems. The northern region, primarily the Russian republic, shows some instability in the regression coefficients, which arises from its considerable diversity and size. When the data become available, the region could be subdivided for considerable gain in estimating

Table 8.2   Prodution Functions, Soviet Union, National and Regions, 1965–75

	N	Land	HP	CHEM	LABOR	HERDS
National	165	.28	.03*	.27	.34	.06*
North	22	− .45*	− .52*	.30*	.19*	1.18*
West	66	.23	.32	− .00*	.27	.13*
South	77	− .00*	.04*	.35	.30	.33

*: coefficient does not differ significantly from zero
R^2 = .99 in all estimates

Definitions:
   N: number of observations
   CHEM: chemical fertilizer
   HP: capital equipment, in horsepower
   HERDS: productive livestock inventory

Sources: Computed by the author. Data are from *Narkhoz SSSR* (Moscow: Statistika) various volumes, 1965 to 1975.

accuracy. Since the estimates were made in logarithms, each coefficient represents an output elasticity for each input in each region, e.g., the input coefficient for land in the west of 0.23 means that a 10-percent expansion of land there would increase output by about 2.3 percent.[17]

From these estimates, some early judgments can be made about the possibility of increasing agricultural output from reallocating inputs between regions. First, any expansion of sown area seems most warranted in the traditional farming areas of the west, even though their land utilization is already high. At prevailing prices, and at the margin, more land use there would increase the value of output more than it would elsewhere. While a knowledge of costs and prices would temper the extent of this judgment, the omission has no serious consequences as to its direction, because any investment in a western hectare (for clearing, drainage) would be considerably less expensive than one in a southern hectare, where irrigation is exceedingly expensive.[18]

The western region shows further prospects for growth from reallocation of machinery (measured in horsepower) to that region. The machinery both complements and substitutes for labor; it replaces the labor moving from agriculture to industry, and it improves the productivity of the remaining labor. It modernizes the Soviet western agriculture in the western tradition, making it more labor-saving than land-saving. This result is indicated by the continuing high-output elasticity of both machinery and labor in the Soviet west. A quite different picture is found in the Soviet south, where an expansion of machinery would be less productive (its output elasticity is low) and there are fewer prospective gains from that input.[19]

Apparently, the western region has reached a barrier to the effective use of mineral fertilizer, and the prospects for gains from it appear to be minimal. The reasons for the limit can be only conjectural, but include the lack of fertilizer-responsive varieties of grain, inadequate use, or improper timing.[20] On the other hand, the south continues to benefit from increased fertilizer supplies, despite its high present use. This finding is quite consistent with the south's need for land-saving technological modernization and its continuing labor-using methods of production.

Finally, an increase in breeding livestock inventories would be clearly productive only in the south. (The other regions' coefficients are also positive, but not significant.) One possible reason for this southern advantage is their reliance on grazing animals, particularly sheep and goats, whose feed supplies are more dependable. The Soviets intend to expand cattle and pork production by large-scale feedlots, but have encountered problems in manufacturing and delivering feed. Until these problems are resolved, greater inventories would not affect the value of output.

The manufactured inputs selected for the regional analysis are the basic ones, but the omissions might be noted. Most critical for the southern region is the omission of water supplies. The consequences for the estimation of an omitted variable depend on the decision-making model behind the equation. If the variable cannot be foreseen, such as rainfall, then the decision maker has no special information that would bias these results. If however, an omitted variable can be predicted—irrigation water would be in this category—then the actual decisions will bias upward the estimated coefficients; e.g., south's labor productivity is overstated, in the sense that its product can be partly attributed to the unmeasured water input. There are two barriers to the inclusion of water. First, the data are skimpy at best, and the technical relationships are barely investigated.[21] Second, the irrigation water is often in private use, as much as 40 percent of its area in some republics. Without other data for the private sector, this use cannot be meaningfully attributed to output there.

Another omission is the inputs formerly from the farm but now from outside. These include manufactures, where only chemical fertilizers and capital were included and where others also contribute to agricultural output. This list might expand to add the hydrologists in the Ministry of Water Supply, the research scientists in a seed institute, the chemists in a herbicide factory, and the mechanics in a repair facility. These omissions affect the estimation as would any other, i.e., by overstating the productivity of measured factors. More problematic are the omitted inputs from the state sector, such as central planners, whose consequence might be the understatement of measured factors.

A final omission is the effect of labor quality, particularly from education, which did not contribute to the measured productivity. Ordinarily, education has two effects. The first is its own effect, where an educated worker is more productive than a poorly educated one. By ignorance or malice, an uneducated worker can waste modern inputs by inaccurate or inappropriate use, e.g., fertilizer. This effect is absent in the Soviet estimates. A second effect is the complementarity between education and manufactures. This effect is present, in that a Soviet study shows that new capital equipment will not increase output where the labor force has fewer than 10 percent skilled.[22] However, the complementarity means that either the manufactures or the education is statistically redundant, so education was omitted.

Despite these omissions, the production functions show considerable regional variation in technical efficiency and indicate some prospective gains from factor reallocation.

CONCLUSION

The Soviet search for technical efficiency in agriculture is by no means limited to the two natural factors of production and their manufactured complements, which were examined here. It is more complicated than that, but the regional factor endowments will affect the adaptation of more sophisticated, new methods where the Soviet Union has unique and unexplored requirements, and even the adaptation of methods that have been successful abroad.

Some further complexities are more political. One is the policy that Thane Gustafson has named "the southern strategy," which diverts northern waters to the south and expands land use there.[23] The Soviet southern leaders favor this investment, their power is considerable, and the required investment is massive. In terms of the technical efficiency examined here, the investment seems misplaced. The outcome is not worth the expenditure, as compared to the west. A second alternative regional strategy is the decision to invest in the Non-Blackearth Zone (NBZ), a project that has received extra investment in the past decade.[24] The NBZ was not separated from the RSFSR for this study, but seems unlikely to rival the west in its return on investment. It should be noted that these judgments apply only to production and ignore the demands that would be made for transport and storage if the west were to improve its specialization in agriculture.

Another political concern for Soviet modernization strategists is the longstanding policy of regional equalization in both production methods and labor income. In production methods, it is clear from this study that a single policy is not everywhere appropriate and that any regional equalization that ignores the differences in factor endowment would worsen efficiency. In the past, there was a stated policy of equalizing the production differences between regions, but not surprisingly this is fading away.[25]

The equalization of labor income is another matter and a national goal. The basic tool for interrepublic agricultural income equalization is differentiation of procurement prices by area in order to extract land rent.[26] The intent is to subtract income from the farms that have natural advantages in fertility and climate and to add it to poorer farms that are not so well endowed. It is difficult to differentiate these prices completely, even though the number of zones has proliferated over the years, and the errors can reduce investment and labor incentives. They can also prejudice the longterm decision to migrate from agricultural areas to cities and industry. All will bias the most correct resource allocation decisions.

Finally, Soviet agricultural efficiency could increase from further specialization of output according to factor endowments, but this would require substantial infrastructure in transportation, storage, and processing.[28] The Eleventh Five-Year Plan envisages this prospect, but the need is immense and the decision must be implemented at the highest level. In addition, this investment competes with the southern strategy, food subsidies for consumers, interregional wage equalization, and other political goals.

NOTES

1. Sylvan Wittmer, "U.S. and Soviet Agricultural Research Agendas," *Science* 208, no. 4441 (18 April 1980). p. 245.

2. Using an index 1950 = 100, Soviet agricultural output grew to 247 in 1977, while U.S. output achieved only 164, but the Soviet level in the terminal year was only 82 percent of the U.S. level. Douglas B. Diamond and W. Lee Davis, "Comparative Growth in Output and Productivity in U.S. and U.S.S.R. Agriculture," in *Soviet Economy in a Time of Change,* (Washington, D.C.: U.S. Government Printing Office, 1979), 48–49 (hereafter cited as *JEC*). In the same volume, see also David Schoonover, "The Quest for Efficiency," in his "Soviet Agricultural Policies," pp. 107–12.

3. Vladimir Treml, *Agricultural Subsidies in the Soviet Union,* (Washington, D.C.: U.S. Bureau of the Census, U.S. Government Printing Office, 1978). In 1981 the subsidy for meat and dairy alone was 25 billion rubles, *Ekonomicheskaia Gazeta* 6 (February 1981), p. 2. This almost equaled total productive agricultural investment in 1980, which was 26.9 billion rubles, *Narodnoe Khoziaistvo SSSR v 1980 g.* (Moscow: 1981), p. 341. (Hereafter cited as *Narkhoz* for the relevant year.)

4. On the rationality of Soviet agricultural pricing, see Michael Wyzan, "Soviet Agricultural Production and Policy," *American Journal of Agricultural Economies* 63, no. 3 (August 1981): pp. 475–83.

5. The production function estimated in this paper is:

$$Q^* = a + b_1L^* + b_2Z^* + b_3CHEM^* + b_4HP^* + b_5HERDS^* + e, \text{ where}$$

asterisk (*) denotes a logarithm
Q = output
L = labor
Z = land
$CHEM$ = chemical fertilizer
HP = capital stock measured in horsepower
$HERDS$ = the productive livestock inventory measured in equivalent units
e = an error term
See also Pan Y. Yotopoulos and Jeffrey B. Nugent, *Economics of Development: Empirical Investigations* (New York: Harper & Row, 1976), pp. 43–124. The data and further definitions used in this paper are given in note 16.

6. National agricultural estimates were compared between the Soviet Union and developing countries in my "Productivity in Soviet Agriculture," *Slavic Review* 39, no. 3 (September 1980): 446–59. Estimates for the developing countries are from Yujiro Hayami and Vernon Ruttan, "Agricultural Productivity Differences Among Countries," *American Economic Review* 60, no. 5 (December 1970): 895–911 and their more complete study *Agricultural Development: An international Perspective* (Baltimore: Johns Hopkins University Press, 1971).

7. See Hayami and Ruttan, *Agricultural Development.* Defining regions depends on data availability, limited to the fifteen Soviet republics, and the purpose of the analysis. The factor endowment (or Hayami-Ruttan) method was chosen here to focus on long-run development strategy. Others have used different methods, e.g., weather patterns, for short-run forecasts.

8. Both correlation coefficients are significant, in that the probability that either equals zero is only 0.0001, but there is a partial identity.

9. R. A. Berry and W. R. Cline, *Agrarian Structure and Productivity in Developing Countries* (Baltimore: Johns Hopkins University Press, 1979).

10. W. Flinn and Frederick Buttel, "Sociological Aspects of Farm Size: Ideological and Social Consequences of Scale in Agriculture," *American Journal of Agricultural Economics* 62, no. 5 (December 1980): 946-53.

11. Data are from *Sel'skoe Khoziaistvo SSSR* (Moscow: Statistika, 1971), pp. 98-99, 102-5; and *Narkhoz 1980,* pp. 221, 223, 226-27.

12. *Wall Street Journal,* 3 March 1981, p. 1.

13. Barney Schwalberg kindly pointed out the residual characteristic of agriculture and construction in the Soviet labor force.

14. *Narkhoz Azerbaidzhanskoi SSR za 60 let* (Moscow: Statistika), p. 119.

15. Frank Durgin, "The Inefficiency of Soviet Agriculture versus the Efficiency of U.S. Agriculture: Reality or an Idol of the Mind?" *ACES Bulletin* 20, nos. 3-4 (Fall-Winter 1978): 1-36.

16. The variables are:

Z = land, sown area in hectares, all categories of economic organization
L = labor, agricultural workers on state and collective farms, unadjusted for days worked
HP = capital equipment in horsepower units
$CHEM$ = fertilizer deliveries, in 100-percent nutrient units, excluding feed supplements
$HERD$ = livestock inventories in cattle-equivalent units (cattle = 1, swine = 0.5, sheep and goats = 0.1, poultry = 0.02);
Q = output, in 1965 ruble prices, all categories of economic organization
(Source: *Narkhoz SSSR,* (Moscow: Statistika) various volumes, 1965 to 1975.) The estimating equation is shown in note 5.

17. Elasticities are expressed in percentage changes of outputs and inputs and may be evaluated at the means to calculate marginal physical products (MPP) and average products (AP), e.g., for land:

	MPP	AP
North region	−.14	+.30
West region	+.15	+.64
South region	−.01	+.96

The incremental (MPP) is still most valuable in the west, despite the high average (AP) of the south.

18. M. N. Loiter, *Prirodnye resursy i effektivnost' capital'nykh vlozhenii* (Moscow: Izdat Nauka, 1974), p. 165, calculates an artificial agricultural land value of 955 rubles per hectare for "rich but unirrigated" land and 3293 rubles for irrigated land.

19. In all likelihood, the north is overmechanized.

20. Karl-Eugen Wädekin, "South Agriculture's Dependence on the West," *Foreign Affairs* (Spring 1982): pp. 882-903, provides an excellent prospective view.

21. Jerry D. Hill, Norton D. Strommen, Clarence M. Sakamoto, and Sharon K. LeDuc, "LACIE—An Application of Meteorology for United Staes and Foreign Wheat Assessment," *Journal of Applied Meteorology* 19, no. 1 (January 1980) relates climate to yield. Weather and yield are examined in Donald Green, "Soviet Agriculture: An Econometric Analysis of Technology and Behavior," U.S. Congress, Joint Economic Committee, *Soviet Economy in a Time of Change* (Washington, D.C.: U.S. Government Printing Office, 1979), pp. 116-132. Padma Desai, "Soviet Grain and Wheat Import Demands in 1981-85," *American Journal of Agricultural Ecnomics* 64, no. 2 (May 1982): pp. 312-22.

22. V. N. Iakimov, *Tekhnicheskii progres i vosproizvodstvo rabochei sily v kolkhozakh* (Moscow: 1975), p. 90. This same effect is found in Hayami and Ruttan, *Agricultural Development,* and Zvi Griliches, "The Sources of Measured Productivity Growth: United States Agriculture 1940-60," *Journal of Political Economy* 71, no. 4 (August 1963): p. 336.

23. Thane Gustafson, "Technology Assessment: Soviet Style," *Science* 208 (June 1980): 1343-48, and his more complete work *Reform in Soviet Politics* (Cambridge: Cambridge University Press, 1981), especially chapters 3 and 5.

24. David W. Carey and Joseph F. Havelka, "Soviet Agriculture: Progress and Problems," surveys the prospects for the NBZ. U.S. Congress, Joint Economic Committee, *Soviet Economy in a Time of Change* (Washington, D.C.: U.S. Government Printing Office, 1979), pp. 71-9.

25. Alfred Evans, Jr., "Interrepublic Inequality in Agricultural Development in the USSR," *Slavic Review* 40, no. 4 (Winter 1981): pp. 570–84.

26. Kenneth Gray, "Soviet Agricultural Prices, Rent, and Land Cadastres," *Journal of Comparative Economics* 5, no. 1 (March 1981): pp. 43–59.

27. Wage-income calculations indicate that the rural-urban income gap diminished between 1970 and 1978 in the RSFSR but increased in Uzbekistan (*Narkhoz RSFSR 1979,* pp. 160, 220; *Narkhoz Uzbekskoi SSR 1978,* pp. 135, 204; both adjusted for days worked). These data are not available for all republics.

28. A Soviet author estimates that agricultural output could be increased 11–12 percent simply by highway improvements (Carey and Havelka, "*Soviet Agriculture*," p. 75).

9

The Kolkhoz and the Sovkhoz: Relative Performance as Measured by Productive Technology

Michael L. Wyzan

INTRODUCTION

One of the more striking aspects of the Soviet agricultural sector is its characterization by three basic organizational forms: the collective farm or *kolkhoz,* the state farm or *sovkhoz,* and the "personal auxiliary holding" or private plot. All three institutions have unique places, both in Marxist-Leninist ideology and in practical Soviet policy. In this paper, an empirical look is taken at the productive technology (as defined below) employed on kolkhozy and sovkhozy. This is carried out in an attempt to ascertain whether significant differences in that technology exist, and if so, whether this divergence can be explained by differences in the behavior or treatment of the two types of farm. More specifically, and as discussed and reported below, this paper is built around the estimation, separately by type of farm, of three-input translog production functions for five Soviet crops. The data employed are at the level of the union republic, are in physical units, and cover the period from 1960 to 1976.

The results of a study such as this are of interest to Soviet planners who must decide on the rate at which the kolkhoz is to be integrated into the state sector of the economy. They thus also bear on Western understanding of the motivations and effects of Soviet agricultural policy, an understanding that has become so important given the huge presence of the Soviet Union in international grain markets. The findings should interest other policy makers as well, especially those in less-developed countries, who are choosing among organizational forms in their attempts to improve the performance of their agricultural sectors. Finally, a study of this type can shed

The author would especially like to thank Robert Stuart for valuable comments on the first draft of this paper. During the conference, I benefited considerably from remarks by Clark Chandler, Edward Cook, Donald Green, and the late Arcadius Kahan. Of course, none of the aforementioned is in any way implicated in the methods or conclusions. All statistical calculations were performed via the Statistical Analysis System on data gathered at the Foreign Demographic Analysis Division of the Commerce Department.

light on a number of questions of largely academic interest, such as whether the kolkhoz behaves like the dividend-maximizing, self-managed firm of Western economic theory.

This paper is organized into five sections, including this introduction. In the second one, I briefly summarize the extant institutional differences by type of farm, as filtered through Western perception and the revelations of official policy contained in Soviet economics journals. This section contains five subsections. First, a summary of the numbers and dimensions of the two types of farm is provided. Second, the current differences and similarities in their operation are discussed, and the question of their convergence, as state farms are granted more autonomy and collective farms come more to enjoy the fruits of inclusion in the state sector, considered. In the third and fourth subsections, that variation in practice that bears specifically on the estimation of production functions is outlined. In the former, I look at divergence in the treatment of land and capital inputs, and in the latter I isolate for separate consideration the treatment of labor; the putative existence of self-managed and democratic aspects of kolkhoz practice is also considered. The fifth subsection briefly examines the question of which variant has generally been deemed "superior" by Soviet and Western observers and the criteria by which such a determination might be made.

The third major portion of the paper contains a discussion of the data set and specific functional form used in the estimation. In the fourth section, the empirical results are presented and discussed, with emphasis on three specific questions: whether there are statistically significant differences by type of farm in the estimated technology; whether the kolkhoz in any way resembles a self-managed firm; and whether any presumption of superiority might be bestowed upon either type of farm. The fifth section concludes by addressing the implications and limitation of the findings.

THE INSTITUTIONS COMPARED

Numbers and Dimensions

Table 9.1 provides a summary of a number of aspects of the two types of farm during and slightly beyond the relevant time period. Several trends immediately catch the eye. The number of collective farms fell steadily over the two decades, while the number of state farms grew. The former became increasingly large over time as measured by sown area per farm, households per farm, and either of the two estimates of capital per farm. On the other hand, sovkhozy became smaller from the standpoint of land and labor force; they have stagnated for twenty years in the per-farm number of tractors, although total horsepower has grown on a per-farm basis. The total sown area and total labor force on kolkhozy have fallen, while similar figures rose over time on sovkhozy. In fact, in 1973, for the first time, total sown area on sovkhozy exceeded that on kolkhozy.

The falling number of kolkhozy is explained by amalgamation, whereby two collective farms are merged, and conversion of (generally weak)

Table 9.1 Numerical Summary

Year[a]	Numbers	Sown Area[b]	Kolkhozy (not including fisheries) Sown Area Per Farm[c]	Labor Force[d]	Labor Force Per Farm	Tractors Per Farm	Total Engine Power Per Farm[e]
1960f	44,900	123.0	2739.4	17,555,900	391	13.8	----
1965	36,300	105.1	2895.3	15,463,800	426	20.8	964.2
1970	33,000	99.1	3003.0	14,355,000	435	28.5	1515.2
1975	28,500	98.2	3445.6	13,480,500	473	37.3	2315.8
1980	25,900	95.2	3675.7	12,742,800	492	40.8	2934.4
				Sovkhozy			
1960	7,375	67.2	9113.0	5,800,000	786.4	54.6	----
1965	11,681	89.1	7624.5	8,230,000	704.6	58.3	2885.0
1970	14,994	91.8	6119.1	8,888,000	592.8	53.6	3161.3
1975	18,064	107.2	5936.7	10,260,000	568.0	57.5	3924.9
1980	21,057	111.8	5309.4	11,600,000	550.9	56.5	4321.6

aAll data refer to the end of the relevant year unless otherwise noted.
bMillion hectares.
cHectares.
dFor kolkhozy, number of kolkhoz households; for sovkhozy, annual average number of workers employed in all branches thereof.
eHorsepower.
f In 1960, the number of kolkhozy includes fisheries and is hence slightly oversized to be strictly comparable to the other years.
Source: Narkhoz 1980 (Moscow: Statistika, 1981), pp. 254, 255, 270, 271; *Narkhoz* 1972 (Moscow: Statistika, 1973), pp. 388, 389, 398, 399.

kolkhozy into sovkhozy (Stuart 1973, p. 47ff). Conversion was especially important before 1965, with peak years in 1957 and 1959–1960 (Wädekin 1971, p. 516), largely before the period of the relevant data set. Table 9.1 contains evidence of similar processes still at work. Indeed, the demise of the kolkhoz has long been anticipated (Miller 1976; Osofsky 1974), the modus operandi thereof during the 1970s perhaps being the various increasingly popular forms of interenterprise cooperation.[1] Amalgamation and the oft-noted fact that it is the weaker (and undoubtedly smaller) kolkhozy that are converted (Stuart 1972, p. 50) probably account for the rising area and labor force per collective farm; the decline in total sown area most likely reflects conversion.

During the period covered by the data set, the rising number and total sown area of sovkhozy reflect the aforementioned conversion process. There has also been the development of new state farms, both near large cities to provide them with milk, potatoes, and vegetables, and in areas of large-scale irrigation. Fully 70 percent of the total number of sovkhozy (as of 1977) had been created between 1955 and 1974 (Morozov 1977, p. 73).[2] The declining sown area and labor force per state farm are most likely evidence of the fact that kolkhozy converted into sovkhozy are smaller than preexisting examples of the latter. It is also possible that newly created sovkhozy near large cities are smaller than their predecessors.

A General Comparison of the Types of Farm

In this section the legal, social, and economic differences between the institutional variants are briefly outlined. Matters related specifically to production functions are postponed until later subsections. Although in Soviet law and by official asseveration the collective farm has always been a unique form of socialist property, Western observers have generally been skeptical with regard to its singularity. Moreoever, it seems that the kolkhoz and sovkhoz are converging toward each other from different directions. This occurs, as argued below, as collective farms receive more of the benefits of full membership in the state sector and as state farms are granted more independence in their decision making. Nonetheless, it appears to me that there remain some interesting differences, the manifestations of which are worth looking for in the empirical results.

A *kolkhoz,* according to the 1969 restatement of the 1935 Model Rules, is " . . . a cooperative organization of farmers who have joined their efforts voluntarily in undertaking large-scale socialist agricultural production on the basis of social means of production and of collective labor" (Morozov 1977, p. 50). Even though most non-Soviet observers reject the cooperative image of this institution, it is nevertheless clear that the kolkhoz's being a "collective" rather than a "state" institution has had a great impact on its treatment by the authorities. Osofsky (1974, p. 97) calls the kolkhoz an "institutionalized ideological concession to practicality"—one that the Soviets would just as soon eliminate if they could. The Marxian legacy has been interpreted as suggesting that agricultural production can be "rationalized," i.e., that agricultural enterprises can be run on a controlled industrial basis.

The sovkhoz is the instrument of this conception and the kolkhoz a concession to an obdurate peasantry.[3]

How has this ideological divergence been visited upon practical policy? It
seems to me that this has occurred primarily by way of the expectation that
kolkhoznik exhibits a greater degree of independence relative to the state
than virtually any other member of Soviet society. This has (historically, at
least) meant a greater degree of autonomy in decision making, but also an
inability to receive many important social benefits. Much of the truly important distinction inheres in the treatment of labor, a topic to be discussed
in the fourth subsection. For the present, there are four basic areas of
divergence.

First, the kolkhozniki were historically ineligible for all the social benefits
to which the state employee was entitled. Even today, they cannot possess
an internal passport, which means, at least formally, that they cannot live in
an urban area, leave the farm without managerial permission, or change
jobs. Before 1966, the kolkhoznik received a share of farm net income,
often in kind, and only after the harvest; this share was generally far less
than the pay of an equivalent employee on a sovkhoz. Kolkhozniki were not
entitled to state retirement pensions, maternity benefits, or illness benefits
and were ineligible for retirement and maternity benefits. Since 1970, they
have received sickness benefits. Finally, in 1975, it was promised that they
would receive identity cards by 1981 (McAuley 1979, pp. 30–31). So this
area of divergence is probably no longer very important.

Second, the two variants have differed in the extent to which their
members have relied on private plots. Over the years, because kolkhozniki
were poorer than state employees, and maybe also because of their location
outside of the state sector, they have relied for subsistence more on these
plots than sovkhozniki. Although the latter often have such plots (like many
other state employees), they are reputed to be smaller and the money income therefrom a less significant share of total income than for kolkhozniki
(Wädekin 1973, p. 4). They may even be less productive, as evidenced by officially imputed income figures used in determining entitlement to the family income supplement (McAuley 1979, p. 358). This difference is, however,
also not considered to be overly significant any more. If this is true, it is
probably a result of increased social-sector income for collective farmers.
There is also the fact that a good number of state farms are converted collective farms on which members were allowed to keep their plots.

Third, there is the manner in which the two institutional forms conduct
their affairs, more specifically their relations with the state planning
authorities. Kolkhozy have generally exhibited a greater degree of
autonomy, although Western scholars are somewhat divided on the extent
to which such independence is genuine. This de facto autonomy is mani-
fested in the following ways:

1. It is officially a self-governing producer cooperative.

2. Its members collectively own its fixed and working capital, although
none of the so-called indivisible fund can be alienated by members upon
withdrawal.

3. It does not have access to interest-free capital grants or subsidies from

the state, so that investment is financed by retained net income and loans. Although the conventional wisdom is that kolkhoz managers have been reluctant to borrow for investment purposes (Millar 1971, p. 289), the level of borrowing relative to the value of output rose steadily during the seventies on both types of farm (Galsanov 1980). There is some evidence that sovkhozy are more heavily in debt relative to their ruble value of output, despite their eligibility for direct government subsidy. (Galsanov 1980, p. 24, provides evidence of this from the Buriat ASSR near Lake Baikal.)

4. Its profit is not withdrawn into various funds but is subject to a flat tax. (a through d are from Millar 1971, pp. 277–278).

5. It is officially subject to fewer indicators in the planning process. Kolkhoz plans contain targets for the volume of agricultural products to be sold to the state, deliveries of machinery, fertilizer, and equipment from the state, and the volume of credit made available. Sovkhozy are also responsible for their overall wage fund, their overall volume of profit, their level of payment for basic productive assets, and their assignments for the introduction of new technological processes. They are also informed of the volume of state subsidies and centralized capital allocations they are to receive (Morozov 1977, p. 107).

The sovkhoz is hence rather more under the tutelage of the authorities than the kolkhoz. As in the other areas discussed, however, one might expect the divergence by type of farm to diminish over time, in the present instance because of the introduction of *khozraschët* on sovkhozy. Morozov (1977, p. 78) defines this concept as follows:

> This refers to a system under which all expenditures that are incurred in carrying out [the sovkhozy's] planned production and delivery assignments are met from their own revenues. This includes a level of profit that will permit the state farm to expand its output. Financing from the state budget is no longer required, and whenever such funds are still given they play an auxiliary role.

Conversion of sovkhozy to this system began as per a decree of 15 April 1967, and over the next nine years all of them were so transformed (Osofsky 1974, p. 108). Between 1967 and 1974, about one-half of state farms adopted khozraschët, with the remainder switching over in 1975 (Morozov 1977, p. 78).[4]

The fourth and final area of divergence to be discussed concerns the level of purchase prices the two variants receive for their outputs. Inasmuch as kolkhozy have been to a large degree self-financing (especially after the demise of the Machine Tractor Stations in 1958), they have needed to be paid higher prices. For example, in 1965, grain prices on sovkhozy averaged 39 percent, and cotton prices 17 percent, below the corresponding kolkhoz averages. The lower prices resulted in lower profitability for given crops on state farms (Bornstein 1969, p. 15). As sovkhozy are transferred to khozraschët, they are supposed to receive the same prices as kolkhozy (Morozov 1977, p. 79; Treml 1978, p. 32). Indeed, as of 1973, two separate Soviet sources reported negligible differences in average prices by type of farm (Bornstein 1976, p. 39). On the other hand, a more recent Soviet source confirms that "[a]t the present time the structure of purchase prices in kolkhozy and sovkhozy differs, which contradicts the principle of one price" (Borkhunov 1976, p. 39). This last author notes that prices paid to kolkhozy must still be higher because their profit must go to pay for such items as social insurance and contributions to funds unrelated to production, such as for housing.

In concluding this subsection, it seems appropriate to observe that although the kolkhoz has approached the sovkhoz in its relations with the state authorities, and the reverse has occurred as the latter has received more operational autonomy, some residual differences may remain. This divergence inheres in such areas as methods of finance, price setting, and the promulgation of plan indicators. The next two subsections treat those differences that specifically relate to the production process.

The Production Process: Capital and Land Inputs

Inasmuch as the empirical work described below consists of the estimation of production functions, in this section and the next, the focus is on the relative treatment by type of farm of the three inputs on which there are data, capital, land, and labor. Turning first to capital inputs, it is quite possible that the still somewhat disparate methods of finance have engendered differences in the usage of these inputs. In view of the unavailability of direct government subsidies and centralized investment funds to kolkhozy, one would expect a higher "shadow price" of capital on these enterprises. Although such a price is, of course, unobservable, note from Table 9.1 that sovkhozy are better endowed (on a per-farm basis) with both tractors and total horsepower. This squares well with the notion that the opportunity cost of funds is lower on sovkhozy, despite the fact that the official interest rates—1 percent for short-term and 0.75 percent for long-term debt—are equal for the two variants (Morozov 1977, pp. 99–101).[5]

Turning to land utilization, Stuart (1972, pp. 114–15) observes that the extent to which managers of kolkhozy can shift portions of their farm's total sown area among crops is very limited; among collective farms, specialization has always been rare. On the other hand, sovkhozy frequently specialize in such fields as vegetable growing or milk production. This specialization cannot, however, be viewed as an optimal response to variable natural conditions, inasmuch as land is provided gratis to both types of farm. Indeed, economic rents accruing to better-situated farms are withdrawn through zonal differentiation of purchase prices (Gray 1979).[5] The result is that, as Buzdalov (1965, p. 9) observes, sovkhozy specializing in the production of a given product often do so no more efficiently, in terms of yield, cost, or productivity, than unspecialized state farms. In any case, it should prove interesting to observe whether productivity (average or marginal) figures for land differ on the two types of farm. One thing that can be said with certainty is that the greater sown area per state farm worker (see Table 9.1) implies that each of them has more land input with which to work.

The Production Process: Labor Inputs and Kolkhoz Democracy

Before turning to the important and interesting question of whether or not the kolkhoz in any way resembles a self-managed firm, a few observations on other aspects of agricultural labor inputs are in order. *Ceteris paribus,* one would expect the average and marginal productivity of labor to be higher on sovkhozy for two reasons. First, as noted already, each sovkhoznik has more capital and land with which to work than the counterpart on the kolkhoz. Second, the conventional wisdom is that the collective farm has an inferior (by qualification) labor force relative to the state farm. There is a prevailing impression that much of collective farm work is performed by elderly women, whereas state farms employ a workforce not dissimilar to that on industrial enterprises.

Evidence on this differentiation is not easy to find, however. In fact, Wädekin (1971, pp. 524–25) asserts that the sovkhoz suffers from the same problems of age and sex structure, although they are possibly less severe in view of the greater mechanization of field work on state farms. McAuley (1979, pp. 63–64) notes that income distribution figures for sovkhozniki are virtually nonexistent. He further avers that although they are state employees with internal passports, full access to the social security system, and so on, sovkhozniki are still rural employees who " . . . to a large extent share the lifestyle of the collectivized peasantry" (p. 64). This is especially true insofar as the labor force on many sovkhozy consists of the former members of weak kolkhozy that have been converted.

Soviet data reveal only slight differences in the educational levels of two variants. Table 9.2 shows that neither kolkhoz managerial personnel nor oridinary members have demonstrably lower educational levels. Both groups are much inferior to the rural clerical-staff category in terms of the possession of higher education. Hence, it may well be that differences in qualification by type of farm are no longer very important.

As far as wages are concerned, kolkhoz labor payments were, at least before 1966, much lower than sovkhoz wages; they were also irregularly paid out and largely in kind. A decree of May 1966 made labor payments a prior charge against kolkhoz gross income, recommended that collective farms adopt sovkhoz wage scales, and allowed Gosbank to extend credits to them to cover the higher wage fund (McAuley 1979, p. 33). Nonetheless, there is much evidence that earnings of collective farmers continue to lag wages on state farms (Osofsky 1974, pp. 60–61, Gray 1979, p. 543). In the empirical results, it will be interesting to compare the average and marginal products of labor by type of farm.

Finally, a few words concerning the extent to which the kolkhoz may be deemed a self-managed firm are necessary. As described in official Soviet publications, the collective farm is indeed a very democratic institution, in which members have the right (even the legal obligation!) to " . . . participate in the management of collective farm affairs, elect its administrative bodies and be elected to them, convey proposals for improving the activities of the collective farm and overcome shortcomings in the work of its board

Table 9.2 Educational Levels of Kolkhoz and Sovkhoz Personnel in 1979

A. Managerial Personnel
Percent Having Completed Higher and Middle Specialized Education[a]

	Kolkhoz	Sovkhoz
Managers[b]	95.1	98.7
Chief Specialists	96.4	97.4
Agronomists	96.8	94.7
Zootechnicians	94.6	91.4
Veterinarians	75.8	81.4
Engineers	65.1	66.4
Crop Brigade Leaders	43.2	41.6
Livestock Farm Leaders	47.0	45.5

B. Workers and Kolkhozniki
Percent Having Completed Given Level of Education[c]

Total Agricultural Population[d]		Workers[e]		Kolkhozniki	
H,IH,MS[f]	MG[g]	H,IH,MS	MG	H,IH,MS	MG
15.1	24.8	3.1	27.9	5.8	22.0

[a]As of April 1, 1979 (*Narkhoz 1978* (Moscow: Statistika, 1979), pp. 290, 292). Table excludes categories of kolkhoz vice-presidents and sovkhoz department heads, who do not seem to have counterparts on the other type of farm.
[b]Kolkhoz president or sovkhoz director.
[c]These data are from *Vestnik Statistiki* (February 1981): p. 63, and refer to the census of 1979.
[d]This category includes workers, kolkhozniki, and clerical staff, the latter of which has a much larger percentage of highly trained individuals than the other groups.
[e]This category includes all rural state workers engaged in production.
[f]Higher, incomplete higher, and middle specialized educational levels.
[g]Middle general educational level.

and its official persons" (Morozov 1977, p. 60). In fact, in the 1960s there was a series of theoretical articles by well-known Western economists in which the kolkhoz was treated as a self-managed firm (Domar 1966; Oi and Clayton 1968). On the other hand, most Western observers today believe that there are few democratic features to this institution. Stuart (1972, p. 189) finds it to be "almost wholly subservient to the planning apparatus" and operating under a set of controls "differing little from those of regular state organizations."

This question is important for the present purposes because the familiar theory of the self-managed firm implies that such a firm strives to maximize profit per worker. In doing so, it makes labor a more expensive input to other factors of production than it would otherwise be. *Ceteris paribus,* this would imply less use of labor on kolkhozy and hence higher labor productivity thereupon.[6] This might conceivably be sufficient to counteract the aforementioned tendencies for such productivity to be lower on collective farms.

Is there any evidence that the kolkhoz has cooperative aspects? There are some minor respects that may present such evidence—it does have more financial independence, as pointed out earlier. More importantly, it is necessary to know whether labor is paid on the basis of residual shares of net revenue. Before the abolition of the labor-day system in 1966, this question was easy to answer in the affirmative: kolkhozniki was paid via small, often arbitrarily determined, and usually in kind, shares of net (of plan fulfillment) output. Since then, kolkhozniki have received monthly cash payments, almost entirely in rubles, and they are subject to a minimum wage.

This might end the matter once and for all, except that there remain features of the payment system on collective farms that suggest that the kolkhoznik remains something of a residual legatee. Millar (1971, p. 278) notes that the introduction of a guaranteed annual wage only "modifies this feature" and that "total earnings of farm members still represent a residual share in farm income." Soviet authors continue to write as though kolkhoz wages depend crucially (and much more so than sovkhoz wages) on profitability; see, for example, Borkhunov (1980).

A recent Soviet source (Morozov 1977, pp. 142–43) outlines three methods of labor payment on collective farms—by the job, by the piece, and by means of a portion of the value of output. As described, all of them depend to some extent on the actual output produced, which is, of course, only known after the harvest.

> Many farms divide their total wages fund into two parts. The first (usually 70–80 percent of the fund) is intended for regular monthly payments, while the second (20–30 percent) is employed for payments *at the end of the year, when the final results of productive activities are known* [p. 144, emphasis mine].

Labor payment on state farms, as described by the same author (pp. 148–50) is fairly similar to the remuneration of industrial labor. There are both a centrally assigned wages fund and a material incentives fund financed out of net revenue.[7]

It thus seems that there remain cooperative aspects of the kolkhoz. Before moving on, however, two caveats are in order. First, it is entirely possible that the collective farm, consisting as it does of members receiving residual shares and a salaried managerial staff, might behave in just the opposite fashion from a classic labor-managed firm. Rather than treating labor as a particularly expensive input, the kolkhoz chairman might (at least before 1966) view labor costs as "infinitely collapsible." Net output could be divided among however many workers had contributed labor days, and as long as the marginal product of labor was positive, there was no reason not to add to the workforce (Nimitz 1967, pp. 195–196). Today the cost of labor can be collapsed around the minimum wage—insofar as it is below sovkhoz wage rates, labor should still be cheaper, and hence employed until its marginal product is lower, than on sovkhozy.

Second, the standard theory of the self-managed firm is based on the assumption that the firm is freely able to change the size of its labor force. In reality, of course, the kolkhoz chairman is hardly empowered to hire and fire in the manner of a capitalist manager. These two factors, along with the assertions above that the kolkhoznik is possibly less qualified and certainly endowed with fewer nonlabor inputs, may be sufficient to eradicate any vestiges of higher labor productivity on the kolkhoz.

The Question of Superiority

Thus far, this section has dealt with differences between the institutional variants without reference of superiority or inferiority. Before going on to describe the data set and econometric techniques used in this paper, the issue deserves mention. At the ideological level, it is true, of course, that the kolkhoz is considered an inferior form of property (Stuart 1972, p. 8), and this notion has no doubt been behind the conversion campaigns. On the other hand, expert Soviet opinion has not always supported this viewpoint. Writing in 1965, Buzdalov notes that "despite a more technically armed labor force, [sovkhozy] receive less gross output from each hectare of land than kolkhozy . . . . The same can be said for indices of productivity, and likewise cost" (p. 3). He goes on to observe that this relatively poor performance even applies to "older" sovkhozy, as well as newly converted ones.

What light can the estimation of production functions shed on this question? It is obviously moot with respect to such matters as which form of property is ideologically superior. Nonetheless, in providing indirect evidence on such questions as the usage (and hence shadow prices) of individual factors of production, it enables one to compare the productivity of the types of farm. If one variant exhibits higher productivity for all inputs, this may be viewed as a sign of greater efficiency of resource use on its part. If, on the other hand, some inputs are more productive on one variant and others are on the other, this does not bear on the superiority issue. Instead, this result invites the comparison of relative factor productivity with relative (conjectural, in this case) shadow prices. For example, a higher marginal product of labor on sovkhozy would suggest that labor is more expensive to them.

The estimation of production functions also provides us with other comarative information about the organizational types that bears on the superiority/inferiority issue. We can compare estimated returns to scale, output growth prospects as embodied in the possibilities for factor substitution, rates of neutral technical progress, and overall technical efficiency.[8] One might (very tentatively) award the laurel of superiority to a form that consistently outperformed its counterpart in all of these respects. From the standpoint of practical policy—if, for example, it could be shown that the kolkhoz "scored" better in all or most of these categories—the Soviets might be advised to slow down their efforts to eliminate it.[9] One must, of course, be prepared for the finding that neither form is clearly superior.

DATA AND METHODS

The data set used in this study, some econometric considerations engendered by its idiosyncracies, and the translog production function are discussed in Wyzan (1981) and are only briefly described here. Figures gathered from official Soviet sources are available on five crops, grain, sugar beets, cotton, potatoes, and vegetables. Other crops, such as sunflowers and flax, are not included because there are no published data on labor inputs into their production. For each type of farm, the data on each crop are in the form of a pool of cross-sectional and time-series observations, with each time series covering some fraction of (or in some cases all of) the period 1960–1976.

The cross-sections are formed by nine Soviet republics: Armenia, Azerbaidzhan, Estonia, Lithuania, Moldavia, RSFSR, Tadzhikistan, the Ukraine, and Uzbekistan. The other six republics, including the important agricultural areas of Byelorussia and Kazakhstan, are omitted from this study because it is impossible to divide total crop outputs by type of farm on the basis of the contents of their statistical yearbooks.[10] Altogether, there are 243 observations for grain (121 kolkhoz and 122 sovkhoz), 143 for sugar beets (71 kolkhoz and 72 sovkhoz), 74 for cotton (evenly divided by farm type), 229 for potatoes (114 kolkhoz and 115 sovkhoz), and 147 for vegetables (74 kolkhoz and 73 sovkhoz), for a total of 836 cases.

As already mentioned, all figures come from official Soviet sources and are not qualitatively adjusted. Land is measured in thousands of hectares of "sown area" and labor in thousands of man-hours.[11] The latter are found in the annuals as labor-intensity data—man-hours per center of output; total direct labor inputs are obtained by multiplying these intensities by appropriate physical output data, which are available in thousands of metric tons.[12] Capital services pose a particularly difficult problem, in that no crop-specific Soviet capital data are available. In this study, the number of a certain type of machine in existence in each year is used as a proxy for capital inputs. Grain combines are used in grain cases, cotton machines in cotton cases, and tractors elsewhere.[13]

The three input translog production function used in the estimations is written:

$$(1) \quad \ln Q_i = b_0 + \lambda t + b_1 \ln R_i + b_2 \ln L_i + b_3 \ln K_i + b_4 (\ln R_i)^2 + b_5 (\ln L_i)^2 + b_6 (\ln K_i)^2 + b_7 (\ln R_i)(\ln L_i) + b_8 (\ln R_i)(\ln K_i) + b_9 (\ln L_i)(\ln K_i) + \epsilon_i$$

where the subscript i indexes a particular observation; Q is output; R is land, L is labor; K is capital; t is a time index equal to 1 for the first year of the data set, 2 for the second year, and so on, meant to capture neutral technological change; and the vector of disturbances (ϵ) satisfies the full ideal conditions (Berndt and Christensen 1973). Table 9.3 summarizes this information.

This function is probably most appropriately viewed as a second order Taylor-series expansion around the means of output and each input, rather than as an exact representation of the productive technology. It allows one to estimate the nature of returns to scale and factor substitution, instead of imposing untested restrictions on them. Regions of nonconvex isoquants are present whenever any coefficient, $b_4, \ldots, b_9$, is significantly different from zero. Neutral technical progress can be treated in an additive manner, as demonstrated in equation (1).

Before we move on, a number of features of this functional form deserve mention. In line with the definition of the translog function as a Taylor-series expansion, all output and input data were divided by their respective means before estimation. This causes the means of R, L, and K all to become one, and hence the means of $\ln R$, $\ln L$, and $\ln K$ all become zero. This procedure has several implications, in view of the fact that estimated scale and substitution effects, being variable, must be evaluated at the means of the data set.

First, the output elasticities (factor shares under cost minimization) are linear functions of the logs of each input. For example,

(2) $\quad \delta \ln Q / \delta \ln R = b_1 + 2b_4 \ln R + b_7 \ln L + b_8 \ln K.$

Because the means of $\ln R$, $\ln L$, and $\ln K$ are all zero, the mean value of the output elasticity of land is simply b_1. It follows directly that b_2 is the mean estimated output elasticity of labor, and b_3 plays this role for capital. Second, returns to scale, m, being the sum of the output elasticities, are also a linear function of all inputs. It is easy to show that they are given by

(3) $\quad m = b_1 + b_2 + b_3 + (2b_4 + b_7 + b_8)\ln R + (2b_5 + b_7 + b_9)$
$\ln L + (2b_6 + b_8 + b_9)\ln K.$

Table 9.3   Variables Used in Production Function

Symbol	Variable	Measurement
Q	Output	Centners (100 kilograms)
R	Land	Hectares of sown area
L	Labor	Direct man-hours
K	Capital	By proxy: numbers of a given type of machine[a]
ϵ	normally distributed disturbance term	
t	time[b]	

[a]Grain combines for grain, cotton machines for cotton, tractors elsewhere.

[b]An index equal to 1 in the first year of the data set, 2 in the second year, and so on.

This function is evaluted at every point in the data set on a crop, and then these calculations are averaged to obtain the mean scale effects for that crop.

Finally, the three partial elasticities of substitution, σ_{RL}, σ_{RK}, and σ_{LK}, are calculated according to a formula given by Berndt and Christensen (1973, p. 97), evaluated at each point in the data set on a crop, and then averaged. The translog function is specially suited to this purpose, in that (unlike the CES function, for example) it allows three different partial elasticities of sustitution to be estimated, two of which can be negative. This makes it possible to have complementary factor pairs.

RESULTS

In this setion, the data and methods described are applied to the institutions being compared. There are essentially three questions to be studied. First, the differences by type of farm in the basic productive technology are examined separately by crop. By obtaining estimates of the parameters of production functions, one is able to examine the nature of certain important technological relationships, such as returns to scale and factor substitution, which constrain the choices of decision makers. For example, a decision to construct huge enterprises may be judged in the light of whether or not estimated returns to scale are increasing or decreasing. Two methods of ascertaining whether the production function parameters are statistically significantly different by type of farm are presented. Such differences, if found, would suggest that kolkhoz and sovkhoz authorities make their decisions subject to divergent technological constraints.

Second, it is of interest to examine empirically the question of whether or not the kolkhoz in any way resembles a self-managed firm. Finally, the estimated prodution functions, factor productivity comparisons, and estimated scale and substitution effects are used in a tentative attempt to discover whether one or the other institution might be deemed the superior one.

On Differences

The first question of interest is the possible existence of statistically significantly different production functions by type of farm. Translog estimates for both types of farm for each crop are reported in Table 9.4. The coefficient on land, labor, and capital (the second through fourth columns) are especially interesting; they are the mean estimated output elasticities of the respective inputs. The coefficient λ denotes the estimated rate of neutral technical progress. At first glance, it appears that for three crops, grain, cotton, and potatoes, the mean output elasticities are quite similar for kolkhozy and sovkhozy. Further, for the latter two crops, estimated neutral technical progress is virtually identical. For the other two products, sugar beets and vegetables, the differences between comparable coefficients are quite large.

There are two ways to be more precise about this matter. First, the production functions, fit separately by type of farm to data on each crop, are estimated "together" as a pair of seemingly unrelated regressions (Zellner 1962). This allows the production function parameters to be more efficiently estimated, taking into account the correlation between disturbances in observations that are identical except for type of farm. It allows a nonzero covariance between "matched" disturbances representing, say, potatoes on Armenian kolkhozy in 1963 and potatoes on Armenian sovkhozy in that year, and a zero covariance for every "unmatched" pair. More important than increased efficiency (the efficient estimates are not presented here) is the fact that this procedure makes possible the performance of an F-test for coefficient equality across farm types. The interest here is in simultaneously testing the ten hypotheses that the coefficients on land are equal, those on labor are equal, and so on, up to and including the hypothesis of equal coefficients on technical progress.

The results of this procedure are contained in Table 9.5. Statistically, the crops for which the greatest differences exist are sugar beets and vegetables, with moderate divergence for the other three crops. The results of the second method of ascertaining differences by type of farm are presented in Table 9.6. Here, a dummy variable set equal to zero for all kolkhoz observations and one for all sovkhoz observations is included in regression estimated for the entire data set on a crop. As can readily be seen, this dummy variable is never statistically significant. In sum, by both methods, only modest technological differences by type of enterprise are observed.

It is interesting to speculate as to why the extent of technological differences by institutional variant varies among crops. The relative significance of the two institutions diverges considerably by product. Total grain output in 1978 was 52 percent from kolkhozy (and 47 percent from sovkhozy); while sugar beet output was 90 percent from kolkhozy (and 10 percent from sovkhozy); and cotton production was 70 percent from kolkhozy (and 30 percent from sovkhozy). Potatoes come predominantly from the private sector (61 percent), with the remainder being 23 percent from kolkhozy and 16 percent from sovkhozy, and vegetables (of which 29 percent come from the private plots) are 28 percent from the collective farm and 43 percent from the state farm (*Narkhoz* 1978, p. 196).

A regional explanation may be useful in shedding light on this question. The division of the output of a crop by type of farm for the nation as a whole reflects the prevailing division in the republics that dominate the production of that crop. A particularly interesting case is sugar beets, the percentage of which obtained from kolkhozy is the highest of all crops. Recall that the most significant difference in technology by type of farm was found for this crop. Most of sugar beet output (60 percent in 1978) coms from the Ukraine, where the kolkhoz predominates; another 4 percent derives from Moldavia and Lithuania, both of which are dominated by the collective farm. The small percentage of sugar beet output that does come from the sovkhoz most likely is obtained from relatively newly utilized areas

Table 9.4 Translog Results Separately by Type of Farm

Crop	Intercept	Land	Labor	Capital	Land²	Kolkhozy Labor²	Capital²	(Land)(Labor)	(Land)(Capital)	(Labor)(Capital)	λ[c]
Grain	−.361**[a] (−5.51)[b]	.757** (5.59)	.137 (1.61)	.362** (2.79)	.576 (1.29)	.182 (1.11)	.019 (.105)	.010 (.018)	−.934 (−1.31)	.200 (.452)	.034* (5.09)
Sugar Beets	−.206** (−2.85)	.255 (1.38)	.875** (6.91)	.929** (.187)	3.26*[a] (2.03)	−.652 (−1.43)	−.307 (−.850)	−1.47 (−1.00)	1.02 (.704)	−1.62** (−2.78)	.023* (3.10)
Cotton	−.196** (−4.71)	.450 (1.01)	.294 (1.13)	.063 (.920)	−15.30 (−1.07)	.880 (.262)	.039 (.390)	12.17 (.915)	−2.48 (−1.47)	.432 (.494)	.020** (5.90)
Potatoes	−.162* (−1.99)	.007 (.044)	.790** (5.56)	.481* (2.46)	−.846 (−1.53)	−.776 (−1.54)	−1.48* (−2.51)	.679 (.916)	−1.73 (−1.86)	−1.40 (−1.46)	.021* (2.58)
Vegetables	−.261 (−1.76)	−.085 (−.460)	.929** (6.51)	.737* (2.12)	.178 (1.34)	.164 (.435)	1.09* (2.24)	−.222 (−.290)	2.95* (2.26)	−1.92* (−2.40)	.016 (1.14)

Note: The heading of each column refers to the logarithm of the relevant variable, with, for example Capital² denoting the coefficient on the square of the log of capital, and (Land)(Labor) denoting the coefficient on the product of the logs of land and labor, and so on.
[a]Two asterisks (**) indicate that the regressor is significant at 0.01; one indicates that it is significant at 0.05.
[b]*t*-statistics are in parentheses below each estimated coefficient.
[c]λ is the coefficient on the time index *t*.

Table 9.4 (continued)

Crop	Intercept	Land	Labor	Capital	Land²	Labor²	Sovkhozy Capital²	(Land)(Labor)	(Land)(Capital)	(Labor)(Capital)
Grain	.089 (−1.23)	.840** (5.12)	.040 (.490)	.380** (3.09)	−2.02 (−1.76)	−.375 (−1.21)	−.279 (−1.16)	2.13* (2.03)	1.35 (1.50)	−.37 (−1.20)
Sugar Beets	−.700** (−5.14)	−.012 (−.07)	1.03** (7.36)	−.516* (−2.27)	−.046 (−.100)	−.199 (−.412)	−.510 (−1.91)	−.110 (−.146)	.190 (.438)	.0001 (.0003)
Cotton	−.200** (−3.38)	.862** (5.26)	.187 (1.36)	.109 (1.06)	.864 (.725)	.413 (.411)	−.239 (−1.09)	−1.71 (−.795)	.606 (1.38)	.153 (.317)
Potatoes	−.224* (−2.15)	.101 (.668)	.724** (6.05)	.483** (2.82)	.084 (.310)	−.094 (−.473)	.413* (2.11)	.123 (.321)	−1.00 (−1.62)	.221 (.571)
Vegetables	−.477** (−4.20)	.137 (.839)	.924** (7.47)	.095 (.431)	.360 (.567)	.425 (1.94)	.550 (1.80)	−.205 (−.193)	−1.44 (−1.68)	.591 (.700)

Note: The heading of each column refers to the logarithm of the relevant variable, with, for example Capital² denoting the coefficient on the square of the log of capital, and (Land)(Labor) denoting the coefficient on the product of the logs of land and labor, and so on.
[a] Two asterisks (**) indicate that the regressor is significant at 0.01; one indicates that it is significant at 0.05.
[b] t-statistics are in parentheses below each estimated coefficient.
[c] λ is the coefficient on the time index t.

Table 9.5

Crop	F-value	Degrees of freedom	Significance level[a]
Grain	2.17	10 and 220	.05
Sugar Beets	5.75	10 and 120	.01
Cotton	2.01	10 and 52	—
Potatoes	2.02	10 and 206	.05
Vegetables	2.56	10 and 122	.01

The numbers in this column mean that the difference is significant with *at most* the given probability of Type 1 error. "—" means that the difference is not significant at .05.

in Kazakhstan and Kirghizia. Hence, for sugar beets, divergence by type of farm may really be regional differentiation (Hultquist 1967).

Grain, for which relatively small differences by organizational form were found, is split about evenly in the country as a whole between collective and state farms. In 1978, the RSFSR was responsible for 58 percent of grain output, and grain output tends to be quite evenly split by variant in this huge republic. If the two organizational types are about evenly distributed across the landscape of the RSFSR, this might explain the failure to find particularly significant technological differences between them. Similarly, the lack of difference by type of farm for cotton might be attributed to the fact that all of it is grown in Central Asia (and Azerbaidzhan), and hence regional differences are unlikely to be significant.

The significant divergence in the technology of vegetable growing may have a different sort of explanation. It may reflect the comparison of specialized suburban sovkhozy and nonspecialized ubiquitous kolkhozy whose primary enterprises are other crops. Vegetables are the only crop for which the sovkhoz dominates social-sector production, and it is quite possible that different production methods are employed on these specialized farms from those used on ordinary kolkhozy. These explanations are taken up again below in the context of the superiority question. For now, the following observation seems appropriate: divergence in estimated technology by type of farm may not reflect any endemic differentiation in production methods between them, so much as variability of a regional or other plausible nature.

On the Kolkhoz as a Cooperative

The next question is whether or not the kolkhoz resembles a self-managed firm. Specifically, the magnitudes of the average and marginal products of labor are of interest. Because the translog function, having been estimated on predivided data (see "Data and Methods"), forces the mean marginal products and mean output elasticities of each input to be approximately equal, it is best not to use it to find mean factor productivities. Table 9.7

Table 9.6 Translog Results With a Dummy Variable Denoting Farm Type

Crop	Intercept	Land	Labor	Capital	Land²	Labor²	Capital²	(Land)(Labor)	(Land)(Capital)	(Labor)(Capital)	λ[c]	Dummy[d]
Grain	−.253**[a] (−6.02)[b]	.696** (6.98)	.053 (.296)	.283** (3.60)	.308 (.831)	.145 (1.25)	−.066 (−.789)	.149 (.358)	−.490 (−1.58)	.055 (.322)	.023** (5.93)	.008 (.319)
Sugar Beets	−.496** (−6.56)	.097 (.749)	.894** (8.49)	−.067 (−.481)	.106 (.261)	−.129 (−.355)	−.231 (−1.27)	−.428 (−.689)	.328 (.889)	−.349 (−.981)	.055** (6.95)	−.004 (−.108)
Cotton	−.181** (−5.02)	.694** (5.28)	.379** (3.36)	.029 (.662)	−.090 (−.095)	−.697 (−.825)	−.093 (−1.36)	.718 (.420)	.064 (.195)	.159 (.520)	.019** (6.44)	−.030 (−1.50)
Potatoes	−.167*[a] (−2.57)	−.021 (−.212)	.788** (9.30)	.569** (5.11)	−.236 (−1.14)	−.056 (−.346)	.293* (2.29)	.258 (.807)	−.417 (−1.19)	−.042 (−.158)	.017** (2.61)	−.013 (−.527)
Vegetables	−.315** (−3.46)	−.048 (−.434)	.960** (10.84)	.523** (2.76)	.406 (1.06)	.370 (1.95)	.516* (2.24)	−.471 (−1.10)	−.434 (−.885)	.178 (.399)	.026** (3.02)	−.009 (−.315)

Note: The heading of each column refers to the logarithm of the relevant variable, with, for example, Capital² denoting the coefficient on the square of the log of capital, and (Land)(Labor) denoting the coefficient on the product of the logs of land and labor, and so on.
[a]Two asterisks mean that the regressor is significant at 0.01; one means that it is significant at 0.05.
[b]*t*-statistics are in parentheses below each estimated coefficient.
[c]λis the coefficient of the time index *t*.
[d]The variable Dummy = 0 if the observation comes from a kolkhoz; Dummy = 1 if it comes from a sovkhoz.

Table 9.7   Mean Average and Marginal Products
              of Land and Labor

	Kolkhozy			
	Land		Labor	
	MP	AP	MP	AP
Grain	1.053	1.491	− .0062	.0331
Sugar Beets	18.95	22.72	.0109	.0515
Cotton	1.312	2.699	.0008	.0025
Potatoes	6.178	7.921	.0067	.0204
Vegetables	1.390	10.61	.0051	.0081
	Sovkhozy			
	Land		Labor	
	MP	AP	MP	AP
Grain	.8585	1.257	.0129	.0065
Sugar Beets	.2965	9.265	.0417	.0452
Cotton	.6529	2.127	.0023	.0031
Potatoes	6.638	8.722	.0112	.0305
Vegetables	18.19	18.96	− .0127	.0158

Note: As estimated from a Cobb-Douglas production function
run on undivided data.

presents the mean marginal products of land and labor, as estimated from a
Cobb-Douglas production.[14] Observe that the estimated marginal product
of labor is higher on sovkhozy for every crop but vegetables and that the
average product of labor is higher on sovkhozy for all crops but grain and
sugar beets. This finding suggests that the impacts of more complementary
inputs with which to work and a higher-quality labor force (among other
things) outweigh any tendency to conserve on hiring in the manner of a self-
managed enterprise.

On the Question of Superiority

In this subsection, attention is turned to the issue of whether either type of
farm can be deemed superior. A number of angles from which this problem
can be approached have already been mentioned: factor productivities can
be examined and returns to scale, factor substitution, and the rate of
technical progress compared. Unfortunately, because capital inputs are
measured by proxy, it is impossible to obtain estimates of its productivity
that can be readily interpreted. As far as land and labor inputs are concerned, Table 9.7 suggests that neither type of farm enjoys higher marginal
or average productivity for both factors—the comparisons of labor productivity tend to favor the state farm and those of land productivity the collective farm.

Rather than impinging upon the superiority issue, this result may reflect a
response (although not necessarily a cost-minimizing one in the Soviet con-

text) to different relative factor prices. Given the data on factor endowments in Table 9.1, it might be conjectured (following a similar analysis by Clayton (1980) in a regional context) that capital and land are "cheaper" relative to labor on sovkhozy than they are on kolkhozy.[15] If so, lower marginal productivity of these inputs and higher marginal productivity of labor would be expected on state farms. Furthermore, the two agricultural sectors seem to behave as if they were virtually autarchic countries; there is little evidence of productivity-equalizing mobility of factors.

However, some of the more striking results do have a certain plausibility. For example, if, as conjectured earlier, sugar beets grown on kolkhozy are largely from the Ukraine, and sovkhoz sugar beets mostly from Central Asia, and if the two systems are essentially closed with respect to each other, then the much higher marginal product of land on collective farms is very credible. Intensive application of labor and capital to Ukrainian sugar-beet production seems to have resulted in very high marginal land productivity and relatively low marginal labor productivity. The converse may be true on Central Asian sugar-beet-growing sovkhozy; marginal land productivity is very low and marginal labor productivity rather high. A similar explanation might apply to the very noticeable variation in productivity for vegetables. Small, specialized suburban vegetable-growing state farms seem to have much higher land productivity and lower labor productivity than unspecialized kolkhozy. For the other crops, the productivity differentials are relatively modest.

Returning to the issue of superiority, the estimated scale and substitution effects reported in Table 9.8 would seem slightly to favor the kolkhoz.

Table 9.8 Mean Estimates of Scale and Substitution Effects Derived from the Translog Production Function

| | | Kolkhozy | | |
| | | Elasticities of Substitution | | |
Crop	Returns to Scale	σ_{RL}	σ_{RK}	σ_{LK}
Grain	1.25	.382	−.769	.262
Cotton	.926	.025	−.302	.323
Potatoes	1.53	.389	−.823	−.198
Vegetables	1.49	−.533	.729	.350

| | | Sovkhozy | | |
| | | Elasticities of Substitution | | |
Crop	Returns to Scale	σ_{RL}	σ_{RK}	σ_{LK}
Grain	1.22	.311	.035	−.832
Cotton	1.15	−.208	.245	.810
Potatoes	1.33	.573	−.791	.170
Vegetables	1.15	.133	−.680	.169

Note: Results for sugar beets were unreliable and are not presented.

Returns to scale are very high for both variants (a similar finding was reported in Wyzan 1981) and are higher on kolkhozy for three of the four crops reported.[16] Looking at the estimated partial elasticities of substitution in the same table, it is of interest to know how many of these elasticities are negative or greater than one. In such cases, optimistic growth forecasts can be made for the relevant crop, because the growth weight (output elasticity) of the faster-growing factor will rise. For kolkhozy, five of the twelve elasticities of substitution are negative; whereas for sovkhozy, four are (none is greater than one for either crop). This result suggests that the outlook for future output growth is at worst no bleaker on collective farms than on state farms. Finally, recall from Table 9.4 that the estimated rate of neutral technical progress is higher on kolkhozy for four of the five crops.

CONCLUSION

At the beginning of this paper, a brief look is taken at the extant institutional differences between the types of farm. Although most divergence seems to have been eliminated, there continues to exist some dichotomy in areas such as finance, the planning process, and perhaps price levels. At the same time, there remain aspects of kolkhoz practice that are suggestive of the behavior of a self-managed firm. There also seems to persist some disagreement among Soviet and Western scholars (although this is probably no longer a major issue) as to whether one form or the other is superior.

Three-input translog production functions are estimated for the period from 1960 to 1976 for five Soviet crops. The chief finding is that only relatively minor differences in productive technology exist. Where significant divergence is found, such as for vegetables and sugar beets, plausible institutional explanations are suggested—a regional one for the latter and one involving specialization for the former. No evidence that the kolkhoz resembles a self-managed firm is found. Finally, to the extent that one form may be said to outperform the other, the laurel might very tentatively be awarded to the collective farm, which seems to have slightly higher returns to scale, somewhat greater possibilities for factor substitution, and faster technological progress.

In conclusion, a word or two are in order on the limitations of the approach. First, the focus has entirely been on the two (historically) major institutional variants. The various relatively new forms of interenterprise cooperation—interkolkhoz associations, sovkhoz-factories, and, most notably, mixed kolkhoz-sovkhoz associations—have been ignored (Miller 1976). There is also no treatment of the technological divergence between the private sector and either of the two types of farm, even though these may be the most interesting comparisons of all. The Soviets do not publish data that would make this possible. Any reference to the important subunits of enterprises, especially the kolkhoz "link," which itself was being placed on khozarschët during the seventies (Osofsky 1974, pp. 74–75), is also omitted, for similar reasons.

Second, there are all manner of limitations inherent in the utilization of production functions. It sharply limits the questions one is able to ask; for example, in wondering whether the kolkhoz is a self-managed firm, the only evidence marshalled concerned labor productivity. One can, of course, also look at such items as labor migration, Phillips curves, structural change, savings rates, and so on, in examining this issue. Further, only three inputs have been utilized, and such important factors as fertilizer, irrigation, and material inputs have been omitted. A reduced number of inputs is a cost of having a large data set in the form of a pool of cross-sectional and time-series observations at the republic level. A smaller national data base would allow for more inputs, but would have its own difficulties, such as multicollinearity (Desai 1982). The method of measuring capital is also problematic; although it can be justified econometrically (Wyzan 1981), it makes it possible to measure capital productivity reliably.

Finally, there are a couple of limitations inherent in the time period chosen. As already mentioned, the data set only covers years after the major conversion campaigns; therefore pertains to a period for which the relevant divergence had perhaps already been sharply reduced. The nature of the results in the presence of data on the 1950s is purely conjectural. Second, time and space constraints precluded dividing the data into subperiods. Table 9.1 shows that kolkhozy on the average have become increasingly large in terms of all inputs, while the average sovkhoz has diminished in its labor force and sown area (and slightly augmented its use of capital as measured in horsepower). Subdivision of the data set, perhaps around the reforms of the mid-1960s, might yield interesting results. It is left for a future study.

To reiterate, the basic finding is that for most crops, the technological divergence by type of farm is rather insignificant. Where it is not, explanations involving differentiation by region or in the degree of specialization are offered; it is difficult to discern variation that inheres specifically in the organizational forms per se. Although this is something of a negative result, it does have one interesting implication. Campaigns to eliminate the kolkhoz, either through conversion or various forms of integration, cannot be based on an inherent economic inferiority of this institution. Instead, they may well be expressions of a purely ideological nature.

NOTES

1. Miller (1976) describes the operation of the so-called MO's (interkolkhoz associations) and their similarity to organizations in the state sector (the "sovkhoz-factories," which combine agricultural and industrial functions). For example, in Moldavia, grape-growing kolkhozy have been merged and transformed into sovkhoz-factory complexes that both grow grapes and make wine, and oilseed kolkhozy have been similarly converted into sovkhoz-factories specializing in the production of vegetable oil.

2. During the period prior to that covered by the data set, the Virgin Lands program was implemented mostly through the creation of sovkhozy. In the RSFSR 1267 state farms were created and another 588 were organized in Kazakhstan, between 1953 and 1960, bringing into cultivation 42 million new hectares of land. See Morozov, *Soviet Ariculture*, p. 72.

3. Certainly the most sophisticated proponent of the notion that agricultural production is qualitatively different from that of industry is Georgescu-Roegen, *Entrophy Law,* especially Chapter 10.

4. As in the industrial sector, the supposed reduction in the official number of targets has sometimes been ignored. Efremov (1976) cites the provision of quarterly assignments in addition to annual ones, withdrawal of the farms' power to channel depreciation charges into its investment fund, and the lack of responsibility on the part of suppliers of industrial machinery for the final results of production.

5. Gray ("Soviet Agricultural Specialization," p. 547) reports that, by some measures, the degree of specialization among sovkhozy increased from 1965 to 1973.

6. See Steinherr ("On the Efficiency," pp. 546–547) for a clear description of this phenomenon. Sapir (1980) uses a CES production function to demonstrate how a rising capital-labor ratio, attributable for the introduction of self-management in the mid-1960s and a low elasticity of substitution between capital and labor, combined to cause a slowdown in Yugoslav economic growth. His study is a good example of how the estimation of production functions can be used to examine questions of this type.

7. Such a system of remuneration does make for some connection between output and wages, inasmuch as bonuses from the incentives fund are based on the level of output. But it seems that the output-wage nexus is less obvious on state farms than on collective farms, and, as mentioned in the text, Soviet writers tend to confirm this.

8. There now exist methods by which production "frontiers" can be estimated. These are standards of technical efficiency to which observations (or sets thereof) can be compared. Inasmuch as these methods are best suited to data at the level of the firm, they are not employed on the aggregative data in this paper. See Aigner and Chu "On Estimating," pp. 826–839, Aigner, Lovell, and Schmidt "Formulation and Estimation," pp. 21–38. In the present instance, overall efficiency is estimated by means of a simple dummy variable included in the production functions.

9. It must be emphasized that the results that follow are strictly limited in their implications to the specific empirical matters just mentioned. A further limitation is worth noting. The data set employed cover the years from 1960 to 1976; as such, it pertains to a period that followed an era of massive conversions of (generally) relatively "weak" kolkhozy into sovkhozy. It is quite possible that, if the kolkhoz were the "inferior" economic unit (however defined), these conversions reduced or even eliminated what had been major differences between the variants. This divergence would hence be much more evident if one examined data from, say, the 1950s. Inasmuch as such data are unavailable, this is not possible, and our results are hence confined to the relatively stable postconversion era. Other limitations are mentioned in the concluding section.

10. The absence of data on Kazakhstan is particularly bothersome because it is the region in which the sovkhoz is the most dominant. In 1978, the republic had 2035 state farms and only 418 collective farms; the former has 82.6 percent of the republic's labor force and 91.1 percent of its sown area. Of the remaining five excluded republics, in Belorussia and Turkmenistan, the kolkhoz is somewhat more important; whereas in Georgia, Latvia, and Kirghizia, both types of farm are about equally significant (*Narkhoz* 1978, pp. 266, 267, 279).

11. The failure qualitatively to adjust land inputs, the fertility of which must vary considerably across such a large nation, deserves further comment. Two pieces of evidence suggest that this may not be a major problem. First, regional dummy variables included in estimated (translog) production functions all proved statistically significant for every crop. Second, Clayton ("Productivity," p. 453) notes that Soviet land data adjusted by a method of her own devising, when included in an aggregate production function, give insignificantly different results from unadjusted data.

12. Two comments are in order on the labor data. First, these data permit measurement of only direct labor inputs into the production process. Farm activity, of course, necessitates the expenditure of effort into a variety of common activities that are difficult in principle, and impossible with Soviet data, to attribute to specific crops. The estimation of multioutput transformation functions with total farm labor as an input would be an attractive way to handle this problem. Second, the labor figures measure actual rather than potential inputs; as Donald Green has pointed out to me, the former are closely tied to weather conditions, a fact that tends to make estimates of labor's marginal product and output elasticity abnormally high. This can be remedied somewhat by including weather variables in the estimated functions, something that I hope to do at some future date.

13. Tractors are used in all cases involving vegetables because of the absence of a specific type of machine used in their production. Although some figures are available on beet combines and potato combines, such data cannot be obtained for every republic. It was therefore deemed best to use tractors in each sugar beet and potato observation. For discussions of the econometric implications of the use of a proxy variable and of omitting other inputs such as fertilizer, see Wyzan, "Empirical Analysis," pp. 475–483.

14. To elaborate on this rather arcane point a bit, it has already been mentioned that in using the translog function as a Taylor-series expansion, the data on output and each of the inputs were divided by their means before estimation. Now, the output elasticity of each input (as given by equation (2)) is defined as follows

$$\frac{\delta \ln Q}{\delta \ln B} = \frac{\delta Q}{\delta B} \cdot \frac{B}{Q}$$

where B is an input and $\delta Q/\delta B$ is its marginal product. The translog function provides an estimate of $\delta \ln Q/\delta \ln B$ for each type of farm.

However, because the means of B and Q are both one, the mean of B/Q is about one (for both variants of course). Hence

$$\overline{\frac{\delta \ln Q}{\delta \ln B}} \approx \overline{\frac{Q}{B}}$$

where the bars indicate that the item in parentheses is evaluated at the overall means of the data set; this approximate equality again applies to both types of farm. The practical effect of this is as follows: The marginal product of a certain input into the production of a given crop can differ by organizational form only if the estimated production functions differ. This seems an inappropriate restriction. One would like to allow for the possibility that the types of farm face essentially the same technology, but use different input combinations in response to, say, different relative factor prices.

For this reason, the Cobb-Douglas function is used in the factor productivity comparisons. It is not meant to be construed as a Taylor-series expansion and is therefore not run on predivided data.

15. I am referring, of course, to the unobserved opportunity costs of the factors and not to their actual prices.

16. The high estimated returns to scale merely imply that, for the specific technologies the Soviets have chosen to exploit, large-scale production can be carried out at a lower per-unit cost than small-scale production. They do not tell us anything about the efficiency of smaller farms, such as that of the private plots or hypothetical small enterprises run on a capitalist basis.

REFERENCES

Dennis Aigner and S. Chu, "On Estimating the Industry Production Function," *American Economic Review* 58 (September 1968): 826–839.

Dennis Aigner, C. A. Knox Lovell, and Peter Schmidt, "Formulation and Estimation of Stochastic Frontier Production Function Models," *Journal of Econometrics* 6 (July 1977): 21–38.

Ernst Berndt and Laurits Christensen, "The Translog Function and the Substitution of Equipment, Structure, and Labor in U.S. Manufacturing 1929–68," *Journal of Econometrics* 1 (March 1973): 81–113.

N. Borkhunov, "Zakupochnye Tseny v Mekhanizme Finansovogo Obespecheniia Khoziaistv," *Ekonomika Sel'skogo Khoziaistva*, no. 11 (1980): 39–43.

Morris Bornstein, "The Soviet Debate on Agricultural Price and Procurement Reforms," *Soviet Studies* 20 (July 1969): 1–20.

———, "Soviet Price Policy in the 1970s," in U.S. Congress, Joint Economic Committee, *Soviet Economy in a New Perspective*, (Washington, D.C.: Government Printing Office, 1976), pp. 17–66.

I. Buzdalov, "Problemy Rosta Effektivnosti Sovkhoznogo Proizvodstva," *Voprosy Ekonomiki* no. 3 (1965): 3–12.

Elizabeth Clayton, "Productivity in Soviet Agriculture," *Slavic Review* 39 (September 1980): 446–458.

Padma Desai, "Soviet Grain and Wheat Import Demand in 1981–85," *American Journal of Agricultural Economics* 64 (May 1982): 312–322.

Evsey Domar, "The Soviet Collective Farm as a Producer Cooperative," *American Review* 56 (September 1966): 734–757.

G. Efremov, *Pravda,* 9 January 1976. Translated in *Current Digest of the Soviet Press,* 28, no. 1 (4 February 1976), p. 19.

M. Galsanov, "Kredit i Organizatisiia Sredstv," *Ekonomika Sel'skogo Khoziaistva* no. 2 (1980): 24–26.

Nicholas Georgescu-Roegen, *The Entropy Law and the Economic Process.* (Cambridge, Mass.: Harvard University Press, 1971).

Kenneth Gray, "Soviet Agricultural Specialization and Efficiency," *Soviet Studies* 31 (October 1979): 542–558.

Warren Hultquist, "Soviet Sugar-Beet Production: Some Geographical Aspects of Agro-Industrial Coordination," in *Soviet and East European Agriculture,* ed. Jerzy Karcz. (Berkeley: University of California Press, 1967), pp. 135–151.

Alastair McAuley, *Economic Welfare in the Soviet Union.* (Madison: University of Wisconsin Press, 1979).

James Millar, "Financing the Modernization of Kolkhozy," in *The Soviet Rural Community,* ed. James Millar (Urbana: University of Illinois Press, 1971), pp. 276–303.

Robert Miller, "The Future of the Soviet Kolkhoz," *Problems of Communism* 25 (March–April 1976): 34–50.

V. Morozov, *Soviet Agriculture.* Translated by Inna Medova. (Moscow: Progress Publishers, 1977).

Nancy Nimitz, "Farm Employment in the Soviet Union, 1928–1963," in *Soviet and East European Agriculture,* ed. Jerzy Karcz (Berkeley: University of California Press, 1967), pp. 175–205.

Walter Oi and Elizabeth Clayton, "A Peasant's View of a Soviet Collective Farm," *American Economic Review* 58 (March 1968): 37–59.

Stephen Osofsky, *Soviet Agricultural Policy: Toward the Abolition of Collective Farms* (New York: Praeger Publishers, 1974).

Andre Sapir, "Economic Growth and Factor Substitution: What Happened to the Yugoslav Miracle?" *Economic Journal* 90 (June 1980): 294–313.

Alfred Steinherr, "On the Efficiency of Profit Sharing and Labor Participation In Management." *Bell Journal of Economics* 8 (Autumn 1977): 545–55.

Robert Stuart, *The Collective Farm in Soviet Agriculture* (Lexington, Mass.: D.C. Heath & Co., 1972).

Vladimir Treml, "Agricultural Subsidies in the Soviet Union," U.S. Department of Commerce, Bureau of the Census, Foreign Economic Report No. 15, December 1978.

Tsentral'noe Statisticheskoe Upravlenie. *Narodnoe Khoziaistvo SSSR V—Godu.* Moscow: "Statistika," various years. Referred to in the text as *Narkhoz.*

Karl-Eugen Wädekin, "Soviet Rural Society: A Descriptive Stratification Analysis," *Soviet Studies* 22 (April 1971): 512–538.

———. *The Private Sector in Soviet Agriculture.* Translated by Keith Bush. (Berkeley: University of California Press, 1973).

Michael Wyzan, "Empirical Analysis of Soviet Agricultural Production and Policy," *American Journal of Agricultural Economics* 63 (August 1981): 475–483.

Arnold Zellner, "An Efficient Method of Estimating Seemingly Unrelated Regressions and Tests for Aggregation Bias," *Journal of the American Statistical Association* 57 (June 1962): 348–368.

10

Improved Agricultural Location: Econometric Evidence from the Ukraine

Kenneth R. Gray

INTRODUCTION: PRODUCTION COSTS AND AUTARKY

During the past twenty years several attempts have been made to quantify the comparative efficiency and trends in performance of Soviet agriculture. One methodology has been to compare partial productivity indices (such as labor productivity and yields) for Socialist and non-Socialist analogue regions that are chosen to minimize climatic differences.[1] Yet another approach has in effect created a historical analogue, by making comparisons of Soviet agriculture with itself over time, through aggregate production function formulations applied to time-series data.[2] These latter studies relate output indices to measured input indices and attribute residual growth of aggregate output (total factor productivity) to "technological change."

The present paper is a disaggregated production function study of an available time series of data related to production of individual crops grown in the twenty-five oblasts of the Ukraine. What is sought is evidence of improvement over time of particular microeconomic decision making: the locational distribution of crop production. While agricultural location in the West is generally considered to be within the competency of decentralized decision making, it is an object of deliberate policy making in the Soviet Union, where marketing and many production decisions continue to be largely centrally planned. The many unresolved and perplexing issues that plague Soviet decision making in this (for them) difficult area have been described by this author elsewhere.[3]

This paper will examine indirectly production cost, to see if it has been reduced for given output growth in the Ukraine, or alternatively, if agricultural specialization has been improved to get more output growth from resources located throughout the Ukraine.

Unlike analogue studies and aggregate production function studies, the present methodology relates measured trends in Soviet performance in this

The author acknowledges helpful commentary by Robert Stuart, Michael Zahn, David Granick, and Earl Brubaker on an earlier version of this study.

area against absolute standards of allocative efficiency suggested by the logic of price theory.[4] These standards are absolute in the sense that they transcend economic systems and hold for production everywhere.

The problem of efficient agricultural specialization is, however, terribly complex. It involves multiproduct, spatial, and temporal aspects that are imperfectly captured, even by the most refined linear programming models.[5] There is an irony involved in any attempt such as this one, since the motivation to "check up" on Soviet resource allocation is frequently skepticism that central decision makers have enough information to make efficient decisions. Yet Western observers may have much less information about production possibilities and constraints than do planners.

The present study is justified because there are available many relevant data for the Ukraine for a period in which we know Soviet efforts have been concentrated on improving agricultural specialization. Second, relevant theory exists to organize these data. Last, the present analysis can be meaningfully simplified to examination of trends in interregional production costs alone, a subset of the full problem, which also involves the cost of transporting state procurement.

It is a common perception that Soviet agriculture has been characterized by a high degree of regional self-sufficiency, or *autarky*.[6] The historical record provides evidence that this has been the case. For instance, a single-minded desire to minimize transportation costs, accompanied by professed skepticism about previous capitalist patterns of specialization, led in the 1930s to the expansion of cotton and sugar beet cultivation to regions where these crops had not been previously grown.[7] Steps were taken to eliminate entirely the interoblast transportation of potatoes after 1939 and to reduce significantly the interoblast transportation of sugar.[8] Cotton production soon proved unsuited for the new areas of the RSFSR and Ukraine to which it had been extended, but sugar beet cultivation remained scattered in the Far East, Eastern Siberia, and elsewhere until the transportation minimization goal yielded to broader economic calculations in the mid-1960s.[9] There were reports in Soviet publications in the mid-1960s of continued restrictions on the interoblast shipment of vegetables and fruit, which were thought to have contributed to decisions to locate winter greenhouse production near northern industrial cities. These investments have recently been reconsidered, as the other examples above have, because they led to inordinately high production costs.[10]

The 1960s brought a reorientation toward regional specialization evidenced by official decrees and the commissioning of research institutes, Gosplan, and the Ministry of Agriculture to find correct patterns of specialization.[11] The growing rejection of transportation cost minimization as the prevalent criterion of agricultural location is evident also in the blossoming in the mid-1960s of linear programming models, which concentrated on the minimization of production costs through increased specialization, with only slight formal inclusion of transportation considerations. Such an applied modelling effort was executed by M. E. Braslavets and the Ukrainian Republic Gosplan in the course of preparing oblast agricultural procurement quotas for twenty products for the 1966–1970 Five-Year Plan.[12]

Production cost can clearly be reduced up to a point through increased specialization and expenditure of transportation resources. The effects of such a policy would be potentially observable in measured increased "total" factor productivity (especially were the study not to include transportation inputs). A policy emphasizing production cost reduction could, of course, be overdone to the detriment of efficiency at the economywide level. Only insofar as Soviet criticism is correct, that past autarky was excessive, is evidence of increased interregional specialization evidence, within limits, of increased general cost-efficiency.

THEORETICAL ANALYSIS

In neoclassical terms, a change in emphasis from transportation cost to production cost minimization, a move away from relative regional autarky in farm procurement, would be reflected in a convergency of marginal rates of product transformation among regions. This idea is illustrated in Figure 10.1. Here ($t_1-t'_1$ and $t_2-t'_2$) represent the net product transformation curves of two agricultural regions. The relative shapes of these two curves indicate that Region 1 is a relatively more able livestock producer than

Figure 10.1
Dispersion of Marginal Rates of Product Transformation

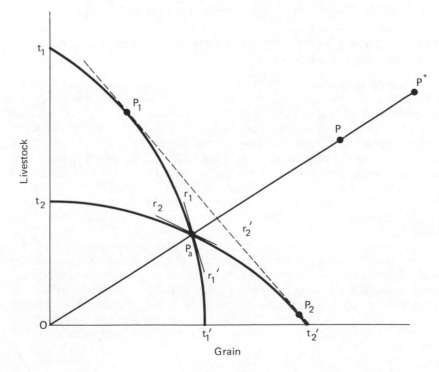

Region 2, which is better suited for grain production. A policy limiting the specialization of the two regions might have each producing equal quantities of both products, represented by P_a, a point on both curves. (An overall combination, $P = 2P_a$, is produced.) With this outcome the marginal rates of product transformation (MRPT) of the two regions are not equal, as is indicated by the intersection at P_a of the lines $r_1-r'_1$ and $r_2-r'_2$, whose slopes are equal to the respective rates of transformation. An effort to reduce overall production cost would result in greater livestock specialization by Region 1 and greater grain specialization by Region 2. If transportation costs were totally ignored, production cost minimization (for the overall combination P^*, which has more of both grain and livestock than P) would result in production of combinations P_1 and P_2. These combinations would be characterized by identical marginal rates of product transformation (MRPT) in both regions (indicated by the dotted line). Specialization could go too far. Put simply, efficient specialization, producing the right amount of goods in regions best suited for them, will lead to an increase in total output.

Our interest essentially is whether there has been convergence of the MRPT's of twenty-five oblasts over time, which would indicate support for the hypothesis that Ukrainian procurement policy has succeeded in rectifying a situation of relative agricultural autarky. Given immobilities in capital stocks, this process, if it occurs, should be strung out over and observable in the years for which data are available. Measurements of MRPT and devised, and the dispersion across regions of these is computed (for the period 1956 to 1973). The trends of disperson are then found.

PRODUCTION FUNCTIONS AND THE MARGINAL RATE OF PRODUCT TRANSFORMATION

Were Soviet agriculture a market economy, questions about interregional efficiency might be resolved by specifying a neoclassical technology and firm behavior such that MRPT would be equated to price ratios adjusted for transport costs. Relative prices would then be observed and some empirical conclusion drawn. However, in the Soviet case there are two problems. First, no continuous series of regionally differentiated procurement price data is available to the investigator. Secondly, Soviet farms pursue profit or output maximization under the constraint of fulfillment of plan. In many cases the existence of separate penalties for nonfulfillment of plan means that relative procurement prices ratios (even if available) will reveal little about MRPT.

Another approach taken in a preliminary fashion by western commentators has been to examine changes in regional growth rates of procurement in the light of burgeoning quantity of *sebestoimost'* (or prime) cost data.[13] While *sebestoimost'* data can be useful (they include conceptually all normally thought-of costs except rent and interest), they are particularly inadequate for agriculture, in that *sebestoimost'* does not include the opportunity cost of land. This point is illustrated in Table 10.1, wherein *sebestoimost'*

Table 10.1

Sugar Beet Shadow Prices

Region & Republic	Full cost (otsenka) (ru./cent.)	Cost (sebestoimost') (ru./cent.)
Kirgizhia	1.26	1.09
Ukraine-Forest Steppe	1.26	1.16
Ukraine-Polesye	1.30	1.19
Armenia	1.32	1.32
Ukraine-Steppe	1.35	1.21
Moldavia	1.41	1.29
North Caucasus	1.56	1.39
Central-Blackearth	1.65	1.60
Kazakhistan	1.86	1.85
Georgia	1.90	1.90
Volga-Viatsky	1.90	1.90
Latvia	2.10	2.08
Lithuania	2.11	2.07
Polvolzh	2.14	2.08
Central	2.20	2.20
Urals	2.32	2.26
Belorussia	2.38	2.36
West Siberia	2.48	2.40
East Siberia	2.54	2.50
Far East	3.00	3.00

Buckwheat Shadow Prices

Region & Republic	Full cost (otsenka) (ru./cent.)	Cost (sebestoimost') (ru./cent.)
Central Blackearth	5.46	4.22
Latvia	5.62	5.20
Estonia	5.63	5.40
Urals	5.70	4.73
West Siberia	5.78	4.10
Lithuania	5.97	5.22
Polvolzh	6.44	5.20
East Siberia	6.45	5.62
Kazakhistan	6.80	6.36
North Caucasus	7.23	2.33
Belorussia	7.23	6.87
Volga-Viatsky	8.10	8.10
Central	8.17	8.17
North-West	8.50	8.50
Ukraine-Polesye	8.61	4.93
Ukraine-Forest Steppe	8.63	5.29
Far East	8.80	8.80

Source: V. S. Mikheeva, *Matematicheskie metody v planifovanii razmeshcheniia sel'skokhoziaistvennogo proizvodstva* (Moscow: Ekonomika, 1966), p. 64.

cost is given for both sugar beet and buckwheat for a number of regions of the USSR. A full cost measure (*otsenka*), which includes a rental element calculated in a Soviet linear programming exercise is given in the first column. The table illustrates that, especially for crops (like buckwheat), which are land intensive, and especially in areas of great fertility (like the North Caucusus), *sebestoimost'* differs from full cost significantly.

The approach taken here is to combine *sebestoimost'* together with available data on land inputs, in a specified neoclassical production function in order to deduce marginal products and proxies for MRPT. Because of data stringencies, there is not much room for experimentation in the specification of technology. The particular approach is to use Cobb-Douglas production functions for each product, in each region (*oblast'*). A production function technology is needed in order to derive measurement of margins from available average product data.*

The assumptions of this approach are outlined below.

Assumption about the Regional Production Functions

The form below represents the deterministic production function for a product i, produced in the jth oblast at year t, with inputs subscripted, k; $k = 1, \ldots, n$.

(1) $\quad Z_{ijt} = A'_{ijt} N_{1ijt}^{C_{1ij}} N_{2ijt}^{C_{2ij}}, \ldots, N_{kijt}^{C_{kij}}, \ldots, N_{nijt}^{C_{nij}}$

or, dropping i, j, and t subscripts for notational convenience:

(1a) $\quad Z = A' N_1^{C_1} N_2^{C_2}, \ldots, N_k'^{C_k}, \ldots, N_n^{C_n} = A' \prod_{k=1}^{n} N_k^{C_k}$

Variations of Land Quality

The nth input, N_n, called land, is assumed to be homogeneous within a region, but heterogeneous among regions. Land in an area j is denotable $q_j L_j$, where L_j is the land area in hectares in region j, and q_j adjusts for differential quality among regions.

---

*Another possible technology for getting MRPTs (other than separate production functions for each product) would be the specification of an entire transformation function, as done by Y. Mundlak for an investigation of the transformation relationships of several products in Australian agriculture. His function was a translog production function, which can be separated into one function of the inputs and another of the outputs. This procedure has three consequences: (1) In this specification MRPT are not affected by input intensities; this means that transformation curves shift homothetically with changes in any or all inputs. This is unrealistic for a situation where the ratio of other resources to land increases over time. (2) This formation almost always means that outputs are produced jointly, which is realistic for agriculture; however, this specification does not allow for use of average product data, which attribute inputs directly to outputs (as available data do). (3) Specification of an entire transformation function as done by Mundlak requires estimation of several parameters, for which the data used are less than adequate. Thus even though it violates the spirit of the discussion of joint costs in Gray (1979), the present exercise specifies individual production functions and uses the average cost data available. (cf., Y. Mundlak, "Specification and Estimation of Multi-product Functions," *Journal of Farm Economics* [May 1963].)

Aggregation of Nonland Inputs

The subset of nonland inputs, $k = 1, \ldots, n-1$, expressed in monetary units with prices P_k so that $R_k = P_k N_k$ (Eq. 1)′ can be written as:

(1b′) $\quad Z = A'\, (qL)^{C_n} \left(\prod_{k=1}^{n-1} P_k^{-C_k} \right) \cdot \left(\prod_{k=1}^{n-1} R_k^{C_k} \right)$ by substitution.

(2) $\quad R_j = \sum_{k=1}^{n-1} P_{kj}\, N_{kj}.$

R will be referred to as the *ruble* input, or alternatively, as *nonland* input. Money prices, P_{kj}, used for aggregation are assumed proportional to the marginal products of each input in natural units for each crop within each region j. That is:

(3) $\quad (\delta Z/\delta N_k)/P_{kj} = (\delta Z/\delta N_{k'})/P_{k'j} \quad$ for $k \neq k'$.

Ruble and Land-input Production Function

Assumptions (b) and (c) make possible the writings of the production function give in Equation (1) in natural units, in ruble terms (restoring all superscripts) as:

(4) $\quad Z_{ijt} = Z_{ijt}\, R_{ijt}^{\alpha_{ij}}\, L_{ijt}^{\beta_{ij}}$

where $A_{ijt} = A'_{ijt}\, q_j^{c_n} \prod_{k=1}^{n-1} P_{kijt}^{-C_{kij}}$,

$\quad \alpha_{ij} = \sum_{k=1}^{n-1} C_{kij}$ and $\beta_{ij} = C_{nij}$

If it is assumed that $\alpha + \beta = 1$, Equation (4) can be rewritten in "per-hectare" form.

(5) $\quad Z/L = A(R/L)^\alpha \quad$ i.e., Yield $= A$ (rubles/hectare)$^\alpha$.

Intraregional Mobility of all Inputs

Within a region both land and nonland inputs are mobile among crop and livestock processes.

Definition of the Marginal Rate of Product Transformation
Through the kth input

By the assumption of mobility (e), within a single region, j, one product, z, can be transformed into product z′, by transfering a unit of any one input k from one production process to the other, leaving all other input assignments unchanged. We here define the *marginal rate of product transformation through the kth input* (MRPT-k) to be the transformation thus achieved. It is expressed as the ratio of marginal products of the input k in producing the two products z and z′.

(6) $\dfrac{\delta z}{\delta z'}\bigg|dN_k = (\delta Z/\delta N_k)/(\delta Z'/\delta N_k)$

If a region distributes inputs efficiently among crops, it is on its production transformation frontier, and a single marginal rate of product transformation, as we normally speak of it, exists. In this case, in that region:

(7) $\dfrac{\delta z}{\delta z'}\bigg|dR = \dfrac{\delta z}{\delta z'}\bigg|dL$

Assumptions (b) and (c) (concerning the homogeneity of land and the form of aggregation of nonland inputs) assure that the partial derivatives of the production functions with respect to the aggregates L and R are nonambiguous.*

Given these assumptions, the *marginal rates of product* transformation for two products, z and z' in a region j are given as:†

(8) MRPT-land $= \dfrac{\delta z/\delta L}{\delta z'/\delta L'} = \dfrac{\beta}{\beta'}\,\dfrac{Z/L}{Z'/L'}$

for land, and

(9) MRPT-nonland $= \dfrac{\delta z/\delta R}{\delta z'/\delta L'} = \dfrac{\alpha}{\alpha'}\,\dfrac{Z/R}{Z'/R'}$

A ratio of average products will be called an *average of product of transformation through the input k* (ARPT-k). These are easily calculable from published Soviet data on yields and nonland cost (*sebestoimost'*).

AVERAGE PRODUCT DATA AVAILABLE

Relatively long series of both agricultural yields and *sebestoimost'* data for collective farms are available in the statistical handbooks published by the Central Statistics Administration. However, the most graphically extensive cost data available at the Union level are average data for the Soviet republics and the extremely heterogeneous economic regions of the RSFSR. Average data for regions this large are likely meaningless for the purpose at hand. Data from the Ukraine represent the best opportunity to investigate the possible convergences of MRPT. They are available as averages for the (province) oblast' level. Figure 10.2 is a map of the Ukraine depicting its

---

*I.e., the changes in output resulting from the increase of land or nonruble input devoted to a product within a region will be nonambiguous in the sense that it does not make any difference *which* plot, or *which* ruble input increases. The assumption (c), needed to make dR nonambiguous, is strong in that it implies that inputs are not rationed, *or are rationed in a uniform manner* such that their marginal products are proportional to their prices. There remains, of course, the standard Cambridge (England) objection to the use of aggregates in production functions.

†The marginal product of R (or L) in the Cobb-Douglas, $Z = AR^\alpha L^\beta$ is simply the average product of R (or L) multiplied by α (or β). This is true whether or not $\alpha + \beta = 1$.

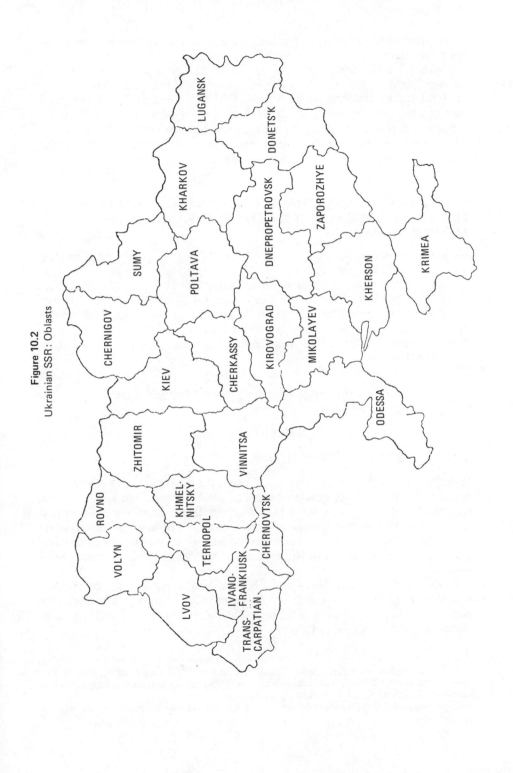

Figure 10.2
Ukrainian SSR: Oblasts

twenty-five oblasts.* These cost data are the most detailed long series that has been found.

Yields (i.e., average land products, Z/L) are available for several crops for the period 1956 to the present. *Sebestoimost'*, essentially average nonland and noninterest resource cost (R/Z), is available for several products (crops and livestock) from 1956 to 1973.† Gray (1976) contains a detailed discussion of the components of *sebstoimost'* and the nature of the Ukrainian time series. A major problem involves the prices used in forming the ruble aggregate and changes in these prices over the period studied.[14]

RELATIONSHIP OF AVERAGE AND MARGINAL RATES OF TRANSFORMATION: TEST OF THE EQUIVALENCE OF THEIR TRENDS

As indicated by Equation (8) and Equation (9), the marginal rate of product transformation through an input k (MRPT-k) equals the ratio of average products of the input k, corrected by a factor that is the ratio of exponents (output elasticities) of the factor k in the production functions for the two products considered. This factor (α/α', for ruble-inputs; β/β', for land inputs) may in general vary among oblasts.

As a possible assumption, in addition to assumptions (a)–(e), we could add the folowing:

Interregional Proportionality of Average and Marginal Rates of Product Transformation

(10) $(\alpha/\alpha')_j = (\alpha/\alpha')_{j'}$ and, $(\beta/\beta')_j = (\beta/\beta')_{j'}$

for $j \neq j'$ (different oblasts).

Whether or not (f) is true is of significant interest for a study of the interregional convergence of marginal rates of product transformation. In fact, if equality of ratios can be assumed, there is no need for econometric estimation of the parameters of each of the production relationships specified above, estimation that is precarious, given the nature of the data and the fact there are only fifteen time-series observations for individual oblasts.

If the proportionality between marginal and average rates of product transformation for two goods is the same in all regions, then the interregional variance of the marginal rate of product transformation is proportional to the average rate. That is:

---

*While an economic region of the RSFSR averages 659,000 square miles, a Ukrainian oblast' averages 9,270 square miles. For comparison, the state of Wisconsin, with an area of 56,000 square miles, would contain about six oblasts.

†Only years 1956–1971 were available at the time of the calculation of production function coefficients.

$$(11) \quad \text{Var} \; (\text{MRPT-R}) = 1/25 \sum_{j=1}^{25} (\text{MRPT-R}_j - \overline{\text{MRPT-R}})^2 =$$

$$(\alpha/\alpha')^2 \; \text{Var}(\text{ARPT-R})$$

where j is the subscript identifying each of the twenty-five regions of the Ukraine, and the rates of transformation are taken to be for the two products z and z'.

This means that if the interregional variance of average rats of product transfromation diminishes over time, so too does the interregional variance of the marginal rates of product transformation.

In a situation of competitive market equilibrium, the condition (f) would be implied were the rental income shares of both crops z and z' identical for all regions. (i.e., were $\alpha_{ij} = \alpha_{ij'}$, and $\alpha_{i'j} = \alpha_{j'i'}$ for all regions $j \neq j'$ and crops i)

In fact, rental income shares deducible from actual landlord-tenant lease agreements in Illinois indicate that for several crops in this state the landlord's share does vary across the state.* Even for Illinois, this does not disprove the validity of (f), however, since where the landlord's share of one crop is less it is generally also less for other crops. Ratios may be unchanged.

Assumption (f) is tested by testing the more stringent conditions that $\alpha_{ij} = \alpha_{ij'}$ for oblasts, j, in the Ukraine. The regression techniques and a form of the "Chow test" are described in detail in the Appendix to this chapter.

This approach indicates that the hypothesis that the "α's" are equivalent interregionally cannot be rejected with great confidence for any of the five crops considered. For grain the probability of error in rejecting equivalence is greater than 75 percent; for vegetables and sunflower it is greater than 50 percent; and for potato and sugar beet it is greater than 25 percent and 10 percent, respectively. This result indicates that information on trends in the interregional dispersion of average rates of transformation may not be valueless.

TRENDS IN INTERREGIONAL DISPERSION OF ESTIMATED AVERAGE RATES OF PRODUCT TRANSFORMATION AMONG CERTAIN CROPS†

Both yield and *sebestoimost'* data are available for the Ukraine for the eighteen years 1956–1973 (except 1967, for which *sebestoimost'* is lacking) for individual oblasts in which five crops are grown. These crops are grain

---

*Deducing Cobb-Douglas shares from actual lease agreements is not easy, since actual farming operations involve several products, and typically the landlord contributes more than just land. However, work by F. J. Reiss of the University of Illinois shows that Cobb-Douglas-like "rent factors" for corn, soybeans, wheat, and "hay and pasture" do vary significantly with location within Illinois and average yields. The rental share is higher where yields are higher.[15]

†Dispersion measures formed from unbiased estimates of stochastic variables are not necessarily unbiased estimates of the dispersion of these variables in the production. (Eg., in

Table 10.2 Ukraine Average Rates of Product Transformation, 1956–1973

Interoblast Range of ARPT-L, 1956–1973

	Sugar beet			Potato			Vegetable			Sunflower seeds		
	Ave	Max	Min	Ave	Max	Min	Ave	Max	Min	Ave	Max	Min
1956	0.66	0.82	0.44	1.65	3.81	0.60	1.38	2.08	0.72	1.38	2.18	0.68
1957	0.77	1.35	0.42	3.43	14.00	0.87	1.65	3.33	0.81	1.73	2.98	1.29
1958	0.62	0.91	0.34	2.21	4.94	0.87	1.53	2.73	0.70	1.39	2.20	0.97
1959	0.86	1.47	0.41	2.92	7.74	1.11	1.86	3.22	0.87	1.84	2.89	1.33
1960	0.71	1.02	0.48	2.18	3.53	0.97	1.52	2.37	0.88	1.78	2.59	1.13
1961	1.06	1.63	0.67	2.97	6.57	1.20	2.02	3.29	1.08	1.62	2.06	1.21
1962	1.06	1.71	0.71	2.50	4.49	1.25	1.63	2.64	0.96	1.50	2.24	1.07
1963	0.93	1.43	0.58	2.22	4.15	1.03	1.46	2.23	0.94	1.27	2.09	0.75
1964	0.73	1.25	0.41	2.31	5.23	0.95	1.44	2.23	0.79	1.34	2.08	1.04
1965	0.89	1.17	0.63	2.65	4.12	1.49	1.77	3.16	1.22	1.61	3.21	0.95
1966	0.95	1.25	0.70	2.45	4.77	1.17	1.88	3.13	0.98	1.58	2.63	0.95
1967	0.85	1.26	0.55	2.58	4.20	1.07	1.75	2.39	1.03	1.45	2.93	0.88
1968	0.63	0.95	0.35	2.26	4.07	1.03	1.49	2.29	1.05	1.28	1.99	0.96
1969	0.93	1.16	0.67	2.65	4.48	1.58	2.14	3.45	1.40	1.69	2.80	0.99
1970	0.79	1.16	0.55	2.61	5.79	1.24	1.91	2.93	1.14	1.94	3.08	1.23
1971	0.95	1.31	0.71	2.53	4.59	1.30	2.03	2.95	1.45	1.98	3.02	1.08
1972	0.86	1.19	0.56	2.51	5.14	1.23	1.84	3.01	1.01	1.67	2.62	1.01
1973	0.97	1.57	0.63	2.94	4.67	1.27	1.97	3.18	1.23	2.21	7.62	1.44

Interoblast Range of ARPT-R, 1956–1973

Year												
1956	0.19	0.33	0.12	0.64	2.08	0.21	0.88	1.57	0.49	0.93	1.58	0.32
1957	0.30	0.76	0.14	1.58	5.88	0.26	1.36	2.59	0.56	1.69	3.29	1.05
1958	0.32	0.56	0.18	2.02	7.33	0.31	1.51	2.69	0.68	1.20	2.15	0.69
1959	0.52	1.09	0.25	2.37	7.85	0.37	2.30	5.31	0.78	1.68	2.40	0.17
1960	0.37	0.72	0.26	1.69	5.58	0.43	1.56	2.83	0.81	1.46	2.68	0.79
1961	0.52	1.32	0.30	3.77	18.48	0.48	2.44	4.50	0.83	1.38	1.93	1.06
1962	0.53	1.55	0.31	2.93	11.73	0.58	1.89	3.17	0.84	1.37	5.70	0.73
1963	0.42	0.78	0.26	1.95	7.42	0.45	1.71	3.09	0.93	1.03	2.91	0.45
1964	0.43	0.65	0.28	1.79	4.78	0.52	1.77	3.21	0.77	0.96	1.65	0.53
1965	0.55	0.79	0.43	1.97	4.09	0.94	2.12	3.34	1.12	1.38	2.51	0.82
1966	0.57	0.79	0.34	1.98	4.78	0.71	2.16	3.92	0.85	1.37	2.36	0.90
1968	0.46	0.64	0.30	1.92	4.27	0.75	1.80	3.05	1.09	1.21	2.10	0.88
1969	0.52	0.62	0.37	2.14	4.00	1.18	2.07	3.09	1.27	1.45	2.57	1.05
1970	0.49	0.70	0.33	2.27	4.71	1.14	2.06	3.36	1.10	1.64	2.90	1.07
1971	0.50	0.69	0.36	2.01	3.67	1.10	2.09	3.33	1.27	1.71	3.71	1.22
1972	0.47	0.69	0.35	1.98	4.28	0.96	1.91	3.23	1.10	1.48	3.75	0.96
1973	0.49	0.68	0.38	2.32	4.84	1.09	1.86	3.59	0.97	1.62	2.53	1.28

(excluding corn), sugar beet, sunflower seed, vegetables, and potatoes. Complete data series are available for all twenty-five Ukrainian oblasts for grain, vegetables, and potatoes. Complete series are available for only nineteen oblasts for both sugar beet and sunflower seeds. Since grain is grown in all areas and occupies the majority land area, it is chosen as the "nummeraire" crop. All rates of transformation are rates of transformation of each of the other four crops into grain.*

Average rates of product transformation (through both land and ruble inputs) for eighteen years are given in Table 10.2. This table gives ARPT for the Ukraine average yield (ARPT-L) and *sebestoimost'* data (ARPT-R), as well as the range of ARPT in the twenty-five oblasts. A considerable amount of variation is indicated. Using either input, the maximum ARPT usually runs about double the minimum ARPT.

The object of the investigation is to see if the dispersion of ARPT diminishes over time. Three dispersion measures are used: The variance, standard deviation, and coefficient of variation.† Each of these dispersion measures is calculated for each year, and then those for all years are correlated with time.

Table 10.3 reports the directions of trends and the levels of statistical significance. Correlations of all dispersion measures for sugar beet, potato, and vegetables are negative (i.e., dispersion decreases over time), indicating increased locational efficiency. For these three crops, eight of the negative correlations are significant at better than the 10 percent level and six at the 5 percent level. Significant decline in dispersion for potatoes is especially striking. Trends in the various dispersion measures for sunflower seed with grain do not display this pattern—there is no significant trend in any direction.

Table 10.4 indicates that the costs of all four crops relative to grain-cost increase with time. The coefficient of variation (which takes into account variation relative to the size of the phenomenon studied) is thus a measure of interest. Trends in this measure are negative and significant for sugar beets, potatoes, and vegetables, but not for sunflower seeds.

---

the linear regression of y on x, the sum of squares of the estimated y is smaller than the sum of squares of y). Therefore, all dispersion measures studied for trends in this chapter are not guaranteed to be unbiased estimates of the dispersion of actual rates of transformation (even in the case that the rates are unbiasedly estimated). Possible bias from this is difficult to analyze, given the complex formation of some of the estimates. Any constant or proportional bias of the dispersion measures would not necessarily cause bias in the trends.

*Throughout this chapter the rate of transformation of products "X" into grain (denoted G) is taken to be dG/dX. (There could be some confusion that it is the inverse.) The rate of transformation is inverse to the price (or marginal cost) ratios. Thus, the expression for ARPT-R is (*sebestoimost'* of X + *sebestoimost'* of G, i.e., $R/X \div R/G$). For ARPT it is (yield X, i.e., $(G/L)/(X/L) = (L/X)/(LG)$. MRPT are these ratios multiplied by the appropriate ratios of elasticities indicated in Equation (8) and Equation (9).

†The *standard deviation* is the square root of the variance. The lesser-known *coefficient of variation* is the standard deviation divided by the mean. The latter statistic is more relevant in expressing variation when the size of the phenomenon is changing.

Table 10.3 Correlation of Time and Interregional Dispersion of Average Rates of Product Transformation (ARPT) Between Four Other Crops and Grain, 1956–1973.

	Variance		Standard Deviation		Coefficient of Variation	
	Nonland	Land	Nonland	Land	Nonland	Land
Sugar beet	− .357	− .037	− .292	.042	− .641	− .195
	(.157)	(.878)	(.255)	(.864)	(.006)†	(.556)
Potato	− .340	− .461	− .414	− .496	− .842	− .681
	(.180)	(.052)*	(.096)*	(.034)†	(.000)†	(.002)†
Vegetables	− .207	− .333	− .124	− .297	− .550	− .692
	(.569)	(.174)	(.639)	(.231)	(.021)†	(.002)†
Sunflower	.091	.337	.107	.329	− .060	.167
	(.727)	(.169)	(.686)	(.180)	(.815)	(.514)

Note: Significance level in parenthesis; correlations with better than 10 percent and 5 percent significance are starred and daggered.

Table 10.4 Time Trends of Average Costs of Four Other Crops Relative to Grain Using ARPT Measures, 1956–1973.

	Land Inputs		Nonland Inputs	
	Intercept (*to*)	Trend (*t*)	Intercept (*to*)	Trend (*t*)
Sugar beet (N = 19)	.742	.010 (.111)	.312	.013 (.002)†
Potato (N = 25)	2.44	.010 (.600)	1.88	(.021) (.518)
Vegetable (N = 25)	1.50	.025 (.014)†	1.55	(.033) (.050)*
Sunflower (N = 19)	1.43	.015 (.128)	1.24	(.011) (.648)

$$(\text{ave. ARPT}_i)_T = to + tT$$
$$T = 1, \ldots, 18$$
$$(\text{ave. ARPT}_i)_T = \sum_{j=1}^{N} \text{ARPT}_{ijT}/N$$

Note: Significance level in parenthesis; levels of 10 percent and 5 percent are starred and daggered.

In summary, the results of this section indicate that ARPT of sugar beets, potatoes, and vegetables (but not of sunflower seed) with grain have converged interregionally over time. If assumption (f) is tenable, these results also imply that MRPT have converged, indicating an interregional movement toward cost minimization in production of the three crops.

ESTIMATION OF INDIVIDUAL COBB-DOUGLAS FUNCTIONS FOR FIVE CROPS: TRENDS IN INTERREGIONAL DISPERSION OF ESTIMATED MARGINAL RATES OF PRODUCT TRANSFORMATION

Although assumption (f), that the ratios of Cobb-Doublas exponents are proportional across regions, could not be strongly disproven by the test described above, neither was it strongly supported. Individual production functions for each oblast can be estimated, however, employing alternative assumptions. These are:

(f') (Alternative Assumptions)

a. *Production functions homogeneous of degree one.*

(12) $\alpha_{ij} = 1 - \beta_{ij}$ for all regions j and products i.

b. *Neutral technological progress a log-linear function of time.*

(13) $A_{ijt} = t^o_{ij} e^{t_{ij}T}$ where T is time.

The first assumption helps to preserve degrees of freedom.*

The second is needed to account in some way for the possibility of technological change.

Still, two circumstances bode ill for attempted estimation of production functions for five individual crops in each of nineteen to twenty-five individual oblasts. (1) There are few years of observation, (2) The assumptions (a)–(f'), especially the assumption (c) about the ruble-input aggregate, are quite strong.† For these reasons, the parameters estimated should best

---

*It also simplifies the regression, allowing estimation of the "perhectare" form, Equation (5) with average product data alone. The assumption of homogeneity of degree one is a common one. "When we try to imagine a situation (which rarely if ever occurs in fact) of an agriculturalist increasing all inputs simultaneously, in uniform proportions, few, if any, of us, expect 'economies of scale,' i.e., an increase in output in greater proportion than the increase in inputs—except perhaps in a few anomalous cases. In constructing production functions for agriculture, therefore, it is customary to introduce the mathematical constraint that the exponents should add up precisely to one." (Colin Clark, "The Value of Agricultural Land," *Journal of Agricultural Economics* (1969): 2.

†Gray (1976) discusses the *sebestoimost'* time series. Individual production function estimates in this section were made with 1956–1971 data only, before 1972 and 1973 *Narodnoe Hospodarstvo* were available. There are fifteen rather than sixteen observations because 1967 *sebestoimost'* data were not published at the oblast level.

be regarded as tentative. Their ratios (i.e., α/α' and β/β') used to adjust the ARPT perhaps approximate the true proportions of ARPT and MRPT and are an alternative to no adjustment at all.

The equation to be estimated, once for each of the five crops, for each of from nineteen to twenty-five regions is:

(14) $\quad \ln (Z_{ijT}/L_{ijT}) - \ln t^{o}_{ij} + t_{ij}T + \alpha \ln (R_{ijT}/L_{ijT})$

$T = 1, \dots, 11, 13, \dots, 16$

Two methods are used to estimate this equation. One is the method of *ordinary least squares* (OLS), in which a separate regression is simply run for each product and region. The other method used is to estimate the equations for all (up to five) crops in each oblast simultaneously. This is a generalized least square (GLS) procedure, which seeks to take advantage of the "seemingly unrelated equations" situation, described by Arnold Zellner.[16] It can be expected that the errors affecting the yield of one crop will be contemporaneously correlated with disturbances affecting the yields of another crop, in the same oblast; i.e., if in a particular year the weather is bad and one crop suffers, so might another. In a situation like this, efficiency may be gained through GLS estimation.

The estimated exponents obtained from these regressions (reported in Appendix tables) were used to calculate the oblast MRPT from the ARPT, which were developed in part five, above. Given assumptions (a)-(f), the results ((α/α') ARPT-R and (β/β') ARPT-L) are conceptually exact, though heroically measured, marginal rates of product transformation, through ruble and land inputs.

The interregional dispersions of these measures were found for every year exactly as for ARPT above and then the resultant dispersion measures were correlated with time. The results are reported in Tables 10.5 and 10.6.

Table 10.5 reports trends of the interregional variances and standard deviations, while Table 10.6 reports trends in the coefficients of (interregional) variation. (Like Table 10.3 these tables present trends in dispersions of rates of transformation through both land and nonland resources. These tables also reflect the proliferation of choice by reporting both GLS and OLS versions.)

Table 10.5 shows no support for the hypothesis of converging rates of transformation, except perhaps for potatoes. The variance and standard deviation of the rate of transformation of potatoes for grain do decline (significantly) with time (in nonland GLS and both land and nonland OLS versions). However, trends in the dispersion of rates of transformation through land are nearly always positive. These positive trends are also significant for vegetables and sunflower seed and, in one instance, for potatoes.

However, trends of the relative measure of variation, reported in Table 10.6, give strong support for the hypothesis, especially for potatoes and also for sugar beets and vegetables, although not for sunflower seeds. There are no significant positive trends for any crop. The decline of interregional

Table 10.5   Correlation of Time and the Interregional Variance and Standard Deviation of Estimates of Marginal Rate of Product Transformation (MRPT) Between Four Other Crops and Grain, 1956–1973.

| | OLS Estimates of MRPT | | | |
| | Nonland | | Land | |
	Variance	Standard Deviation	Variance	Standard Deviation
Sugar beet	− .050 (.842)	.068 (.791)	.253 (.311)	.295 (.233)
Potato	− .433 (.080)*	− .413 (.092)*	− .068 (.785)	− .009 (.972)
Vegetable	− .005 (.983)	.093 (.723)	.445 (.062)*	.550 (.033)†
Sunflower	− .289 (.260)	− .231 (.625)	.415 (.084)*	.441 (.064)*
	GLS Estimates of MRPT			
Sugar beet	.355 (.159)	.435 (.078)*	.253 (.312)	.276 (.268)
Potato	− .296 (.247)	− .247 (.659)	.349 (.152)	.408 (.090)*
Vegetable	.098 (.710)	.146 (.582)	.311 (.207)	.335 (.171)
Sunflower	.121 (.649)	.169 (.522)	.367 (.131)	.370 (.127)

Note: Significance level in parenthesis; levels of 10 percent and 5 percent or better are starred and daggered.

dispersion of rates of transformation through nonland resources is uniformly negative (except for sunflower seed) and significant at the 5 percent level for all these except the GLS estimate of sugar beet. As Table 10.7 indicates, this particular measure of *relative* variation has particular relevance, since the (MRPT) "cost" of all four crops relative to grain increases in the period 1956–1973, for all but one measure used.

REVIEW OF THE EMPIRICAL FINDINGS

The approach followed in the preceding sections seem to indicate that the marginal conditions for interregional production cost minimization are increasingly achieved for potatoes, sugar beet, and vegetables, but not sunflower seed. Given the multiproduct, and multi-input nature of the approach, and the possible choice of estimation techniques and representations of rates of transformation and of dispersion measures, there is a plethora of measures, some of conflicting sign. However, focus on those trends that are "signficant" at the 10 percent level or better reveals the following:

1. All trends using all dispersion measures of the average rates of transformation of sugar beet, potatoes, and vegetables are negative. Several are significant. There are no significant positive trends for sunflower.

2. Every trend of the coefficients of (relative) variation of transformation through nonland input, in each approach (ARPT, MRPT-OLS, and MRPT-GLS) is significantly negative (except the MRPT-GLS formulation for sugar beet, which is negative but significant at only the 12 percent level).

Table 10.6   Correlation of Time and the Coefficient of (Interregional) Variation of Estimates of Marginal Rates of Product Transformation (MRPT) Between Four Other Crops and Grain, 1956–1973.

OLS Estimates of MRPT

	Nonland	Land
Sugar beet	− .691	− .084
	(.002)†	.738
Potato	− .910	− .637
	(.000)†	(.531)
Vegetable	− .755	.160
	(.000)†	(.531)
Sunflower	− .508	.290
	(.036)†	(.243)

GLS Estimates of MRPT

Sugar beet	− .388	− .117
	(.120)	(.647)
Potato	− .625	.257
	(.007)†	(.303)
Vegetable	− .483	− .092
	(.047)†	(.717)
Sunflower	.029	.209
	(.909)	(.589)

Note: Significance level in parenthesis; levels at 10 percent and 5 percent are starred and daggered.

Table 10.7   Time Trends of Average Costs of Four Other Crops Relative to Grain Using Various MRPT Measures, 1956–1973.

	Land Inputs		Nonland Inputs	
	MRPT-OLS	MRPT-GLS	MRPT-OLS	MRPT-GLS
Sugar beet	.062 (.118)	.004 (.133)	.002 (.003)†	.003 (.002)†
Potato	.053 (.211)	.008 (.036)	.000 (.987)	−.007 (.807)
Vegetable	.085 (.005)*	.006 (.013)†	.014 (.119)	.018 (.053)
Sunflower	.015 (.120)	.015 (.129)	.066 (.706)	.019 (.605)

(avg. MRPT$_i$)$_T$ = $to + tT$
$T = 1, \ldots, 18$

(ave. MRPT$_i$)$_T$ = $\sum\limits_{j=1}^{N}$ MRPT$_{ijT}$/N

Note: Regression coefficient (t); significance level in parenthesis; correlations with better than 10 percent and 5 percent significance are starred and daggered.

3. All but one of the contradictory significant *positive* trends in variance or standard deviation occurs with the marginal rate of product transformation through land. Realistic realization of assumption (b), that land is homogeneous within oblasts, would call for discounting trends based on transformations through land in favor of trends based on transformations through more mobile labor, machinery, and materials components of *sebestoimost'*. That is, if the cultivation of grain and potatoes occurs predominantly on different types of land within an oblast, we cannot expect the rate of product transformation occurring through "potato land" to grain production to be measurable by a ratio of the marginal (grain) product of "grain land" to the marginal (sunflower) product of "sunflower land." The effect of nonhomogeneous land within oblasts is an obvious consideration in an attempt to understand the difference in the results between transformation through land and nonland resources, and between sunflower and the other three crops. It needs further study.

Although Section 7's estimation of simple production functions with these kinds of data is precarious, the results achieved are supportable by some separate evidence from a Soviet source. Under the assumption that input shares ("α" and "β" exponents) are equivalent for all oblasts, the best estimates of these shares for the five crops are those achieved from the regressions utilizing the large sample of pooled time-series and cross-section data (see Appendix). The factor share of nonland inputs in sugar beet, vegetables, and potato production are high, while the nonland input shares for grain and sunflower seeds are low. That is, the first crops are not land-intensive, while the latter crops are. The implication of this is that were land rent imputed into the "full cost" of grain and sunflower, this cost would increase significantly over *sebestoimost'*.* Sugar beet, potatoes, and vegetables *sebestoimost'* would not differ so much from "full cost." Indeed these same products are grouped in exactly this way in the contrast of shadow price and *sebestoimost'* contained in the Soviet work from which Table 11.1 is taken, the result of a linear programming formulation that yielded optimal crop distributions with limited land.†.

It is an interesting reflection that these regressions do indicate that the relative marginal costs of grain and sunflower compared to those of vegetables, sugar beet, and potatoes are more than is indicated by relative *sebestoimost'*, and that this neoclassical approach agrees with an independent Soviet calculation done through linear economics.

CONCLUSION

The evidence of this paper is that over the period 1956–1973 adjustments did take place in specialization among Ukrainian oblasts consistent with greater production cost efficiency from the location of potato, vegetable, and sugar beet production within the Ukraine. These findings are consistent with our knowledge of greater Soviet attention paid in the 1960s to lowering production cost through specialization, even at the possible risk of increased transportation cost for agricultural products.

The location of the production of potatoes, which are relatively perishable and difficult to transport, showed the most pronounced effect, while the apparent dispersion of the cost of sunflower seed production was continually the odd case.

In agreement with linear programming models, grain and sunflower seed are shown to be more land-intensive than the others, thus their relative real domestic cost (compared to potatoes, sugar beet, and vegetables) is greater than is indicated by the Marxist cost category, *sebestoimost'*. Consequently, the current Soviet policy of importing both grain and oil seeds may be much more rational than is indicated by comparisons of "low" average *sebestoimost'* to "high" world grain prices.

Lastly, the conclusions of this paper do not constitute an endorsement of Soviet agricultural planning.

---

*The relationship between *sebestoimost'* and full cost can be shown explicitly in the case of the Cobb-Douglas function. Consider a production function for an individual product Z: $Z = R^\alpha L^\beta$. The incremental ruble input required for one more unit of output (other inputs fixed) is $(R/Z)/\alpha$. (Same calculation as that involved for Equation (4). The more land-intensive the crop is (i.e., the smaller α is) the more incremental ruble input exceeds *sebestoimost'*. (This appears to be particularly the case with grain and sunflower seeds.) When agriculture really is efficient (with no unutilized resources and equivalent marginal rates of technical substitution of inputs for all products), this "blown-up" *sebestoimost'* is really orthodox marginal cost; (i.e., on the production frontier, the alternative of producing more Z through more land involves an equivalent opportunity cost of another product Z'.

†Table 10.1 indicates that the full cost of non-land-intensive sugar beets never exceed *sebestoimost'* by more than 15 percent. On the other hand, the full cost of buckwheat grain in some areas of the Ukraine exceeds *sebestoimost'* by around 75 percent.

The paterns of specialization that existed in the 1950s may have been very bad, so bad that crude data and techniques available to planners should correct gross mistakes. Attention paid to specialization may have contributed to the significant increases in total factor productivity in Soviet agriculture observable in the 1960s.[17] At the same time, measurements of total factor productivity do not take account of either transportation costs or the costs of planning agricultural administration.

Also, as intense Soviet discussion continues to indicate, there is much to be gained from the continued improvement of regional and farm specialization.

NOTES

1. Alec Nove, "Agricultural Performance Compared: Belorussia and Eastern Poland", in *Economic Development in the Soviet Union and Eastern Europe: Sectoral Analysis,* ed. Zbigniew M. Fallenbuchl (New York: Praeger, 1975); D. Gale Johnson, "Agricultural Production," in A. Bergson and S. Kuznets, *Economic Trends in the Soviet Union* (Cambridge, Mass.: Harvard University Press, 1963); Karl-Eugen Wädekin and Alec Nove, *Agriculture in Eastern Europe and the Soviet Union: Comparative Studies,* Vol. III of *Studies in East European and Soviet Russian Agrarian Policy,* ed. Alec Nove (Totowa, N.J.: Allanheld, Osmum & Co., 1982).

2. A number of updated productivity studies by Diamond and associates at the CIA date back to Douglas B. Diamond, "Trends in Output, Inputs, and Factor Productivity in Soviet Agriculture," Joint Economic Committee, *New Directions in the Soviet Economy* (Washington, D.C.: U.S. Government Printing Office, 1966); see also D. Diamond and C. Krueger, 'Recent Developments in Output and Productivity in Soviet Agriculture," in *Soviet Economic Prospects for the Seventies* (Washington, D.C.: U.S. Government Printing Office, 1973). Recent production function studies of Soviet agriculture across republics include Michael L. Wyzan, "Empirical Analysis of Soviet Agricultural Production and Policy," *American Journal of Agricultural Economics* 63, no. 3 (August 1981) and Elizabeth Clayton, "Productivity in Soviet Agriculture," *Slavic Review,* 39, no. 3 (September 1980).

3. Kenneth R. Gray, "Soviet Agricultural Specialization and Efficiency," *Soviet Studies,* 31, (4 October 1979): 542–58 and "The Efficient Location and Specialization of Soviet Agricultural Procurement" (Ph.D. diss., University of Wisconsin, 1976).

4. A study, using similar methodology to this article's, but focusing on the marginal product of capital across sectors, is Judith Thornton's "Differential Capital Charges and Resource Allocation in Soviet Industry," *Journal of Political Economy* 79, 3 (May/June 1971): 545–61.

5. See Kenneth R. Gray, "Soviet Agricultural Specialization," for a review of Soviet and US attempts to program this problem.

6. For instance, Jerzy F. Karcz, "An Organizational Model of Command Farming," in *Comparative Economic Systems,* ed. Morris Bornstein (Homewood, Illinois: Richard D. Irwin, 1969), pp. 278–99.

7. A. Libkind, "Sdvigi v razmeshchenii sel'skokhoziaistvennykh kul'tur," *Problemy Ekonomiki* 3 (1938): 62.

8. *Ibid.,* p. 67.

9. Gray, "Efficient Location", pp. 140–145; N. I. Zhukovsky, *Novoe v sel'skom khoziaistve Sibiri* (Moscow: Selklogiz, 1958), p. 49; *Razmeschenie i spetsializatsiia sel'skogo khoziaistva SSSR* (Moscow: Kolos, 1969), pp. 129–30.

10. G. Lisichkin, "Gektary, tsentnery, rubli," *Novy Mir.* 9 (1965): 227; Vasilets, "Zimnii ogorod," *Pravda,* 20 November 1977; G. Gukasov, "Zabytyi tsvet abrikosa," *Izvestiya,* 30 April 1975.

11. Gray, "Efficient Location," p. 98.

12. *Ibid.,* Chapter 4 for review of Soviet use of linear programming in this field; specifically of M. E. Braslavets, *Ekonomiko-matematicheskie metody v organizatsii i planirovanni sel'skogo khoziaistva* (Kiev: Urozhai, 1968), pp. 383–93.

13. For example, after perusal of regional data on prime costs and growth rates of grain procurement, Jerzy Karcz concluded that the latter were "not conducive along cost reducing lines." Jerzy Karcz, "The New Soviet Agricultural Programme," *Soviet Studies* (October 1965): 147.

14. Data used here are from various years of the Ukrainian yearbook (*Narodne Hospodarstvo*). Some shifts in oblast boundaries in the early 1960s were minor.

Principal *sebestoimost'* components for crops are given as direct labor, fuels and lubricants, seed, fertilizers, amortization, current repairs, "other direct expenditures," and general production and farm expenses.

Inputs expressed in money terms should be deflated for price changes, but this was not possible given fragmentary published information. To some extent the ruble category used here has been protected since 1967 by the two-tiered price system, which has maintained constant prices for some farm inputs through subsidies while the prices paid farm suppliers have been increased. Thus fertilizer and many machinery prices have not gone up, while fuel and construction materials have. The most important rate increase has been the labor wage increase.

These and other aspects of the sebestoimost' data used and possible biases are discussed in Gray, "Efficient Location." An argument is made there that for the purposes of this investigation it does not really matter if the α and β are biased estimates, as long as the bias is proportional from one oblast to another.

15. Descriptions of Illinois farm lease practices are contained in a number of University of Illinois College of Agriculture/Agricultural Experiment Station Bulletins (e.g., nos. 728, 745, and 677) authored by Franklin J. Reiss. An information extension service paper by Reiss, titled "Relations of Gross Value of Production and Landlords' Gross Cash Rents," (1975) contains percentage rent factors.

16. Arnold Zellner, "An Efficient Method of Estimating Seemingly Unrelated Regressions and Tests for Aggregation Bias," *Journal of the American Statistical Association* (1967): 348–368.

Equations 14 for all five crops (i) are estimated simultaneously for each region (j) under the assumption that:

$$\sigma_{\epsilon_{ijT}, \epsilon_{i'jT}} \quad \text{is not zero.}$$

The University of Wisconsin's "TSP" program was used to estimate the σ and subsequent α and β. See Gray, "Efficient Location," chapter 5, for more detail on the estimation procedure.

17. See Diamond, "Trends in Output."

APPENDIX: STATISTICAL TEST OF THE PROPORTIONALITY OF AVERAGE AND MARGINAL RATES OF PRODUCT TRANSFORMATION, THROUGH A TEST OF THE INTERREGIONAL EQUIVALENCE OF COBB-DOUGLAS EXPONENTS.*

This test involves the calculation of a Snedecor F statistic for each of the five crops (grain, sugar beet, potatoes, vegetables, and sunflower seed) under a maintained hypothesis. It compares the resultant statistic with tabled critical values to determine with what level of assurance the maintained hypothesis can be rejected. The F-statistic is:

(1) $\quad F(I - 1, 12 - I) = \dfrac{(Q_1 - Q_2)/(I - 1)}{Q_2/(12 - I)}$

---

*This test is based on the "Chow test." (J. Johnston, *Econometric Methods* [New York: McGraw-Hill, 1963], p. 136). Here the test is for equality among coefficients of nineteen or twenty-five rather than two relations.

where I is the number of regions raising a crop (19 for beets and sunflower, 25 for the others). Q_2 and Q_1 are the residual sums of squares from two separate approaches to estimation of the equation

(2) $\ln y_{ijT} = \ln(t^o_{ij}) + t_{ij}T + \alpha_{ij}\ln(R/L)_{ijt} + 1n\ \epsilon_{ijT}$

where

time (T) is incorporated as in assumption (f') (Eq. 5–13 in chapter 5)

y_{ij} is the yield of crop i in region j $(j = 1, \ldots, I)$

(R/L) is the ruble expenditure per hectare

e is the disturbance term

t^c, t, and α are parameters

where α_j holds the most interest for us, since we want only to know if $\alpha_{ij} = \alpha_{ij'}$ for all $j \neq j'$.

The equation (2) is first estimated for a single crop by pooling all data (fifteen years each for either twenty-five or nineteen regions). One huge regression is run, allowing t^2 and t to vary across regions, but constraining the α_{ij} to be equal in all oblasts. (This is the maintained hypothesis; it constrains the regression.) The resultant sum of squares of this regression is Q_1.

Equation (2) is then estimated for each region separately, and the sum of the sums of squared residuals is Q_2. (Because these regressions place no constraint on the α_j, $Q_2 < Q_1$.)

The procedure of the above two paragraphs was repeated for all five crops. The results of these computations (estimates of "α" and R^2 from the constrained equation, number of oblasts, and the residual sums of squares of both regressions, along with the F-statistics and their acceptance level) are reported in the Appendix Table. As can be seen, the maintained hypothesis cannot be rejected for any of the crops with a great deal of assurance.

11

The Effects of the Private Sector on the Labor Behavior of Soviet Collective Farmers

Clark Chandler

INTRODUCTION

Labor is an important input into Soviet agricultural production, and its availability has a great impact upon the performance of the Soviet agricultural sector. Therefore, both Soviet and Western scholars have been concerned with identifying the factors affecting the availability of labor both to Soviet agriculture as a whole and the socialized sector of Soviet agriculture in particular. The labor supply problem will become even more important during the coming decade, as demographic changes led to an increasing scarcity of able-bodied farm workers in many parts of the Soviet Union.

The existence of the private sector is one of the factors that affect the supply of labor to Soviet agriculture. Soviet collective farms are divided into collective and private sectors. As a result of this division, collective farmers must decide not only how to allocate their time between labor and leisure, but also how to distribute their labor time between the collective and private sectors. This study attempts to identify the most important factors affecting these two types of labor decisions.

THEORETICAL MODEL[1]

The Soviet collective farmer's utility is assumed to depend upon income and leisure, and therefore the farmer's utility function may be described as:

(1) $U_i = U_i(W_i, h_i^l)$

where U_i, W_i, and h_i^l represent the utility, income, and leisure time of the ith member of the collective farm.[2]

Leisure is simply the difference between total available time (h_i) and total labor time (h_i^{c+p}). The latter is the sum of time spent working in the collective sector (h_i^c) and time spent working in the private sector (h_i^p). Hence:

(2) $h_i^1 = h_i - h_i^c - h_i^p$

$\quad\quad = h_i - h_i^{c+p}.$

The collective farmer receives income from three sources: (1) wage income earned for work in the collective sector,[3] (2) income earned for work in the private sector, and (3) unearned income. The last of these categories consists of all of the unearned receipts of the collective farmer, whether they come from the government, the social consumption fund of the collective farm, or any other source such as the second economy. Unearned income is assumed to be independent of labor time or the size of the private plot.

Total wage income from work in the collective sector is equal to the product of the wage rate (w_i) offered to the ith member of the collective farm for work in the collective sector and the total amount of labor time that spent in the collective sector. It is therefore equal to $w_i h_i^c$.

Income from the private sector is equal to the net value of privately produced output. Each member of the collective farm is entitled to the use of a small plot of land (m_i). The size of the private plot may vary from one collective farmer to another, but is determined independently of labor effort.[4] The private plot and private labor inputs of the collective farmer are combined to produce a product Y according to the following production function[5]:

(3) $Y_i = F_i(m_i, h_i^p)$

Y is then sold by the collective farmer at an exogenously determined price of P_y to yield $P_y Y_i$ income from employment in the private sector.

Wage income, income from the private sector, and unearned income (W_i') are now added together to obtain total income:

(4) $W_i = w_i h_i^c + P_y F_i(m_i, h_i^p) + W_i'$

Equations (2) and (4) are substituted into (1) to yield:

(5) $U_i = U_i(w_i h_i^c + P_y F_i(m_i, h_i^p) + W_i'; h_i - h_i^c - h_i^p)$

The collective farmer is assumed to maximize utility. Differentiating (5) with respect to h_i^c and h_i^p yields the following first-order necessary conditions:

(6a) $\dfrac{\delta U_i}{\delta h_i^c} = w_i U_i^W - U_i^1 \leq 0$

and $\left(\dfrac{\delta U_i}{\delta h_i^c}\right) h_i^c = 0$

(6b) $\dfrac{\delta U_i}{\delta h_i^p} = P_y F_i^h U_i^W - U_i^1 \leq 0$

and $\left(\dfrac{\delta U_i}{\delta h_i^p}\right) h_i^p = 0$

where
$$U_i^W = (\delta U_i/\delta W_i), \quad U_i^1 = (\delta U_i/\delta h_i^1) \text{ and } F_i^h = (\delta F_i/\delta h_i^p).$$

If the collective farmer works in both the collective and private sectors, h_i^c and h_i^p are greater than zero. This implies that the partial derivatives of U_i with respect to these two variables must be strictly equal to zero. Under these circumstances:

(7a) $\quad w_i = P_y F_i^h$

(7b) $\quad w_i = (U_i^1/U_i^W)$

and (1) the socialized sector wage rate is equal to the marginal revenue product (MRP) of labor in the private sector and (2) both are equal to the marginal rate of substitution between income and leisure.

The effects of changes in the exogeneous variables of the model (w_i, W_i', m_i, and P_y) on total labor time can be determined by totally differentiating (7b) with respect to these variables. Equation (7a) is then differentiated with respect to these variables to determine their impact upon private labor time. This is done in Appendix A, and the results are reported in Table 11.1 Changes in the amount of labor time spent in the collective sector are equal to the difference between changes in total labor time and changes in private labor time ($dh_i^c = dh_i^{c+p} - dh_i^p$).

Changes in the collective sector wage rate have an ambiguous effect on both total and collective labor time due to the familiar countervailing pull of the income and substitution effects. But an increase in collective sector wage rates necessarily reduces private labor time, as the collective farmer transfers labor from private to collective employment until the MRP of labor in the private sector increases until it equals the new wage rate.

An increase in unearned income unambiguously decreases total labor time as income increases while wages do not change.[6] This entire decrease in labor time takes place in the collective sector, as private labor inputs must remain at their initial level to preserve the equality between the collective sector wage rate and the MRP of labor in the private sector.

Changes in m_i and P_y have qualitatively equivalent effects on labor

Table 11.1   Predicted Labor Behavior of Collective Farmers (No Compulsory Minimum Labor Constraints)

	dw_i	dW_i	dm_i	dP_y
dh_i^{c+p}	?	−	−	−
dh_i^c	?	−	−	−
dh_i^p	−	0	+	+

behavior. Increases in either of these two variables lead to an increase in income without changing the marginal wage rate (which is pegged at the wage rate offered by the collective sector) and therefore reduce total labor time. The reduction in collective labor time is greater than the reduction in total labor time, as labor is transfered from the collective to the private sector as a result of the upward shift in the private MRP of labor curve.

The above model describes the collective farmer's labor behavior if the individual is free to make labor decisions according to personal wishes. This has frequently not been the case, however, due to the existence of compulsory labor minimums that require each collective farmer to spend a specified minimum amount of time working in the collective sector. These compulsory minimums are introduced into the model by specifying that each collective farmer must spend at least $h_i^{c'}$ amount of time working in the collective sector.[7] With the introduction of this constraint, equation (5) can be rewritten as:

(5*) $U_i = U_i(w_i h_i^{c'} + h_i^{c*}) + P_y F_i(m_i, h_i^p) + W_i' ; h_i - h_i^{c'}$

$- h_i^{c*} - h_i^p)$

where $h_i^{c*} = h_i^c - h_i^{c'}$ and denotes voluntary labor time spent in the collecttive sector (i.e., labor time in excess of the required minimum). Differentiating (5*) with respect to h_i^{c*} leaves (6b) unchanged, but (6a) becomes:

(6a*) $\dfrac{\delta U_i}{\delta h_i^{c*}} = w_i U_i^W - U_i^1 \le 0$

and $(\dfrac{\delta U_i}{\delta h_i^{c*}}) h_i^{c*} = 0$

The minimum labor constraint $h_i^{c'}$ is binding if it forces the collective farmers to work more in the collective sector than they would choose to do voluntarily. This occurs when the MRP of labor in the private sector is greater than the wage rate offered by the collective sector. $(\delta U_i / \delta h_i^{c*})$ is strictly less than zero under these circumstances, and therefore $h_i^{c*} = 0$ and $h_i^c - h_i^{c'}$.

Using equation (6b):

(8) $P_y F_i^h = (U_i^1 / U_i^W)$

and the marginal rate of substitution between leisure and income is given by the MRP of labor in the private sector. Labor behavior under these circumstances can be analyzed by totally differentiating (8) with respect to the exogeneous variables of the model. Noting that changes in total labor time are the same as changes in private labor time, the results of this differentiation (calculated in Appendix A) are reported in Table 11.2

Increases in the collective sector wage rate and in unearned income reduce both total and private labor time, due to the income effect. This result for

Table 11.2 Predicted Labor Behavior of Collective Farmers
(With Compulsory Minimum Labor Constraints)

	$\dfrac{dw_i}{}$	$\dfrac{dW_i}{}$	$\dfrac{dm_i}{}$	$\dfrac{dP_y}{}$	$\dfrac{dh_i^{c'}}{}$
dh_i^{c+p}	−	−	?	?	+
dh_i^c		0	0	0	1
dh_i^p			?	?	−

wage changes comes about because changes in the collective sector wage rate change income, but do not have a direct effect on the cost of leisure (now given by the MRP of labor in the private sector).

Changes in plot size and in the price of private output now have an ambiguous effect on labor behavior. An increase in either of these variables leads to an increase in both income and the marginal cost of leisure. The income and substitution effects therefore work in opposite directions.

Finally, an exogenous increase in the minimum labor constraint leads to an increase in total labor time and a decrease in private labor time (with the amount of labor time spent in the collective sector changing by the same amount as the change in the constraint). This result is not surprising. If private labor time were to increase after an increase in the minimum labor constraint, the collective farmer's total income would increase and the MRP of labor in the private sector would fall. Both of these effects would tend to decrease total labor time, which is incompatible with a simultaneous increase in both collective and private labor time. On the other hand, if total labor time falls, following an increase in the minimum labor constraint, total income would fall (as $dW_i = w_i dh_i^c - P_y G_i dh_i^p < 0$ under these circumstances) and to the MRP of labor in the private sector would increase (as private labor inputs would necessarily decrease). This once again leads to a contradictory result, as both of these effects would push for an increase in total labor time. Therefore the only feasible result is a decrease in private labor time that is less than the forced increase in collective labor time.

The comparative static results point out the basic incompatibility between economic incentives and institutional constraints on labor behavior. If compulsory minimum constraints are used to secure labor inputs into the collective sector, then the only way of either increasing or decreasing labor inputs into this sector is through the increase or decrease of the statutory minima. The use of other tools has no effect on labor inputs into the socialized sector and may have perverse effects on total and private labor time.

ESTIMATION OF LABOR SUPPLY FUNCTIONS

The total, collective, and private labor supply functions of collective farmers can be derived from equations (7a) and (7b). Linear approximations of these equations are then obtained through a first-order Taylor expansion to yield:

(9a) $h_i^c = a_0 + a_1 w_i + a_2 m_i + a_3 W_i' + e_i^c$

(9b) $h_i^p = b_0 + b_1 w_i + b_2 m_i + e_i^p$

The individual data needed to estimate these labor supply functions are not available. Therefore, grouped data are used, and each observation denotes the mean value of the variables in a particular republic in a given year. The collective sector labor supply function was estimated by using data for fifteen Soviet republics in the years 1963, 1967, and 1970; and the private sector labor supply function was estimated, using data for the fifteen republics in 1968. Separate labor supply functions were estimated for able-bodied men and women.

The labor functions presented in (9a) and (9b) assume that the labor behavior of collective farmers is not restricted by compulsory minimum labor constraints. If such binding constraints exist, then collective labor inputs are determined exogeneously and the coefficients in (9a) should not be significantly different from zero. Therefore the presence of binding minimum labor constraints may bias the coefficient estimates, with the degree of bias depending upon the number of farmers affected by these constraints.

Collective farmers received much lower wages for their work in the collective sector in 1963 than in the second half of the 1960s. Therefore it is possible that while compulsory minimum labor constraints were needed to force collective farmers to work in the collective sector in 1963, wage incentives alone were sufficient in the latter two years. This possibility is acknowledged by introducing a dummy variable into (9a), which allows the coefficient values in 1963 to vary from those in 1967 and 1970.[8] The model to be estimated becomes:

(10a) $h_{gt}^c = a_0 + a_1 w_{gt} + a_2 m_{gt} + a_3 W_{gt}' + a_4 Z_t + a_5 Z_t w_{gt}$

$\qquad\qquad + a_6 Z_t m_{gt} + a_7 Z_t W_{gt}' + e_{gt}^c$

(10b) $h_g^p = b_0 + b_1 w_g + e_2 m_g$

where the subscripts g and t denote the gth republic and the tth year respectively, and Z_t equals 1 in 1963 and 0 in 1967 and 1970.

In these equations, labor time is measured in man-days per year, wages in rubles per man-day (including both monetary payments and payments-in-kind), plot size in hectares per collective farmer, and unearned income in rubles per year.[9] The values of the independent variables denote the average for all able-bodied collective farmers and are therefore assumed to be the same for both able-bodied men and women.[10] The error terms are assumed to be heteroskedastic across specified groups of republics and to follow a first-order autocorrelation scheme over time. The appropriate corrections were made for these problems.

The estimation results are presented in Tables 11.3 and 11.4. The values of the standard errors are reported in parentheses below the coefficient

Table 11.3 The Estimated Coefficients Of The Collective And Private Labor Supply Functions Of Able-Bodied Male Collective Farmers, 1960s

Variable	Collective Sector		Private Sector	
	Coefficient	Elasticity[a]	Coefficient	Elasticity[a]
Constant	181.68**	—	20.635*	—
	(22.578)		(10.546)	
Unearned Income	.026697	.047	—	—
	(.020218)			
Wages	10.500†	.160	− 1.6739	− .189
	(5.4879)		(2.8539)	
Plot	− 21.422	− .025	29.914*	.199
	(27.270)		(14.026)	
Constant (1963)	27.494	—	—	—
	(36.191)			
Unearned Income (1963)	.049549	—	—	—
	(.071396)			
Wages (1963)	− 7.7074	—	—	—
	(17.653)			
Plot (1963)	− 16.403	—	—	—
	(52.675)			

*Significantly different from zero at the 90-percent level.
†Significantly different from zero at the 95-percent level.
**Significantly different from zero at the 99-percent level.
[a]Evaluated at the mean values of the variables.

estimates. One, two, and three asterisks indicate that the coefficients are significantly different from zero at the 90-, 95-, and 99-percent level, respectively. The R^2s reported in the table refer to the transformed equations, and therefore cannot be interpreted as a measure of the share of the labor behavior of collective farmers that is explained by the independent variables. They are not corrected for degrees of freedom.

The estimation of the labor supply functions of able-bodied men provided no surprises. The collective sector wage coefficient and the private sector plot coefficient are both positive and significantly different from zero at the 95- and 90-percent level, respectively. None of the other coefficients is significantly different from zero. This may either be due to the large degree of multicollinearity that exists among the explanatory variables, which weakens the power of the econometric tests, or it may imply that the coefficients are in fact equal to zero. The insignificance of the collective sector plot and the private sector wage coefficients may imply that the two sectors do not compete for labor—able-bodied male collective farmers work full-

Table 11.4   The Estimated Coefficients Of The Collective And Private Labor Supply Functions Of Able-Bodied Female Collective Farmers, 1960s

Variable	Collective Sector Coefficient	Elasticity[a]	Private Sector Coefficient	Elasticity[a]
Constant	117.88** (27.577)	—	32.458** (6.8963)	—
Unearned Income	.00952 (.026172)	.026	—	—
Wages	13.424* (6.9266)	.266	5.0262† (1.8578)	.199
Plot	43.783 (33.308)	.066	43.626** (10.012)	.102
Constant (1963)	91.575† (44.795)	—	—	—
Unearned Income (1963)	.10619 (.081410)	—	—	—
Wages (1963)	− 36.683* (20.604)	—	—	—
Plot (1963)	− 145.65† (63.376)	—	—	—

*Significantly different from zero at the 90-percent level.
†Significantly different from zero at the 95-percent level.
**Significantly different from zero at the 99-percent level.
aEvaluated at the mean values of the variables.

time in the collective sector and only work on their private plots when such work does not interfere with their labor in the collective sector (i.e., in the evenings, on their days off, etc.). And the income coefficient may be equal to zero for either of two reasons. First, the income data used were based on the Soviet definition of income, and the largest part of unearned income consists of free services (medical, educational, recreational, etc.). It is not very surprising that income of this type does not have a strong impact on the labor behavior of able-bodied men. Second, the income levels of collective farmers may be low enough so that income is valued so highly in comparison with leisure that the income effect is negligible.

The fact that none of the dummy variables that have been included in the model to measure the marginal effect of being in 1963 as opposed to the two later years can be shown to be significantly different from zero implies that the labor supply functions of able-bodied men were the same in 1963 as in 1967 and 1970. To corroborate this, an F-test was used to test for the joint effect of the four dummy variables. Their joint effect could not be shown to be significantly different from zero at the 95-percent level. These results suggest that economic factors rather than compulsory minimum labor constraints were the primary determinants of the labor behavior of able-bodied male collective farmers as early as 1963.

As in the case of able-bodied men, the estimated collective sector wage coefficient and private sector plot coefficient were both positive and significantly different from zero for able-bodied women, this time at the 90-and 99-percent level, respectively. Moreover, the estimated income and plot coefficients of the collective sector labor supply function of able-bodied women could not be shown to be significantly different from zero; therefore there is no indication that these variables affect the labor behavior of able-bodied women in the collective sector.

But there are also a number of surprises in the estimation results for able-bodied women. The first of these is that although the predicted wage coefficient of the private sector labor supply function is negative, the estimated coefficient for able-bodied women is both positive and significantly different from zero at the 95-percent level. There are two likely causes of this perverse result. One, women may specialize more in the private sector as wage levels increase. Higher wage rates may increase the comparative advantage of men in the collective sector (as men are more likely to have the skills most needed in the collective sector than women). As a consequence of this, women may be displaced by men in the collective sector and therefore increase the amount of time they spend working in the private sector. A second and complementary explanation is that the private sector production function has been misspecified in the theoretical model. Land and labor are the only inputs in this production function. However, livestock is one of the most important products of the private sector, and the production of livestock requires fodder, foodgrains, etc., which can only be obtained from the socialized sector. If an increase in the collective sector wage rate leads to an associated increase in the ability of collective farmers to acquire such inputs (perhaps via payments-in-kind), then wage increases may lead to increases in both private sector output and associated labor inputs.

The coefficients of three of the four dummy variables included to measure the marginal effects of being in 1963 are also significantly different from zero, indicating that the labor behavior of able-bodied women changed between 1963 and 1967 and 1970. The 1963 collective sector labor supply function for able-bodied women is therefore presented in Table 11.5 to illustrate the nature of these changes.

The observed changes do not appear to be consistent with the hypothesis that minimum labor constraints have become less important in recent years, however. For although the change in the wage coefficient is consistent with this hypothesis, the change in the plot coefficient is not.

Therefore, it seems likely that the differences between the estimated labor coefficients in the early and late 1960s are due to changes in the composition of the female labor force. Soviet writers frequently point out that collective farm women can be divided into two different groups of workers: one group consisting of women who work in highly seasonal occupations (such as unskilled field hands) and the other of women who work in occupations

Table 11.5   The Estimated Coefficients Of The Collective Sector Labor Supply
Function For Able-Bodied Female Collective Farmers, 1963

Variable	Coefficient	Elasticity[a]
Constant	209.45† (35.300)	—
Unearned Income	.11571 (.077088)	.281
Wages	− 23.259 (19.405)	− .266
Plot	− 101.86* (53.918)	− .139

*Significantly different from zero at the 90-percent level.
†Significantly different from zero at the 99-percent level.
[a]Evaluated at USSR levels in 1963.

that demand long hours consistently throughout the year (such as milkmaids, who must be available for morning and evening milkings day after day). Women who fall into the first of these two categories have time to work in the private sector; consequently their labor behavior is likely to be sensitive to changes in private plot size. Moreover, as these women are likely to have children and therefore to be unwilling to work more than a specified amount of time in the collective sector, and as their jobs are highly seasonal and therefore the demand for their labor is likely to be highly inelastic, the labor behavior of these women may not be very sensitive to changes in wage rates. Women belonging to the second of the above groups, on the other hand, do not have time to work in the private sector; therefore their labor behavior should not be affected by plot size but is likely to be affected by wage rates. Given the existence of these two groups, one explanation for the observed changes in the wage and plot coefficients is that the 1960s saw a relative decline in the importance of women who divided their labor time between the private and collective sectors and a corresponding increase in the importance of women who worked exclusively in the collective sector.

SUMMARY

The model that has been developed and tested in this paper is subject to a number of limitations. The model itself is a very simple one and ignores such problems as wage determination, the use of one sector's output as input in the other sector, and the fact that the key decision-making unit on the collective farm may be the household, rather than the individual worker. Moreover, the use of highly aggregated data has necessitated, at least in the case of able-bodied women, grouping together different types of women, who may have different labor supply functions. Finally, regional differences in prices, land quality, etc. have been ignored—something that cannot be done with much comfort in the case of a country as large and as diverse as the Soviet Union.

Despite these limitations, the results of the study have important implications with respect to Soviet agricultural labor behavior and policy. First, the econometric results provide little support for the hypothesis that the two sectors compete for the same labor resources. Supporting evidence for this hypothesis would have been a significant negative private plot coefficient in the estimated collective sector labor supply function and/or a significant negative wage coefficient in the estimated private sector labor supply function. But the plot coefficients for the estimated collective sector labor supply functions of both able-bodied men and women were not signficantly different from zero, nor was the estimated wage coefficient in the private sector labor supply function for able-bodied men. And the estimated wage coefficient in the private sector labor supply function of able-bodied women was positive and significant. These results suggest that collective farmers work predominantly in either the collective or the private sector. This relative specialization probably occurs because working conditions are much different in the private sector than in the collective sector (for example, the collective sector requires more technical expertise, while the private sector conflicts less with the domestic responsibilities of women), and these differences in working conditions determine how any given individual collective farmer distributes labor between the collective and private sectors. Such specialization appears to have increased for able-bodied women during the 1960s.

The econometric results also indicate that economic variables rather than legal restrictions were the key determinants of labor behavior in the 1960s. The collective sector wage coefficient and the private sector plot coefficient are positive and significant for both able-bodied men and women, which implies that increases in wages and plot size increase collective and private labor time, respectively.

Unearned income cannot be shown to have a significant effect on labor behavior. This may be of great interest to Soviet policymakers, as the unearned income of Soviet collective farmers has been increasing rapidly because of Soviet policies to increase rural living standards. This conclusion must be treated with some caution, however, as (1) multicollinearity among the explanatory variables weakens the power of the econometric tests that have been employed, and (2) even though income increased rapidly during the 1960s, it may still have been so low that changes in unearned income did not affect labor behavior.

Finally, the labor behavior of able-bodied women apparently changed between 1963 and 1967 and 1970, while that of able-bodied men did not. The collective sector wage rate could not be shown to have a significant effect on the collective labor time of able-bodied women in 1963, although it did have a significant impact upon their labor in the latter two years; while private plot size had a significant effect upon the labor of able-bodied women in 1963 but could not be shown to affect their collective labor behavior in the other two years. One possible reason for this is that more women tended to specialize in one sector during the second part of the 1960s than during the first part of the decade.

NOTES

1. The work presented in this paper was carried out as part of the author's doctoral dissertation at the University of Michigan. A detailed description of the literature used to develop the theoretical model and the data used in the study is presented in the dissertation.

2. This utility function is assumed to have positive first-order derivatives, negative second-order own partial derivatives, and positive second-order cross-partial derivatives.

3. Collective farmers did not receive a true "wage" prior to 1966. Wage payments prior to this have been obtained from Soviet authors, who have divided total payments for labor to collective farmers by the number of man-days spent in the collective sector. Wages include both monetary payments and payments-in-kind.

4. It should be noted that (a) private plots are granted to households rather than to individuals and (b) even though the size of the private plot is not closely and consistently related to labor effort, the overall level of participation in the collective sector may have an impact on the size of the private plot.

5. This production function is assumed to have positive marginal products and diminishing returns to both factors.

6. This is not strictly true. Private labor inputs decrease as a result of the increase in income, and therefore the MRP of labor in the private sector and the cost of leisure both increase. But since this effect is induced by the initial increase in income, there is no chance that it will outweigh the income effect.

7. This labor constraint is assumed to apply to the individual rather than the household.

8. Several methods of allowing for the possibility of minimum labor constraints were considered. One was to categorize the dummy variable by wage levels. There are two problems with this approach: It is very difficult to select the appropriated wage levels, and wage levels may vary from one group to another. Alternatively, the assumption could have been made that the share of collective farm members bound by the minimum labor constraint was a continuous function of the wage rate during the transition period. This approach envisions a continuous movement of collective farm members from a situation in which their labor behavior is governed by legal restrictions to one in which it is determined by economic factors, rather than the more abrupt transition implied by the use of dummy variables. This approach would require both a specific modelling of the transition function and some knowledge of the beginning and end points of the transition period.

9. The data used in the study were taken from various Soviet sources. The number of man-days worked in the collective sector by able-bodied men and women were taken from M. I. Sidorova, *Vozmeschenie neobkhodmiykh zatrat i formirovanie fonda vosproizvodstva rabochei sily v kolkhozakh; metologiia, uroven', istochniki* (Moscow: Nauka, 1972) for 1963 and 1970; and from F. T. Zemlianskii, *Ekonomika podsobnykh predpriatii i promyslov v kolkhozakh* (Moscow: Kolos, 1971) for 1967. Wage data for 1963 wre obtained from Iu. V. Aruntiunian, *Sotsial'naia struktura sel'skogo naseleniia SSSR* (Moscow: Mysl', 1971); while wage data for 1967 and 1970 were obtained from Sidorova, *op. cit.* Total family income, income obtained from the private sector, and unearned income were all derived from data presented in Sidorova, *op. cit.* Data on the size of private plots were obtained from the statistical yearbooks of the various Soviet Republics.

10. This makes it very difficult to compare the wage coefficients of able-bodied men and women, as these coefficients may differ, due to different skill coefficients as well as (possibly) different income and substitution effects.

APPENDIX A THE DERIVATION OF THE COMPARATIVE STATIC RESULTS

To derive the impact of changes in the exogenous variable on total labor (leisure) time, equation (7a) is totally differentiated with respect to α. This yields:

$$\frac{dw_i}{d\alpha} = \frac{U_i^W[U_i^{W1}\frac{dW_i}{d\alpha} + U_i^{11}\frac{dh_i^1}{d\alpha}] - U_i^l[U_i^{WW}\frac{dW_i}{d\alpha} + U_i^{W1}\frac{dh_i^1}{d\alpha}]}{(U_i^W)^2}$$

$$= \frac{[U_i^{W1}U_i^W - U_i^1 U_i^{WW}]}{(U_i^W)^2}\frac{dW_i}{d\alpha} + \frac{[U_i^W U_i^{11} + U_i^1 U_i^{W1}]}{(U_i^W)^2}\frac{dh_i^1}{d\alpha}$$

Solving this expression for $dh_i^1/d\alpha$ yields:

$$\frac{dh_i^1}{d\alpha} = -\frac{dh_i^{c+p}}{d\alpha} = -\frac{A}{B}\frac{dW_i}{d\alpha} + \frac{1}{B}\frac{dw_i}{d\alpha}$$

where:

$$A = \frac{[U_i^W U_i^{1W} - U_i^1 U_i^{WW}]}{(U_i^W)^2} \qquad B = \frac{[U_i^W U_i^{11} - U_i^1 U_i^{W1}]}{(U_i^W)^2}$$

If the first-order partial derivates of the utility function are positive, the second-order own partial derivates negative, and the second-order cross partial derivates are positive, then $A > 0$ and $B < 0$, and this yields the signs given in Table 1.

The sign of $dh_i^1/d\alpha$ can now be determined if the signs for $dh_i^1/d\alpha$ and $dw_i/d\alpha$ are known. These are:

for $dw_i = d\alpha$:

$$\frac{dW_i}{dw_i} > 0; \frac{dw_i}{dw_i} = 1 > 0 \Rightarrow \frac{dh_i^1}{dw_i} \text{ is } \begin{smallmatrix}\leq\\>\end{smallmatrix} 0$$

for $dW_i' = d\alpha$:

$$\frac{dW_i}{dW_i'} > 0; \frac{dw_i}{dW_i'} = 0 \Rightarrow \frac{dh_i^1}{dW_i'} > 0$$

for $dm_i = d\alpha$:

$$\frac{dW_i}{dm_i} > 0; \frac{dw_i}{dm_i} = 0 \Rightarrow \frac{dh_i^1}{dm_i} > 0$$

for $dP_y = d\alpha$:

$$\frac{dW_i'}{dP_y} > 0; \frac{dw_i}{dP_y} = 0 \Rightarrow \frac{dh_i^1}{dP_y} > 0$$

To derive the effects of changes in the exogenous variables on the allocation of time between the public and private sectors, equation (7b) is totally differentiated with respect to α. This yields:

$$\frac{dw_i}{d\alpha} = P_y \left[G_i^{hh} \frac{dh_i^P}{d\alpha} + G_i^{hm} \frac{dm_i}{d\alpha} \right] + G_i^h \frac{dP_y}{d\alpha}$$

$$\frac{dh_i^P}{d\alpha} = \frac{(dw_i/d\alpha)}{P_y G_i^{hh}} - \frac{G_i^{hm}(dm_i/d\alpha)}{P_y G_i^{hh}} - \frac{G_i^h(dh_i^P/d\alpha)}{P_y G_i^{hh}}$$

where G_i^h, $G_i^{hm} > 0$ and $G_i^{hh} < 0$ by assumption. The sign of $dh_i^P/d\alpha$ can now be determined if the signs of $dw_i/d\alpha$, $dm_i/d\alpha$, and $dP_y/d\alpha$ are known.

for $dw_i = d\alpha$:

$$\frac{dw_i}{dw_i} = 1 > 0; \quad \frac{dm_i}{dw_i} = \frac{dP_y}{dw_i} = 0 \implies \frac{dh_i^P}{dw_i} < 0$$

for $dW_i' = d\alpha$:

$$\frac{dw_i}{dW_i'} = \frac{dm_i}{dW_i'} = \frac{dP_y}{dW_i'} = 0 \qquad \implies \frac{dh_i^P}{dW_i} = 0$$

for $dm_i = d\alpha$:

$$\frac{dm_i}{dm_i} = 1 > 0; \quad \frac{dw_i}{dm_i} = \frac{dP_y}{dm_i} = 0 \implies \frac{dh_i^P}{dm_i} > 0$$

for $dP_y = d\alpha$:

$$\frac{dp_y}{dP_y} = 1 > 0; \quad \frac{dw_i}{dP_y} = \frac{dm_i}{dP_y} = 0 \implies \frac{dh_i^P}{dP_y} > 0$$

To derive the result reported in Table 2, equation (8) is totally differentiated with respect to α. This yields:

$$\frac{dP_y}{d\alpha} F_i^h + \left[F_i^{hh} \frac{dh_i^y}{d\alpha} + F_i^{hm} \frac{dm_i}{d\alpha} \right] P_y = A \frac{dW_i}{d\alpha} + B \frac{dh_i^\ell}{d\alpha}$$

where A and B are defined as before. Except for an exogenous change in the minimum labor constraint (where $d = dh_i^x$), $(dh_i^\ell/d\alpha) = -(dh_i^y/d\alpha)$. Making this substitution and solving for $dh_i^y/d\alpha$:

$$[B + P_y F_i^{hh}] \frac{dh_i^y}{d\alpha} = A \frac{dW_i}{d\alpha} - \left[F_i^h \frac{dP_i^P}{d\alpha} + P_y F_i^{hm} \frac{dm_i}{d\alpha} \right]$$

Or:

$$\frac{dh_i^y}{d\alpha} = \frac{A}{(B + P_y F_i^{hh})} \frac{dw_i}{d\alpha} - \frac{1}{(B + P_y F_i^{hh})} \left[F_i^{hh} \frac{dh_i^y}{d\alpha} + P_y F_i^{hm} \frac{dm_i}{d\alpha} \right]$$

where: $A > 0$, $(B + P_y F_i^{hh}) < 0$, $F_i^h > 0$, and $F_i^{hm} > 0$. Substituting the specific exogenous variables for α now yields the following results:

$$\frac{dW_i}{dw_i} > 0; \frac{dP_y}{dw_i} = \frac{dm_i}{dw_i} = 0 \Rightarrow \frac{dh_i^y}{dw_i} < 0$$

for $dW_i' = d\alpha$:

$$\frac{dw_i}{dW_i'} > 0; \frac{dP_y}{dW_i'} = \frac{dm_i}{dW_i'} = 0 \Rightarrow \frac{dh_i^y}{dW_i'} < 0$$

for $dm_i = d\alpha$:

$$\frac{dW_i}{dm_i} > 0; \frac{dP_y}{dm_i} = 0; \frac{dm_i}{dm_i} = 1 > 0; \frac{dh_i^y}{dm_i} \gtrless 0$$

for $dP_y = d\alpha$:

$$\frac{dW_i}{dP_y} > 0; \frac{dP_y}{dP_y} = 1 > 0; \frac{dm_i}{dP_y} = 0 \Rightarrow \frac{dh_i^y}{dP_y} \gtrless 0$$

This analysis changes somewhat if the minimum labor constraint changes. In this case:

$$-\frac{dh_i}{dh_i^{-x}} = \frac{dh_i^{-x}}{dh_i^{-x}} + \frac{dh_i^y}{dh_i^{-x}} = 1 + \frac{dh_i^y}{dh_i^{-x}}$$

Substituting this equality into the first equation on p. and moving all of the expressions containing dh_i^y / dh_i^{-x} on the left-hand side and all of the remaining terms to the right-hand side of the equation yields:

$$(P_y F_i^{hh} + B)\frac{dh_i^y}{dh_i^{-x}} = A\frac{dW_i}{dh_i^{-x}} - (F_i^h \frac{dP_y}{dh_i^{-x}} + F_i^{hm}\frac{dm_i}{dh_i^{-x}}) - B$$

where $(dP_y / dh_i^{-x}) = (dm_i / dh_i^{-x}) = 0$ and $(dW_i / dh_i^{-x}) = (w_i + P_y F_i^h (dh_i^y / dh_i^{-x}))$. Substituting these expressions into the above equation and solving for dh_i^y / dh_i^{-x} now yields:

$$(P_y F_i^{hh} + B - AP_y F_i^h)\frac{dh_i^y}{dP_y} = Aw_i - B$$

Or:

$$\frac{dh_i^y}{dh_i^{-x}} = \frac{A}{(P_y F_i^{hh} + B - AP_y F_i^h)}w_i - \frac{B}{(P_y F_i^{hh} + B - AP_y F_i^h)} < 0$$

PART FOUR

Contemporary Soviet Agriculture: Performance and Prospects

12

Rural Living Standards
in the Soviet Union

Gertrude E. Schroeder

INTRODUCTION

Recent research has found that per capita consumption of goods and services in the USSR is only about one-third of that in the United States and well below levels in most European countries, both East and West, and in Japan.[1] This research has also demonstrated that real per capita consumption in the USSR has risen at an average annual rate of 3.5 percent since 1950. Although it would be of great interest to make such calculations separately for the urban and rural populations in the USSR, the framework in which relevant data are published, as well as their paucity, precludes our doing so. The weight of the evidence, even with the large lacunae, shows unmistakably, nonetheless, that the level of living of the average rural resident is still well below that of the urban counterpart but also that the gap has been substantially reduced in recent decades. My "ballpark" estimates are that per capita consumption in rural areas at present is between two-thirds and three-fourths of the level in urban areas and that since 1950 real per capita consumption more than tripled in rural areas, and more than doubled in urban areas. During the past thirty years the rural population has declined by 10 percent, while the urban population has doubled. This general assessment of the relative position of rural residents is based on an array of quantitative measures. Much anecdotal evidence, including literary writings of Soviet authors, supports my judgment that when qualitative factors are taken into account, urban-rural differences in living standards are considerably greater than the quantitative evidence suggests. Both quantitatively and qualitatively, the differences vary greatly by region of the country.

The purpose of this paper is to marshall some of the evidence on which these generalizations are based. The second section ("Incomes") considers relative levels and trends in rural and urban incomes, a proxy for which necessarily must be agricultural and nonagricultural incomes. The third section ("Consumption of Goods and Personal Services") assembles the complementary data on expenditures for goods and services by rural and urban households. "Communal Services" considers some fragmentary data on investment in infrastructure serving rural and urban areas and also the role of the state and of the collective farms (through so-called social consumption funds) in providing health, education, and cultural services to the respective populations. A final section comments on some of the qualitative factors bearing on an assessment of living conditions in rural areas relative to the situation in cities.

INCOMES

The Soviet government publishes no direct data on rural and urban incomes. Hence, relative levels and trends in these incomes must be inferred from data on wages paid to agricultural and nonagricultural workers, estimates of incomes in kind and receipts from sales of home-produced agricultural products, and indirect evidence about rural/urban differentials in wages of nonagricultural workers. In addition, both groups receive substantial incomes in money and in kind from transfer payments and free or subsidized services provided by the state. In Soviet statistics, these "incomes" are labelled "payments and benefits from social consumption funds." Although these data are not published separately for rural and urban residents, these social benefits can be estimated with reasonable accuracy for collective farm families, state farm families, and the rest of the population, but only for one year—1977. The data gaps are most unfortunate. Nevertheless, it is clear that (1) such social "incomes" are considerably higher in urban areas than in rural areas, and (2) they have been rising far more rapidly as components of total incomes of collective farm families than of incomes of the state-employed labor force. At the same time, the number of collective farmers has declined by one-half since 1950, while the number of state farmers has more than tripled.

Incomes of Agricultural and Nonagricultural Workers

Table 12.1 presents my estimates of incomes of agricultural and nonagricultural workers in benchmark years in monetary valuations and in real terms.[2] Agricultural incomes are the sums of wages of state farmers, monetary payments to collective farm members for work of all kinds done for the farms, receipts from the sale of farm products by the population, and consumption in kind of farm products valued at average retail prices. Nonagricultural wages are derived from published data, as are wages in state agriculture and wages paid to collective farmers. The weakest component of these estimates is the valuation of incomes in kind, which had to be put together from a variety of sources; nonetheless, the results probably are not seriously off the mark. The price index used to express the incomes of both groups in real terms is an implicit deflator, calculated from indexes of per capita consumption of the Soviet population as a whole in current and in constant prices. This index undoubtedly understates the real rate of price increase, and its use to deflate agricultural incomes is questionable.[3] The

Table 12.1 Incomes of Agricultural and Nonagricultural Workers, Selected Years, 1950-1976

	Average Annual Agricultural Incomes (rubles)	Average Annual Nonagricultural Wages (rubles)	Indexes of Real Incomes (1950 = 100) Agricultural Workers	Nonagricultural Workers
1950	441	794	100	100
1960	651	1002	167	143
1970	1234	1505	280	190
1976	1616	1838	329	208

Sources: Average annual wages of nonagricultural workers and of state farmers are derived from *Trud v SSSR* (Moscow: Statistika, 1968), p. 137 and *Narkhoz SSSR* (Moscow: Statistika, 1977), p. 385. Money payments to collective farmers and incomes of the population from sales of farm produce are given in M. Elizabeth Denton, "Soviet Consumer Policy: Trends and Prospects," in U.S. Congress, Joint Economic Committee, *Soviet Economy in a Time of Change* (Washington: U.S. Government Printing Office, 1979, p. 785. The price index used to deflate incomes of both groups is also given there (p. 766). The values of income in kind of agricultural workers are the writer's estimates, based on a wide variety of quantity and price data. Employment data are taken from Stephen Rapawy, *Estimates and Projections of the Labor Force and Employment in the U.S.S.R., 1950 to 1990,* U.S. Department of Commerce, Foreign Economic Report No. 10, 1976, p. 40. Estimates for 1976 were provided by him.

only other price index available, however, is the officially published index of state retail prices, supplemented with a calculated index of prices in collective farm markets; this composite index is wholly misleading because of the methodology used in its construction.[4]

According to the data in Table 12.1, average annual incomes of agricultural workers rose 5.1 percent annually during 1950–1976 in nominal terms and 4.7 percent annually in real terms. Corresponding annual growth rates for nonagricultural workers were 3.5 percent and 2.9 percent. As a consequence, the differential between the average incomes of the two groups decreased greatly. In 1950, average agricultural incomes were extremely low and averaged only 56 percent of average nonagricultural incomes; the percentage was 88 in 1976. The estimates shown in Table 12.1 somewhat overstate incomes of farmers, because all incomes (in money and in kind) from private farming activity are attributed to agricultural workers.[5] If we assume, for example, that 10 percent of such incomes are earned by nonagricultural workers (surely a maximum), the differential is reduced to 82 percent in 1976. The difference would be greater on a per capita basis, because rural families are larger.[6]

In addition to earnings from work and incomes from private agriculture, the Soviet population receives substantial incomes in the form of money transfer payments (stipends, pensions, aid) and the value of free or subsidized services provided by the state. In 1977, such incomes from "social consumption funds" amounted to 99.5 billion rubles, or 384 rubles per capita.[7] Of this total, 14.0 billion rubles represent vacation pay. Deducting this amount, because it is already counted as a part of wages, leaves 85.5 billion rubles, or 342 rubles per capita. A greatly disproportionate share of these funds accrues to urban residents, but no data are officially published on the distribution among population groups. Information provided in a recent Soviet source, however, makes it possible to estimate roughly the share of the total that benefits agricultural families.[8] The key data relate to the shares of these funds in the total incomes of collective farm families and families of state farm workers (*rabochii*). Using these data and related information, I have calculated that in 1977 about 14.8 billion rubles of social consumption funds (less vacation pay and assuming no such payments for collective farmers) benefitted agricultural families, 17 percent of the total funds. Finally, the population also receives income from interest on savings deposits. In 1977, this income amounted to about 691 million rubles for rural residents and 1,875 million rubles for urban residents,[9] expressed per capita, the respective amounts are 7 rubles and 11 rubles.

A substantial proportion of rural residents is engaged in nonagricultural pursuits.[10] According to data from the 1970 census, 37.6 percent of all gainfully occupied, rural residents were employed in activities other than agriculture and forestry, nearly half in industry, construction, transport, and communications.[11] Judging from indirect evidence, average wages in nonagricultural branches are much lower in rural areas than in urban areas. This conclusion is based on the rather high correlation between average wages in these branches in the republics and various other geographic entites and the shares of rural population in their total populations. To illustrate, with few exceptions, average wages in most nonagricultural branches in the relatively more urban republics of Latvia, Estonia, Armenia, and the RSFSR in 1975 considerably exceeded those in the more rural republics of Georgia, Azerbaidzhan, and Central Asia (except Turkmenia).[12] One explanation for relatively lower wages is that the light and food industries, with their relatively lower wages, tend to be more prominent in the industrial structures in the more rural republics. Also, salary levels of white-collar workers in many branches are related to size of establishments, which tend to be smaller in rural areas than in cities. Inspection of available regional wage data suggests that average wages of nonagricultural workers in rural areas are perhaps about three-fourths of the average in urban areas. In 1970, nearly 20 percent of all nonagricultural workers resided in rural areas.

Assuming that these relationships held in 1976, we can approximate the nonagricultural wage bill for state emloyees in rural areas in that year. Combining that estimate with the data in Table 12.1 and using the relative shares of social consumption funds and interest on savings calculated above for 1977, we can estimate the total incomes in money and in kind received in rural and urban areas, respectively. According to this calculation, per capita incomes in rural areas were 77 percent of those in urban areas. Some heroic assumptions are used in this estimate. That it may not be too far off the mark, however, is suggested by the assertion in a Soviet source that in 1975-76, total income per family of workers on state farms and of collective farms was no more than 15 percent below that of the family of an average industrial worker (*rabochii*) and that the differential was even less in respect to money incomes alone.[13] The difference would be greater, if expressed per capita, rather than per family. Another source states that in 1977 real income per collective farm family had reached 87 percent of that for families of all state workers and employees.[14] In summary, our estimates provide this income profile of the average rural inhabitant: 23 percent of income, most of it in kind, comes from private farming activity; 56 percent comes from wages for work in the socialized sector; and 20 percent is provided by social consumption funds. In contrast, the average urban resident receives 72 percent of income from wages in the public sector, 26 percent from social consumption funds, and less than 1 percent from private plot activity. Our calculations also indicate that the average nonagricultural worker living in rural areas is better off than the average agricultural worker. For both rural and urban residents, the shares of income that comes from private farming activity has been declining, while the shares of both wages and benefits from social funds have been rising, especially in the case of rural residents.

These estimates do not take into account incomes earned and redistributed in the illegal segment of the so-called second economy. These incomes are generated mainly through illegal production and sales of goods and services, black market sales, bribery, and corruption. There is no way to determine whether such activities are more prevalent in rural areas than in urban areas or the size of the differences, if any. We know only that production of *samogon* is largely a rural phenomenon; its production could add a few billion rubles to consumption in kind in rural areas. Black market activities and corruption, perhaps, are more common in urban areas because of greater opportunities to acquire scarce goods as well as the higher incomes there. We do not know. In any event activities of the latter kind merely raise prices and redistribute incomes and existing goods; they do not augment supply.

CONSUMPTION OF GOODS AND PERSONAL SERVICES

The available data preclude even tolerably reliable estimates of levels and trends in per capital consumption of goods and services by rural and urban residents separately. One major difficulty was considered above—the large but declining role of consumption in kind of food products in rural areas and the difficulty of measuring it. Another major problem concerns the use of published retail sales data to indicate the relative purchases of the two groups—a common practice. Such data include purchases by enterprises and institutions (*melkii opt*), as well as so-called productive services such as shoe repair and tailoring, and there are no data with which to remove these items separately from rural and urban sales. Moreover, the data on rural and urban sales represent total purchases in the respective areas, rather than total purchases by their residents. Sample surveys indicate that in the 1970s collective farm families made 38 percent of their purchases of nonfood goods in cities.[15] A sample survey in the Ukraine showed that 44.5 percent of all rural families made trips to cities for the purpose of buying goods and that an average rural dweller purchased about 20 percent of all goods in cities.[16] Similar considerations apply to the published data on sales of personal services (*bytovye uslugi*) in urban and rural areas. As a consequence of these critical information gaps, the available data on retail sales are cited merely as rough indicators of some of the rural-urban differences to be assessed. The statistics are assembled for selected benchmark years in Table 12.2, along with related data on trade and service facilities, housing, and recreation services available in rural and in urban areas.

Food

Although we do not have recent data, it is probable that rural residents consume about the same number of calories daily as do their urban counterparts. The rural diet is qualitatively much inferior, however, in the sense that rural residents obtain much larger shares of total calories from starchy foods such as bread and potatoes than do urban residents. Such a dietary pattern is to be expected, given the relatively lower incomes of the rural population. This judgment is based on data for the 1960s (the latest data were published in 1968) giving per capita consumption of major foods in kilograms by families of state workers and employees and of collective farmers. Selected statistics will show the large differences. In 1968, per capita consumption of meat was 51 kilograms in worker and employee families and 37 kilograms in collective farm families: corresponding figures are 125 and 151 for potatoes, 142 and 172 for grain products, and 83 and 65 kilograms for vegetables.[17] Because of their relatively higher incomes, rural familes other than those of collective farmers may have had a more protein-oriented diet than did the latter. The data also show that dietary quality was improving somewhat more rapidly for collective farm families than for the rest. During 1968–1980, per capita meat consumption for the nation as a whole rose from 48 kilograms to 57 kilograms, while consumption of grain products fell from 149 to 139 kilograms. Unless relative rates of improvement were greatly different in the 1970s from what they were in the 1960s, the diet of collective farm families, and probably also of all rural residents, still lags well behind that of urbanites with respect to the relative share of meat, vegetables, and fruit. Data for 1976 from a sample survey support this conclusion.[18]

As one might expect, economic development in the USSR, as in other countries, has entailed a large shift from consumption in kind and home processing of food to purchases through retail outlets. Virtually all of this shift, primarily affecting rural residents, has occurred since 1950. In that year, collective farm families produced almost all of their own food on their private plots, and rural retail sales of food per capita were a mere 40 rubles, much of it beverages, staples, sugar, and flour. Since then, per capita retail sales in rural areas have risen more than sevenfold, two and six-tenths times as fast as per capita urban sales. Even now, however, the average rural resident produces about 40 percent of the family's food. In the families of collective farmers, private plots supply 95 percent of their needs for potatoes, 75 percent for vegetables, 70 percent for meat, 82 percent for milk, and 97 percent for eggs.[19] According to Western estimates, per capita consumption of food for the entire Soviet population has increased at an average rate of 2.6 percent annually during 1951–79.[20] Progress clearly has been more rapid for the rural population, although the advantage cannot be quantified.

Other Goods

Our information concerning rural and urban purchases and stocks of soft goods and consumer durables is limited to data on retail sales and on household stocks of selected durables. Keeping in mind the limitations of retail sales data noted above, we find that per capita retail sales of nonfood goods in rural areas in 1980 were less than half (43 percent) of those in urban areas. During 1951–80, however, rural sales per capita rose six and four-tenths times in current prices, compared with a fourfold rise in per capita urban sales. There are no data on the composition of these sales in the two areas.[21] Information on household stocks of consumer durables is available with a rural-urban breakdown only since 1965. As these data show (Table 12.2), stocks in 1965 were relatively small for both groups, but have expanded rapidly since then—a little faster in rural areas than in cities. In 1980, there were 42 percent more of the listed durables per urban resident than there were per rural resident. Over three-quarters of all urban families owned the key household items—television set, refrigerator, and washing machine. In rural households, between 58 and 73 percent of families had them. In contrast, a substantially larger share of rural families owned motorcycles, bicycles, and the like than did urban families. Data on stocks of passenger cars are not published. However, during 1975–1980, 2.3 million cars were sold in rural areas through state and cooperative retail trade, compared with 4.4 million in urban areas; both figures include sales of used cars.[22]

As far as is known, retail prices for soft goods and durables are now the same in rural and in urban areas. A surcharge on rural sales was abolished in the 1960s. As for quality, there is no way to determine whether the quality of goods allocated to rural areas is inferior to that in urban areas, but the assortment is not doubt much more limited in rural shops. The Soviet press is rife with complaints from both groups about the poor quality and assortment of goods on sale in stores. Judging from such evidence, it seems that supplies of desired goods, relative to effective demand, are far scarcer in rural areas than in cities. This relative scarcity is the explanation nearly always given for the necessity for rural dwellers to go to cities, especially large ones, to make purchases, mainly of soft goods and durables.

Personal Services

According to Western measures of per capita consumption in the USSR, personal services, although comprising only about one-seventh of total household expenditures, have been one of the most rapidly growing com-

Table 12.2 Indicators of Rural and Urban Consumption and Services, Selected Years, 1950–1980

	Rural				Urban			
	1950	1960	1970	1980	1950	1960	1970	1980
I.								
Retail sales (rubles per capita)	80	174	334	568	383	564	874	1283
Food	40	86	185	295	234	316	485	647
Nonfood	40	88	149	273	149	248	389	636
II.								
Personal services (rubles per capita)			7	21			24	34
III.								
No. of retail stores (000)	190	242	279	283	109	171	221	249
Average size of store (M²)		36	49	69		54	83	110
No. of public dining facilities (000)	26	38	71	95	70	109	166	208
Seats per restaurant		23	28	41		40	57	72
No. of personal service establishments (000)			103	113			136	158
IV.								
Housing (M² per capita)	4.7	6.3	7.8	8.9	4.7	5.8	7.2	8.6
V.								
Paid movie attendance per capita	11	12	16	16	13	21	21	16
Number of clubs (000)	116	114	116	119	9	14	18	19

VI.
Stocks of consumer durables
(per 100 families)

	a			a		
Watches	245	309	418	375	480	570
Radios	49	55	75	67	78	90
TV sets	15	32	71	32	61	91
Cameras	8	12	16	36	36	39
Refrigerators	3	15	61	17	43	99
Washing machines	12	26	58	29	64	78
Vacuum cleaners	1	3	13	11	16	37
Sewing machines	50	54	69	54	57	63
Bicycles and motorcycles	57	71	83	49	49	46

aData are for 1965.

Sources: I. Narkhoz SSSR (Moscow: Finansy i Statistika, 1980), p. 428.; II. Ibid., p. 451.; III. Calculated from data Narkhoz SSSR (Moscow: Finansy i Statistika, 1980, pp. 440, 445, 449, 451.; IV. Midyear stocks of living space per capita. Urban housing stock is regularly published in the annual Narkhozy. Rural housing stock is estimated from data published there, following the methodology used in Willard Smith, "Housing in the Soviet Union: Big Plans, Little Action," in U.S. Congress, Joint Economic Committee, Soviet Economic Prospects for the 1970s (Washington: U.S. Government Printing Office, 1973), pp. 422–23. Basic data are given in M² of "useful space," which includes hallways, kitchens, baths, and closets. Ratios of 0.75 and 0.666 were used to convert useful space to living space in rural and urban areas, respectively.; V. Narkhoz SSSR (Moscow: Statistika, 1965), pp. 724, 731: Narkhoz SSSR (Moscow: Finansy i Statistika, 1980), pp. 478, 483.; VI. Narkhoz SSSR (Moscow: Finansy i Statistika, 1980), p. 407.

ponents of consumption in the postwar years. These services consist of housing and utilities, transportation and communications, repair and personal care, and recreation. Per capita consumption of these services has grown 4.3 percent annually since 1950, compared with 3.5 percent for consumption as a whole. The data available (Table 12.2) permit an urban-rural split only for housing, repair and personal care, and partially for recreation.

Housing, as measured by living space per capita, has been the slowest-growing component of consumption. Rural dwellers have fared a little better than urban dwellers. In 1950, per capita living space was 4.7 square meters for both groups: in 1980, it was 8.9 in rural areas and 8.5 in urban areas. However, the nature of the housing is quite different. The vast bulk (about 80 percent) of rural housing is owned privately and consists of small, two- or three-room wooden farmhouses. Most new rural housing is built and owned privately, whereas most new urban housing is built by the government, which owns about three-fourths of the total stock. During 1951–80, 30 percent of all rural housing was built by the state and by housing cooperatives, which are few in rural areas; and 70 percent was built by private persons and by collective farms. Although the share of the latter has been increasing, it appears to be small for the period as a whole. Housing built in rural areas by the state and collective farms consists mainly of apartment-type buildings and dormitories. In recent years, there has been a lively discussion in the press concerning the kind of public housing that should be constructed in rural areas. The advocates of multifamily units evidently have prevailed, with resulting decisions to build many such units in rural areas. This type of housing, however, has had an adverse impact on private farming. Now that the government is once more pushing the development of that sector, schemes are having to be devised to counteract the disinclination of rural apartment dwellers to organize the tending of animals and the growing of vegetables, when the dwelling unit and the private plot are no longer virtually one and the same.

Far fewer amenities are provided to rural residents than to city dwellers. Although use of electricity is now nearly universal, brownouts and interruptions in power are much more frequent in the countryside. In 1976, some 59 percent of rural homes were supplied with gas, which meant individual propane tanks; in that year, 69 percent of urban housing units were supplied with gas.[23] Other amenities are far more scarce in rural areas. Thus, in the RSFSR in 1980, only 38 percent of state-owned rural housing units were connected to central water supply systems and only 22 percent to sewer lines; 26 percent of the units had some form of central heating.[24] The situation was no doubt worse for housing owned by collective farms, and few individually owned houses have any of these amenities. Thus, according to a sample survey of all rural housing units in Novosibirsk Oblast in 1977, amenities were available as follows: running water—22 percent; hot water—5 percent; indoor plumbing—11 percent; baths—9 percent; central heating—10 percent; telephones—4 percent.[25]

Services for repair and personal care are available in minimal quantities

NKH '77
(za 60 let)

in the USSR, both in cities and in the countryside. These services, described in Soviet statistics as "everyday services" (*bytovye uslugi*), are provided partly by state and cooperative shops and partly by private persons. As shown by the data for 1980 in Table 12.2, the public sector furnished a mere 21 rubles per capita of such services to rural areas, less than two-thirds the level in cities. These services have been developing much faster in rural areas than in cities, however: in 1970, the rural level was 29.2 percent of the urban level, and in 1960 it was 10.7 percent. All of these data overstate both the urban and rural shares and the rates of growth, however, because a substantial and growing percentage of these services were provided to enterprises and institutions, rather than to the population.[26] As compared with cities, such services as laundries, dry cleaning, public baths, photographers, and barber and hairdressing shops are poorly developed in rural areas. Most of the services provided there consist of repair services, tailoring, and construction of housing. In line with the lower volume of services provided, rural areas also have far fewer service enterprises.

Soviet sources repeatedly declare that provision of these "everyday" services by the public sector lags far behind the demand for them and that their quality is poor. Part of the evidently large gap is filled by private purveyors, who seem to supply a larger share of the total in rural areas than in cities. Only fragmentary information is available on the amount of private services. An authoritative survey for the RSFSR found in the early 1970s such services amounted to 6 rubles per capita per year and that in 1971, 47.9 percent of services in rural areas were rendered by private persons, compared with 15 percent in cities; the respective shares in 1960 were 90.4 and 44.3 percent. In 1970, 55 percent of private services related to the construction and repair of housing in rural areas, compared with 41 percent in cities.[27]

The information with which to assess rural/urban differences in recreational patterns is sparse. Table 12.2 provides data on movie attendance and on the number of clubs. As shown there, movie attendance developed rapidly in both areas during the 1950s and 1960s, but this form of recreation was much more common in cities. In the 1970s, however, movie attendance declined (per capita) in cities and leveled off in rural areas. As the data cited earlier suggest, both groups were responding similarly to the rapidly increasing availability of television sets. Clubs are largely a rural phenomenon. They are, in effect, gathering places for rural villagers, providing centers for social and cultural life there. Their number has not changed much in thirty years in rural areas, despite a drop of 10 million in the rural population, relfecting government efforts to upgrade cultural facilities in the countryside. In recent years, this effort has taken the form of establishing cultural centers in villages or on large farms; these centers combine various kinds of social and cultural activities. Relatively few such centers have been built yet, however, and recent sample surveys indicate that about half of the respondents gave a negative evaluation of the activities provided by the cultural and educational facilities available to them.[28]

COMMUNAL SERVICES

Education and health services in the Soviet Union are almost entirely provided by the government. They are financed mainly by the state budget, supplemented by funds from trade unions, enterprises, and collective farms. The latter play a major role in the construction of school and health facilities in rural areas. During 1951–80, they built 61 percent of the rural schools, with 43 percent of the pupil places.[29] During 1956–80, they built preschool facilities for 2.5 million children and hospitals with 161,000 beds.[30] Although statistics on total construction of such facilities in the countryside are not available, the share built by collective farms clearly was substantial.

Data from the three postwar Soviet censuses show that the level of education of the rural population has improved greatly and at a more rapid rate than that of the urban population. The data are given in Table 12.3. In 1979, 47 percent more persons (per 1,000 population) age ten years and over, in urban areas had some higher or secondary education than was the case in rural areas; the corresponding figure was 83 percent in 1959. The number (per 1,000 population) having some higher education in 1979, however, was nearly four times greater in urban areas than in rural areas. The rural/urban differential was smaller for the gainfully occupied population, and rural progress has been relatively greater. Thus, the urban superiority for persons with some higher or secondary education was 25 percent in 1979 and 78 percent in 1959. Three times more persons (per 1,000 population) had some higher education in 1979 in urban areas than in rural areas, compared with five times more in 1959.

Despite notable quantitative progress, much evidence indicates that the

---

Table 12.3   Educational Attainment of the Rural and Urban Population, 1950, 1970, and 1979 (per 1000 Persons)

| | Higher and Secondary, Complete and Incomplete | | of which | | | |
| | | | Higher | | Secondary | |
	Rural	Urban	Rural	Urban	Rural	Urban
Population age 10 and over						
1959	256	469	7	40	249	429
1970	332	592	14	62	318	530
1979	492	723	25	93	467	630
Gainfully occupied population						
1959	316	564	11	59	305	505
1970	499	748	25	90	474	658
1970	693	863	42	130	651	733

Source: Naseleniia SSSR po dannym vsesoiuznoi perepisi naseleniia 1979 goda (Moscow: Politizdat, 1980), p. 21.

quality of rural education is far inferior to that in urban areas,[31] despite the fact that the state spends more per pupil on rural schools than on urban schools. Rural schools are small, poorly equipped, and costly to maintain. In many isolated areas and small settlements, the one-room school is common. On the average, rural teachers are less well educated than their urban counterparts, and turnover is high, despite a pay supplement. Thus, in 1975–76 only 58 percent of the teachers in rural general education schools had a higher education, compared with 73 percent of those in urban areas.[32] In 1950–51, however, the corresponding shares were 8 percent and 29 percent. Apparently, opportunities to attend trade schools and to combine schooling with work are scarce in rural areas. According to survey evidence, the desire to further one's own or one's children's education is one of the main reasons for migration of rural residents to cities in general and for the exodus of young skilled and technically trained workers, in particular.[33]

Another area of rural inferiority lies in the provision of preschool facilities for children, a reason also cited for high turnover of young specialists in rural areas. In 1980, there were 58,700 permanent preschool institutions of all kinds in rural areas, with 3.5 million children accommodated; urban areas had 69,100 such facilities, with 10.9 million children.[34] The share of children in the relevant age group in such child-care facilities is much larger in urban areas than in rural areas. In addition to permanent nurseries and kindergartens, various kinds of seasonal facilities are organized in summer, accommodating nearly 2 million children of preschool age; the share of rural areas in this total is not given.

Although the Soviet government does not publish data to support a quantitative assessment, it is clear that the availability and the quality of medical services in rural areas is far inferior to those in urban areas. In the early 1970s, according to a Soviet source, only 11 percent of all doctors were located in rural areas, and the total number of visits to doctors and house calls by them per capita was three times lower there than in cities.[35] The same source reports that hospital beds per capita in rural areas were 89 percent of those in cities, after allowing for use of urban facilities by rural residents. Another source states that in 1975, urban areas had two and four-tenths times as many medical personnel per 10,000 population as did rural areas, compared with three times as many in 1965 and 1970.[36] Only 20 percent of all middle-level medical personnel were employed in rural areas.[37] In 1975, less than 15 percent of total current expenditures on hospitals and clinics from budgets of the union republics represented outlays in rural areas.[38] Turnover is high among doctors and technicians sent to rural areas upon graduation; most of them evidently leave for the cities at the earliest opportunity. The situation with respect to medical care varies widely among geographic areas. The press reported in 1972, for example, that in Georgia, which had more doctors per capita than any other republic, there were no physicians at all in 25 rural hospitals and 127 rural outpatient clinics.[39] Writing in 1980, the Minister of Health in the Ukraine states, "today, the level of medical care provided to hospital patients in rural areas is often comparable to that received in cities, but it is significantly lower in the outpatient clinics and polyclinics. Almost half of all visits by villagers are being handled at present, not by a physician, but by a paramedic."[40]

AN OVERVIEW

After surveying the evidence for the 1950s, Shimkin concluded that real per capita income of the average rural resident at the end of that decade was about half of that of the average city dweller.[41] My survey of the evidence for the 1960s and 1970s shows conclusively that a sizeable reduction in the rural-urban gap in levels of living has taken place, which leads me to think that at present average rural per capita income (consumption) is in the range of 65 to 75 percent of that of urban residents. This tentative assessment relates to the relative quantities of goods and services available to the two populations on a per capita basis. A large body of evidence, some of it already presented, indicates, however, that many of these goods and services available in the countryside are inferior in quality to those available in urban areas. Certainly, this is true of housing, retail trade, and personal service facilities; education and health services; and cultural and recreational opportunities. Not captured in the quantitative indicators, either, is the relative isolation of much of rural Russia. In general, the road system of the Soviet Union is poorly developed by any modern comparison. At the end of 1980, there were 1.346 million miles of automobile roads, 69 percent of which were paved.[42] Only 9 percent of the populated points in rural areas were located on paved roads in 1976.[43] By all accounts, the dirt roads in most rural areas are virtually impassable during rainy seasons.

It is also evident that conditions of rural life vary greatly among the union republics and within republics and smaller administrative areas. The evidence is indirect. Among the republics, the differences in wages are much wider for state and collective farm wages than for nonagricultural wages.[44] Wide differences among republics are to be found in the incomes that collective farmers receive (in money and in kind) from work on their private plots.[45] Even larger differences in wage payments and social consumption funds exist among collective farms within republics, especially within the highly diverse RSFSR, stemming from differences in the income and profitability of the farms themselves.[46] Without doubt, the same is true for state farms.

Obviously, also, living standards and the quality of rural life in general have much to do with the size of rural settlements. Between 1959 and 1970, the number of rural settlements decreased from 705,000 to 319,000, mainly because of a deliberate campaign to liquidate small, so-called unviable villages. In 1970, 46.3 million persons lived in settlements with fewer than 500 persons—34 percent of the total; some 7.1 percent lived in villages with fewer than 100 persons.[47] In 1970, nearly a third of the rural population resided in settlements described as "points at which are located individual brigades, farms, and production sectors of state farms and collective farms."[48] In 1979, over two-thirds of all rural settlements with 12 percent of the population had fewer than 100 inhabitants.[49] The obvious difficulties of providing social and cultural facilities and other amenities to such small settlements, along with ideological notions about what constitutes "socialist" rural living arrangments, has led to a concerted effort to consolidate rural settlements and to improve the lot of the larger ones. A long-range plan calls for the liquidation of 348,000 small villages, affecting 15.4 million persons, by 1990.[50] In the past year or two, the planners seem to have been reconsidering the scheme, for the program has had adverse effects on the supply of farm products to cities and on migration patterns. One study showed, for example, that not only had the resettlement program failed to halt the exodus of young people from the countryside in general, but many families uprooted under the program simply moved to urban areas instead of to larger rural settlements.[51] Also, some of the consolidated settlements themselves have disintegrated, thus worsening the situation. In October 1980, *Pravda* published a series of articles discussing the program to liquidate small villages,[52] suggesting that things may have been moving too far too fast.

Progress in reducing the differences between rural and urban living standards is slated to continue. The Directives for the Eleventh Five-Year Plan (1981–85) state the intent to overcome the "basic" difference between the village and the city gradually.[53] The plan calls for wages of collective farmers from work in the socialized sector to rise by 20 to 22 percent, compared with 13 to 16 percent for the state labor force as a whole. The plan accords "stepped up priority" to the construction of rural housing, amenities, and child-care and cultural facilities, with investment to be increased by 25 to 30 percent. Further steps also are to be taken to bring the social security system for collective farmers more nearly in line with that for state employees. Many of these programs have become a part of Brezhnev's much-touted "food program," announced in May 1982; a follow-up Party-government decree spells out a spate of measures to be taken during the 1980s to improve rural living standards, with emphasis on developing rural infrastructure on a broad front.[54] Moreover, two recent decrees call for a concerted program to provide improved incentives and material support to the private agricultural sector.[55] If implemented, these measures could materially improve living conditions in rural areas. On balance, the rural population well may fare somewhat better than the urban population in the difficult decade ahead, when both economic growth and gains in living standards in the USSR are likely to slow markedly.

NOTES

1. Gerturde E. Schroeder and Imogene Edwards *Consumption in the USSR: An International Comparison* (Washington, D.C.: U.S. Government Printing Office, 1981).

2. The values in current rubles are presented in my paper, "Consumption," in *The Soviet Economy Toward the Year 2000,* Abram Bergson and Herbert S. Levine, eds. (New York: Allen and Unwin, 1983), pp. 311–49.

3. A description of this price index and its limitations is given in Gertrude E. Schroeder and Barbara S. Severin, "Soviet Consumption and Income Policies in Perspective," in *Soviet Economy in a New Perspective* (Washington, D.C.: U.S. Government Printing Office, 1976), pp. 630–32.

4. See Morris Bornstein, "Soviet Price Statistics," in *Soviet Economic Statistics,* eds. Vladimir G. Treml and John P. Hardt, (Durham, North Carolina: Duke University Press, 1972), pp. 370–84.

5. Incomes from agriculture per se are also overstated, because wages paid by collective farms to their members include pay for nonagricultural work. Rapawy has estimated that 15 percent of collective farmers were engaged in such work in 1974. See Stephen Rapawy, *Estimates and Projections of the Labor Force and Civilian Employment in the U.S.S.R.: 1950 to 1990* (Washington, D.C.: U.S. Department of Commerce, Foreign Economic Report No.' 10, 1976), p. 38. We can ignore this fact, however, since our concern in this paper is to approximate rural incomes, rather than purely agricultural incomes.

6. According to the 1979 census, the average rural family had 3.8 members, and the average urban family had 3.3 members (*Vestnik statistiki* no. 12 (December, 1980): 61). Rural agricultural families likely were larger than rural families in general.

7. *Narodnoe khoziaistvo SSSR v 1977 gody* (Moscow: Statistica, 1978) p. 408 (hereafter *Narkhoz SSSR*).

8. V. M. Popov and M. I. Sidorova, *Sotsial'no-ekonomicheskie problemy proizvoditel' nosti truda i vosproizvodstva rabochei sily v sel'skom khoziaistve* (Moscow: Nauka, 1979), p. 148.

9. Total savings deposits in rural and urban areas are given in *Narkhoz SSSR,* p. 433. An average interest rate of 2.2 percent was assumed for both groups of savers.

10. Wädekin has meticulously examined this matter, using data for the 1950s and 1960s. He concludes that in the late 1960s, the rural population was about three-fifths agricultural and two-fifths nonagricultural and that the latter's share had been rising since 1950 (Karl-Eugen Wädekin, "The Nonagricultural Rural Sector," in *The Soviet Rural Community,* ed. James R. Millar (Urbana, Illinois: University of Illinois Press, 1971), pp. 159–79. This trend continued in the 1970s, according to data given in *Voprosy ekonomiki* no. 8 (August, 1981): p. 59.

11. *Itogi vsesoiuznoi perepisi naseleniia 1970 goda* Vol. V (Moscow: Statistika, 1973), p. 200.

12. The data, gathered from regional statistical handbooks, are cited in Gertrude E. Schroeder, "Regional Differences in Income in the USSR in the 1970s," in NATO, *Regional Development in the USSR* (Newtonville, Massachusetts: Oriental Research Partners, 1979), p. 28.

13. Popov and Sidorova, *Sotsial'no-ekonomicheskie,* p. 148.

14. *Ekonomicheskaia gazeta* no. 34 (August, 1979): p. 10.

15. *Narkhoz SSSR za 60 let* (1977): p. 539.

16. *Ekonomika Sovetskoi Ukrainy* no. 7 (July 1975): p. 48.

17. *Narkhoz SSSR* (1968), p. 595.

18. *Narkhoz SSSR za 60 let* (1977), p. 512.

19. *Ekonomika sel'skogo khoziaistva* no. 1 (January 1980): p. 63.

20. Gertrude E. Schroeder, "Consumption," (1983).

21. The annual statistical handbooks publish data on the distribution of sales by product group in state and cooperative retail trade and in cooperative trade. Although the bulk of cooperative trade takes place in rural areas, state outlets also operate there.

22. *Narkhoz SSSR* (1980), pp. 404–405.

23. *Narkhoz SSSR za 60 let* (1977), p. 502.

24. *Planovoe khoziaistvo* no. 10 (October 1981), p. 95.

25. A. Aganbegian, ed., *Sibir' v edinom narodno-khoziaistvennom komplekse* (Novosibirsk: Nauka, 1980), p. 116.

26. *Pravda,* 29 September 1980.

27. V. I. Dmitriev, *Metodologicheskie osnovy prognozirovaniia sprosa na bytovye uslugi* (Moscow: 1975), pp. 44, 46, 49.

28. *Sovetskaia kul'tura,* 19 September 1980, p. 2.

29. *Narkhoz SSSR* (1980), p. 396.

30. *Ibid.,* p. 398.

31. Susan Jacoby, *Inside Soviet Schools* (New York: Mill and Wang, 1974), pp. 134–69.

32. *Narodnoe obrazovanie, nauka i kul'tura v SSSR* (Moscow: Statistika, 1977), pp. 97–98.

33. For example, T. I. Zaslavskaia, (ed.), *Migratsiia sel'skogo naseleniia* (Moscow: Mysl', 1970), p. 160.

34. *Narkhoz SSSR* (1980), p. 409.
35. *Voprosy ekonomiki* 6 (1974): p. 50.
36. *Voprosy ekonomiki* 8 (1979): p. 67.
37. Cited in A. G. Sultanov, *Sovershenstvovanie sotsialisticheskikh proizvodstvennykh otnoshenii v derevne* (Kazan': 1978), p. 192.
38. *Gosudarstvennii biudzhet i biudzhety soiuznykh respublik 1971–*1975 gg (Moscow: Finansy, 1976), pp. 63, 65.
39. *Izvestiia,* 26 July 1972.
40. *Pravda,* 19 October 1980.
41. Demitri B. Shimkin, "Current Characteristics and Problems of the Soviet Rural Population," in *Soviet Agricultural and Peasant Affairs,* ed. Roy D. Laird (Lawrence, Kansas: University of Kansas Press, 1963), p. 100.
42. *Narkhoz SSSR* (1980), p. 307.
43. Sultanov, *Soverghenstvovanie,* p. 194.
44. Schroeder, "Regional Differences" p. 36.
45. Popov and Sidorova, *Sotsial'no-ekonomicheskie,* p. 152.
46. *Ibid.,* p. 184, for example.
47. *Itogi perepisi naseleniia 1970 goda* vol. I (Moscow: Statistika, 1972), pp. 146–47.
48. R. S. Golovin, ed. *Problemy rasseleniia i urbanizatsiia v razvitom sotsialisticheskom obshchestve* (Moscow: 1980), p. 41.
49. *Planovoe khoziaistvo'* no. 1 (January, 1981): p. 93.
50. *Voprosy ekonomiki* no. 5 (May, 1978): p. 85.
51. *Sovetskaia rossiia* 12 September 1980.
52. *Pravda,* 20, 27 October 1980.
53. *Pravda,* 2 December 1980.
54. *Leninskaia agrarnaia politika KPSS: sbornik vazhneishykh dokumentov, Mart 1965-Iul' 1978* (Moscow: Politizdat, 1978), pp. 632–40; *Sel'skaia zhizn',* 18 January 1981.
55. *Pravda,* 30 May 1982.

13

Agro-Industrial Complexes: Recent Structural Reform in the Rural Economy of the USSR

Valentin Litvin

INTRODUCTION

Since the Communist revolution of October 1917 and the nationalization of land declared at the same time, the Soviet rural economy has undergone a number of important structural reforms.

The first major structural reform was the collectivization of Soviet agriculture during the period 1927–1933. This reform resulted in the formation of kolkhozes (collective farms) and sovkhozes (state farms), the two main types of agricultural enterprises persisting to the present day in the USSR.

A second major reform of more recent vintage has been the amalgamation of kolkhozes. This reform has resulted in the enlargement of kolkhozes and the transformation of many of them into sovkhozes.

Finally, the year 1976 marks the formal beginning of a third major structural reform of the Soviet rural economy, namely the development of *inter-farm cooperation and agro-industrial integration,* a program that will generate far-reaching changes in Soviet rural society.

The decade prior to the introduction of this third structural reform, that is, the period 1966 through 1976, may be characterized as one of routinization of Soviet economic life, a period with no structural changes and only incremental functional changes in the Soviet rural economy. However, the turn of the Brezhnev leadership from bureaucratic inertia to structural reform was necessitated by both serious economic problems and political pressures.

Agriculture continued to consume larger and larger amounts of investment but with diminishing returns and concomitant low productivity. The inevitable result has been low living standards for the Soviet people, along with the political implications that result from such a situation. Finally, it was necessary to spend ever-growing amounts of hard currency to pay for the imports of food products from capitalist countries.

The reform focusing upon agro-industrial integration was sanctioned by a special resolution of the Politburo in May of 1976.[1] Thereafter, this resolution was supplemented by a series of central directives to Party and agricultural organs in 1976, 1977, and in 1978.[2]

The historical importance of this reform is indicated by the fact that the Politburo resolution of 1976 described it as "the second collectivization."[3]

STRUCTURAL ASPECTS OF THE REFORM

The Politburo resolution of 1976 charged local Party organs and agriculturalists to reorganize both kolkhozes and sovkhozes to form three broad types of agricultural organizations: interfarm enterprises, interfarm associations, and finally agro-industrial complexes. Let us examine the main characteristics of all three types.

Interfarm enterprises (*mezhkhoziaistveonoe predpriatie*) are agricultural enterprises built by both kolkhozes and sovkhozes on a sharing basis. Considered the property of the cooperating farms, the interfarm enterprises are managed by a general meeting of the representatives of shareholders (*sobranie upolnomochennykh*). In reality, however, interfarm enterprises are managed by an elected chairman or an appointed director, the degree of managerial freedom depending upon the particular agreement.

Profits of interfarm enterprises are shared by the cooperating farms proportionally to their initial investment.

An example of an interfarm enterprise, visited by the author in 1977, is "Timashevski," located in the Krasnodar region of the USSR. Timashevski was constructed by nineteen kolkhozes, allocating 6,500 acres of farm land and 1.25 rubles of capital investment per acre of arable land for initial construction and the purchase of capital equipment.

Timashevski is an interfarm enterprise specializing in the fattening of cattle, a function that ceased on the cooperating farms when the interfarm enterprise was organized. The cooperating farms specialize in dairy farming and calf rearing, sending their fatteners to the interfarm enterprise.

Another example of an interfarm enterprise is the "Pamiat' Il'icha," established by the kolkhozes of several districts in Moldavia. This enterprise, very different from Timashevski, is in fact a huge orchard consisting of 12,500 acres planted anew to serve as a replacement for numerous small and unprofitable kolkhoz orchards. In addition to the orchard, this enterprise has a container-producing factory, several storage facilities, and a trucking service.

Interfarm associations (*mezkhoziaistvennoe ob'edinenie*) should be considered a further step in the development of interfarm cooperation. In the case of interfarm associations, kolkhozes and sovkhozes are amalgamated under a common administrative management. The association is managed by a general director, who is appointed to this position by the state. The board of the association (*soviet ob'edinenia*) includes chairmen of the kolkhozes and the directors of the sovkhozes, and functions as an adivsory body.

The farms that cooperate in the formation of an interfarm association pool their funds and other material resources, developing common construction facilities, repair services, etc. Interfarm associations are widespread in dairy, beef, hog, and poultry farming and in vegetable, fruit, and grape growing.

In 1977–1978, the author visited a number of interfarm associations in the Ukraine, Moldavia, Leningrad, Novosibirsk, and Omsk regions. All of these associations were in the process of structural and technological reconstruction based upon the requirements of the central directives, and all might be considered representative of the transformation process.

For example, the "Novyi Svet" interfarm association brought together six hog-producing sovkhozes of the Leningrad region. In addition, on the basis of the program of technological specialization, the "spirinski" and "Druzhba" farms were reconstructed to produce fatteners. "Vostochni," "Romanovka," and the remaining interfarm associations specialize in hog fattening. This program provides for specialization in feed production, but all sovkhozes continued to produce feedstuffs.

Another example of the interfarm association is the "Leninskoe" association in the Novosibirsk region of Western Siberia. This association united three sovkhozes, all of which keep dairy cows, produce milk, and cultivate feeding crops. The purpose of the reform in this case was the placement of the feedlotting operation on one of the farms.

The third stage of this reform of the Soviet rural economy calls for the inclusion of canning and food-processing plants directly in the interfarm associations. This development is designed to create the third major type of agricultural organization on the basis of interfarm associations, the *agro-industrial complex (agrarno-promyshlennyi kompleks)*.[4]

The agro-industrial complexes integrate under a common administrative management—for example, fruit and vegetable farming with canning, grape growing with wine making, sugar beet production with sugar production, poultry farming with the egg and broiler industry, etc.

The author visited "Moldvinprom" and "Moldplodoovoshchprom" in Moldavia, the largest and one of the best-known vertically integrated farm organizations in the Soviet Union.

"Moldplodoovoshchprom" and "Moldvinprom" are republican agro-industrial associations that manage district agro-industrial complexes. For example, "Moldplodoovoshchprom" operates thirty-two agro-industrial complexes, "Tiraspolskoe," "Kagulskoe," and others. Each such agro-industrial complex integrates fruit and vegetable production with canning. In the aggregate, the association comprises twenty-six sovkhozes, twenty-six canning factories, storage facilities, refrigeration capacity, two package-container plants, procurement facilities, marketing and transportation services, and stores and vocational schools.

Another example of vertical integration is the "Moldvinprom" organization, which runs thirteen district agro-industrial complexes, such as "Ungienskoe," "Kotovskoe," and others. This association integrates grape growing and wine making and consists of grape-growing sovkhozes, winemaking plants, storage facilities, refrigeration capacity, technical services, and grape and wine stores.

Both "Moldvinprom" and "Moldplodoovoshchprom" are vertically integrated systems of the so-called complete (*posledovatelnyi*) type. Integration of this type is designed to bring together farming, processing, and the retailing of both fresh and canned farm products. "Konservplodoovoshch" in the Chechen-Ingush ASSR and "Donkonserv" in the Rostov region are other agro-industrial complexes of this complete type. Most agro-industrial complexes include farms and processing (canning) plants, while few include stores.[5]

Agro-industrial enterprises, like interfarm associations, are managed by a general director, with a *soviet ob'edinenia* functioning as an advisory body. However, there are no special administrative personnel to run the agro-industrial complex. Rather, the complexes are managed by the administration of the head enterprise (*golovnoe predpriatie*). This head enterprise is typically the leading industrial enterprise (integrator). Thus the director of this leading enterprise is the general director of the agro-industrial complex.

In the central directive sent out to the republics and regions in 1976, interfarm cooperation and agro-industrial integration were interpreted as consecutive stages of the transformation of the Soviet rural economy. Thus interfarm cooperation was viewed as an initial stage and necessary precondition of subsequent agro-industrial integration. In fact the picture is rather diverse, and interfarm associations, interfarm enterprises, and agro-industrial complexes have been formed by local authorities following the Party directive rather than utilizing local experience.

In the Ukraine, Moldavia, and Bylorussia for example, canning and processing facilities were erected directly on kolkhozes and sovkhozes. Agro-industrial enterprises of this type were classified as *kolkhoz-zavod* (collective farm plant) or *sovkhoz-zavod* (state farm plant). However, a single farm typically cannot provide enough raw products to load a processing facility to capacity, so the *kolkhoz-zavod* and the *sovkhoz-zavod* have been found to be "unpromising" and are usually transformed into agro-industrial complexes.[6]

To turn to a different issue, the question of the legal status of the kolkhozes and sovkhozes under integration is one of importance. The Politburo resolution of 1976 provided that kolkhozes and sovkhozes would retain their legal status in the earlier stages of agro-industrial integration. However, at the latter stage of the development of the agro-industrial complex, the cooperating farms were to lose their legal independence and become production units (divisions and branches) of the new complexes. In fact in Moscow, Leningrad, Odessa, Minsk, and some other regions, sovkhozes, kolkhozes, and processing facilities were deprived of their legal independence and their separate economic status at the time of their amalgamation. In some such cases, the agro-industrial complexes had proven to be unworkable, and the kolkhozes and sovkhozes are disintegrated and returned to their former status.[7]

ECONOMIC ASPECTS OF THE REFORM

By the end of the year 1979, there were 9,000 interfarm associations and 800 agro-industrial complexes in the USSR. The experience gathered from the operation of these new organizations allows the evaluation of the basic economic issues of the reform program. There are a number of important issues.

First, interfarm cooperation and ultimately agro-industrial integration are considered effective instruments of farm specialization. Historically, the large absolute dimensions of Soviet farms have tended to hide what in fact is a high level of concentration of agricultural production. Thus it has traditionally been assumed that Soviet "collectivized" agriculture would be based upon large-scale units. In 1979, for example, kolkhozes averaged 16,700 acres of land, while sovkhozes averaged 44,000 acres of land. On the average, kolkhozes had 1,818 cattle and sovkhozes 1,911 cattle. At the same time, however, most kolkhozes and sovkhozes have the so-called branch or division structure, with relatively small dairy units, hog operations, and vegetable and potato plantations in each of the production divisions. Thus the average number of livestock per animal farm or the average acreage per each crop is in fact relatively small.

However, the system of obligatory state procurements has blocked the natural process of farm specialization in the USSR. Thus, since the 1930s, kolkhozes and sovkhozes have been developing as unspecialized multi-product farms oriented toward self-sufficiency.

In 1979, more than 90 percent of Soviet farms had plan targets for beef and dairy cattle, while 87 percent of farms (many under unfavorable soil and climatic conditions) had to grow grain crops. Milk is produced on 90 percent of farms, potatoes on 80 percent, and vegetables on 60 percent. In fact, only 20 percent of kolkhozes and 30 percent of sovkhozes in the Soviet Union may in fact be classified as specialized.

Thus a major objective of interfarm cooperation and agro-industrial integration is to overcome the conservatism of state procurement planning and to increase the degree of farm specialization. In part, this objective will be achieved by a change in plan procurement arrangements. When kolkhozes and sovkhozes are united in an inter-farm association or an agro-industrial complex, state procurement plans are sent out not to each kolkhoz and sovkhoz as before, but to the interfarm association or agro-industrial complex. These plans include targets for the output of industrial (final) products (together with the planned wage bill, gross income, and gross investment) and for the output of farm products to be delivered to the state, but without the turnover of intermediate products (*vnutrennii oborot*).

As part of the plan process, the *ob'edinenie* is authorized to distribute plan quotas among member farms. This means that a kolkhoz or sovkhoz may specialize, while the total amount of produce to be delivered to the state (obligatory state procurements) does not change.[8]

Second, the Soviet pricing system has been a serious constraint on the rational specialization of kolkhozes and sovkhozes.

In spite of widely divergent levels of profitability among different products, the number of products in the mandatory state procurements plan did not decline. Thus farms were required to produce according to the procurements plan, quite apart from variations in profitability. Periodical adjustment of the state procurement prices (*zakupochnaia tsena*) did not alter this situation.

The introduction of interfarm associations and agro-industrial complexes is designed to improve the pricing arrangements, since these organizations are authorized to set their own prices for intermediate products. Thus intermediate prices (*raschetnaia tsena*) are to be utilized to level the profitability of cooperating farms and to facilitate their specialization.

In addition to changes in the mechanism for setting intermediate prices, the so-called centralized funds (*tsentralizovannye fonds*) will be developed. At least two of these centralized funds, an investment-and-development fund (*fond razvitia*) and a material incentive (premium) fund (*fond materialnogo pooshchrenia*), will be used to level the profitability of cooperating farms and to create equal incentives for all farms.[9]

Third, the massive allocation of resources to the input industries (producer goods) and to agricultural production resulted in the neglect of other important sectors of the Soviet food economy, in particular processing, transportation, storage, and marketing. As a result of this neglect, the annual waste of produce in Soviet agriculture averages 20–25 percent of output, increasing proportionally in good years.

Traditional forms of economic relationships based mainly upon administrative agreements have proven ineffective in dealing with this loss problem. Agro-industrial complexes are considered to be an effective organizational form with which to optimize interindustry relationships and to cut down losses in the intersectoral flows.[10]

Fourth, the development of specialized interfarm and agro-industrial organizations is designed to transform the traditional system of management in Soviet agriculture. Under this new system, territorial agricultural organs, such as regional and district departments of agriculture, are to lose a great deal of their former administrative power over specialized kolkhozes and sovkhozes, not to mention power over interfarm associations and agro-industrial complexes.

Interfarm associations and agro-industrial complexes will be formed at the district, regional, and republican levels, as is the case with the organizations that we have examined, for example "Moldvinprom," "Molplodo-ovoshchprom," and "Konservplodoovoshch."

As a result of this managerial reform, extensive sectors of agricultural production in the agro-industrial complexes will be run by specialized trusts, which function in the same manner as a linear (vertical) industrial management system. In fact, there has already been a gradual shift away from the mainly territorial management system toward the mainly sectoral management system in Soviet agriculture.[11]

SOCIAL ASPECTS OF THE REFORM

The development of interfarm cooperation and agro-industrial integration can be expected to result in a significant social transformation of the Soviet rural economy. A number of dimensions of this social transformation should be noted.

The first major aspect of this social transformation is the fundamental distinction between the kolkhoz and the sovkhoz.

The two basic forms of agricultural enterprise have existed in the Soviet Union since the 1930s, with the sovkhoz as a completely socialist enterprise and the kolkhoz as an "artel" (commune). In terms of practical differences between the two forms of organization, the kolkhoz has had the means of production and production resources (except land) in collective ownership, receiving a comparatively limited number of plan targets from the state. In a formal sense, the income of the kolkhoz belongs to the collective, wages being set by kolkhoz management without any labor or wagebill limitations from above.

In addition, the management systems of the two forms of organization differ. The kolkhoz is run by a general meeting of the collective farmers (with an elected chairman), while the sovkhoz is run by a director appointed by the state. Finally, kolkhozes and sovkhozes have different relations with the state budget, the State Insurance System (Gosstrakh), and the State Bank (Gosbank).

Of course many of the differences between the kolkhoz and the sovkhoz as noted above exist on a purely nominal or formal basis. Nobody believes that a kolkhoz works out its own plan targets or disposes of its own income. Furthermore, the evolution of both kolkhozes and sovkhozes over a period of many years has resulted in a partial rapprochement between the two forms of organization.

In spite of this basic structure and its evolution through time, real social differences do in fact exist. According to the Leninist philosophy, socioeconomic differences between kolkhozes and sovkhozes reflect the basic social difference between the two forms of property that exist in the Soviet Union, namely cooperative-collective property and state property. The inclusion of both kolkhozes and sovkhozes in interfarm associations and agro-industrial complexes may result in the complete socialization of Soviet agriculture.

It should be noted that the trends discussed above vary considerably from one region to another. In the Ukraine, for example, many kolkhozes retain their legal independence and cooperate with sovkhozes and processing enterprises within the framework of an agreement or contract (dogovor).

In yet another variation, the collective sector in Moldavia is not only preserved, but also is administratively isolated.[12]

Even when operating on a contractural basis, however, the kolkhozes undergo a radical transformation. Thus, as a result of the development of interfarm cooperation and agro-industrial integration, the kolkhoz as a specific social type of production enterprise in the Soviet rural economy may well disappear.

A second important aspect of the social reform is the changing status of the kolkhoznik (collective farmer) and the sovkhoz worker (state farmer). Thus in the agro-industrial complexes, kolkhozniks and sovkhoz workers classified in Russia as peasants (*krestianin*) acquire some of the social characteristics typical of industrial workers (*rabochii*).

In a practical sense, this means that kolkhozniks and sovkhoz workers who come to work in the *ob'edinenie* submit to the same labor legislation as that applied to industrial workers.

At the present time, kolkhozniks and sovkhoz workers should both have a forty-one-hour work week, with two holidays, annual paid vacation, the same system and level of wages, and the same system of old-age and disability pensions. Indeed the process of rapprochement of the social status of kolkhozniks and sovkhoz workers to industrial workers has proceeded especially rapidly in those agro-industrial complexes utilizing the "labor exchange" (*trudoobmen*). What does the "labor exchange" mean? Basically, the administration of the agro-industrial complex sends workers of processing plants to help farmers during the harvesting peaks, while farmers who have accomplished their seasonal obligations in the fields are transferred to processing plants to moderate the seasonal production peaks in these plants. As a result of this polytechnization of labor, farmers and workers master "adjoining" professions and acquire an intermediate "agro-industrial" social status.

There are, however, complications. Farmers working at processing enterprises risk losing those benefits that are due to farm labor. At the same time, workers who are sent to farms lose a part of their incomes, since workers' wages are significantly higher than farmers' wages. These complications necessitate the unification of two different social systems.

In agro-industrial complexes that do not practice *trudoobmen* the problem is much the same. Different levels of payment do not create equal incentives for those who produce intermediate (farm) products and those who produce final (food) products. The economic outcome of the *ob'edinenie* is negatively affected along with increased pressure for speeding up social reforms.

In yet another dimension, the rapprochement of the social status of farmers and workers had led to the unification of their living conditions. This process has necessitated development of the network of roads, the construction of schools, improvement of medical services, etc.[13]

IMPEDIMENTS TO THE REFORM

There are a number of serious impediments that have in the past limited the progress of the agro-industrial reform program and will continue to do so in the future. A number of these impediments should be noted if we are to assess the future potential of this reform program.

First, both interfarm associations and agro-industrial complexes suffer from a shortage of capital investment with which to carry out the reconstruction of the farms. In fact, the government has shifted this problem to local Party and government organs, who are called upon to utilize "local resources."

Second, interfarm associations and agro-industrial complexes are usually formed within existing administrative boundaries of regions and districts, a policy that results in technological disproportions. For example, fattening farms with large feedlots have more fatteners than can be produced by reproduction farms; or to take another example, canning factories need more raw materials (vegetables) than can be supplied by cooperating kolkhozes and sovkhozes.

A specific example of this type of disproportion would be the "Vinnitskoe" agro-industrial complex in the Ukraine, a complex that includes twelve canning factories but only three sovkhozes. Another example is the "Kubanvino" complex in the Krasnodar krai, a complex that includes twenty-two sovkhozes, capable of supplying only one-half of the raw materials needed for the "Kubanvino" processing capacity. The same situation has been observed by the author in the Moscow and Leningrad regions, in the Altai krai, and in Western Siberia.

Third, there is an unresolved problem pertaining to the manner in which specialization will be defined and implemented. Specialization of farm units in interfarm associations and agro-industrial complexes usually touches only one or two leading branches, for example cattle or hog farming, horticulture, vegetable or porato growing, etc. Thus specialization is encouraged in cattle raising in an effort to separate dairy farming from beef production, two sectors that until recently have been developing in the Soviet Union as a dual-purpose branch of agricultural production. But what is to be done with "auxiliary" branches that are of vital importance for the self-sufficiency of districts and the proper nutrition of the local population? There are a number of examples of this problem. For instance, the "Kotovskoe" complex, formed as a specialized grape-growing and wine-making complex, continued to keep 2,000 dairy cows, 12,000 hogs, and also cultivates both potatoes and vegetables. Another example, the "Kagulskow" complex, formed as a specialized fruit and vegetable and canning complex, continues to keep hogs, sheep, and poultry.

Unfortunately, prevailing planning arrangements tend to worsen this problem. Thus territorial planning organs continually increase the plan targets of kolkhozes and sovkhozes for the "auxiliary" products. Thus the interfarm associations and the agro-industrial complexes tend to develop as unspecialized multiproduct production units, a result very different from that originally envisaged.

Fourth, pricing problems, and in particular an evident contradiction between intermediate prices (*raschetnaia tsena*) and state procurement prices (*zakupochnaia tsena*) affects the economic mechanism of the interfarm associations and agro-industrial complexes. Specifically, when the state procurement prices are lower than the intermediate prices, a typical situation, the *ob'edinenie* cannot function as a profitable organization. In the Altai krai, for example, one-third of feedlots in the interfarm associations can manage to survive only on the basis of regular state subsidies. Indeed, a recent government directive says that intermediate prices set by interfarm associations and agro-industrial complexes should be "approved" by the government.[14] Unfortunately, this means that the government imposes its administrative control over the most sensitive element of the economic mechanism of interfarm associations and agro-industrial complexes.

Fifth, the departmental structure of the Soviet economic system turns out to be an insurmountable barrier to the progress of agro-industrial reform. Soviet kolkhozes and sovkhozes belong to the USSR Ministry of Agriculture, food-processing plants to the Ministry of Food Industry, and meat-packing plants to the Ministry of the Meat and Dairy Industry. In addition to this organizational complexity, there are separate and different systems of planning, financing, and providing material supplies for industry and agriculture.

The formation of agro-industrial complexes necessitates the amalgamation of several ministries and the radical reorganization of others, not to mention changes in the State Planning Committee (Gosplan), the State Committee of Material and Technical Supply (Gossnab), and other upper-level bodies.

In fact, interfarm cooperation and agro-industrial integration, initiated as a radical structural reform of the Soviet rural economy, has continued to demonstrate a tendency of routinization in the Soviet economy, a tendency typical of the Brezhnev leadership during the last decade.

Economic and political pressures have certainly speeded up the reform process, and yet the Soviet leadership has been reluctant to transform the existing conservative systems of planning and pricing. The problem of increasing the productivity of the Soviet food economy is approached by a partial reorganization of the "production link" (*proizvodstvennoe zveno*), while the bureaucratic superstructure is left intact.[15]

Sixth, impediments to the social transformation of Soviet rural society turn out to be even more serious than those impediments that inhibit the structural and economic reorganization of the Soviet agrarian sector.

The unification of the social status of kolkhozniks, sovkhoz workers, and industrial workers with regard to their wages, regular paid vacations, and welfare benefits may require 7–8 billion rubles of additional spending on an annual basis from the state budget. But this is not the basic point. Before the social status of the kolkhoznik and the sovkhoz worker can be unified in this sense, it is necessary to bring the kolkhozes and sovkhozes to a similar economic level. To achieve such an economic levelling might require additional state investment on the order of 35–40 billion rubles. Such an additional commitment would amount to one-fourth of all capital investments planned for the Soviet rural economy for the period 1980–1985.

Achieving parity in the living conditions of the population in the villages and in urban settlements ("overcoming the distinction between the town and the country" in Soviet parlance) is a task that seems grandiose and unfeasible. The implementation of this program through the year 1990 will require 85–90 billion rubles, or an amount equal to almost four times the annual gross income of all of the country's kolkhozes. To the extent that such investments are to be made for the social transformation of Soviet rural society, funds inevitably must be diverted from the program for the development of interfarm associations and agro-industrial complexes.

PROSPECTS FOR REFORM: 1981-1985

What are the real prospects for the implementation of this unprecented reform in 1981-1985?

Analysis of "Basic Guidelines for the Economic and Social Development of the USSR in 1981-1985 and in the Period up to 1990," a document recently published in the USSR, would indicate that the reform is in progress and is assumed to continue during the next five-year plan period. The "Guidelines" call upon the nation "to constantly develop the specialization and concentration of agricultural production on the basis of interfarm cooperation and agro-industrial integration." Furthermore, they require attention "to improve the administration of agriculture," that is, to develop interfarm cooperation and agro-industrial complexes.[16]

In the "Guidelines," the Soviet rural economy is interpreted as a specific economic area within a larger sector of the economy of the USSR, namely the agro-industrial complex. The latter is meant as the unified planning and proportional and balanced development of the related branches of the Soviet food economy and the organization of efficient cooperation among them.[17]

In fact, this program signifies a shift in Soviet economic policy away from agricultural policy and toward food policy, a shift that is assumed to be achievable through agro-industrial integration.

Turning to the social side of the reform, the "Guidelines" call for the further social development of Soviet rural society, including a rapprochement between the level of collective farmers' pay and the pay level of personnel working on "state agricultural enterprises," that is sovkhozes. In addition, collective farmers are to receive minimum annual paid vacation time at the same minimum vacation time established for workers and office employees.

The "Guidelines" require improvement in the system of social security for collective farmers, namely raising the minimum old-age and disability pensions. This measure is considered in the document as part of the program "to continue the process of making the conditions under which collective farmers receive social security 'more nearly equal' to those for the personnel of state enterprises."[18] Finally, there is provision in these "Guidelines" for improvement in the housing and general living conditions, including higher standards for all types of services.[19]

There is incontrovertible evidence, however, that the impediments to reform discussed above cannot be overcome. Most notably, the key problem of investment and development funds is not discussed. The "Guidelines" do not suggest any figures for 1981-1985, saying that appropriate capital investments to agriculture as a percentage of total investment in the development of the national economy "should be no lower than the level already achieved."[20] If so, how will it be possible to obtain the substantial additional sums required to implement the reform program?

The inconsistency between the objectives and the available resources is all too evident. Furthermore, the "Guidelines" do not provide any resolution, suggesting that it will be necessary "to expand opportunities for construction using the incentive funds of interfarm associations and agro-industrial complexes, to popularize the 'do-it-yourself' method of carrying out construction and installation work, etc."[21]

The latest Party directive document—"The Food Program of the USSR for the Period up to 1990 and Measures for its Realization"—is further evidence that the process of interfarm cooperation and agro-industrial in-

Of course "the proportional and balanced development of the agri-industrial complex" is considered to be one of the basic preconditions of the implementation of the Food Program.[22]

In the section entitled "The Increase of the Efficiency of Operation of Kolkhozes, Sovkhozes and Other Enterprises and Organizations of the Agri-Industrial Complex," there is a demand "to provide the transition to planning of the operation of the agri-industrial complex and its management as an integral unity at all levels."[23]

Almost all sections of this document contain direct reference to the agro-industrial complex, and yet a thorough analysis of the entire program brings the reader to the conclusion that it is pure rhetoric.[24]

Problems of interfarm cooperation and agro-industrial integration are in fact not discussed in the program. Assignments for the development of agricultural branches, for example, for beef and pork production do not contain any reference to the new type of organization in this branch, once considered "the most progressive."[25] Nor do we find such reference in the assignments for union republics, for example, Moldavia, a republic that has recently been considered the main experimental region for cooperation and integration.[26]

Moreover, instead of integration, there is evidence of disintegration, for example in the case of the formation of the USSR Ministry of Fruit and Vegetable Production as a disintegrated part of the USSR Ministry of Agriculture.[27]

Other "directive" documents approved by the May 1982 session of the Central Committee of the Communist Party in fact dwell to a great extent upon problems of cooperation and agro-industrial integration, especially in the decree "On the Improvement of the Management of Agriculture and other Branches of the Agri-Industrial Complex." Here, we find a resolution to form task forces at different administrative levels to study the problems of economic integration.[28] The latter is interpreted basically as a function of economic coordination.[29]

The May 1982 Party session emphasized the need to raise the efficiency of kolkhozes and sovkhozes, to utilize more specialists and technicians on the farms and at a higher level of responsibility, and to improve material incentives.[30]

In fact, however, the new pattern for the reallocation of resources, in particular capital investment, ignores the needs of the reform.

Finally, about 16–17 billion rubles will be spent mainly for the purpose of raising state procurement prices in order to strengthen "weak" farms through the use of special "premium" payments.[31]

Turning to yet another dimension, further evidence that the reform is not

expected to be effective is the nationwide campaign for the expansion of the private sector of the Soviet rural economy. The economic importance of private farming ("personal auxiliary farming" in Soviet parlance) in the Soviet Union is well known. Thus farmers' private plots account for only 4 percent of public lands, but supply 28 percent of the gross output of agriculture.

The share of income obtained from private plots averages 5 percent of the median aggregate income of Soviet industrial workers and employees, while it represents one-fifth for sovkhoz workers and above one-third for kolkhozniks. Kolkhozniks obtain 95 percent of the potatoes they need, 75 percent of the vegetables, 79 percent of the meat, 82 percent of the milk, and 97 percent of the eggs from "personal auxiliary farming."[32] The contraction of private plots in interfarm associations and agro-industrial complexes (an inevitable issue in the socialization of Soviet rural society) threatens the well-being of the Soviet rural population.[33]

The expansion of the private sector, noted above, suggests that the Soviet leadership is unwilling to place great faith in the achievement of the structural reform program. This expansion indicates that the private plots are indispensible at the present time and indeed that they will continue to be important for the "foreseeable future.[34] Indeed the "Guidelines" require the development of a network of private markets in the USSR and the provision of assistance to the population in the delivery and sale of products from the private plots.[35]

In the past, there have been many examples of economic and social reforms declared to be "historical," but which have in due course simply faded away. Such was the case, for example, with the agrarian reform declared by the CPSU Plenum in March of 1965, and such is the case with the program for the development of agriculture in the non-chernozem zone of the RSFSR declared by the Politburo in March of 1974.

Will the latest and most far-reaching economic and social reform of Soviet rural society have the same destiny?

NOTES

1. O dalneishem razvitii spetsializatsii i kontsentratsii selskokhoziastvennogo proizvodstva na baze mezhkhoziaistvennoi kooperatsii i agropromyshlennoi integratsii. *Postanovlenie TsK KPSS* (Moscow: 1976).

2. See, for example: *Plenum Tsentralnogo Komiteta KPSS* (25 October 1976); *Pravda*, 2 June 1976; *Ekonomicheskaia gazeta* no. 20 (1977); *Ekonomika se'lskogo khoziaistva*, May 1978 (Moscow); See also: *Materialy XXV s'ezda KPSS* (Moscow 1977).

3. *O dalneishem razvitii spetsializatsii . . .*, p. 7.

4. Soviet economists and agriculturists use different terms to define these vertically-integrated units: *agrarno-promyshlennoe ob'edinenie* (agro-industrial association), *agrarno-promyshlennyi kombinat* (agro-industrial combine works), etc.

5. A detailed classification of production types of vertically integrated formations in the Soviet rural economy was worked out by the author in 1975–1976. The results of this research are published Valentin Litvin, *Agrarnopromyshlennye ob'edinenia* (Moscow 1976), chapter 4–5.

6. See Valentin Litvin, "Novyi formy organizatsii proizvodstva," *Mezhdunarodnyi Se'lskokhoziaistvennyi Zhurnal* (May 1975): p. 13.

7. Litvin, "Novyi formy . . ." pp. 13–14.

8. Plan targets are not also sent out to interfarm enterprises. The output of an interfarm enterprise is counted as a part of the plan quota set for shareholding farms.

9. See, for example: A. Esin, "Printsipy postroenia khozraschetnykh otnoshenii v agropromyshlennykh ob'edineniakh," *Ekonomika Se'lskogo Khoziasistva* (1 January 1981): pp. 18–26.

10. The idea of the systems approach, or vertical integration, becomes more and more popular in the Soviet leadership. This concept has been partially borrowed from U.S. practices (Delmarva Poultry Industries, Perdue & Son, and other American integrated systems). The author has carried out extensive research on vertical integration in the USA for the Academy of Agricultural Sciences of the USSR since the mid-1960s. The results of these studies have been published in Moscow. See Valentin Litvin, *Strukturnye sdvigi i osnovnye napravlenia nauchno-tekhnicheskogo progressa v agropromyshlennom komplekse kapitalisticheskikh stran* (Moscow 1978); Valentin Litvin, "Sotsialno-ekonomicheskaia sushchnost' agrarno-promyshlennoi integratsii v kapitalisticheskikh stranakh," *Trudy Akademii Sel'skokhoziaistvennykh Nauk* (Moscow, 1976).

11. See E. Gubin, "Formy meshotraslevykh sviazei," *Ekonomika Sel'skogo Khoziaistva* no. 5 (May 1978): pp. 37–45. See also I. Shamiev and Feizullaev, "Ob'edinenie Azplodoovoshchprom," *Ekonomika Sel'skogo Khoziaistva* no. 5 (May 1978): pp. 45–50.

12. Moldavia is the only Soviet republic where the Council of Collective Farms ("Soviet Kolkhozov") does not serve as an adivsory body but has the administrative power to plan, finance, and control the republic's kolkhoz sector.

13. The author reported these trends to the National Conference of the Institute of Economics, Academy of Sciences of the USSR; see V. M. Litvin and N. A. Khiluk, *Mekotoryi sotsialno-ekonomicheskie problemy truda v usloviakh agrarno-promyshlennoi integratsii.* (Moscow: Nauka 1975), pp. 211–15.

14. See, for example *Ekonomika i organizatsia selskokhoziastvennogo proizvodstva* (Moscow: 1979), p. 156.

15. The author suggested the partial reorganization of the Soviet economy to adjust it to the needs of the agro-industrial integration in the draft Legal Status of Agro-Industrial Complexes in 1979. Yet the Council of Ministers of the USSR refrained from approving it.

16. "Proekt osnovnykh napravlenii ekonomicheskogo i sotsialnogo razvitia SSSR v 1981–1985 godakh i na period do 1990 goda," *Pravda,* 2 December 1980, pp. 1–2.

17. *Ibid.,* p. 2.

18. *Ibid.,* p. 3.

19. *Ibid.,* p. 3.

20. *Ibid.,* p. 2.

21. *Ibid.,* pp. 2–3.

22. *Proizvodstvennaia Programma SSSR na Period do 1990 goda i Mery po yego Realizatsii* (Moscow: 1982), p. 32.

23. *Ibid.,* p. 54.

24. See, for example, *Proizvod stvennaia,* pp. 30, 42, 47, 52, etc.

25. *Ibid.,* pp. 34–35.

26. *Ibid.,* pp. 60–61.

27. *Ibid.,* pp. 38, ff.

28. See *Kommunist,* no. 6 (June 1982): pp. 46–47 ff.

29. *Ibid.,* pp. 44–49.

30. See, for example, "O merakh po sovershenstvovaniyu ekonomicheskogo mekhanizme i ukrepleniyu ekonomiki kolkhozov i sovkhozov," *Kommunist,* no. 6 (June 1982): pp. 40–52; "O Merakh po usileniyu materialnoi zainteresovannosti rabotnikov sel'skogo khoziaistva v uvelichenii proizvodstva produktsii i povyshenii yego kachestva," *Kommunist,* no. 6 (June 1982): pp. 56–57.

31. "O merakh po sovershenstvovaniyu ekonomisheskogo mekhanizme i ukrepleniyu ekonomiki kolkhozov i sovkhozov," p. 50.

32. G. Diachkov i A. Sorokin, "Rol' lichnogo podsobnogo khoziaistva," *Ekonomika se'lskogo khoziaistva,* no. 1 (January 1981): pp. 62–29.

33. We should stress an important fact: kolkhozniks and sovkhoz workers are not paid

premiums for above-the-plan produce in interfarm associations and agri-industrial complexes. According to the author's calculations, only grape growers of sovkhozes of Moldavia lose about 1 mill rubles of additional income. See V. M. Litvin and N. A. Khiluk, *Nekotorye sotsialno-ekonomicheskie problemy truda v usloviakh agrarno-promyshlennoi integratsii* (Moscow: Navka, 1975), p. 214.

34. *Ibid.,* pp. 68–69. See also *Pravda,* 4 February 1981, p. 7.

35. See also *Voprosy Ekonomiki,* no. 6 (June 1980), pp. 118–24; *Sovetskaia Kultura* 21 October 1980, p. 6.

14

Soviet Agricultural Management and Planning and the 1982 Administrative Reforms

Everett M. Jacobs*

After the frequent changes in Soviet agricultural management and planning in the Khrushchev era, Brezhnev's policies, especially since his March 1965 reforms, have evidenced considerable stability. Brezhnev himself drew attention to this at the July 1978 Central Committee Plenum, stressing the continuity of agricultural policy relating to planning, price policy, economic incentives, capital investments, mechanization, chemicalization, land improvement, increasing productivity, etc.[1] Nevertheless, some notable departures from, or embellishments to, the March 1965 program have occurred in recent years, the most outstanding being the encouragement and development of interfarm cooperation and agro-industrial integration in an effort to improve administrative and production efficiency. In this respect, the May 1982 administrative reforms build on the experience of the 1970s and try to overcome the management and planning problems that have bedevilled Soviet agriculture.

COOPERATION AND INTEGRATION

Emphasis on the concentration and specialization of production as the "main line" of Soviet agricultural development had become a slogan by the mid-1970s. The decision to move in this direction was based on an assessment of foreign (particularly American) experience, the operation of large-scale specialized farms in the USSR, and the developments that had occurred in creating inter-kolkhoz associations.[2] It was claimed at the June 1976 Central Committee Plenum that in the USSR, labor inputs on nonspecialized farms per unit of output were two and one-half to three times higher than on specialized interfarm animal husbandry units, and that production costs on nonspecialized farms were one and one-half to two times

*The author acknowledges the assistance of the University of Sheffield Research Fund in carrying out research for this work.

higher. A resolution was therefore passed to develop further, in the soon-to-be well-worn phrase, the specialization and concentration of agricultural production on the basis of interfarm cooperation and agro-industrial integration.[3]

The allied processes of interfarm cooperation and agro-industrial integration had developed slowly in the late 1960s and early 1970s,[4] but were now to become the main means of achieving production concentration and specialization. The June 1976 resolution dealt with both horizontal and vertical integration of farming. At the first stage, horizontal integration was to occur as kolkhozes and sovkhozes created large specialized inter-kolkhoz, inter-sovhoz, kolkhoz-sovkhoz, sovkhoz-kolkhoz, and other industrial-type state-kolkhoz enterprises and associations. As detailed below, by 1982 there were about ninety-six hundred such inter-farm enterprises, which as a rule specialize in a single activity, such as the production of meat, milk, eggs, wool, mixed and other kinds of feeds, pedigree stock breeding, seed growing, fruit and vegetable growing, agro-chemical services, construction, land reclamation, manufacture of building and other materials, the joint use of equipment and the means of transportation, etc.

When horizontal integration had been achieved, the June 1976 resolution envisaged that the process of specialization and concentration would lead to a further deepening of the division of labor among farms and the development of vertical integration through the establishment of agro-industrial enterprises. These would link agricultural and industrial production and could involve kolkhozes, sovkhozes, poultry factories, and interfarm and other enterprises that, besides producing agricultural products, also process, pack, and store them. Typical agro-industrial enterprises up to mid-1982 were sovkhoz factories (and more rarely, kolkhoz factories) producing and processing grapes, fruit, vegetables, sugar beets, flax, hemp, eggs, poultry, milk, and meat and other livestock products. This type of organization is not yet particularly widespread in the Soviet Union, though it is a feature of farming in Moldavia, Azerbaidzhan, Krasnodar and Stavropol krais, and Rostov, Crimea, and Odessa oblasts.[5] According to the June 1976 resolution, the creation of agro-industrial enterprises would gradually create conditions to bring kolkhoz-cooperative property closer to state property, in the long run leading to their fusion into the property of the whole people.

The June 1976 resolution envisaged interfarm and agro-industrial enterprises based on the territorial-branch principle (i.e., within the boundaries of one raion) or on the branch principle (i.e., spanning administrative regions, but within one republic). However, preference has usually been given to the territorial-branch principle because it is administratively easier for the raion's Party, Soviet, and agricultural organizations to supervise such bodies, and it is easier to resolve questions of material-technical supply, construction, transportation, services, etc. Moreover, "gigantomania" can more easily be avoided.[6] The resolution specifically cautioned that the development of specialization and concentration was not a one-time measure but an extended process designed for the long term and linked with specific economic conditions and the level of development of productive forces. Party, Soviet, and economic organizations were warned against "decreeing from above" on specialization and concentration and against the imposition of forms of production organization and management that had not been tested by science and practice. At the same time, these bodies were told to curb resolutely any attempts to impede the process or to stall, and to prohibit a departmental or parochial approach to the work.[7]

The interfarm and agro-industrial enterprises are supposed to be formed voluntarily by kolkhozes and sovkhozes on their own initiative and using their own funds. A meeting of representatives of the shareholding farms is to determine the size of each member's contributions and the procedures for assessing them. The interfarm or agro-industrial enterprise itself functions on *khozraschet* (full economic accountability) and is a legal person. According to the Minister of Agriculture, the enterprise's main task is to achieve a maximum, systematic increase in output. The chief criteria in establishing either type of enterprise are to be the level of labor productivity, the unit cost of output, the profitability, and the rate of return on capital investment to be achieved—in short, the degree of growth in production efficiency.[8]

Kolkhoz-Sovkhoz Cooperation

The specific regulations on interfarm enterprises (organizations) were spelled out in a General Statute published in mid-May 1977.[9] Before this time, cooperation between kolkhozes and sovkhozes in interfarm or agro-industrial arrangements was hindered because of a number of obstacles. On the kolkhoz side, it was reported at the end of 1975, without explanation, that kolkhozes virtually never participated in agro-industrial cooperation (as distinct from interfarm enterprises).[10] This was probably due to four main reasons. First, such projects were (and are) expensive, and kolkhozes, interested in maximizing funds for the payment of wages to their members and financing their "own" operations, were not eager to lash out in projects in which they would have little say and little, if any, profit to make. Second, the existing rules for managers offered little financial or other incentives for kolkhoz managers to favor participation in the projects. Third, kolkhozes at that time were involved mainly in horizontal integration, primarily through inter-kolkhoz associations. Last, there were undoubtedly administrative problems in organizing kolkhoz-sovkhoz enterprises: kolkhozes were subordinate to the USSR Ministry of Agriculture, whereas sovkhozes could be subordinate directly to that ministry or, through sovkhoz trusts and associations, to either the USSR Ministry of Agriculture or to the USSR Ministry of the Food Industry (or, in the Ukraine, to the Ukrainian Ministry of Sovkhozes).[11]

On the sovkhoz side, it is more than likely that sovkhoz trusts, which fulfil many of the functions of interfarm enterprises, had acted (and continue to act) as a block to kolkhoz-sovkhoz cooperation. The importance of sovkhoz trusts in some areas is considerable, as in Kalinin oblast in 1980, when 151 of the 316 sovkhozes (47.8 percent) were subordinate to sovkhoz trusts.[12] According to the regulations on sovkhoz trusts published at the start of 1975, the *trust* is a unified production and management complex consisting of sovkhozes and other state agricultural enterprises and organizations (including enterprises processing agricultural products or raw materials, producing building materials or consumer goods, providing transport, or performing specialized operations and services for sovkhozes). Sovkhozes and other enterprises and organizations entering a trust retain their independence and legal entities. The trust operates on the basis of khozraschet and also is a legal entity. On the basis of economic advisability, and with the consent of the members (although administrative fiat is not unknown in practice), the trust management wholly or partly centralizes the fulfilment of specific production and management functions. These include, in particular, feedlot operations, provision of highly productive animals and high quality varieties of seed, processing of agricultural raw materials, transportation, and other activities of the members that can be centralized to economic advantage. The main type of trust is a specialized trust uniting sovkhozes and other state agricultural enterprises engaged in a single type of production or cooperating with one another by performing different phases of a production process. If local conditions warrant, territorial trusts can be formed to unite sovkhozes and other state agricultural enterprises involved in different types of production.[13]

Another factor hindering sovkhoz participation in kolkhoz-sovkhoz enterprises undoubtedly was the restriction, until May 1977, that sovkhozes engaging in such cooperation could finance this only through funds earmarked for strengthening and expanding production, which funds existed only on sovkhozes making substantial profits.[14] However, under the May 1977 General Statute, sovkhozes can now use planned budget appropriations, bank credits, and their own funds to help create interfarm enterprises.

Data on the number of interfarm or agro-industrial enterprises involving both kolkhozes and sovkhozes are unavailable; but it is clear that between the end of 1977 and the end of 1980, the number of sovkhoz members of such organizations grew more quickly (by 62.0 percent, from 16,433 to 26,629, with some multiple memberships) than did the number of kolkhoz members (by 27.6 percent, from 95,942 to 122,469, with considerable multiple memberships).[15] At least in part, this may have been due to the new financial arrangements for sovkhozes. However, as discussed below, administrative pressure apparently also had a role in the rate of growth of sovkhoz members.

Agricultural Production Associations

A form of vertical integration more comprehensive in scope than the agro-industrial enterprise is the agricultural production association, whose statutes did not appear until February 1979.[16] The association's members can include kolkhozes, sovkhozes, interfarm enterprises (organizations), enterprises for processing farm output, and transportation and other state and cooperative enterprises and organizations (whatever their type of work). The agricultural production association centralizes a number of economic and production functions and resources in order to form a single production-economic complex.

The main task of the association is to increase the production and sale to the state of farm output, to fulfill plans and contracts for the purchase of this output, to improve its quality and reduce costs, to increase labor productivity and production efficiency, to ensure economically sound specialization and concentration of production, and to make more effective use of the resources and potential of members. Membership in the association is supposed to be voluntary; as in the interfarm enterprise, the members retain their economic independence and the rights of a legal person. The agricultural production association itself operates on khozraschet and is a legal person. It may be created on either the territorial-branch or the branch principle.

Shortcomings

Although the number of kolkhozes and sovkhozes involved in interfarm or agro-industrial enterprises over the years has grown steadily, the results of the program have fallen far short of Soviet expectations. At the July 1978 Central Committee Plenum, Brezhnev complained of "shortcomings and negative phenomena" in the work on the specialization and concentration of agricultural production, particularly that "a good many people" give their own interpretation to the Central Committee's warning about the impermissibility of haste, seeing this as an opportunity to drag out the work over many years. Also, frequently narrow departmental positions are taken by "individual officials" of ministries and departments (especially the food industry and the meat and dairy industry). They were said to hold back the progressive process and sometimes, in Brezhnev's words, "to put it mildly," failed to recommend that their farms enter into interfarm cooperation or seek to create isolated associations.[17] In spite of this criticism, the number of interfarm enterprises and organizations grew by a mere 381 (4.3 percent) between the end of 1978 and the end of 1979, and by a scant 351 (3.8 percent) between the end of 1979 and the end of 1980.[18] In the next eighteen months, the number of interfarm enterprises hardly rose, standing at "9.6 thousand" in mid-1982 (against 9,638 at the end of 1980). In mid-1982, the number of advanced agro-industrial formations was still relatively small, totalling "more than 600" agro-industrial enterprises and "more than 150" agricultural production associations, indicating almost no growth since the end of 1980.[19]

Even with the slow development of interfarm cooperation, the Soviets report that "in some places" the creation of interfarm enterprises has proceeded artificially, without sufficient technical and economic foundation, and that in some raions, the establishment of such enterprises had been used to swell the number of bureaucrats.[20] This naturally suggests that joining such associations is not a voluntary matter for the farms. Reluctance of farms to join or participate fully is further evidenced by the complaint that at the start of 1982, interfarm enterprises and organizations accounted for only 2.9 percent of kolkhoz and sovkhoz agricultural production funds and involved less than 2 percent of the agricultural workforce. Furthermore, the interfarm associations are said to have failed to devote sufficient attention to increasing their members' production effectiveness, specifically in relation to decreasing labor and material expenditure per unit of output.[21] The production specializations of the interfarm enterprises illustrate this point. At the end of 1980, only 18 percent of interfarm enterprises were devoted to agricultural production (15.8 percent were involved in livestock production and 2.2 percent in crop production). By contrast, agricultural services accounted for 26.9 percent of enterprises (including 14.8 percent for electrification), and the remaining 55.1 percent of enterprises were devoted to nonagricultural purposes (including 29.7 percent for construction, 5.8 percent for production of mixed fodder, and a mere 0.4 percent—only thirty-eight interfarm enterprises—for processing of agricultural products). A mere 4,611 nonfarm state and cooperative enterprises and organizations belonged to interfarm enterprises at the end of 1980, showing the reluctance of such bodies to invest or involve themselves in this type of project.[22]

In his work on inter-kolkhoz associations in the early and mid-1970s, Miller found that support for these bodies was not uniform throughout the country, being strongest in the Ukraine, Moldavia, and Estonia, and weakest in Armenia and Tadzhikistan.[23] The data for 1980 in Table 14.1 show that participation in interfarm enterprises and organizations was by far strongest in the Ukraine, Moldavia, and Georgia (for both kolkhozes and sovkhozes), and in Lithuania (for sovkhozes). By comparison, the other republics had poor records, regardless of their general agricultural production orientation and the average size of their kolkhozes and sovkhozes. Brezhnev did caution against rushing into things, but it is apparent that in seven of the republics, many of the sovkhozes do not yet belong to even one interfarm enterprise. In this respect, it is interesting to note that the number of sovkhozes belonging to interfarm enterprises grew particularly quickly in Kazakhstan in the course of 1980 (from 298 to 1,169), suggesting an administrative campaign there to increase sovkhoz participation in these bodies.

The interfarm enterprises were of course designed to foster specialization, and an unwanted effect of their creation has been the premature abandonment of branches of production in nonspecialized farms. Livestock production seems to have been particularly affected by this, even though Brezhnev spoke strongly against the phenomenon at the October 1976 and July 1978 Plenums of the Central Committee. The attempt of farms to abolish their livestock sections is understandable, since the tendency over the years has been to require most farms to produce milk and pork regardless of main farm specialization, and these and other livestock products usually have low rates of profitability or are produced at a loss.[24] The producer price increases taking effect in January 1983 may help to correct this situation.

Table 14.1   Membership of Farms in Interfarm Enterprises and Organizations, by Union Republic, End of 1980

	No. of interfarm enterprises	No. of Kolkhoz members	No. of Sovkhoz members	Av. no. of memberships per farm Kolkhozes	Av. no. of memberships per farm Sovkhozes
USSR	9638	122469	26629	4.7	1.3
RSFSR	4034	38989	15671	3.3	1.3
Ukraine	3510	60585	3572	8.6	1.7
Belorussia	376	5208	1219	2.9	1.4
Uzbekistan	313	2258	342	2.7	0.4
Kazakhstan	190	937	1169	2.4	0.6
Georgia	316	4266	1214	6.2	2.5
Azerbaidzhan	158	1669	452	2.7	0.7
Lithuania	118	2202	824	2.9	2.6
Moldavia	228	2833	623	7.2	1.8
Latvia	49	527	208	1.6	0.9
Kirgizia	99	479	196	2.7	0.8
Tadzhikistan	82	448	85	2.7	0.4
Armenia	67	678	592	2.2	1.3
Turkmenistan	65	941	78	3.0	0.7
Estonia	33	449	384	3.1	2.4

Note: All data include multiple membership
Source: Narodnoe khozyaistvo SSSR v 1980 g. (Moscow: Finansy i statistika, 1981), pp. 260, 264–65, 272.

LARGE-SCALE INTEGRATION EXPERIMENTS

The kind of cooperation and specialization projects reviewed above have existed for the most part on a relatively small scale. Even if there were a considerable number of members in one or another project, the project's impact would be mainly local, seldom affecting an entire raion, let alone an oblast or republic. Moreover, as mentioned, most of the cooperation schemes did not deal with agricultural production and thus did not foster the kind of agricultural integration most sought. In these circumstances, it was natural that attempts would be made to integrate agricultural production over a wider territorial area. Because these experiments had a bearing on the May 1982 administrative reforms, a number of the more important innovations will be summarized here. It will be obvious that the emphasis of these experiments was on interfarm integration and specialization over a relatively large territory and that, while nonagricultural activities were encompassed in the experiments, the main stress was on increasing the efficiency of agricultural production.

The Moldavian Experiment

In an effort to foster interfarm cooperation, agricultural administration was completely revamped in the small Moldavian republic in March 1973. The reform affected both kolkhozes and sovkhozes, but was more far-reaching in the kolkhoz sector.

Kolkhoz councils had been created at all-Union, republic, krai, oblast, and raion levels throughout the country in 1969 but were largely ineffectual, merely advising on legislation and general questions of farm policy. In the reform, Moldavia's republic and raion kolkhoz councils (Moldavia has no oblasts) were given responsibility for policy making and operational management over the republic's kolkhoz sector. The raion kolkhoz councils were to receive procurement assignments from the state, distribute them, and ensure fulfilment in the kolkhoz sector; plan production and manage it directly; introduce scientific and technical developments; distribute material and technical resources and ensure their rational utilization; ensure the correct proportions between accumulation and consumption on the kolkhozes and inter-kolkhoz enterprises, as well as the growth of fixed production assets and their effective use; concentrate and distribute capital investments allocated for the development of inter-kolkhoz enterprises; and lastly, resolve questions of setting output norms, the pay system, the training of cadres, and the solution of urgent social problems in the countryside. Moreover, the councils were to have full administrative powers over inter-kolkhoz enterprises and associations and over creating centralized capital investments.[25]

As a result of the reform, the former inter-kolkhoz councils (for construction, livestock fattening, and the design and reconstruction of perennial plantations) were abolished, and the inter-kolkhoz organizations themselves became structural subdivisions of the republic kolkhoz council.[26] Horizontal cooperation became the order of the day, for instance in vegetable growing, where the size of fields sown to a particular crop in the interfarm rotation in 1975 reportedly reached 700, 800, or more hectares, producing a profitability (on direct cost) as high as 60 percent to 80 percent (in contrast to losses in conditions of multibranch, fragmented production).[27] By the end of 1976, kolkhoz agro-industrial associations had been set up for livestock production, grain production, tobacco production, freight haulage, and construction.[28]

At the same time, Moldavia's sovkhoz sector underwent further specialization and concentration (sovkhoz factories had for a number of years been prominent in wine production). Sovkhozes specializing in grapes, vegetables, and essential oil crops were merged with canning, winemaking, and other processing enterprises. Territorial agro-industrial associations were established on the basis of sovkhoz factories, with the largest enterprise becoming the head of the association and having the function of production coordinator. For example, in Kotovsk raion, one agro-industrial association in 1976 included eleven sovkhoz factories for winemaking, and their vineyards covered almost 10,000 hectares. The association established an interfarm enterprise for the production of espalier poles, a land reclamation detachment, a truck column, and an accounting service.[29] Besides territorial agro-industrial associations for sovkhozes, three were created at the republic level, for winemaking, fruit and vegetable production, and essential oils.[30] However, the Moldavian Agro-Industrial Association for Fruit and Vegetable Production lost 20 million rubles in 1976 because about one out of every five tons of produce it shipped went bad before reaching the customers because of slow delivery.[31]

An interesting and important part of the Moldavian experiment was the creation of interfarm associations for mechanization and electrification, which, having been first set up in 1973, by the start of 1978 functioned in thirty of the republic's raions.[32] The associations, having their own budget, operating on khozraschet, and with the rights of a legal person, were made responsible for the operation, maintenance, and repair of all the kolkhoz farm machinery in the raion. The associations were subdivisions of the raion kolkhoz councils and could deal not only with kolkhozes but also with sovhozes and other organizations. The shareholder farms paid the interfarm mechanization association for mechanized work performed by the latter on the basis of a planned, uniform rate per standard hectare. This rate was calculated on the basis of planned unit cost and the member's pro rata contributions for capital investments and to the economic incentive fund and personnel training fund. Contracts between the farms and the association determined the amount and time period of the work. The Soroki raion interfarm association for mechanization in 1976 was said to have raised the average daily output of the raion's farm machinery by approximately 60 percent and to have reduced fuel consumption per hectare of standard plowing by over 20 percent. Also, the value of spare parts used was cut in half.[33] Another report stated that under the old system, some 480 workshops, about 1,100 technical stations, and 320 garages would have been required for the kolkhoz machinery, but under the new system, only 34 central bases and 278 territorial technical stations were needed. Additional benefits were that every farm, regardless of economic level, had the chance to use the full range of equipment it needed, and differences between the farms in power available per worker were eliminated, at least on paper.[34]

In spite of the reported advantages of interfarm enterprises in Moldavia, the fact remains that the system, as it operated there for kolkhozes, marked the abandoment of efforts at decentralization of farm management, tried briefly in the mid- and late 1950s and then for another somewhat longer period after 1965. The sweeping powers of the kolkhoz councils made the republic Ministry of Agriculture almost redundant in the kolkhoz sector, although it was claimed that the role of the ministry had grown, since it could now concentrate its efforts on the main, decisive areas of technical policy, the introduction of scientific innovation, and the training of cadres.[35] There were all the makings of a conflict of interest between the ministry's organs in the localities (the raion agricultural production administrations of the raion Soviet executive committee) and the raion kolkhoz councils, as each tried to assert its legitimate role of leadership of the raion's kolkhozes. Moreover, the kolkhoz chairmen lost much of their freedom of independent action, being so much involved in cooperation schemes and having been stripped of their ability to allocate their own machinery. There was an extremely high turnover of farm leaders in Moldavia in 1976–1981, especially of kolkhoz chairmen and sovkhoz directors,[36] suggesting either that they opposed the trend of developments or that they were found unequal to new challenges. Another shortcoming of the Moldavian experiment was that it did little to foster kolkhoz-sovkhoz cooperation.

The degree of economic success of the Moldavian experiment is difficult to determine. Gross agricultural output for 1976–1978 was 36 percent above that that of 1966–1970, which compares favorably with the simultaneous all-Union average increase of only 24 percent. However, Moldavian agriculture received above-average investment during that time and also had more abundant labor than most other parts of the USSR. It is therefore doubtful whether Moldavia's better performance is valid for net output as well, and if so, whether it may be attributed to the integration measures.[37]

Raion-wide Experiments

The Moldavian experiment covered an entire republic, whereas the other large-scale agricultural integration experiments given prominence in the Soviet Union in recent years encompassed much smaller territorial areas—individual raions. The three main raion-wide experiments were in small republics lacking oblasts: Georgia (Abasha raion), Estonia (Viljandi raion), and Latvia (Talsi raion).

The three experiments involved the creation of agricultural production associations (the Abasha and Viljandi models) or, apparently to signify a greater degree of vertical integration, a raion agro-industrial association (the Talsi model). The associations incorporated the raion's kolkhozes, sovkhozes, interfarm formations, and all services directly connected with agricultural production (e.g., raion branches of the republic farm machinery association, the land reclamation and irrigation administration, and, at least in Abasha and Talsi raions, the agricultural procurement agency.[38] As in Moldavia, no attempt was made to introduce product specialization beyond the limits of one raion.

The Abasha association, as well as the others, was responsible for the "functions of planning, finance, assignment of personnel, allocation of material and technical resources, and overall supervision of kolkhozes, sovkhozes, and other agricultural enterprises and institutions" belonging to it.[39] In keeping with these functions, the associations incorporated the staffs of the raion agricultural administrations, which formerly were part of the raion Soviet's bureaucracy. At the same time, the associations were subordinate to the republic Ministry of Agriculture and to the raion Soviet.[40] Having lost most of their economic responsibilities to the associations, the republic Ministry of Agriculture and the raion Soviet retained general supervisory functions, although their lowest-level agency for this (the raion agricultural administration) was abolished. There was thus a shorter (though ill-defined) chain of command from the center to the raions, and the raion's agriculture was subject to closer control through the raion association than it was under the various authorities of the old system. As in Moldavia, the effect was to retreat from earlier attempts to foster decentralization in agricultural management.

The associations operated on khozraschet, and their activities were financed from contributions from member farms and enterprises or, in some cases, from centralized funds. The Talsi association centralized and spent money to finance construction of interfarm production activities; drafted and implemented measures to even out economic conditions between members; organized specialized production units and enterprises; centralized a number of service functions; and even designated areas to grow raw materials for specific processing industries.[41] The Viljandi association had extensive jurisdiction and powers in allocating available resources and inputs among members and in creating new interenterprise projects such as feed mixing mills, repair workshops, warehouses, health and cultural centers, etc. To help equalize economic conditions among members and raise the production capacity of those in less favorable circumstances, the Viljandi association redistributed income through a joint development fund, formed from contributions from profits of the association's members.[42] In carrying out similar functions, the Abasha association and others in Georgia apparently relied mainly on special centralized funds for investments to achieve the "well proportioned and balanced economic development" of the members.[43]

The "highest administrative body" of the various associations was a council, but there were differences between the models. The Talsi association's council was composed of representatives of the constituent members and also of raion Party, Soviet, and other public organizations.[44] Representatives of Party, state, and other public organizations were not directly mentioned in connection with the Abasha association council, but it is clear that from the outset, Party control of the Abasha experiment had been strong and direct.[45] By contrast, detailed reports on the Viljandi raion association put scant emphasis on the role of political and administrative organs, stressing instead the economic side of the association's operations.[46] On 10 March 1982, that is, before the May 1982 reorganization of agricultural administration, the Presidium of the USSR Supreme Soviet adopted a decree on agro-industrial associations. In it, only the Talsi and Abasha models were specifically endorsed, not only for "improving the management of agricultural production" but also "for increasing the role of the raion organs of state power."[47] The Viljandi model's failure to accent political and administrative control over the association seems to be one important reason that it did not find favor with the Presidium.

In all three models, the association's members retained, at least formally, their economic independence and legal personality. Nevertheless, with so much power centered in the hands of the association, the members' independence was restricted to some extent. In this respect, it is interesting to note that joining an association was supposed to be voluntary, and decrees up to now have not used the word "all" when stating that raion associations are composed of kolkhozes, sovkhozes, processing enterprises, etc. in the raion. However, it is likely that joining an association is not in fact a voluntary matter. *Izvestia* reported that members of the Viljandi association were "included by order, according to a list," although the Parnu association, formed later in Estonia on the Viljandi model, was said to have been established on a voluntary basis.[48] Within an association, member enterprises that were previously subordinate to an economic branch ministry were put under dual subordination, to the association as well as to the ministry. In Abasha at least, in an apparent effort to simplify administration, a number of such enterprises only nominally formed part of the association, with their operations and decisions governing them remaining the responsibility of the appropriate ministry.[49]

Apart from the issues of political and administrative control, there were other features differentiating the models. A distinctive feature of the Abasha experiment was its emphasis on incentives to the farmers, in the form of payments in kind set at 10 percent of planned output and as much as 70 percent of above-plan output. The system of remuneration was particularly suited to the conditions of Abasha raion, where corn production was largely unmechanized at the time of the experiment's inception, an ample workforce was available, and the work was carried out by small or extended family groups. Starting from relatively low production figures (Abasha was one of the most backward raions in Georgia), the experiment helped the raion to increase gross agricultural output by 162 percent during 1974–1980, and farmers' average monthly incomes reportedly roughly doubled.[50] The greater availability of corn to feed livestock on the private plots spurred the development of this sector of production. This is illustrated by the fact that state and cooperative purchases of meat from individuals in the raion rose from 400 tons in 1971 to 830 tons in 1978, and free-market sales and personal consumption also rose substantially.[51]

In spite of what appears to have been the specificity of the Abasha experiment, it was considered to be universally applicable in Georgia and was to be adopted in all of the republic's raions (having been tried over some years in fourteen of them) during 1982. However, the Georgian authorities were aware of certain problems. For example, the Georgian Party Central Committee was said to be dissatisfied that in some raions where the Abasha experiment had been introduced, the restructuring had been only pro forma and there were still areas in which the activity of all enterprises and organizations connected with agriculture was not supervised and directed by agricultural production administrations. Moreover, not all raion Party committees appeared willing to give up some of their previous economic functions and to "improve purely Party methods of influencing the raion's economic mechanism."[62] Thus, at the time of its intended adoption throughout the republic, the Abasha model was experiencing significant difficulties going far beyond teething troubles. Especially in view of the May 1982 reforms, one should note that in the first part of 1982, in order to coordinate the activities of the raion agricultural production administrations, a special interdepartmental Coordinating Council for the Management of the Agro-Industrial Complex was set up under the Georgian republic Council of Ministers. The Coordinating Council was headed by the deputy chairman of the republic Council of Ministers in charge of agriculture.[53]

An important emphasis of the Talsi raion agro-industrial association was the central direction of specialization, concentration, and industrialization of production. In keeping with this, a special feature of the association was its ability to set settlement (*raschetnye*) prices for goods exchanged between farms and charges for reciprocal services. Thus, the association reduced the profit margin on seed grain production in order to increase the profitability of producing grain for marketing.[54] While this procedure may help some members of the association (in this case, those producing grain for marketing), it naturally penalizes those association members who could get higher prices for their output (in this case, seed grain) by selling it outside the association. Consequently, although the association as a whole might benefit from the use of settlement prices, their application is bound to cause conflict between individual members, since each member operates on khozraschet and in practice is out to maximize profits.

An incentive scheme did not receive the prominence in Talsi's experiment that it did in Abasha's. Perhaps by way of compensation, a declared responsibility of the Talsi association was to develop agricultural production and increase its efficiency not only in the communal sector but also in private farming operations.[55] In short, the Talsi model was quite different from the Abasha model, as one would expect from the differences in climate and socioeconomic conditions between the republics. The Talsi model for raion agro-industrial associations was to be adopted in all raions in Latvia during 1982.[56]

The Viljandi model (which did not receive an approving mention in the March 1982 decree of the Presidium of the USSR Supreme Soviet, but nonetheless continued to operate) was somewhat more administratively complex in its operations than the other two models. In trying to equalize economic conditions among the raion's farms, the Viljandi raion agricultural production association organized member farms into eight regions, comprising clusters of two to five farms each. In each region, one farm was chosen as a base farm, denoting a leader for the group and an initiator of its activities.[57] The problem of raion, oblast, republic, and all-Union economic supervision of such a system if it were to be employed nationwide, plus the apparent underemphasis of political control, undoubtedly account for the center's lack of enthusiasm for the Viljandi model. Moreover, since Viljandi raion is one of the best farming areas in a republic with the most intensive and progressive agriculture in the USSR, the model may have been thought to be inappropriate for conditions prevailing in most other localities in the USSR.

THE MAY 1982 REFORMS

Soviet agriculture's disappointing performance in recent years (as evidenced by a declining rate of growth, food shortages and rationing, and persistent large imports of grain, meat, and other foodstuffs from the West) was the main matter of concern at the May 1982 Plenum of the Party Central Committee. Brezhnev's long-awaited "Food Program" set out the tasks for Soviet agriculture up to 1990 and announced a number of economic and administrative measures to aid in achieving the goals. Among the program's principal points on the economic side is increased investments (to approximately one-third of all investments in 1986–1990), with greater emphasis on infrastructural development. It was also decided to raise procurement prices for virtually all major crops and livestock products from 1 January 1983 (amounting to an extra 16 billion rubles a year), to write off kolkhoz debts of 9l7 billion rubles and defer repayment of a further 11 billion rubles, and allocate 3.3 billion rubles for housing and social-cultural projects on low-efficiency and loss-making kolkhozes. On the administrative side, the program called for the creation of agro-industrial associations at the raion level, with counterparts at all higher administrative levels.[58]

The new management system combined elements from the agro-industrial experiments undertaken in the Russian Federation, Ukraine, Georgia, Latvia, and Estonia. The Moldavian experiment, concentrating as it did on the kolkhoz sector, was presumably too narrow in its scope to be a suitable model for the new reform and presumably will now be superseded.

In keeping with Brezhnev's call at the November 1981 Central Committee Plenum,[59] the new measures are designed to strengthen the raion level of agricultural management, provide for the "rational" combination of the territorial and branch principles" of management, eliminate departmental fragmentation, and reduce the size of the administrative apparatus.[60] Throughout the country, raion agro-industrial associations were to be set up, incorporating kolkhozes, sovkhozes, interfarm formations, and other agricultural enterprises, as well as enterprises and organizations providing services to them and connected with agricultural production and the processing of produce. Enterprises and organizations serving several raions can be included in the association with the agreement of the appropriate higher agencies. The decree does not state that "all" of a raion's farms, interfarm formations, etc. must join the agro-industrial association, but this is clearly implied. In this respect, not even for the sake of form is the "voluntary principle" of membership mentioned in the decree. All enterprises and organizations belonging to an association are supposed to preserve their economic independence, the rights of a juridicial person, and their departmental affiliation.

The "highest management agency" of the raion agro-industrial association is the association council, formed by the raion Soviet. The council is chaired by the director of the raion agricultural administration (who is simultaneously first deputy-chairman of the raion Soviet executive committee) and includes the kolkhoz chairmen, sovkhoz directors, and leaders of other member enterprises and organizations. The council's composition suggests that in practice it may be too large and contain too many unequal elements to be a genuine decision-making body, and that therefore the real authority will rest with the chairman and his staff. The council's staff is that of the existing raion agricultural administration, plus personnel from enterprises and organizations serving the farms.

The duties of the raion association council exhibit many of the features of the earlier experiments. The council is responsible for determining, on the basis of control figures transmitted to it, plan indicators for the established product lists of kolkhozes and sovkhozes; presenting draft state plans for purchases of agricultural products for confirmation by the raion Soviet; and examining the draft plans of nonfarm members of the association and submitting proposals on the drafts to the appropriate higher agencies. Also, the council has power to distribute centrally allocated capital investments, budget appropriations and credits, and material and technical resources (tractors, combines, agricultural machinery, equipment, fertilizers, building and other materials) to designated kolkhozes, sovkhozes, and other agricultural enterprises. The council can redistribute, when necessary, 10–15 percent of allocated material and technical resources among association members, with their consent. It can also centralize, in accordance with members' proposals, the performance of certain economic-production functions and assign the performance of centralized economic-production functions to individual enterprises (organizations) regardless of their departmental affiliation (or create specialized subdivisions for these purposes on the basis of interfarm cooperation). The methods by which the council is supposed to resolve the inevitable disputes arising from its important allocation functions are not explained in the decree.

As in the Talsi experiment, the council can approve charges for work and services performed by enterprises and organizations within the association, regardless of their departmental affiliation, and moreover can establish settlement prices for livestock, feed, materials, and other resources supplied by kolkhozes and sovkhozes to each other. In addition, the council is supposed to work out, on the basis of members' proposals, long-range plans for the specialization and siting both of the production of agricultural output and also of enterprises for its receipt and processing. It is also to redistribute, if necessary, capital investments not put to use by different state enterprises and organizations belonging to the association, with the agreement of higher-level departmental agencies; create and distribute centralized funds for material incentives, social and cultural measures, housing construction, and production development; and to confirm, on the basis of standard regulations, conditions for the payment of bonuses to leading workers and specialists of sovkhozes and other enterprises and organizations belonging to the association, regardless of their departmental affiliation.

The May 1982 administrative reform goes beyond the earlier experiments by creating a complete hierarchy over the raion agro-industrial associations. In the oblasts, krais, and autonomous republics, agro-industrial associations are to be set up to include oblast, krai, or autonomous republic organizations of the agro-industrial complex and enterprises under their jurisdiction. The association's highest management agency is a council, made up of executives of oblast, krai, or autonomous republic organizations of the agro-industrial complex, plus "other officials" approved by the oblast (krai) Soviet or autonomous republic Supreme Soviet. The council's staff is that of the existing agricultural administration of the oblast (krai) Soviet executive committee or of the autonomous republic Ministry of Agriculture. In each union republic, a Commission on Questions of the Agro-Industrial Complex under the Presidium of the union republic Council of Ministers (or an agency similar to the Commission) is to be created. Derived from the Georgia experiment, the Commission is composed of ministers and executives of departments belonging to the republic's agro-industrial complex, as well as other officials confirmed by the republic Council of Ministers. The Commission's chairman is a deputy chairman of the union republic Council of Ministers. At the top of the hierarchy, there is a Commission on Questions of the Agro-Industrial Complex under the Presidium of the USSR Council of Ministers, chaired by a deputy chairman of the USSR Council of Ministers. The decree establishing this Commission stipulated that the membership should include ministers from seven all-Union ministries concerned with agro-industrial production (agriculture, fruit and vegetable farming, procurements, meat and dairy industry, food industry, land reclamation and water resources, and rural construction), plus the chairmen of two USSR state committees (forestry and supply of agricultural machinery), the director of the USSR Council of Ministers' Chief Administration for the Microbiological Industry, and other officials named by the USSR Council of Ministers. When the Commission was appointed, the last category took in the USSR Minister of Fisheries, together with the first deputy chairmen of USSR Gosplan, the USSR State Committee of Supply (Gossnab), and the USSR State Committee on Science and Technology.[61]

The councils of the oblast, krai, and autonomous republic agro-industrial associations are responsible for (1) reviewing the basic indictors of plans for the development of members of the territory's agro-industrial complex as well as the volume of sales to the state of agricultural products by raions and categories of farms and (2) submitting proposals to the oblast (krai) Soviet executive committee or autonomous republic Council of Ministers. The councils can also redistribute centrally allocated capital investments, material and technical resources, and other resources among branches of the territory's agro-industrial complex, with the agreement of the appropriate union republic ministries and departments. Another important function is checking on the fulfilment by members of the agro-industrial complex of plans for the production, processing, and state purchase of agricultural produce and its delivery to all-Union and republic stocks. In this connection, they also supervise the supplying of food to the territory's population. Covering large areas, these councils can work out and implement comprehensive special-purpose food and other programs. On the other hand, they overlap to some extent with the raion councils in a number of tasks: fully or partially centralizing certain administrative and economic-production functions, and assigning their performance to individual enterprises or organizations belonging to the territory's association; working out a plan for the development and siting of agricultural production and of other branches of the agro-industrial complex; and creating, in the basis of interfarm cooperation, industrial enterprises and shops for the production of mixed feed, local construction materials, production equipment, and consumer goods. The union republic commissions, whose duties are not spelled out in the decree, presumably oversee the work of the raion, oblast, krai, and autonomous republic councils under them; ensure that the aggregated plans fit in with the republic and all-Union plans; and take measures to foster agro-industrial development and specialization within and across the smaller territorial units of the republic.

The duties of the Commission of the Presidium of the USSR Council of Ministers include coordinating the activities of ministries and departments belonging to the agro-industrial complex and supervising their implementation of Party and government decisions, assignments established by state plans, and assignments for procurements of agricultural products and deliveries of machinery, equipment, and chemical agents. It is also responsible for supervising the rational use of material, financial, and labor resources; the production of output of the food branches of industry; and raising the quality of this output and getting it to the consumers. In addition, the Commission examines the draft annual and long-range plans for the agro-industrial complex submitted by Gosplan and also prepares (in accordance with assignments of the USSR Council of Ministers) proposals on questions of the further development of the agro-industrial complex. Among a long list of other general duties (e.g., strengthening the material-technical base of the farms, continuously perfecting the economic mechanism, etc.), the Commission is charged with implementing measures to develop further personal subsidiary plots of citizens and subsidiary farms of industrial enterprises as a component part of the country's food complex. It is clear from the high-powered membership of the Commission that most of these time-consuming responsibilities will have to be delegated to a staff.

That the May 1982 system owed more to the Talsi and Abasha models than to the Viljandi model is illustrated by the provisions for political supervision and for financial incentives. In his speech to the Plenum, Brezhnev noted tersely that "in view of the complexity and diversity of tasks tackled at raion level, it has been decided to carry out a number of measures to strengthen the raion Party committees, and specifically to establish agricultural departments within raion committees."[62] At the time of writing, the composition and precise duties of these departments had not yet been announced, but it can be assumed that among their main tasks will be checking (and, in practice, undoubtedly directly supervising) the operations of the raion agro-industrial associations and councils, as well as increasing the raion Party committee's role in the selection, training, and placement of management personnel and other farm leaders and workers. It is not known whether the raion Party committee agricultural departments will have counterparts at oblast or higher level.

Relating to incentives, Brezhnev declared that "there has been a tendency in recent years to underestimate the importance of payments in kind," and that the practice of payment in kind would be extended.[63] In the event, while the Abasha model made payments in kind amounting to 10 percent of planned output and up to 70 percent of above-plan output, the May 1982 decree on incentives was considerably less generous. For grain production, workers are to be paid up to 1.5 kilograms of grain for fulfilling a shift-norm and up to 15 percent of gross above-plan output. For production of potatoes, vegetables, fruit, berries, grapes, melons, and feed crops, workers are to be paid in kind up to 15 percent of the planned gross harvest and, at the farm manager's discretion, no more than 30 percent of the above-plan gross harvest. These rates apply specifically to sovkhozes and other state agricultural enterprises, with a recommendation that kolkhozes also should adopt them.[64] It remains to be seen whether kolkhozes will use the provisions and whether distributions under this system will approach the stated maxima.

PROSPECTS

The May 1982 administrative reforms were specifically designed to eliminate many long-standing deficiencies in Soviet agricultural management. As enumerated by Brezhnev at the Plenum, these include insufficient incentives to farm managers and workers; "excessive" reliance on administrative methods and petty tutelage; demanding that farms should carry out assignments not envisaged by the state plan; requiring farms to submit information other than that required under existing procedures for accounting to the state; the widespread operation of farms under "formal" rather than "real" khozraschet, thereby allowing "many" kolkhozes and sovkhozes to operate at a loss; the widespread failure to hold regular general meetings of kolkhoz members; and the "unjustifiably frequent" change of kolkhoz and sovkhoz leaders in many places.[65] Further, as stressed by the decree on the administrative reform, the old management system was excessively cumbersome and fragmented, the managerial apparatus had grown to an unwarranted size, the "necessary combination" of the branch and territorial principles of management had not been ensured, and there was unacceptable parallelism and duplication in agricultural administration.[66] Moreover, according to a report in *Pravda,* the old system was plagued by the return of local planning and economic agencies to using "long-condemned methods" such as planning "from the achieved level," failing to observe the territorial principle in planning, seeking to dictate to farms how much of what crops to sow and how many head of livestock of each type to raise, imposing recommendations that do not take local conditions into account, and scattering capital investments and material resources among the various ministries and departments because of departmental barriers.[67] To this list of woes could be added overcentralization of planning and administration and over-large farms and enterprises, but these faults (as perceived in the West) of the old system were not referred to in the debate, and the new reform, instead of alleviating them, in fact worsens them.

It is just possible that the 1982 reform will improve the coordination of agricultural production within and between raions. On paper at least, the raion councils can now look at their territories and determine what is best to produce where, how best for association members to integrate their activities, how most efficiently to shift resources, etc. Likewise, the oblast councils can foster cooperation between raions. However, in practice there are bound to be many obstacles to achieving the reform's aims. First, in many areas, the process of creating agro-industrial associations began only in mid-1982,[68] and it will take some time before these bodies can efficiently come to grips with the tasks facing them. Second, and hardly less important, the size of the councils and the nature of their composition (encompassing farms and enterprises of widely differing economic importance in the raion, and with differing and sometimes conflicting interests), would seem to make them unsuitable as genuine or efficient decision-making bodies. For example, it may be relatively easy for the council to fix a settlement price between members for feed deliveries but, given the desire by most farms to maximize income, it may be rather more difficult to decide at a council meeting which farms must "voluntarily" sacrifice income by making such deliveries. It is a fair bet that any such decisions will be made behind the scenes, through "the usual channels," as they traditionally have been. The council chairman and his staff—and also the raion Party agricultural department, not to mention superior councils and Party bodies—will undoubtedly carry most of the burden of local decision making. In this respect, one recalls Brezhnev's criticism of "excessive" reliance on administrative methods and petty tutelage in agricultural management, almost as if he were saying that some reliance on these is necessary to make the system work. In the last analysis, there is no guarantee that the councils will make agricultural planning, decision making, and management more rational or efficient than they have been to date. Furthermore, the new reform is a significant centralization measure, in that it takes away many planning and decision-making responsibilities from the 47,000 kolkhozes and sovkhozes, 9,600 interfarm enterprises, and 750 existing agro-industrial undertakings of various kinds. The problems of the diseconomies of scale encountered in the past in administering the country's farms are likely to be exacerbated if the new reform leads to increasingly large economic units.

Another obstacle is the problem of getting the bureaucracy to operate the new system as intended. The difficulty of changing old attitudes and methods, overcoming local opposition to particular reforms, and providing enough well-trained personnel to carry out the new tasks has been a persistent problem in Soviet agricultural administration.[69] A report on the introduction of the new program states openly that major efforts are being made to "surmount narrow departmentalism and regionalism, antiquated working methods, and inertia and sloth in economic thinking."[70] However, since most of the personnel from the old system will be employed in administering the new one, we can expect the old practices to die hard. Similarly, the ritual calls to (1) correct shortcomings in the selection, placement, and training of cadres; (2) transfer specialists from management work to production work on the farms; and (3) reduce the replacement rate for kolkhoz chairmen, sovkhoz directors, and farm specialists[71] are unlikely to be better heeded now than they were in the past.

On the economic side, the reforms appear to do little to improve the efficiency of Soviet agriculture. The price increases and debt write-offs may reduce a farm's losses or raise its profits, but they need not lead to increases in productivity. The promised boost in infrastructural and other investments, together with a planned growth in fertilizer and tractor deliveries, potentially could lead to improved farm efficiency; if so, this would be a departure from the experience of the past few years. In terms of incentives to the farmers, the provisions for payments in kind seem somewhat niggardly, given the recent difficulties in increasing the workers' motivation. Brezhnev's continued advocacy at the May 1982 Plenum of the "more socialist," less individualistic forms of labor organization and incentives schemes (team and collective piece-work, and an aggregate job piece-rate plus bonus system) in preference to the "normless link" (*beznaryadnoe zveno,* which gives small production teams an area of land without assigned norms and pays the teams according to results) also indicates a relatively conservative approach toward incentives. All in all, it is highly unlikely that the economic measures will secure fulfilment of the Food Program's target for 1990 of rises of at least 33 percent in agricultural output per hectare of arable land and of about 50 percent in labor productivity on the farms.

In 1963, Swearer pinpointed a number of factors hindering local agricultural administration under Khrushchev: "the ponderous bureaucracy, the absence of a rational system of priorities on which local cadres could base decisions, the inability to define precisely the responsibilities of various regional and local officials, the constant intervention by political cadres at all levels of administration, and unrealistic agricultural production targets . . . ."[72] It can be argued that the system of priorities became more rational under Brezhnev, but it is a sad commentary that the rest of the faults have remained prominent features of Soviet agricultural administration. The May 1982 Food Program and administrative reform pay lip service to removing these shortcomings, but there is no reason to suppose that the new remedies will be any more successful than the old. The Soviet

Union's food problem is a consequence not only of unfavorable weather conditions but also of bad economic and administrative management. Until the overall management system is fundamentally improved, we cannot expect to see a long-term, domestically generated solution to the Soviet food problem.

NOTES

1. *Pravda,* 4 July 1978.
2. For an example of inter-kolkhoz associations, see Robert F. Miller, "The Future of the Soviet Kolkhoz," *Problems of Communism* 25, no. 2 (1976): pp. 34–50.
3. *Pravda,* 2 June 1976.
4. See Arcadius Kahan, "The Problems of the 'Agrarian-Industrial Complexes' in the Soviet Union," in *Economics Development in the Soviet Union and Eastern Europe,* vol. 2, ed. Zbigniew Fallenbuchl (New York: Praeger, 1976), pp. 205–22; Robert C. Stuart, "Aspects of Soviet Rural Development," *Agricultural Administration* 10, no. 2 (1975): pp. 165–78; and Karl-Eugen Wädekin, *Agrarian Policies in Communist Europe: A Critical Introduction* (Totowa, N.J.: Allanheld, Osmun & Co., 1982), pp. 234–57.
5. V. A. Dobrynin, ed., *Ekonomika, organizatsia i planirovanie sel'skokhozyaistvennogo proizvodstva* (Moscow: Kolos, 1980), p. 33.
6. *Izvestia,* 21 August 1976.
7. *Pravda,* 2 June 1976.
8. *Izvestia,* 21 August 1976.
9. *Izvestia,* 19 May 1977.
10. *Pravda,* 6 December 1975. At the end of 1975, the number of kolkhozes (including multiple memberships) in interfarm enterprises was 81,940 *Narodnoe khozyaistvo SSSR v 1975 g.* (Moscow: Statistika, 1976), p. 422.
11. L. Ya. Zribnyak, *Planirovanie sel'skokhozyaistvennogo proizvodstva* (Moscow: Kolos, 1979), p. 85.
12. *Ekonomika sel'skogo khozyaistva,* no. 4 (April 1980): pp. 53–54.
13. *Izvestia,* 6 January 1975.
14. *Ekonomika sel'skogo khozyaistva,* no. 5 (May 1977): pp. 9–17.
15. *Narodnoe khozyaistvo SSSR v 1977 g.* (Moscow: Statistika, 1978), p. 280; and *Narodnoe khozyaistvo SSSR v 1980 g.* (Moscow: Finansy i statistika, 1981), p. 264.
16. *Izvestia,* 7 February 1979. See also Dobrynin, 33–4, and N. M. Savenko, N. A. Dobrolyubova, and N. A. Koluzanova, *Ekonomika, organizatsia i planirovanie sel'skokhozyaistvennogo proizvodstva* (Moscow: Kolos, 1981), pp. 32–33.
17. *Pravda,* 4 July 1978.
18. *Narodnoe khozyaistvo SSSR v 1978 g.* (Moscow: Statistika, 1979), 270; *Narodnoe khozyaistvo SSSR v 1979 g.* (Moscow: Statistika, 1980), p. 294; *Narodnoe khozyaistvo SSSR v 1980 g.,* p. 264.
19. *Ekonomicheskaya gazeta,* no. 25 (June 1982): pp. 12–14. There were 640 agro-industrial enterprises and 140 agricultural production associations at the end of 1980 *Khozyaistvo i pravo,* no. 6 (June 1981): p. 13.
20. *Ekonomika sel'skogo khozyaistva,* no. 6 (June 1980): p. 22.
21. *Ekonomika sel'skogo khozyaistva,* no. 6 (June 1982): p. 54.
22. *Narodnoe khozyaistvo SSSR v 1980 g.,* pp. 264–46.
23. Miller, p. 40.
24. See Everett M. Jacobs, "Recent Developments in Soviet Agricultural Planning," in *Jahrbuch der Wirtschaft Osteuropas,* vol. 3 Franz-Lothar Altmann, ed. (Munich: Olzog, 1972), p. 323; and U.S. Department of Agriculture (Economics, Statistics, and Cooperatives Service), *USSR Agricultural Situation: Review of 1978 and Outlook for 1979* (Washington, D.C.: U.S. Government Printing Office, 1979), p. 30. The profitability from sales to the state (including premia) in 1977 by kolkhozes and sovkhozes under the USSR Ministry of Agriculture was as follows: cattle (live weight), 10.7 percent and 9.9 percent, respectively; hogs (live weight), 2.3 percent and 12.1 percent; poultry, – 3.9 percent and 5.6 percent; milk and milk products, – 0.1 percent and – 6.3 percent.

25. *Sovetskaya Moldavia,* 10 March 1973, translated in *Current Digest of the Soviet Press,* XXXV, 10, (4 April 1973): 1–8 (hereafter *CDSP*).

26. *Izvestia,* 30 January 1974.

27. *Pravda,* 10 June 1976.

28. *Pravda,* 9 December 1976.

29. *Pravda,* 9 December 1976.

30. *Pravda,* 10 June 1976.

31. *Pravda,* 24 February 1977.

32. *Pravda,* 10 January 1978.

33. *Ekonomicheskaya gazeta,* no. 1 (January 1977): p. 19.

34. *Pravda,* 10 January 1978.

35. *Pravda,* 9 December 1976.

36. See *Radio Liberty Research* 104/81 (6 March 1981).

37. Wädekin, p. 247.

38. For Abasha raion, see *Radio Liberty Research* 125/82 (17 March 1982) and *Ekonomicheskaya gazeta,* no. 21 (May 1982): pp. 7–8; for Talsi raion, *Planovoe khozyaistvo,* no. 7 (July 1979): pp. 82–5, abstracted in *CDSP,* XXXI, 42 (14 November 1979): pp. 14–15; for Viljandi raion, *Radio Liberty Research* 130/81 (25 March 1981); for Abasha and Talsi raions together, see *Pravda,* 11 March 1982. The Abasha association included the raion state seed-inspection service and a station for combatting animal diseases. The Viljandi association included a dairy combine, a meat-packing combine, and a grain products combine.

39. *Sovetskaya Rossia* (15 September 1981), cited in *Radio Liberty Research* 125/82, (17 March 1982).

40. *Radio Liberty Research* 125/82, (17 March 1982); *Ekonomicheskaya gazeta,* no. 21 (May 1982): p. 7.

41. *Planovoe khozyaistvo,* no. 7 (July 1979): pp. 82–85, abstracted in *CDSP,* XXXI, 42 (14 November 1979): pp. 14–15; *Izvestia,* 6 December 1981.

42. *Radio Liberty Research* 130/81, (25 March 1981).

43. *Ekonomicheskaya gazeta,* no. 21 (May 1982): p. 7.

44. *Izvestia,* 30 April 1980.

45. *Radio Liberty Research* 170/82 (22 April 1982); *Ekonomicheskaya gazeta,* no. 21 (May 1982): p. 7.

46. *Radio Liberty Research* 170/82, (22 April 1982).

47. *Pravda,* 11 March 1982.

48. *Izvestia,* 8 January 1981.

49. *Radio Liberty Research* 125/82, (17 March 1982).

50. *Ekonomicheskaya gazeta,* no. 21 (May 1982): pp. 7–8.

51. *Radio Liberty Research* 48/82 (29 January 1982).

52. *Ekonomicheskaya gazeta,* no. 21 (May 1982): pp. 7–8.

53. *Ibid.,* p. 8.

54. *Planovoe khozyaistvo,* no. 7 (July 1979): pp. 82–85, abstracted in *CDSP,* XXXI, 42 (14 November 1979): pp. 14–15; *Izvestia,* 6 December 1981.

55. *Ibid.*

56. *Izvestia,* 6 December 1981.

57. *Radio Liberty Research* 130/81, (25 March 1981).

58. *Pravda,* 27 May 1982.

59. *Pravda,* 17 November 1981.

60. *Pravda,* 28 May 1982.

61. *Ekonomicheskaya gazeta,* no. 25 (June 1982): p. 3.

62. *Pravda,* 25 May 1982.

63. *Ibid.*

64. *Pravda,* 28 May 1982.

65. *Pravda,* 25 May 1982.

66. *Pravda,* 28 May 1982.

67. *Pravda,* 6 August 1982.

68. *Ekonomicheskaya gazeta,* no. 25 (June 1982): p. 14.

69. Jerzy F. Karcz, "Seven Years on the Farm: Retrospect and Prospects," in U.S. Congress, Joint Economic Committee, *New Directions in the Soviet Economy,* Part II-B

(Washington, D.C.: Government Printing Office, 1966), pp. 427–428; Alec Nove, "Peasants and Officials," in *Soviet and East European Agriculture,* ed. Jerzy F. Karcz (Berkeley: University of California Press, 1967), pp. 57–76; Robert F. Miller, "Continuity and Change in the Administration of Soviet Agriculture Since Stalin," in *The Soviet Rural Community* ed. James R. Millar (Urbana: University of Illinois Press, 1971), pp. 73–102.

70. *Pravda,* 6 August 1982.

71. *Pravda,* 29 May 1982.

72. Howard R. Swearer, "Agricultural Administration under Khrushchev," in *Soviet Agricultural and Peasant Affairs,* ed. Roy D. Laird (Lawrence, Kansas: University of Kansas Press, 1963), p. 37.

15

Prospects for Soviet Agriculture in the Eleventh Five-Year Plan: Econometric Analysis and Projections

Daniel L. Bond
Donald W. Green

RECENT DEVELOPMENTS IN THE ECONOMETRIC ANALYSIS OF SOVIET AGRICULTURE

In the last several years there has been much greater interest in the use of econometric methods for the analysis of Soviet agriculture. A major contribution has been the application of regional information to improve the parameter estimates for agricultural production functions. In this paper, we shall summarize the earlier analysis presented in Bond[1] and compare those results with recent estimations by Clayton.[2] This cross-sectional information is then used in constraining certain parameters in the estimation of aggregate production functions for total crops and total grain. The relationship between Soviet grain production and the livestock sector has concerned a number of Western economists in recent years, and a condensed grain-balance system is estimated to determine grain fed to livestock, grain imports, and inventory change. Then, the aggregate determination of animal production and meat production is reconsidered in this paper in order to obtain better output elasticities for feedgrain and total livestock. Finally, the deviation in feedgrain is introduced in the determination of livestock investment functions for various animal categories.

Pooled Estimation of Agricultural Production Functions Using Regional Data

The objective of this portion of the study was to estimate output elasticities for capital, labor, and land in Soviet agriculture, using annual data for the fifteen republics for the period 1960 through 1975. The estimates obtained from this analysis were used as a guide when developing parameters for the agricultural production functions used in SOVMOD V.[3]

Production function estimation can be carried out using time-series data, cross-sectional data (where the units of observation are most commonly subsectors of production or firms or regions), or a combination of the two types of data. A common problem in time-series analysis is the frequent presence of multicollinearity among variables. This is a particularly severe problem in the Soviet case, where centralized planning has created a pattern of input and output growth that is relatively constant over time. A high degree of multicollinearity makes it very difficult to separate the influence of technological progress from the influences of scale effects and elasticities of output.

Estimation problems are somewhat lessened when cross-sectional data are used. In this case the technological change parameters are excluded from the equation, and usually there is less multicollinearity among the variables. Also, the greater variation in capital to labor ratios found in cross-sectional data significantly improves the opportunities for obtaining significant estimation results.

At the same time, these wide differences in cross-sectional input-output combinations raise the question whether it can be assumed that the same production function is appropriate to the different regions or sectors.. That this can not be assumed is an objection frequently raised against cross-sectional estimation. The issue must be decided separately in each case, of course, depending on whatever evidence is at hand. This problem is also to be found in time-series analysis, in that the relative shares of subsectors, each with different production function characteristics, may be changing over time.

It is often the case with cross-sectional data that the variance of the error term is much greater than is normally found in time-series data. By combining both time-series and cross-sectional data, it is possible to reduce distortion that random errors cause if data for only one year are used. From an empirical point of view, the usefulness of pooling across regions for the study of production functions has been demonstrated by a number of studies using international data. This is particularly useful in cases where the cross-sectional sample is rather small. An additional attractive feature of the "pooling" approach is that the number of observations can in this way be greatly increased.

In estimating the agricultural production functions in this study, it was assumed that the shape of the function was the same across all regions. The function chosen for the study was the Cobb-Douglas form.[4] Technical progress was represented as being disembodied and Hicks-neutral, with a linear trend. Versions with both nonconstant and constant returns to scale were tested.

Three approaches were utilized for the parameter estimations. First, each set of functions (with nonconstant and constant returns to scale) was estimated by simply pooling the time-series and regional data and estimating the parameters, using OLS with no correction.

In a second approach, the "covariance model" was used to allow for the possibility of differing intercepts and differing rates of technical growth among regions.[5] In order to minimize the loss in degrees of freedom, the fifteen republics were grouped together into seven larger regions according to prior notions of economic similarity.[6] In this way some account was made for constant effects associated with both the time direction and cross-sectional units not readily attributable to the identified causal variables. This serves to lessen possible bias in the estimates of the output and scale elasticities.

In the third set of estimations, an attempt was made to recognize possible correlations among error terms and to account for these in order to increase the asymptotic efficiency of the estimates of the causal parameters. Various correction techniques have been developed for pooled estimations, each depending upon the assumed pattern among the correlations. Here only one such approach has been used. It is assumed that there is autoregression in the time dimension, and heteroscedasticity in the cross-sectional observations. These are the most common assumptions made concerning time-series and cross-sectional observations. In the particular case at hand, it is possible to provide an economic rationale for their presence. The timewise correlations can be explained as resulting from the fact that in the Soviet Union the effect of harvest deviations has a significant impact on the performance of agriculture and other sectors, both in the current year and in the following year. And the necessity of corrections for heteroscedasticity arises from the great differences among regions in level of output, which make it unlikely that the variance in error terms will be of equal magnitude. The approach used to correct for these effects is the "cross-sectionally heteroscedastic and time-wise autoregressive (CSH/TWA) model."[7]

Each regression was carried out by using pooled data for fifteen regions and sixteen time periods—a total of 240 observations. A net agricultural output measure was used, together with data on the primary inputs—land, labor, and capital. (The data are described in Appendix A.) The estimation results are presented in Table 15.1.[8] Estimates of the following parameters are given:

β = output elasticity of capital
α = output elasticity of labor
ψ = output elasticity of land
v = scale elasticity (in some cases assumed equal to 1)
ζ = constant rate of disembodied technological progress

The coefficients of determination indicate that the specifications used explain most of the variation in the dependent variables. Considering that cross-sectional information is used, the $\bar{R}^2$ values are quite good.

In all cases, there is little support for either increasing or decreasing returns to scale. The point estimates for the scale parameter in the unconstrained versions range from 0.982 to 1.033. Although the fit statistics worsen in all cases when the functions are constrained by the assumption of constant returns to scale, this is to be expected because of the specification of the function—logs of ratios instead of logs of levels are used in the constrained case.

The parameter estimates for capital and labor were significant, and the variation in values obtained using the various regression methods was

Table 15.1 Production Function Estimation Results for Agriculture

	$\hat{\beta}$	$\hat{\alpha}$	$\hat{\upsilon}$	$\hat{\zeta}$	$\hat{\psi}$	$\bar{R}^2$	S.E.
Cobb-Douglas with nonconstant returns to scale	0.404 (7.21)	0.523 (14.84)	0.982	-0.019 (-3.64)	0.055 (2.22)	0.979	0.174
Cobb-Douglas with constant returns to scale	0.455 (11.96)	0.545	1.	-0.023 (-5.78)	0.034 (1.91)	0.503	0.174
Cobb-Douglas with nonconstant returns to scale, covariance model	0.379 (6.26)	0.626 (9.56)	1.033	-0.025* (-2.73)	0.028 (0.66)	0.987	0.140
Cobb-Douglas with constant returns to scale, covariance model	0.327 (5.92)	0.621	1.	-0.021* (-2.36)	0.052 (1.24)	0.677	0.141
Cobb-Douglas with nonconstant returns to scale, CSH/TWA model	0.360 (5.22)	0.654 (10.54)	1.000	-0.020 (-3.05)	-0.014 (-1.08)	0.998	0.825
Cobb-Douglas with constant returns to scale, CSH/TWA model	0.332 (5.59)	0.668	1.	-0.017 (-2.81)	0.002 (0.09)	0.552	0.863

*$\hat{\zeta}$ are for the RSFSR in the covariance forms. Values for $\hat{\zeta}$ ranged from -.026 to 0.005 in the nonconstant returns to scale form and -0.021 to 0.008 in the constant returns to scale form.

limited—the output elasticity estimate for capital varies between 0.327 and 0.455, while that for labor varies between 0.523 and 0.668.

However, greater variation in the output elasticity for land is apparent. The estimated coefficient of this variable ranged from −0.014 to 0.055. Also the t-statistics of the estimates were relatively low, indicating that little in the way of explanatory power was added by the inclusion of land in the production function.

The effect of using either the covariance model or the CSH/TWA model for the pooled regressions was primarily limited to improving the fit of the regressions and had little effect on the value of the parameter estimates.

It has been suggested that when the results of cross-sectional estimations are to be for analyzing changes over time, then it is wise to test the stability of the estimates over various time periods. For this reason a series of additional regressions was run over shorter time spans of pooled data. The Cobb-Douglas covariance model was used (with only capital and labor included in the function). The parameter estimates are reported in Table 15.2. The values of the reported parameters exhibit some instability across the time periods. However the sudden drop in the value of the capital coefficient in the last period is likely caused, in part at least, by the unusually bad harvests in 1972 and 1975.

A test to see if the estimated parameters were constant across regions was also undertaken. Another set of regressions was run on the pooled data, using the Cobb-Douglas specification (in both nonconstant and constant returns to scale form), but with separate factor output elasticity parameters provided for the northern republics (RSFSR, Baltic republics, Belorussia, Ukraine, and Moldavia) and the southern republics (Kazakhstan, Transcaucasian and Central Asian republics.) These regression results are presented in Table 15.3. The fact that the two estimated elasticities are very close in value in each case gives additional support to the view that the two sets of observations are from the same population and thus can be usefully pooled.

The above results indicate that increases in capital may have played a more significant role, and increases in land and labor a less significant role, in growth of agricultural output than previous studies have indicated—such, for example, as the studies by Diamond,[9] Diamond and Krueger,[10] and Clayton (see note 2).

The earlier two of these studies used estimated factor shares in value-added as a guide in setting output elasticities. Since this is equivalent to assuming cost-minimization in Soviet agriculture, they represent a conditional hypothesis about production relations, rather than an empirical test of these relations.

The more recent study by Clayton is more directly comparable to that described here. Clayton also used a statistical estimation approach based on pooling time series of republican data. Two significant differences between the studies may account for their different results. First, Clayton used gross regional output rather than net output. Appropriately to the use of a gross output measure, she included intermediate inputs, represented by fertilizer, as well as primary inputs, represented by land, labor, and two forms of

Table 15.2   Time Series of Pooled Estimations

Cobb-Douglas Nonconstant
Returns to Scale (Covariance Model)

	$\hat{\beta}$	$\hat{\alpha}$
1960–1963	0.490 (4.95)	0.516 (5.33)
1964–1967	0.462 (3.98)	0.575 (5.29)
1968–1971	0.477 (4.05)	0.576 (5.51)
1972–1975	0.336 (2.62)	0.737 (6.36)
1960–1975	0.387 (6.53)	0.649 (11.80)

Cobb-Douglas Constant
Returns to Scale (Covariance Model)

	$\hat{\beta}$	$\hat{\alpha}$
1960–1963	0.486 (5.08)	0.514
1964–1967	0.407 (3.76)	0.593
1968–1971	0.382 (3.71)	0.618
1972–1975	0.180 (1.55)	0.820
1960–1975	0.334 (6.06)	0.666

Table 15.3   Regional Disaggregation of Pooled Estimations

Cobb-Douglas Nonconstant Returns to Scale

$\hat{\beta}$		$\hat{\alpha}$	
North	South	North	South
0.420 (10.98)	0.436 (9.15)	0.540 (16.13)	0.624 (12.13)

Cobb-Douglas Constant Returns to Scale

$\hat{\beta}$		$\hat{\alpha}$	
North	South	North	South
0.490 (14.65)	0.474 (9.88)	0.510	0.526

capital—livestock and machinery. However, a rough approximation of the output elasticities of primary inputs to net output can be obtained from Clayton's results. But from these it would still seem that land played a substantially more significant role in agricultural output growth than indicated in the present study.

A second difference is likely to arise from Clayton's use of observations for only each fifth year in the period 1960 to 1975, rather than annual data. Since 1965 and 1975 were years of poor agricultural performance in the Soviet Union (that is, they were below the trend-line for output over the entire period), this may have biased the estimation results obtained. Lowering the apparent growth rate of output would tend to impact most negatively on the estimated elasticity for a faster-growing input such as capital and push up that of the more slowly growing, or declining, factors such as land and labor.

Aggregate Determination of Total Crops and Grain Production

Even when an agricultural output series has been appropriately smoothed by linked-second-peak interpolation, the econometric estimation of production functions remains difficult.[11] Output elasticities for labor are sometimes negative, and other parameter estimates are often unreasonable when three or more factor inputs are included as dependent variables. Consequently to obtain reasonable production functions for analysis and forecasting, one must often introduce additional information by imposing elasticities for particular inputs. As discussed in the previous section, there now exist two major sources of additional information: (1) cross-section estimation results at the Republican level in the USSR and (2) Western estimates of factor shares in agricultural value-added.

Various estimates of output elasticities are presented in Table 15.4, along with the output elasticities actually used in the 1981 version of our econometric model of Soviet agriculture. In comparing the 1966 factor shares with the output elasticities for net agricultural production, the combined output elasticities for labor and land are smaller in most estimations than the factor shares, 60 percent compared with 70 percent. The combined elasticities for fixed capital and current purchases are correspondingly larger in the estimations than in the factor share vector.

The complete estimations for normal output are presented in Table 15.5. The serial correlation, suggested by the low Durbin-Watson statistics, arises from the methodology of linked-second-peak interpolation and is corrected in the second step of the estimation procedure.

The second step of the estimation procedure determines the deviation of actual output from normal output as a function of three simple weather variables:

1. Spring-summer precipitation (JPS9): Average precipitation during the growing months (April to September) for five representative grain-growing regions. Precipitation averages are weighted by relative grain output for those areas.[12]

Table 15.4 Factor Shares and Output Elasticities

	Factor Shares in Value-Added[a]	Regional Estimations		SOVMOD V Aggregate Production Functions	
		Bond[b]	Clayton[c]	Total Crops	Total Grain
Labor	0.58	0.67	.37	0.49	0.465
Land	0.12)	-	.20	0.15*	0.15*
Fixed Capital	0.15)	0.33	.14	0.20*	0.185
Productive Livestock	0.03)	-	.05	-	-
Current Purchases	0.12	-	.21	0.16	0.20*
Sum	1.00	1.00	.97	1.00	1.00

*Imposed in the estimation.

[a]Diamond and Krueger (1973); output variable is total agricultural production net of animal feed.
[b]Bond (1979); output series is national income originating in agriculture.
[c]Clayton (1980); fixed-capital variable is machinery in horsepower and current-purchases variable is fertilizer in nutrient units.

Table 15.5 The Determination of Normal Output

Category	Constant	Sown Area (ASGR9)	Employment (NAT)	Fixed Capital (KAIR)	Current Purchases (AVCP70)	$\bar{R}^2$	S.E.	D.W.
Total Crops (XCROPN)	-0.0238 (1.52)	0.1516*	0.4892 (6.79)	0.20*	0.1592 (10.35)	0.828	0.025	0.29
Total Grain (XGRTN)	1.4959 (1.32)	0.15*	0.4634 (1.61)	0.1849 (8.41)	0.20*	0.941	0.018	0.53

All estimations are in log-linear form. Sample periods: 1955–77 for XCROPN and 1961–77 for XGRTN.
*indicates an imposed elasticity.

Note: These equations are actually the definitions of normal output. The statistical properties are those from regressing the linked-second-peak series on factor inputs. The low values of Dublin-Watson statistics are a consequence of the smoothing procedure adopted, and any bias is partially corrected in the estimation of the deviation equations below.

Weather Determination of the Deviation from Normal Output

Category	Constant	Dummy 1975	Spring-Summer Precipitation	Winter Temperature	Winter Precipitation	$\bar{R}^2$	S.E.	D.W.
Total Crops	-0.0122 (0.51)		0.1447 (3.85)	0.0061 (1.36)	0.0996 (2.23)	0.598	0.063	1.66
Total Grain	-0.0263 (0.80)	-0.3006 (3.14)	0.1848 (3.74)	0.0110 (1.83)	0.0452 (0.73)	0.717	0.08	3.28

The dependent variable is the difference between the log of actual output and the log of normal output. Sample period is 1962–1976.

2. Winter temperature (JTW9T): Mean monthly temperature (January to March) for the Southern Ukraine, an important region for winter wheat. This series has now been truncated so that mean temperatures above zero degrees centigrade are set equal to zero; the impact, therefore, is only on the downward side for winter-kill.
3. Winter precipitation (JPW9): Mean monthly precipitation (January to March) for the Southern Ukraine. Winter precipitation contributes snow cover for winter wheat and soil moisture for early spring crops.

Considerable work remains to be done in refining such indexes and developing alternatives, but we have found that these three indexes explain more than half of the deviation of actual output from normal output.

Estimation results for the deviation of actual agricultural production are presented in the second part of Table 15.5. The sample period of these estimations includes only fifteen observations, 1962–1976, because of the limited availability of weather data. For total crops, the standard error in predicting actual output is 6.3 percent; the largest percentage errors appear in 1964 (12 percent below the actual value), 1969 (7.5 percent above), and 1975 (7 percent above). For total grain, the three weather variables did not explain the very low yields in 1975; with a dummy variable for that year, the standard error of prediction is 8 percent, or around 12–18 million metric tons in the 1970s.

The final component in the crop sector is the determination of agricultural current purchases from other sectors. Earlier analysis had found that the two major determinants of current purchases were normal crop production and the output of chemicals and petrochemicals (lagged one year). There does not appear to be any systematic relationship between the harvest deviation (current or lagged) and deliveries of fertilizer and fuel to agriculture. It may be that the application of such inputs does fluctuate with the state of the harvest (as does employment), but the inventory adjustment takes place within the agricultural sector and is not directly observed. In SOVMOD V, the output of industrial materials (XIMA—which includes chemicals) is used in the determination of current purchases as given below:

$$AVCP70 = -8.26 + 0.346 \ XCROPN + .057 \ XIMA_{-1}$$
$$\quad\quad\quad (5.70) \quad (4.20) \quad\quad\quad (3.79)$$

$\bar{R}^2 = 0.998$ \quad\quad S.E. $= 0.14$ \quad\quad D.W. $= 0.77$
Sample period: \quad 1961–1977

A Grain Balance System for SOVMOD V

The Soviet livestock sector, described in the next section, depends crucially on the availability of grain for livestock feeding. In this section, we shall describe a seven-equation grain balance system introduced to determine feedgrain and grain imports for SOVMOD V. These equations are presented in Table 15.6 and depend on total grain production (XGRT) and normal grain production (XGRTN).

Grain wastage (XGRW), which averages 10 percent of production over the sample period, is positively related to summer precipitation (JPS9).

Table 15.6 Grain Balance Equations for SOVMOD V

1. Grain Wastage   (XGRW)

$$XGRW/XGRT = 0.0988 + 0.0436\ JPS9$$
$$(17.82)\quad (3.51)$$
$$\bar{R}^2 = 0.41 \qquad\qquad S.E. = 0.02 \qquad\qquad D.W. = 1.49$$

2. Non-Feed-Grain Usage   (XGROTH)

$$XGROTH = 42.96 + 9.695\ QLT28 + 0.0608\ (XGRT - XGRTN)$$
$$(2.97)\quad (2.49)\qquad\quad (2.92)$$
$$+ 0.0387\ (XGRT_{-1} - XGRTN_{-1})$$
$$(1.83)$$
$$\bar{R}^2 = 0.41 \qquad\qquad S.E. = 1.9 \qquad\qquad D.W. = 2.04$$

3. Grain Imports   (MTGR)

$$MTGR/XGRTN = 0.3655 - 0.2061\ ISGR_{-1}/XGRTN$$
$$(7.12)\quad (4.50)$$
$$- 0.1791\ XGRT/XGRTN$$
$$(4.37)$$
$$\bar{R}^2 = 0.70 \qquad\qquad S.E. = 0.02 \qquad\qquad D.W. = 1.51$$

4. Feedgrain Demand   (XGRLD)

$$XGRLD/ALVR_{-1} = -5.5810 + 1.8053\ QLT28 + 0.2753\ QSH68_{-1}$$
$$\phantom{XGRLD/ALVR_{-1} =\ }(2.55)\qquad (2.99)\qquad\quad (1.93)$$
$$\bar{R}^2 = 0.85 \qquad\qquad S.E. = 0.15 \qquad\qquad D.W. = 1.73$$

5. Actual Feedgrain   (XGRL)

$$XGRL = -38.2 + 1.0125\ XGRLD + 0.305\ ISGR_{-1}$$
$$(2.20)\quad (15.90)\qquad\qquad (2.19)$$
$$+ 0.380\ (XGRT + MTGR - XGRW - XGROTH - XGRLD)$$
$$(3.26)$$
$$\bar{R}^2 = 0.94 \qquad\qquad S.E. = 6.6 \qquad\qquad D.W. = 1.52$$

6. Change in Grain Stocks   (IGR)

$$IGR = XGRT + MTGR - XGRW - XGROTH - XGRL$$

7. Grain Stocks (End-Year)   (ISGR)

$$ISGR = ISGR_{-1} + IGR$$

Notes: Sample period: 1961–1977. Data resource for grain balance is U.S. Department of Agriculture," The U.S. Sales Suspension and Soviet Agriculture: An October Assessment," Supplement 1 to WAS = 23, October 1980. Feedgrain demand equation (4) estimated with actual feedgrain (XGRL) as the dependent variable; the estimated equation becomes the definition for XGRLD.

Other uses of grain—direct human consumption, industrial use, seedgrain, and total exports—have been combined in a single variable (XGROTH) and determined by a log trend and grain harvest differences, current and lagged one year. Grain imports are determined by a simple demand equation, with negative impacts from initial stocks and current grain production; all variables have been scaled by normal grain output.

The determination of feedgrain is a two-step procedure in this specification. A feedgrain demand function has been estimated in relation to initial livestock on January 1. The intensity of feeding has been regressed on a log trend and a shift variable for the 1970s. This equation, estimated using actual feedgrain (XGRL) as the dependent variable, is then used to define feedgrain demand (XGRLD). Actual feedgrain is determined in a second equation from feedgrain demand (coefficient 1.01), the grain balance in the current year if feedgrain demand were met exactly (coefficient 0.38), and the initial level of grain stocks (coefficient 0.30). This equation indicates that a shortfall in grain availability of 10 million metric tons will result in a reduction in actual feedgrain of 4 million metric tons; the remaining adjustment will take place in imports (+ 2 mmt) in stocks (− 4 mmt). This pattern of adjustment will vary, depending upon the level of grain stocks when the disturbance occurs.

Once the actual feedgrain is determined, the change in grain stocks (IGR) becomes the residual category in the balance (Equation 6). Changes in grain stocks in turn determine the end-year level of stocks (Equation 7). One major advantage in determining feedgrain by a two-step procedure is that it provides an explicit indicator of feedgrain scarcity for use in the estimation of livestock growth equations.

Livestock Output and Growth

The production of animal product output depends upon the size of livestock herd, the volume and composition of feed fed to livestock, and the allocation of other factors to livestock production. However, efforts to construct separate data on capital and labor services to the livestock sector are quite difficult, primarily because of intrafarm allocation of such factors between crop production and livestock production. Consequently, in our macroeconomic determination of livestock output there are three separate sources of information:

1. The size and composition of the herd, with Soviet livestock data available for cattle, swine, sheep and goats, and poultry
2. The volume of grain fed to livestock and the value of feed fed to livestock, calculated using 1970 prices for different components
3. The harvest deviations for total grain and total crops, which influence the timing of animal slaughtering as well as the efficiency of livestock management

The basic approach begins with a log-linear production function:

$$\text{Livestock Output} = A \, (\text{Herd size})^\alpha \, (\text{Feedgrain})^\beta$$

Aggregate production functions for total animal product output (including net additions to herds), total meat production, and residual animal products (dairy, eggs, hides, etc.) are presented in Table 15.7. In contrast to an earlier study, the USDA estimate of grains fed to livestock (XGRL) in physical units (mmt) has been used instead of the value of total feed (AFEED70). One important observation is the contrast between elasticity estimates for total animal product output and estimates made for the two noninventory

Table 15.7　Output from the Livestock Sector

	Constant	Livestock	Feedgrain	$\bar{R}^2$	D.W.
Total Animal Product Output (XANIM70)	−0.0284 (0.03)	0.5416 (2.34)	0.3194 (6.22)	0.961	1.99
Total Meat Production (XMEAT70)	−3.1776 (6.46)	1.4380 (9.61)	0.1518 (4.30)	0.971	2.13
Residual Animal Products (Nonmeat, Noninventory)	−2.1835 (3.02)	0.9288 (5.04)	0.1960 (4.80)	0.970	1.52

Sample Period: 1961–1977
Specification is log-linear in livestock and feedgrain; assumption of unitary elasticity of substitution between livestock and feedgrain.
Livestock variable is in 1970 value. The initial level of livestock is used in the determination of meat production, while the average of initial and end-year levels is used in the determination of total animal product output (including additions to livestock inventories) and residual animal products.

components. The latter specifications are closer to technological functions where the livestock elasticity is quite high (0.9 to 1.4) and the feedgrain elasticity is rather low (0.15 to 0.20). Because total animal production includes inventory change, the estimated impact of feedgrain is larger, since feed availability is a major determinant of additions to the herd.

In our revised model of the Soviet agricultural sector, physical counts of the livestock herd are determined for cattle, hogs, sheep and goats, and poultry. In addition, there is the value measure of productive livestock (ALVR70), computed by aggregating those stocks using 1970 prices. Under our specification, livestock growth is a function of long-term policy (the constant term and a shift variable for the 1970s), the feedgrain deviation, and specific policy interventions in certain years. The estimated growth-rate equations are presented in Table 15.8.

Livestock growth during the 1961–1977 period was highly volatile in the Soviet Union. Growth rates slowed down during the 1970s in all categories despite the official commitment to increase the supply of meat to the domestic market. The impact of feedgrain availability is most pronounced for hogs, with an impact multiplier of 0.75; i.e., a 10 percent deviation from feed requirements results in a 7.5 percent drop in the swine herd. The feedgrain impact is much less for cattle (0.14) since rebuilding cattle herds is so difficult. It is also low for sheep and goats (0.16), since most sheep and goats are maintained on pasturage and not prepared feeds. The feedgrain impact on poultry stocks is also large at 0.50, and for the total value of livestock the impact is 0.28.

Certain specific interventions were important for the livestock sector during the 1960s. There was an amplified swing in the swine herd during 1963–64 of 24 percent due to panic slaughtering after the 1963 grain harvest failure. This is a swing beyond that which could be attributed to a linear harvest impact. The problem may be that in this range (where the crop

Table 15.8 Growth of Livestock

Category	Constant	Feedgrain Deviation	1970s Shift	Specific Interventions		$\bar{R}^2$	S.E.	D.W.
Cattle	0.0098 (1.44)	0.1365 (3.83)	0.0241 (2.63)	−0.0583 (4.84)	$\bar{Q}$6769	0.654	0.017	2.58
Hogs	−0.0030 (0.13)	0.7555 (5.32)	0.0482 (1.52)	−0.2420 (5.03) −0.2030 (4.09)	(Q63-Q64) $\bar{Q}$6768	0.862	0.061	1.75
Sheep and Goats	−0.0045 (0.78)	0.1612 (5.27)	0.0131 (1.70)	−0.0729 (4.59) −0.0934 (5.95)	$\bar{Q}$64 $\bar{Q}$69	0.836	0.015	1.59
Poultry	0.0123 (1.32)	0.5044 (9.39)	0.0419 (3.26)			0.861	0.026	1.90
Total Livestock (OER Measure)	0.0078 (1.11)	0.2802 (6.80)	0.0215 (2.27)	−0.0371 (2.67) −0.0642 (5.13)	(Q63-Q64) $\bar{Q}$6769	0.858	0.018	2.76

Sample Period: 1961–1977
Dependent variables: Growth rates of end-year stock over previous end-year. Total livestock calculated from stocks and 1970 prices.
Feedgrain deviation: Deviation of actual feedgrain from requirements: (XGRL-XGRLD)/XGRLD.
1970s Shift: A dummy variable equal to 1 through 1970, 0 thereafter; for poultry, the shift occurs two years earlier.
Interventions: Dummy variables for years indicated; a bar indicates that the dummy variable has been adjusted to a mean of zero over the sample period.

shortfall exceeds 10 percent) the impact may be nonlinear. A smaller swing did occur after the 135 million metric ton harvest of 1975. In 1964, there was a 7 percent additional reduction in the herd of sheep and goats, i.e., beyond the expected reduction due to the 1963 harvest. In 1967 to 1969, there were significant reductions in herd size despite reasonably good harvests. This restraint, imposed by financial restrictions on collective farms and a decision not to import Western grain, was felt most sharply in the swine and cattle herds. That strategy, which proved very costly in the late 1960s, was decisively abandoned during the 1970s.

SOVIET LONG-RANGE TARGETS
AND WESTERN PROJECTIONS

At the July 1978 Plenum of the CPSU Central Committee, President Brezhnev presented a major report on the general objectives for agricultural growth during the Eleventh Five-Year Plan (1981–1985).[13] As indicated in Table 15.9, the principal targets for grain and meat were ambitious but not unreasonable at the time: (1) an average of 238–243 million metric tons of grain during 1981–85; and (2) 19.5 million metric tons of meat in 1985. In particular, the 1985 meat target was much less ambitious when compared with the official target for 1980 introduced in the Tenth Five-Year Plan, rather than with achieved production during 1980. Concerning major inputs to crop production, Brezhnev placed his greatest emphasis on mineral fertilizer and machinery. In the livestock sector, priority was given to beef and poultry and the stress was on livestock productivity, i.e., slaughter weight rather than herd size.

Early in 1979, the Central Intelligence Agency issued a revised outlook for Soviet grain imports and production.[14] They concluded that the Plenum grain goal was quite high and would depend on (1) a continuation of favorable weather conditions, or (2) more rapid growth in technical progress. The broad range of their grain projection is presented in Table 15.9; their higher projection exceeds by 13 million tons the midpoint of the Soviet goal, while their lower projection is 13 million tons below the midpoint. To achieve the Soviet meat target of 19.5 million metric tons in 1985, they concluded that the USSR would have to import at least 15 million tons of grain annually through 1985 and that average grain imports could remain in the 20–30 million ton range during the 1981–85 period.

Next, Table 15.9 presents a projection based on the analysis given in Green (1979). The grain projection range was based on the growth of normal output given certain assumptions for productive inputs. The range of output was then calculated from normal output, using deviations for favorable weather (average deviation of −4.5 percent for 1955–1977) and less favorable weather (average deviation of −8.5 percent for 1962–1965). The projection for meat was based on 1978–1985 growth rates expected for livestock and feed. Those calculations suggested that only the cattle herd would expand significantly in the 1980s, although the growing contribution of poultry was not considered in that paper.

Table 15.9 Agricultural Projections to 1985

Alternative Projections	Total Grain Output (Average 1981–85) (m.m. tons)	Annual Growth Rate	Total Meat in 1985 (m.m. tons)	Annual Growth Rate
1. Soviet Official Targets of the July Plenum (1978)	238–243	1.8 percent (over plan for 1976–80)	19.5	3.5 percent (over 1977) 2.5 percent (over 1980 plan)
2. Central Intelligence Agency (1979) (Range: Favorable weather and long-term average weather)	228–254	2.2 percent (from 1980 to 1985)	— (Soviet target accepted as reasonable)	—
3. Earlier SOVMOD Projections				(over 1977)
a) SOVMOD III Projection (1978)	234–246	2.2 percent	15.2–19.2	0.3–3.3 percent
b) SOVMOD V Projection (1979)	238–248	2.5 percent	17.6–18.3	2.2–2.7 percent
4. Guidelines for the 11th Five-Year Plan (1981)	238–243	3.2 percent (over average 1976–1980)	18.2	3.8 percent (over 1980)

Note: Range constructed for CIA (1979) by applying 11 percent adjustment to standardized grain weight and assuming a linear growth path from 1980 to 1985.

Sources: 1. Report delivered by L. I. Brezhnev, 3 July 1978; *Reprints from the Soviet Press*, 31 July 1978.
2. Central Intelligence Agency, *USSR: Long-Term Outlook for Grain Imports*, ER 79-10057, January 1979.
3. Donald W. Green, "The Soviet Union and the World Economy in the 1980s: A Review of Alternatives," in *The Future of the Soviet Economy: 1978–1985*, ed. Holland Hunter, (Boulder, Col., Westview Press, 1978).
4. Green, "Soviet Agriculture."
5. N. A. Tikhonov, "Guidelines for the Economic and Social Development of the USSR for 1981–1985 and the Period Ending in 1990," unofficial translation, 1981, L. I. Brezhnev, "Report of the Central Committee of the CPSU to the 26th Congress of the CPSU, 23 February 1981.

In February 1981, the Soviet leadership announced the Guidelines for the Eleventh Five-Year Plan at the Party Congress. In Brezhnev's "Report of the Central Committee," he announced that meat production was now planned to reach 18.2 million tons by 1985. He acknowledged that the major constraint was the shortage of feed and announced that the target for grain production over the five-year-plan period would be an average of 238–243 million tons. It was pointed out by many observers that this average was higher than the record harvest of 1978 and that it was identical to the target announced earlier at the July 1978 Plenum. The Chairman of the Party also stressed priorities of pasturage, storage, and distribution, and the need to encourage private agriculture and reduce central interference in the decisions of collective and state farms.

Tikhonov, the new Chairman of the Council of Ministers, was more explicit in his presentation of the Guidelines, but many features of the Plan were still left unclear. One of the highest targets in the industrial sector is the 44–49 percent growth projected for mineral fertilizer, but targets for agricultural machinery were not announced. Tikhonov did state, however, that capital assets per worker would rise 40 percent in the five-year period. Besides the 18.2 million target for meat production in 1985, he announced that average meat production over the period would be 17–17.5 million tons. No specific targets for livestock inventories were given in the Guidelines, and the emphasis was rather on efficiency in feedgrain and livestock. Particular attention was directed to the cultivation of "fodder grain, pulses and other high-protein crops." To improve storage facilities, 15 billion rubles were to be allocated in the capital investment plan, an increase of 60 percent over the allocations in the previous five-year plan. Tikhonov's speech contained much less attention to private agriculture and did not echo Brezhnev's criticisms of Party and Government officials supervising the agricultural sector.

CURRENT PROJECTIONS OF GRAIN PRODUCTION, GRAIN IMPORT REQUIREMENTS, AND MEAT PRODUCTION

In working with a new version of SOVMOD V, we have devoted most of our attention to preparing a plausible baseline projection for the early 1980s. As a consequence, we can present in Table 15.10 the main features of our current baseline for comparison with earlier forecasts in Green (1979) and the Eleventh Five-Year Plan. On the input side, the major assumptions are at least consistent with known targets in the Plan, although the growth rates projected for fixed capital and current purchases are 1 percent lower than our previous analysis. On the basis of those input projections, determined in the full solution of SOVMOD V, the normal outputs of total crops and grain are projected to grow at 1.6 percent annually over the five-year-plan period.

Because of the depressed harvest in 1980, the growth rates for actual production through 1985 are somewhat higher. Still, the baseline projection indicates that average grain production in the 1981–85 period will only be 217 million metric tons, or 6 percent above the average for 1976–80. Our baseline projection is therefore less than the Eleventh Five-Year Plan and our earlier projections. The adjustment in our macroeconometric projection is due to two major factors: (1) a downward adjustment in the trajectory of normal grain output in the late 1970s, using an average over the 1976–1980 period; and (2) the higher labor elasticity used in the production function based on cross-sectional information described in the section "Pooled Estimation of Agricultural Production Functions Using Regional Data."

In the grain balance system, the lower level of grain production and the low level in grain stocks result in strong import demand for grain during the Plan period—an average of 26 million metric tons costing $4.5 billion annually. The system rebuilds stocks in 1981–82 and reaches a level of 130 mmtons by the end of 1985. In this smooth projection for the early 1980s, grain fed to livestock averages 138 mmtons during the Plan and sustains modest growth in livestock and meat production. The new model suggests, therefore, that the commitment to build herds will push the Soviet Union to expand average grain imports in the early 1980s.

Livestock inventories expand modestly in this baseline projection to 1985, growing 1.5 percent on average during the Plan period. The growth in cattle is quite steady, while a rebuilding of swine and poultry in the early 1980s increases the growth rates for those categories. This projection for total livestock is quite similar to the assumptions used in forecasting meat production in Green (1979).

The final aspect of this baseline is the implications of the feedgrain balance and livestock growth on the increase in meat production. In the baseline, meat production averages 16.7 million metric tons over the Plan and reaches a level of 17.7 mmt in 1985; both levels are below the targets in the Eleventh Five-Year Plan. Average meat production in 1981–85 is still 10.5 percent above the average during the previous five years, but that will certainly fall far short of domestic demand at current prices.

To evaluate the properties of the model, we have constructed an alternative projection with assumptions of more favorable weather. These weather assumptions do not increase normal output, but do increase realized output for total crops (+4 percent) and total grain (+7 percent). The major agricultural indicators of this scenario are compared with the baseline projection in Table 15.11. One important feature of the model is that the 15 million tons in additional grain each year result in only a 6-million-ton increase in average grain fed to livestock. Average annual grain imports are cut by 4 million tons, and the average annual increment to grain stocks is increased by 1.5 million tons. The missing 3.5 million tons is lost in grain wastage and moisture content each year. The saving on grain imports over the five years amounts to $3.5 billion, some of which would probably be spent on Western capital goods.

The dynamics of the livestock sector are also illustrated in this more favorable scenario. Average meat production is only increased 3 percent over the plan period, but by 1985 sustainable meat production has been

Table 15.10   A Baseline Projection for 1981–1985 (Normal weather assumed)

	Annual Growth Rate 1980/85	Level 1985	Average Level 1981–1985	Percent Increase over 1976–1980
Major Inputs				
Total Employment (million)	−0.6%	34.9		
Capital Investment	3.9%			
Capital Stock	6.5%			
Sown Acreage	0.4%			
Current Purchases (bn R)	3.3%	17.4		
Crop Production				
Normal Crop Production (bn R)	1.6%	47.6	46.1	8.7%
Normal Grain Production (mmt)	1.6%	244.3	236.4	8.9%
Total Crops (bn R)	2.7%	45.8	44.4	6.2%
Total Grain (mmt)	3.5%	224.5	217.0	5.9%
Total Feed (bn R)	3.3%	16.8	15.9	10.3%
Grain Fed (mmt)	6.2%	148.4	138.	16. %
Grain Imports (mmt)			26.2	22. %
Change in Grain Stock (mmt)			4.9	
Grain Stocks (end-year) (mmt)	4.3%	129.9		

Livestock Sector				
Total Livestock (bn R)	72.0	1.5%		
- Cattle (m head)	121.7	1.3%		
- Hogs (m head)	71.0	1.6%		
- Sheep and Goats (m head)	145.	0 %		
- Poultry (m)	1052.	2.5%		
Animal Products				
Meat Production (mmtons)	17.7	3.1%	16.7	10.6%
Total Animal Output (bn R)	70.5	2.3%	67.7	7.2%
Other				
Total Agricultural Output (bn R)	99.5	2.3%	96.2	5.8%
Grain Purchases (bn $)	4.8		4.6	
Net External Debt (bn $)	15.6	7.2%		

Table 15.11 The Impact of Favorable Weather on Soviet Agricultural Performance

Category	Units	Baseline: Normal Weather	Scenario: Favorable Weather	Percent
Average Grain Production (1981–1985)	mmt	217	232	(6.9)
Average Grain Fed to Livestock (1981–1985)	mmt	138	144	(4.3)
Average Grain Imports (1981–1985)	mmt	26	22	(– 15.4)
Grain Stocks (End–1985)	mmt	130	137	(5.4)
Average Meat Production (1981–1985)	mmt	16.7	17.2	(3.0)
1985 Meat Production	mmt	17.7	18.6	(5.1)

boosted by over 5 percent and the Plan target for that year is actually achieved. Consequently, even though grain production targets are not achieved (results are 3.5 percent below the midpoint of the target range) the purchase of grain imports allows an expansion in the herd, which achieves the meat production target by 1985.

APPENDIX A: REGIONAL DATA USED IN THE ESTIMATION OF PRODUCTION FUNCTIONS

In order to estimate production functions, data are needed for both inputs and output of agriculture for each republic over the time period 1960–1975.

Because of the difficulties involved in obtaining usable series on the value of total material inputs into agriculture by republic, it was decided to use production functions expressed in terms of primary factors (land, labor, and capital) and net output.

The basic measure of net output used in Soviet statistics is national income (*natsional'nyi dokhod*). In Marxian terms national income is the sum of labor earnings and surplus value. It is computed as a residual by subtracting from the gross value of output the cost of materials, services (such as communication, transportation, and trade) required to bring goods to consumers, and depreciation allowances. This measure is usually referred to as *net material product* (NMP) by Western economists.

Indexes of aggregate produced national income by republic in constant prices are available in both the republican and national statistical handbooks for all years under study. Considerably less-complete information is available for these series for the various sectors of the economy. The methods used to compute these series are described in detail in Bond (1979).

In only a very few cases are capital stock data in value terms available for republics. Thus most of data used are estimated on the basis of growth indexes obtained from republican handbooks and estimates of the value of capital stock by republic and branch for end-of-year 1965 prepared by Gillula (1979).[15] These series are based on constant 1955 prices and are gross of depreciation. The capital series coverage is limited to fixed capital. This includes buildings, structures, equipment, productive livestock, and long-term plantings. Working capital is excluded.

The data for labor inputs come directly from tables published in the national statistical yearbooks. The accounting unit is average annual employment. For employees in the state sectors (which includes workers on the state farms), this measure is computed in such a way as to reflect the actual amount of work done during the year, by making adjustment for the number of workdays put in by the labor force. It is somewhat deficient, in that changes in the length of the workweek are not reflected. However, for the period under study this change has been rather insignificant.

The estimate of collective farm workers is much less reliable as a measure of labor input. Monthly employment in this sector is calculated as the number of persons who have done at least one day's work in the kolkhoz during the month. The annual figure is then a simple, unweighted average of these monthly figures. No attempt has been made to include in the measure of agricultural labor persons working in private agriculture. (This latter group covers family members of collective farms and others working exclusively on private garden plots.) In 1970 they made up 17 percent of total agricultural employment. Unfortunately there is no reliable way in which the known national totals can be distributed by republic.

The measure of land use in agriculture used is total sown areas (*posevnye ploshchadi*).

APPENDIX B: LIST OF AGRICULTURAL VARIABLES IN SOVMOD V

Symbol	Description	Units	Source
AFEED70	Value of feed fed to livestock, 1970 prices	B. 1979 Rubles	SAIOER
ALVCT	Cattle Inventory (End-Year)	m. head	USDA
ALVHG	Swine Inventory (End-Year)	m. head	USDA
ALVPL	Poultry Inventory (End-Year)	m. head	USDA
ALVR	Value of Productive livestock (End-Year), 1970 prices	B. 1970 Rubles	SAIOER
ALVSG	Sheep and Goats Inventory (End-Year)	m. head	USDA
ASGR9	Area sown to grain	Index	SAIOER
AVCP70	Value of agricultural current purchases	B. 1970 Rubles	SAIOER
IGR	Change in Grain Stocks	m.m. tons	USDA
ISGR	Grain Stocks (End-Year)	m.m. tons	USDA
JPS9	Spring-summer precipitation index	Centimeters	SOVMOD
JPW9	Winter precipitation index	Centimeters	SOVMOD
JTW9T	Winter temperature index (truncated)	Degree Cent.,	SOVMOD
KAIR	Agricultural fixed capital (mean year), 1955 prices	B. 1955 Rubles	N.Kh.
MTGR	Total grain imports	m.m. tons	USDA
NAT	Total agricultural employment	m. persons	FDAD

APPENDIX 3:   (continued)

Symbol	Description	Units	Source
XAGT70	Net agricultural production, 1970 prices	B. 1970 Rubles	SAIOER
XANIM70	Animal product output	B. 1970 Rubles	SAIOER
XCROP70	Total crop output, 1970 prices	B. 1970 Rubles	SAIOER
XCROPN	Normal crop output	B. 1970 Rubles	SOVMOD
XGRL	Grain fed to livestock	m.m. tons	USDA
XGRLD	Grain requirements for livestock	m.m. tons	SOVMOD
XGROTH	Other grain usage (seed, industry, food and exports)	m.m. tons	USDA
XGRT	Total grain production	m.m. tons	USDA
XGRTN	Normal grain production	m.m. tons	SOVMOD
XGRW	Grain wastage	m.m. tons	USDA
XMEAT70	Total meat production, 1970 prices	B. 1970 Rubles	SAIOER
XIMA	Output index, industrial materials	1970 = 100	OER

Sources:
FDAD   Foreign Demographic Analysis Division, Department of Commerce
N.Kh.   Soviet Official Statistics, Annual Handbook
OER   Office of Economic Research, Central Intelligence Agency
SAIOER   Soviet Agricultural Index Databank, OER
SOVMOD   SRI-WEFA Soviet Econometric Model Databank; data presented in Green (1979)
USDA   U.S. Department of Agriculture Databank

NOTES

1. Daniel L. Bond, "Multiregional Development in the Soviet Union: 1960–1975," (ph.D. diss., University of North Carolina at Chapel Hill, 1979).

2. Elizabeth Clayton, "Productivity in Soviet Agriculture," *Slavic Review* 39 (September 1980): 446–58.

3. Gregory C. Chow, *Econometric Analysis by Control Methods* (New York: John Wiley & Sons, 1981).

4. A preliminary set of estimations using a CES specification indicated that the assumption of unitary elasticity of substitution could not be rejected at any reasonable level of significance. In these tests, the point estimate of the elasticity of substitution in the CES case with a non-constant returns to scale specification was 0.86; for a CES with constant returns to scale case, the elasticity was 0.93.

5. The "covariance model" is one of the simplest approaches used for correcting for possible bias in pooled estimation. In addition to the identified causal variables, special dummy (binary) variables are incorporated into the specification to estimate possible intercept difference associated with each time period or cross-sectional unit. This has the effect of isolating in the dummy variable coefficients the influence of unidentified factors related to time or region. If the model is correctly specified and standard assumptions satisfied, the ordinary least squares (OLS) estimation technique is appropriate.

6. The groupings used were (1) Russian republic (R.S.F.S.R.); (2) Baltic region: Estonia, Latvia, and Lithuania; (3) Belorussia; (4) Ukraine and Moldavia; (5) Transcaucasian region: Armenia, Georgia and Azerbaydzhan; (6) Kazakhstan; and (7) Central Asian region: Kirgizia, Tadzhikistan, Turkmenistan, and Uzbekistan.

7. This approach, which also requires the use of only OLS estimation techniques, is used when it is expected that autoregression and heteroscedasticity are present in the data. The first step in this approach is to make an OLS estimation of the parameters from the uncorrected

pooled data. The regression residuals obtained from this step are used to calculate estimates of the autoregression coefficients for each cross-section variable, which are then used to transform the original data set. OLS estimation is then applied to these transformed data, and the regression residuals from this step are used to calculate values to transform the pooled data again, this time correcting for heteroscedasticity. A third OLS regression on the twice-transformed data is then used to obtain final parameter estimates, where the disturbance terms are now asymptotically nonautoregressive and homoscedastic.

8. In Table 16.1 the values in parentheses under the coefficient estimates are Student's *t*-statistics. $\bar{R}^2$ is the coefficient of determination, corrected for the degrees of freedom.

9. Douglas B. Diamond, "Trends in Output, Inputs, and Factor Productivity in Soviet Agriculture," in U.S. Congress, Joint Economic Committee, *New Directions in the Soviet Economy* (Washington, D.C.: U.S. Government Printing Office, 1966), pp. 339-81.

10. Douglas B. Diamond and Constance B. Krueger, "Recent Developments in Output and Productivity in Soviet Agriculture," in U.S. Congress, Joint Economic Committee, *Soviet Economic Prospects for the Seventies* (Washington, D.C.: U.S. Government Printing Office, 1973), pp. 316-339.

11. Donald W. Green, "Soviet Agriculture: An Econometric Analysis of Technology and Behavior," in U.S. Congress, Joint Economic Committee, *Soviet Economy in a Time of Change* (Washington, D.C.: U.S. Government Printing Office, 1979), pp. 116-32.

12. See Donald W. Green and Christopher I. Higgins, *SOVMOD I: A Macroeconomic Model of the Soviet Union* (New York: Academic Press, 1977), pp. 259-62, for a more complete description of JPS9 and JTW9.

13. L. I. Brezhnev, "Report to the Plenum of the CPSU Central Committee," translated in *Reprints from the Soviet Press,* 31 July 1978.

14. Central Intelligence Agency, "U.S.S.R.: Long-Term Outlook for Grain Imports," ER79-10057, January 1979. In Green (1979), these standardized projections by the CIA were misrepresented since the adjustment for standardized weight (11 percent) was not applied.

15. James W. Gillula, "The Regional Distribution of Fixed Capital in the U.S.S.R." Unpublished working paper (Washington, D.C.: U.S. Bureau of the Census, Foreign Demographic Analysis Division, 1979).

Index

List of Contributors

Robert C. Stuart, Professor of Economics, Rutgers University, New Brunswick, New Jersey, and Visiting Professor of Economics, Princeton University, Princeton, New Jersey.

Paul R. Gregory, Professor of Economics, University of Houston, Houston, Texas.

Mark Harrison, Lecturer in Economics, University of Warwick, Coventry, England.

S. G. Wheatcroft, Research Fellow, Soviet Industrialization Project, Centre for Russian and East European Studies, University of Birmingham, Birmingham, England.

Eugène Zaleski, Professor of Economics, Centre National de la Recherche Scientifique, Paris, France.

James R. Millar, Professor of Economics, University of Illinois, Urbana, Illinois.

Frank A. Durgin, Jr., Professor of Economics, University of Southern Maine, Portland, Maine.

Alfred Evans, Jr., Professor of Political Science, California State University at Fresno, Fresno, California.

Elizabeth M. Clayton, Professor of Economics, University of Missouri, St. Louis, Missouri.

Michael L. Wyzan, Assistant Professor of Economics, Illinois State University, Normal, Illinois.

Kenneth R. Gray, Associate Professor of Economics, North Texas State University, Denton, Texas.

Clark J. Chandler, Senior Economist, Economic Consulting Services, Inc., Washington, D.C.

Gertrude Schroeder Greenslade, Professor of Economics, University of Virginia, Charlottesville, Virginia.

Valentin Litvin, Professor of Russian Studies, University of Alabama, Birmingham, Alabama.

Everett M. Jacobs, Senior Lecturer, The University of Sheffield, Sheffield, England.

Daniel L. Bond, Director, CPE Projects, Wharton Econometrics, Washington, D.C.

Donald W. Green, Vice-President, Chase Manhattan Bank, New York, New York.

Barbara Severin, Central Intelligence Agency, Washington, D.C.

Joseph Berliner, Professor of Economics, Brandeis University, Waltham, Massachusetts.